THE FINAL ROMAN EMPEROR,
THE ISLAMIC ANTICHRIST,
AND THE VATICAN'S LAST CRUSADE

THE FINAL ROMAN EMPEROR,
THE ISLAMIC ANTICHRIST,
AND THE VATICAN'S LAST CRUSADE

IN THIS SIGN CONQUER!

THOMAS HORN & CRIS PUTNAM

DEFENDER

CRANE, MO

THE FINAL ROMAN EMPEROR, THE ISLAMIC ANTICHRIST, AND
THE VATICAN'S LAST CRUSADE
Defender
Crane, MO 65633
©2016 by Thomas Horn
A collaborative work by Thomas Horn and Cris Putnam.

Printed in the United States of America.

ISBN: 9780996409544

A CIP catalog record of this book is available from the Library of Congress.

Cover illustration and design by Jeffrey Mardis.
All Scripture quotations from the King James Version; in cases of academic
comparison, those instances are noted.

Editor's Note:

Readers will note that the authors use both "ISIS" and "IS" frequently throughout the book. By way of explanation, "ISIS" refers to the Islamic State of Iraq and Syria (ISIS), also known as the Islamic State of Iraq and the Levant (ISIL). "IS," as the pop-savvy branding experts now prefer, refers to the Islamic State as well: a Muslim terrorist group governing large portions of territory in Iraq and Syria, with growing territories in Libya, Nigeria, and cells within Pakistan, Algeria, Egypt, Philippines, Lebanon, Indonesia, Jordan and Israel.[1, 2]

CONTENTS

Foreword

THIS BOOK IS ABOUT a prediction involving war and the complex web of philosophy by which men indulge themselves in order to make sense of battle. Glory, power, respect, fear, and even the worship of their peers motivate such men. We take the reader on a survey of ethical theories of war, the secret motives behind wars, and, as our primary focus will hone in on the ultimate war, we forecast the "great day of God Almighty" (Revelation 16:14), a battle that, according to biblical prophecy, will be waged at "a place called in the Hebrew tongue Armageddon" (Revelation 16:16). While we will discuss psychological and military war, we ultimately forecast a heavenly battle. What we see played out on earth is a pale comparison to the war that is coming, described in Revelation 12. A Singularity is near, but it marks the Tribulation and return of Jesus. The tension of Israel's mere presence amongst its Muslim neighbors is a constant threat. Since 1948, this remains the top unsolvable conundrum of generations of diplomats and statesmen at the United Nations, and underlies an undeclared Third World War (undeclared at the time we are sending this manuscript to the printer), yet one that has already begun, according to people with as diverse backgrounds as Pope Francis and the American politician Lyndon LaRouche. We think it likely that this Third World War will soon be an acknowledged fact rather than the attention-grabbing sound bite Pope Francis has been banding about for years now. In fact, we are writing this introduction just after the Paris attack, and Jordan's King Abdullah has declared: "We are facing a Third World War against humanity."[3]

We believe this so-called Third World War is coming in earnest and will lead the entire planet to oppose Jesus as He returns triumphant, defies the apostasy, destroys the Antichrist, and prevails over the strong delusion imprisoning the end-time minds of men (2 Thessalonians 2:3; 2:11). The position of these political pieces on the chessboard strongly favors a scenario described in ancient Scripture as well as in long-forgotten prophecies that were once held in high esteem by early Church Fathers, which we will uncover in this fourth and final entry into our four-year investigation, which culminates now with *The Final Roman Emperor, the Islamic Antichrist, and the Vatican's Last Crusade.*

Introduction

WE HAVE FACED more opposition in the form of nebulous calamity during this project than all of the others combined. The text you are reading is the fruit of much spiritual warfare. Our lives have been changed as a result. In the end, we believe it was worth it. In chapter 1, we go out on a limb and offer some specific predictions. We were as shocked as everyone else when our prediction that Pope Benedict would step down came to pass. After all, we documented our sources. While this is dangerous business, we offer some new predictions in all sincerity for the reader to critically (and prayerfully) examine. By attacking Paris, the Islamic State (IS) has drastically changed the geopolitical landscape. Although their days are numbered, the IS serves as the quintessential antithesis to Western values and likely serves its purpose as a globalist dialectic more than the kingdom of Antichrist.

In order to fully understand the signs of the times, we address the necessary background knowledge and terminology in chapter 2, "Theories of War." With a solid foundation in ethical theory, we delve into the realm of conspiracy and prophecy. We believe we have something unique to offer that no other book currently available offers about what radical Islam represents. Our analysis is filtered through a supernatural worldview, a perspective seldom adopted in nonfiction. In particular, we examine conspiracy, Islam, post-Vatican II (luciferic enthronement ceremony) Catholicism and geopolitics from the perspective of an Immortal. Muhammad was given the Qur'an by an angel (allegedly Gabriel), and we see no reason to doubt it was indeed a spirit of some kind. However, the content explicitly inoculates one from believing the true Gospel (1 Corinthians 15:3–7). The Qur'an explains that Jesus never died on the cross, so it is impossible for a Muslim to even imagine He died for one's sins, if the Qur'an is true. We are forced to conclude that Muhammad was deceived by a fallen angel—that is, *if* his vision was genuinely supernatural. More interestingly, we suggest the same *fallen ones* are driving both Freemasonry and Roman Catholicism toward globalism, Marxism, and the pantheistic monist religion of Pierre Teilhard de Chardin.

We demonstrate that the Qur'an's understanding of Christian theology is so sophomoric that its narrative seems to be a product of contrived ignorance rather than preternatural revelation. Accepting a challenge almost certainly laden with misinformation, sophistry, and intrigue, chapter 4 reveals that the Islamic State existed long before 2014 and Baghdadi. More disturbingly, we examine the painful truth that US policy virtually created the IS, we believe *de facto,* but not likely intentionally. Initially, the IS may have seemed to serve our strategic interest against Assad, but allowing the IS to blossom into a poisonous flower, an actual State, that takes in over one million dollars a day in oil revenue alone, quickly embarrassed the Obama administration after the troops left Iraq. Obama and his revisionist henchmen have been covering their heels since the fall of Mosul in 2014.

Considerable effort was taken to carefully document our contentions. When ordering from SkyWatch TV, we provide scans of original source documents acquired via the press or WikiLeaks. We reveal via leaked government documents that the intelligence community (and Obama administration) well knew the IS declared statehood back in 2007.[4] In 2014, they simply defined what "statehood" meant (the final *caliphate*) and put forth their man Baghdadi—a virtually unknown jihadist detainee who held a PhD in Islamic Studies from Baghdad University and the correct prophetic pedigree. Unbeknownst to the largely spoon-fed press, Abu Bakr al-Baghdadi amounts to a hired hand who had the right credentials to be caliph; the caliphate was long declared in anticipation of the imminent arrival of the Mahdi.

We examine Pope Francis, his socialist politics and liberation theology. We argue that nothing has falsified our original thesis presented in *Petrus Romanus* back in 2012. While it remains to be seen if he is *the* False Prophet, it is documented to be true that he is *a* false prophet. Surprising details have surfaced about his election by Jesuit conspiracy. Some are asking if his election was canonical… (opening the way for yet another Petrus?). Even so, after the unmitigated slaughter of the oldest Christian groups in the world, the peacenik pope called for a war to stop the Islamic State.

We believe all of these tensions will one day be decided in Jerusalem. Rome and the United States will likely also be the brunt of terrorism. The vast majority of Iraqis, Iranians, and Malaysians believe that the Mahdi is to arrive within a few years or less. This book documents that preparations for his worldwide introduction are now in place. Fortunately, we argue it's all in vain. We have a shocking surprise that will not only challenge their worldview but will keep Muslim scholar-apologists busy learning to read Syrian to their ultimate dismay—and, we pray, conversion.

We take a detailed look at Muslim beliefs and eschatology in chapter 9. In addition to the Qur'an and countless *Hadiths*, we consulted works by the top scholars in the field: Bernard Lewis, PhD, oriental studies; Timothy Furnish, PhD, Islamic history; William McCants, PhD, Near Eastern studies; James White, ThD, theology; and David Cook, PhD, Islamic literature. Regarding the collision course Islam's apocalyptic scenario has plotted with Christian premillennial belief, we relied heavily on the work of Michael Heiser, PhD, Hebrew Bible; Samuel Shahid, PhD,

Middle Eastern studies; John Weldon, PhD, comparative religion; and Chuck Missler, PhD, biblical eschatology. After consulting the original source documents and opinions of scholars, we examined the popular Islamic Antichrist debate as reflected in recent books by Christian eschatology author Joel Richardson and countering Christian apologist, Chris White. After much study and reflection, we conclude that Islamic eschatology is an incoherent, plagiarized mess. Most likely, there is no actual Mahdi, nor will there ever be, he is merely a literary *topos*.

We turn back to examine the "the battle of that great day of God Almighty" (Revelation 16:14) from a Hebrew Bible perspective because John specified "a place called in the Hebrew tongue Armageddon" (Revelation 16:16). Next, our friend Derek Gilbert presents an intimately plausible case for why so many people will accept the Antichrist. Finally, we show how all of this fits together under one occult umbrella through the ancient pagan prophecies of the Sibyl. When we began digging, we had no idea we would find a tunnel leading right back to *Apollyon Rising*, but, indeed, that's what we found.

The final chapter reveals how the discussed prophecies: The Great Monarch of Catholic eschatology, the Mahdi of Islamic eschatology, and the Antichrist of Christian eschatology all work together driving the world toward a globalist totalitarian socialism under the thumb of one man, whether he is seen as king, messiah, or both. In the end, the world will be deceived into opposing Jesus Christ when He returns to the Mount of Olives and crushes them at what has come to be called the "Battle of Armageddon," although some translators prefer "*War* of Armageddon," we contend the battle for the Mount of Assembly, otherwise known as Mount Zion in Jerusalem.

1

The Prediction

MANY YEARS AGO, I, Tom Horn, died and woke up in heaven. Contemplating my surroundings, I wondered where I was, where I had come from, how long I had been here, and why I had no memories of getting here… wherever *here* was.

At that moment, I knew this was no dream; it was too vivid to be anything less than real. In fact, it felt *realer* than any previous reality I had known.

I barely became aware of this supernatural backdrop when I abruptly found myself standing somewhere before a spectacular pillar of light (*or was it a throne?*). It was so bright, so intense and penetrating—glistening with vibrant streams of silver and blue and gold emanating with the most unexplainable yet awe-inspiring presence—that I could hardly keep my eyes open or my face toward the radiance.

And I was urgently exclaiming something I couldn't possibly understand: "Please, Lord, don't let me forget. Please don't let me forget! IT"S TOO WONDERFUL!"

How much time had I spent in this surreal place, what had I just observed that so profoundly influenced my desire to remember it, and what was it I was even talking about? Why was I so desperate to recall something I had obviously feared forgetting? And how had I known I was standing before the LORD?

Suspended there like a marionette hanging on wires, I was somehow aware that "memories" from only moments before stood just beyond my ability to summon them back into my conscious mind again. (But were "moments" or "time" even a factor in this place?) Whatever had been revealed to me was already gone, leaving a hungry void in the place of what had just been a great revelation.

But I *had* known something…of that I was sure. A disclosure of vast importance had dawned within my cognition like a great, vibrating bell, alerting the depths of my very soul to a certainty that trumped any knowledge I've ever held in my finite brain…and it had come through no invitation of my own. It hadn't been *my* idea. That much was clear. It had been a truth that electrified my deepest consciousness…something about *the future.* The data was there, I had visualized it, I had *seen* it, and then it was immediately blocked from being accessed again; I had been told I would not remember the details.

But why? What would be the purpose in that?

Something else had happened, too. Somehow I knew that a scroll of some kind had unrolled before me with scenes of a distant tomorrow, a hereafter, a time ahead—*my* time ahead—playing out on what looked like a silvery parchment. It had been as clear and as believable as if I were watching a movie, with rich depictions of a destiny, or a possible future, where something extraordinary and miraculous was taking place. A cinematic conveyance of a personal fate. A "potential existence" that had been downloaded into my subconscious mind—or *soul.* And then, for some reason, it departed my intellect as quickly as it had appeared.

Had a revelation of some type been sealed within me? Something intended for a later time?

My thoughts raced, and I started to repeat, "Lord, please, don't let me forget," but I stopped short as, just then, a deep, still, small voice countered, "You will not remember…and it is time for you to go back now."

I heard a thunderclap and found myself falling backward, gliding rapidly, as if I had been dropped out of an airplane window or was let loose by some heavenly hands that had been holding me above, my arms and legs gliding up and down now against a cloudless sky.

As I fell, I gazed unblinkingly upward in amazement. The brilliance, which had just been in front of me, was moving swiftly away into the distance, and yet I wasn't afraid. A high-pitched whistling sound began rushing in around my ears, and I thought it must be the air carrying me aloft as I plummeted toward the earth. A moment later, I observed the oddest thing: the roof of my house literally enveloped around me as I passed effortlessly through it, and then it felt as if I had landed on my bedroom mattress with a thud...

I sat straight up, took a desperate, shuddering, deep inhalation, and then slowly let it out, realizing something extraordinary had occurred. Wherever I had been, whatever I had seen, I was back now to the so-called real world, and this material, earthly substance all around me straightaway felt far less authentic to me than the other place I had been. It was like *this* cosmos, *this* dimension, *this* realm that everyone calls "life" was merely a temporal and trivial matrix of existence that I was now being required to return to after tasting the marvelous phenomenon of a genuine, superior domain.

It was the middle of the night and I sat there for a few seconds, possibly in shock, trying to determine what had happened.

I could feel my chest burning...and then I heard something.

Sobbing. Right next to me. My young wife, Nita, with her head in her hands.

As my eyes adjusted to the darkness, I found her isolated stare. She looked as if she had been crying desperately, and had an unfamiliar expression conveying what I somehow already understood—we both had experienced something far more irregular than we ever could have prepared for.

"Nita," I said softly, "what's going on? Why are you crying?"

It took a while for her to collect herself, but once she did, she tearfully described how she had awakened to find me dead. I had no pulse, no breath, and no heartbeat; I was cold to the touch—and not just for a few seconds. I had remained in that condition for approximately fifteen minutes, she estimated, while she screamed for me to wake up, pounded on my chest, and attempted something like CPR.

We didn't have a phone in those days, and it was in the middle of the night. Nita had been unsure what to do and was about to try pulling me outside to the car to take me to the hospital when I jerked up, took a deep breath, and looked at her.

For the reader, no matter how incredible the narrative above seems, it really did happen to me a long time ago. Later, and since then, I understood why God had allowed my wife to wake up and find me in that condition. Without her eyewitness account that night, uncertainties about the supernaturalism of the experience would have undoubtedly crept into my mind over the years. That I had been dead for a significant period of time—not breathing and therefore not taking in oxygen, and yet experiencing no brain damage (though I'm sure some would argue otherwise)—also attested to the preternatural virtues of the event.

But why would God show me something and then not allow me to remember it? What would be the point in that, right? I can tell you that this was *the* question pressing me in the days immediately following the incident, and in my youthful naiveté and impatience I first went about trying to find the answer to that mystery in the wrong way. I learned a valuable and biblical lesson as a result. In fact, that early mistake is why most have never heard this story until now.

A couple days after my death and return from "over yonder," I told the pastor of our local church that I had an important question to ask him. In private, I recounted my episode and probed him for its potential meaning. "Why would God show somebody something and then tell them they would not remember the vision?" I had inquired earnestly. His response was shocking for an honest and sincere young Christian man. Basically, he offered that I had probably eaten too much spicy food, or maybe had accidently been poisoned and was therefore delusional or had a vivid dream.

No kidding. That was his response.

Of course, I was not yet familiar with such admonitions as, "Give not that which is holy unto the dogs, neither cast ye your pearls before swine, lest they trample them under their feet..." (Matthew 7:6). Understand that I am not saying my pastor back then was a dog, but that this was a lesson I would not soon forget about sharing sacred and holy things with those who have not had similar supernatural experiences and therefore cannot appreciate or comprehend the otherworldly significance. In fact, besides my closest friends and family, from that day forward I kept the event (and what I would soon understand about its measurable implications) a secret between me and them. Then, just a few years ago, after sharing my story with the well-known television personality Sid Roth—who, unlike some ministers, actually *believes* in the miraculous—he asked me to repeat the story on his syndicated program, *It's Supernatural.* I agreed that it was time to tell at least a part of that history. However, as legendary radio broadcaster Paul Harvey used to ponder, *what was the rest of the story?*

Tom Horn and Cris Putnam on Sid Roth's *It's Supernatural*

After the disappointing experience of my pastor's less-than-enthusiastic response to my question regarding why God would give somebody a vision then not allow him to remember it, I struggled to make sense of what had obviously been an extraordinary incident in mine and Nita's life. I prayed daily, seeking understanding, and it was during this same period (undoubtedly God had all this timing in control from the very beginning) that I happened to be reading through the Bible from cover to cover for the first time in my life. I had made it to the book of Job, and it was during these devotions that one day my eyes suddenly fell upon Job 33:15–17, and the Word of God dramatically came to life in what some charismatics might call a *Rhema* moment: a time in which the Scripture went from being ink on paper to *the living Word of God.* The text that instantly conveyed the dynamic truth behind what had happened to me that fateful night read:

> In a dream, **in a vision of the night**, when deep sleep falleth upon men, in slumberings upon the bed; Then he openeth the ears of men, and **sealeth their instruction** [within them], **That he may withdraw man from his purpose, and hide pride from man.** (emphasis added)

Though I was a very young and inexperienced believer, I clearly understood what this text was saying to me. Like the apostle Paul who could not tell whether he was "in the body…or out of the body" when he was "caught up to the third heaven" (2 Corinthians 12:2), God, on that momentous night, had taken me to a heavenly place and "sealed instructions" within me. These directions would be there when I needed them during life, as they were like a roadmap that the Holy Spirit would "quicken" when, at different times, I needed guidance or information. Nevertheless, I was not to remember these details ahead of time; other-wise, I might be drawn away into my "own purpose" and lifted up in "pride" according to this oldest book in the Bible—Job.

In other words, if, as a young believer, I had seen the ministries that God would later allow me and Nita to participate in—from pastoring large churches and owning a Christian publishing house and syndicated television ministry to speaking at major conferences as a best-selling author or any of the other opportunities He would give us permission to be associated with—I very likely would have made two huge mistakes: First, I would have immediately aimed at these later ministries and started working toward making them happen all without the benefit of the struggles, trials, setbacks, sideroads, and experiences that are necessary for "seasoning" and (hopefully) qualifying one to eventually operate in them (thus God "withdrew me from *my* purpose"); and second, I would have been tempted by pride to think of myself as more than I should have as a young man, if I had seen myself winding up in high-profile ministries, and so God in His benevolence also "hid pride" from me by keeping the revelations "sealed" until the appropriate times.

The Quickenings

In the Bible it is clear that God does "seal" knowledge, wisdom, and revelations in the hearts of those who follow Him. That these concealed truths can be "quickened" or made alive at the right moments as they are needed is depicted in such texts as Matthew chapter 10:19–20, where Jesus says to His disciples: "But when they deliver you up, take no thought how or what ye shall speak: *for it shall be given you in that same hour* what ye shall speak. For it is not ye that speak, but the Spirit of your Father which speaketh *in you*" (emphasis added). That this reflects a deep partnership between our personal devotions and studies (2 Timothy 2:15; Psalm 119:11) and the indwelling Holy Spirit as part of the mystical union God holds with all members of the true Church—the Body of Christ—can also be seen in Proverbs 3:6, which says, "In all thy ways acknowledge him [that's us doing our part], and he shall direct thy paths [His part]." Again in the book of John (6:63) it refers to the Holy Spirit as the one "that quickens" (Greek *zōopoieō*—"to cause to live, to make alive at that moment") the Word of God as well as those "sealed instructions" that Job talked about.

11

I'm not sure how this experience plays out for others, but several times in my life and at times completely unexpected, I have been jolted from my sleep at night in bed with an astonishing glimpse that I believe is taken from that original storyboard God gave me years ago, and about which I begged Him to not "let me forget." On one occasion, for example, I was shaken from sleep by a very powerful and detailed list of things that would happen in the former religious institution I had been an executive in. I jumped from bed, wrote down the vision as I had seen it—including names of people who would be involved and exactly what they would do and how it would greatly damage the ministry if the district leaders did not intervene (they didn't, and it did damage the ministry)—and then I sent that detailed letter to the state superintendent. I also gave a copy to my son, Joe Ardis, and to my wife, Nita. Within three years, everything played out exactly as I had seen it, down to the smallest particulars. In fact, it was so precise that it shook Joe deeply, causing him to come to me afterwards to express his utter amazement as to how it could have been possible for me to foresee such comprehensive events with such accuracy.

A more recent quickening revelation is one that the world somewhat knows about now involving how me and Cris Putnam were able to very precisely predict the historic resignation of Pope Benedict in our book, *Petrus Romanus: The Final Pope Is Here*, as well as on television and radio a year in advance.

This began with a series of preternatural events too long to list in this book, but of which ultimately brought me and Putnam together to investigate and write our first best-seller, *Petrus Romanus*. During the research phase of that work, Putnam uncovered the obscure manuscript of a Belgian Jesuit, Rene Thibaut, who predicted sixty years in advance that the papacy would change hands in 2012 based on his understanding of the nine-hundred-year-old prophecy by St. Malachy that we were studying. Putnam worked diligently to translate Thibaut's work into English and to verify his mathematical (and mystical) calculations using a software spreadsheet and language translator.

At first, we found Thibaut's speculations interesting partly because of the year 2012, which the world was abuzz about in the lead-up to that date. But as we made inroads behind the scenes with Catholic academics and historical artifacts, we began to believe something much bigger was afoot and that either the Malachy prophecy was genuine (that is, it was either divinely or demonically inspired) or that some of the Cardinal electors *believed* it was genuine and were consequently electing popes down through the years who could somehow be seen as fulfilling their lines in the prophecy, and therefore it had become a self-fulfilling oracle.

It was during this time that one night I was, once again, rattled from sleep and instantly convinced that Putnam had been led by God to make this discovery and that, in fact, Pope Benedict would indeed step down in April 2012 using "health reasons" as a cover for abdication. We went on television and radio in 2011 (and out on a limb, quite frankly) as the book was being written and rushed through editing, typesetting, and print, so that it could be in stores before the anticipated resignation of the pope. We wrote specifically on page 470 of *Petrus Romanus* that Pope Benedict would "likely" step down in April, 2012, but in media (which people can watch on YouTube in numerous interviews from 2011) we were more insistent that not only "could" it happen, but, we predicted, it *would*.

As the year 2012 came and went and neither Pope Benedict nor the Vatican made any announcement that he was stepping down, I thought—perhaps, for the first time since I had woke up dead in heaven years earlier—the "sealed," Job-like "instructions" mechanism had either not worked or that I had been mistaken. Yet as the months passed I somehow remained convinced that we had seen the vision correctly...I would email Putnam, declaring, "It's not over till it's over," while at the same time saying to myself, *What are you talking about? Benedict is still the pope!*

Then something happened that the world now knows about—on February, 28, 2013, at 8 o'clock in the evening, the resignation of Pope Benedict was announced by the Vatican, which immediately gave the

New York Times an interview in which they made the following astonishing admission: Pope Benedict had *secretly and officially* tendered his resignation to select members of the Curia in April 2012…just as Putnam and I (and Thibaut, *and the quickening!*) had said he would. (This was an event that had not happened for hundreds of years, and one that everybody was telling us would never happen again…that is, until it did.) This was immediately confirmed by Giovanni Maria Vian, the editor of the authorized Vatican newspaper, *L'Osservatore Romano*, who wrote that the pope's decision "was taken many months ago," after his trip to Mexico and Cuba ended in March 2012, "and kept with a reserve that no one could violate"[5] (meaning it was to remain top secret and was to be known only to a handful of trusted Vatican cardinals until preparations for Benedict's housing and the public announcement was ready).

This revelation was astounding! Putnam had been led by God to uncover the trail, Thibaut had mystically speculated the event sixty years in advance, and the quickening had confirmed for me this historic event with pinpoint accuracy all ahead of time. Media everywhere went crazy! My office phone did not stop ringing for weeks with top media from around the world (including major outlets within Rome) wanting to interview us to ask "who our insider at the Vatican was." CNN begged me to come on their program, which I declined. The History Channel pleaded with us to participate in a special series, and Putnam agreed, and so on. But why am I talking about this now? Is it so we can pat ourselves on the back and brag about how incredibly accurate our prediction was?

No.

I'm raising this issue now because there has been another quickening, and this time it involves the current Pope Francis—the last Pope, Petrus Romanus, according to the Malachy list. (*Or is he!?* More on that question later.) This quickening also encompasses the revelation I will shortly detail as being much bigger and more concerning than the last one was, and yet it is with the same level of confidence I had when we foresaw that Pope Benedict would step down that I, Tom Horn, will now convey what I predict is going to happen over the next few years.

ISIS, the Final Roman Emperor, and the Next Great Awakening

Further along in this book, and in much greater detail, we will examine the apocalyptic beliefs—both Muslim and Catholic—of a final war between Islam and the "Army of Rome," which we believe is currently guiding the actions of some of the major global players in both of these institutions and that is tied to a startling revelation that no other modern writers or researchers have made involving an ancient prediction about a "last Roman emperor."

But more on that later.

As for the role ISIS (Islamic State of Iraq and Syria; sometimes "ISIL": Islamic State of Iraq and the Levant) will play in the prediction that I am set to make, I need to briefly consider the "hows" and "whys" of our modern world's fears over this mysterious group.

Our Facebook newsfeeds have been inundated with blurred images of bloody beheadings. When we visit YouTube, unsolicited videos pop up off to the side with the latest reporting of death tolls by men in black clothing carrying threatening firearms with their faces covered. When we Google-search something entirely unrelated, articles appear declaring that the seemingly unnecessary and irrational executions of non-hostile men in orange jumpsuits are still underway. Our confidence in national security has been rattled by the threat, the American collective consciousness lives in nail-biting suspense, and even our children have picked up on the fact that nameless and faceless "bad guys" are fulfilling repulsively dreadful feats of bloodshed that makes the boogeyman look like a comparative saint.

Unbelievably, however, there lies a group of central questions at the forefront of our minds that even our country's leaders have not been able to effectively answer: What is ISIS' motivation? Where did they come from? Why are they killing? And what in the world is "the Islamic State"?

Reasonable questions, no doubt, and simple enough that one would assume they would render equally simple answers. Despite convoluted explanations, however, our government, as well as the American public, is largely mystified. Though many theories have surfaced, some of which are popularized as the most likely, getting in touch with ISIS and understanding the purpose behind their mission is puzzling to even Maj. Gen. Michael K. Nagata, former US Army commander of the Special Operations Command Center, who said in an interview with *The New York Times*, "'We do not understand the movement, and until we do, we are not going to defeat it,' he said, according to the confidential minutes of a conference call he held with experts. 'We have not defeated the idea. We do not even understand the idea.'"[6] Former Defense Intelligence Agency Michael T. Flynn reacted to this comment: "The fact that someone as experienced in counterterrorism as Mike Nagata is asking these kinds of questions shows what a really tough problem this is."[7]

Firstly, the Islamic religion is monotheistic and Abrahamic, and it holds its roots in the Qur'an (Arabic: "the recitation"), which Muslims (followers of the Islamic faith) believe to be the exact and literal words of Allah (Arabic: "the God [of Abrahamic religions]"). There are many common elements between fundamental Islam and Christianity, such as beliefs in: only one God; the message and teachings of the prophets Noah, Abraham, Moses, David (and others), as well as Christ; Christ as a prophet (but not divine in Islam); Old and New Testaments are holy; wickedness of Satan; appearance of Antichrist; and heaven and hell… and so on. A peaceful start, one might think. However, just like there are different denominations within Christianity in which fundamental beliefs and lifestyle practices fluctuate, there are varying sects of Islam (Sunni, Shia, Sufi, Kharijites, Ahmadiyya, etc.), under each of which exist numerous different schools of thought—and all with their own views on violence.

To which does ISIS belong? It is said they subscribe to Wahhabism, a branch of Sunni Islam. Wahhabism is described by neutral and unbiased sources as a "religious reform movement…[in which] followers believe that they have a religious obligation…for a restoration of pure monotheistic worship."[8] Even among many Muslims, however, such as those behind the As-Sunnah Foundation of America (ASFA) whose mission statement on the front of their webpage says "Unity, Knowledge, and Understanding for the Muslim Community,"[9] Wahhabism is "[t]he most extremist pseudo-Sunni movement today."[10] The ASFA goes on to say, "Irrespective of what they think, they [Wahhabis] are not following the Islamic sources authentically."[11]

Other experts say the "best" way to describe ISIS' belief system is Salafist, a belief in the literal interpretation of the words and deeds of Muhammad and his early successors (*salaf* being Arabic for "ancestor") and that while all Wahhabists are Salafists, not all Salafists are Wahhabists. In fact, "Wahhabi" is apparently considered an insult by Salafists.

"Wahhabism," referring to the subset of Salafism founded by Muhammad ibn 'Abd al-Wahhab (d. 1792), was allied to the House of Saud in the late-eighteenth century and remains as such today. In a nutshell, Wahhabism rejected modern influences on Islam.

Salafism emerged at al-Azhar University in Cairo (according to Tim Furnish, the most influential Islamic academic institution in the world) in the second half of the nineteenth century. Contra the Wahhabists, Salafists tried to reconcile Islam with modernism. ISIS rejects leadership of the House of Saud because they are not the religious or political heirs to Muhammad. (ISIS declared war on Saudi Arabia in December, and the Saudis have been building a high-tech fence along its border with Iraq.)

What they have in common is a "fundamentalist" interpretation of the Qur'an and Hadiths, a belief that mainstream Sunnis have been wrong about their faith for about a thousand years. And both see themselves as the legitimate, "true" Muslims. ISIS especially engages in takfiri, the practice of excommunicating those who aren't with the program, but for both groups Shias are right out, absolute heretics.

In 2010, Abu Bakr al-Baghdadi became the leader of ISIS, and has since strived for domination. Aggressively, he has led ISIS to control huge land masses in Iraq, Syria, Libya, Nigeria, and Afghanistan, among many other territories of Asia and Africa. In 2014, official ISIS spokesman Abu Muhammad al-'Adnani declared Baghdadi the "Caliph Ibrahim":

> 'Adnani demanded that all jihadi factions, not only those in Iraq and Syria, but everywhere, pledge allegiance to the Islamic State, for the "legality" of their organizations is now void. He stated: "Indeed, it is the State. Indeed, it is the khilāfah. It is time for you to end this abhorrent partisanship, dispersion, and division, for this condition is not from the religion of Allah at all. And if you forsake the State or wage war against it, you will not harm it. You will only harm yourselves."[12]

Many may read these words and believe they are—*at least*—the most emphatic definition of hubris fathomable, if not complete totalitarianism. Nevertheless, though the world caliphate is a self-proclaimed authority (which numerous Muslim groups find controversial), and though Baghdadi is the self-proclaimed caliph (of whom numerous Muslim groups deny support), ISIS continues to gain assistance from fellow terrorists-in-training; American intelligence officials have estimated that one thousand foreign fighters *per month* travel to Iraq and Syria to join ISIS,[13] with Baghdadi now standing as dictatorial commander over every Muslim community in the world.

While their clandestine motives—political and religious—have baffled even US intelligence officials, their actions are loud and clear. They may be reclusive in keeping communication lines limited to themselves, allowing the rest of the world to draw whatever conclusions they will about the *whys*, but leaders of ISIS are social media savants, and at every turn they have blasted the Internet with execution videos, propaganda videos, rejections of peace, and articles of demands, as well as photos of their destruction of Christians, artifacts, and buildings, etc. Genocide, the likes of which this world has not seen since the domination of Nazi Germany, is one of ISIS' goals:

> The Nazi destruction of stolen art was an act of gratuitous violence against Europe's cultural heritage, undertaken in service to a demented ideology… Similarly gratuitous destruction of ancient cultural centers and artifacts is now underway wherever the black flag of the Islamic State, ISIS, is raised in Iraq and Syria. And so is another genocide, this time of Christians.…
>
> As the indefatigable human rights campaigner Nina Shea wrote…the wanton destruction of a sacred place is also a metaphor for "the genocide of Iraq's Christian people and their civilization."[14]

Nina Shea is not the only one who sees this horror for what it is. For example, the European Parliament "passed a resolution declaring that the Islamic State terror group…'is committing genocide against Christians and Yazidis…(and) other religious and ethnic minorities.'"[15] Even Democratic presidential candidate Hillary Clinton said a few months ago, "I am now sure we have enough evidence, what is happening is genocide deliberately aimed at destroying lives and wiping out the existence of Christians and other religious minorities."[16]

Is ISIS so far out in left field that their cries for dominance are driven by an apocalyptic landscape? Some rational minds would believe this to be an immediately sensationalistic notion, but if we look at how dramatic ISIS is in every other aspect, we begin to not only accept, but *expect*, their ideologies to be ceaselessly and recklessly grandeur…and we are not alone. ISIS is in fact driven by very specific and ancient eschatological apocalypticism.

To begin, Islam's central figure, the prophet Muhammad, allegedly predicted the invasion and defeat of both Constantinople and Rome. The first of these two cities fell into the hands of the Muslims in the

1400s, bringing the prophecy to fruition. Rome has yet to be dominated. Sheikh Yousef Al-Qaradhawi, "one of the most influential clerics in Sunni Islam,"[17] explained this prophecy:

> The Prophet Muhammad was asked: "What city will be conquered first, Constantinople or Romiyya?" He answered: "The city of Hirqil [i.e. the Byzantine emperor Heraclius] will be conquered first"—that is, Constantinople... Romiyya is the city called today "Rome," the capital of Italy. The city of Hirqil [that is, Constantinople] was conquered by the young 23-year-old Ottoman Muhammad bin Morad, known in history as Muhammad the Conqueror, in 1453. The other city, Romiyya, remains, and we hope and believe [that it too will be conquered].[18] (brackets and ellipses in original)

The idea that ISIS plans to wage war against Rome is more than clear through all of their speeches, posts, articles, and propaganda. To quote Baghdadi, himself, in a speech to fellow Muslims just two days after he was pronounced the caliph (translated by ISIS' subsidiary media company Al-Hayat; as quoted by the Middle East Media Research Institute):

> So congratulations to you, O slaves of Allah, as Allah has allowed you to reach this noble month. Praise Allah and thank Him for having granted you long lives, thereby giving you a chance to correct your past deeds.... As for the religion of Allah, then it will be victorious. Allah has promised to bring victory to the religion....
>
> So take up arms, take up arms, O soldiers of the Islamic State! And fight, fight!... So raise your ambitions, O soldiers of the Islamic State!...
>
> Soon, by Allah's permission, a day will come when the Muslim will walk everywhere as a master, having honor, being

revered, with his head raised high and his dignity preserved. Anyone who dares to offend him will be disciplined, and any hand that reaches out to harm him will be cut off.

So let the world know that we are living today in a new era. Whoever was heedless must now be alert. Whoever was sleeping must now awaken. Whoever was shocked and amazed must comprehend. The Muslims today have a loud, thundering statement, and possess heavy boots. They have a statement that will cause the world to hear and understand the meaning of terrorism, and boots that will trample the idol of nationalism, destroy the idol of democracy, and uncover its deviant nature....

So listen, O ummah [Arabic: "community"] of Islam. Listen and comprehend. Stand up and rise. For the time has come for you to free yourself from the shackles of weakness, and stand in the face of tyranny, against the treacherous rulers—the agents of the crusaders and the atheists, and the guards of the Jews....

O Muslims everywhere, glad tidings to you... Raise your head high, for today—by Allah's grace—you have a state and caliphate, which will return your dignity, might, rights, and leadership....

Therefore, rush, O Muslims, to your state. Yes, it is your state. Rush, because Syria is not for the Syrians, and Iraq is not for the Iraqis. The Earth is Allah's... The State is a state for all Muslims. The land is for the Muslims, all the Muslims....

Know that today you are the defenders of the religion and the guards of the land of Islam. You will face tribulation and epic battles....

So prepare your arms, and supply yourselves with piety. Persevere in reciting the Koran [Quran] with comprehension of its meanings and practice of its teachings.

This is my advice to you. If you hold to it, you will conquer Rome and own the world.[19]

Besides the aforementioned parallels between Nazi Germany and ISIS' genocidal agenda is the blatantly obvious parallels between Hitler's declaration-of-war speeches and this—Baghdadi's declaration of war against Rome and all enemies of Islam. His intonations are sometimes so Hitlerian that one could swap out the relative ethnic groups and enemy groups and post it online as a "lost speech by Hitler" and people would believe it. But I digress...

Under the leadership of Baghdadi, radical Muslim terrorist factions are, *in fact*, "raising up arms" for war. Islamic eschatology (from the Hadith) points to the town of Dabiq, Syria, as a fester-pot of the *Muslim Malahim* (apocalypse; Armageddon). The "Romans" (or "Roman Christians," as some scholars put it) will "land" in Dabiq, wage war against the Muslim soldiers, the Muslims will win, and the "Last Hour" heralds the arrival of Isa (Christ) and Dajjal (Antichrist). (Note, also that ISIS' official magazine is also called *Dabiq*.) From "The Only Quran" website, the prophecy reads:

Abu Huraira [Muhammad's recorder and companion] reported Allah's Messenger (may peace be upon him) assaying: The Last Hour would not come until the Romans would land...in Dabiq. An army consisting of the best (soldiers) of the people of the earth at that time will come from Medina (to counteract them).... They will then fight and a third (part) of the army would run away, whom Allah will never forgive. A third (part of the army), which would be constituted of excellent martyrs in Allah's eye, would be killed and the third who would never be put to trial would win... And as they would be busy in distributing the spoils of war (amongst themselves) after hanging their swords by the olive trees, the Satan would cry: The Dajjal [Antichrist] has taken your place among your family. They would then come out, but it would be of no avail. And when they would come to Syria, he would come out while they would be still preparing themselves for battle drawing up the ranks. Certainly, the time of prayer shall come and then Jesus ["Isa"] (peace be upon him) son of Mary would descend and would lead them in prayer. When the enemy of Allah [Dajjal; Antichrist] would see him, it would (disappear) just as the salt dissolves itself in water and if he (Jesus) were not to confront them at all, even then it would dissolve completely, but Allah would kill them by his hand and he would show them their blood on his lance (the lance of Jesus Christ).[20]

For some time, ISIS has been goading worldwide military powers to bring vicious attacks against Dabiq, believing that the Muslims will win, and subsequently take the battles therefore outward to Rome. These provocations have been seen in a number of recent terrorist activities, and now they have raised the incitement even higher, baiting up to sixty countries across the globe.

Not long ago, a serious ISIS threat-video was released called *See You in Dabiq*, relating imagery of this upcoming war. The media specialists in ISIS used some digitally altered stock footage to make the film, since the war has not yet happened, as well as original footage filmed in Iraq. At one point in the video, the ISIS flag is raised over sixty other nation flags, representing its domination over opposition. Another scene shows an armored battle tank driving toward the Roman Coliseum, with the voiceover saying, "This is your last crusade, the next time it is us who will take the battle on your own land."[21] From *Heavy News*:

> In the video, tanks can be seen driving towards the Coliseum crumbled in the sand. Footage then cuts to outside buildings of the Italian capital, before zeroing in on the Vatican....
>
> The film's dialogue makes claims that the "Dabiq Army" will race into Rome, destroy crucifixes, and enslave Christian women.[22]

This video trails another, which was released last December (2015). Two ISIS radicals sit on a peaceful beach, facing the camera. One speaks in (somewhat broken) English, regarding the November 2015 ISIS terrorist attacks in Paris, France, and goes on to list other targets, including the US:

> It is a state [referring to the Islamic State]. When you violate its right, your hand is bound to get burned.... All you Crusaders, you claim to want to degrade and fight the Islamic State, while you fail to secure your nations and your capitols. How come shall you degrade us? You call your armies, like France called their armies in the streets of Paris, but rest assured, they will avail them nothing. We will come to them from where they do not expect.... The revenge has started, and the blood will flow. France was the beginning. Tomorrow will be Washington. It will be New York, and it will be Moscow. You Russians, don't you think that we forgot you! Your time is coming! It is coming! And it will be the worst.... You will not have safety in the bedroom of your houses.... Allah! This event healed our hearts.[23]

The article, "ISIS Releases Chilling New 'End of the World' Video Showing Final Battle with Crusaders," from *Mirror News* has no problem linking all their past violence to their latest unsettling *See You in Dabiq* bait, calling forth all powers of the world to challenge them on their own soil, and then taunts that nonbelievers will "burn on the hills of Dabiq."[24]

How the Vatican Is—and Will—Play Right into ISIS' Hands

Over the last few years and on more than one occasion, Pope Francis as well as top Vatican diplomats and spokespersons have argued in favor of a coordinated international force to stop so-called Islamic State (ISIS) atrocities against Christians and other minorities throughout the Middle East. In 2015, this included Italian Archbishop Silvano Tomasi calling on the United Nations to "stop this kind of genocide.… Otherwise we'll be crying out in the future about why we didn't do something, why we allowed such a terrible tragedy to happen."[25] Pope Francis, himself, has tried to parse words between "stopping" ISIS and distancing himself from US-led bombing sorties, yet he, too, has used very specific language in recent days that has not gone unnoticed by these writers. These are hermeneutical efforts undoubtedly cultivated for theologians and knowledgeable persons to encourage them to see beneath his judiciously chosen phrases to his deeper *sotto voce* ("under voice") communication, which clearly expresses his and Rome's intentions to sanction a coming war, using terms like "unjust aggressor," "genocide," and even the very idiom, "Just War,"[26] which are directly connected not only to specific activities of ISIS but are particular vocabulary extracted from the "Just War" theory and "Just War" doctrine (the latter is derived from Catholic Church 1992 Catechism, paragraph 2309, which lists strict conditions for "legitimate defense by military force").

Both "Just War" traditions mentioned above (thoroughly examined later in this book by Putnam as it involves definitions by theologians, policy makers, and military leaders) repeatedly employ the very terms "unjust aggressor" and "genocide" for the purposes of ratifying those doctrines whenever "war is morally justifiable through a series of criteria, all of which must be met for a war to be considered *just*. The criteria are split into two groups: 'the right to go to war' (*jus ad bellum*) and 'right conduct in war' (*jus in bello*). The first concerns the morality of going to war and the second moral conduct within war," which postulate that "war, while terrible, is not always the worst option. There may be responsibilities so important, atrocities that can be prevented or outcomes so undesirable they justify war."[27]

The fact that Pope Francis and other high-ranking churchmen have explicitly used precise "Just War" terms is telling and supports the *prediction* made later in this chapter. It also serves to clarify why Archbishop Tomasi, in his call to the UN for greater military action against ISIS, admitted his request for engagement was derived from "a doctrine that's been developed both in the United Nations and in the social teaching of the Catholic Church."[28] This is the dictum I believe certain power brokers at the Vatican (what Father Malachi Martin called the Masonic "Superforce") and the pontiff will knowingly use to eventually engage the self-proclaimed caliph of the ISIS regime, who wants nothing less than a final, end-times Holy War leading to the arrival of the Islamic Mahdi (Messiah).

I Predict

Once the proper balls are rolling, both ISIS and the Vatican will see themselves in the midst of unfolding prophecy. For their part, all the Vatican needs at this moment are the right trigger events.

PREDICTION #1—Weapon of Mass Destruction

Sometime over the next forty-eight months, the Islamic State and/or their associates are going to use a weapon of mass destruction. It will be of such scope and impact as to raise the international outcry sufficient for Rome to play its first card, which, as we noted in the previous pages, has been primed by subtle references to the Just War theory in the lead-up to this predicted event. When this WMD (electromagnetic pulse, biological weapon, chemical weapon, dirty radiological bomb, or nuke that causes widespread damage) is used by ISIS, the Roman pontiff will call for the revitalization of the Christian rules for "Just War."

A coalition army similar to the 2003 invasion of Iraq will be formed to seriously engage the Islamic radicals. Geopolitics aside, the jihadists will see the Vatican's sanction of war as a new and final religious crusade—indeed, an actual fulfillment of their thirteen-hundred-year-old Hadith, which allegedly quotes the sayings of the prophet Mohammed concerning a last-days caliphate that goes up against "the army of Rome" to initiate "Malahim"—the equivalent to Armageddon in Christian teachings, a battle that ISIS believes they will ultimately win. This war will, according to ISIS, provoke the coming of Mahdi (their Messiah), the Al-Masih ad-Dajjal (Antichrist), and Isa (Jesus), who spears the Antichrist figure and fights on behalf of the Muslim army.

It is my belief that Pope Francis (or whatever pontiff is sitting on St. Peter's throne at the Vatican at that time) likewise will view himself—and Rome—as amidst unfolding prophecy, which the current pope has alluded to on several occasions, including connecting ISIS terrorism with the end of the world.[29] Francis has even recommended that people read *Lord of the World*—a related 1907 book by Monsignor Robert Hugh Benson that depicts the reign of Antichrist and the Vatican's relationship to the end of the world, which both Francis and emeritus Pope Benedict have called "prophetic." This is not surprising, as the reigning pope is an avowed prophecy believer and knows that he is "Petrus Romanus," the final pope (#112) from the famous "Prophecy of the Popes" attributed to St. Malachy (that is, unless Francis was *not* canonically elected, which we will discuss later, an intriguing possibility that presents additional strange and prophetic alternatives to the narrative). The best-selling work by Putnam and myself titled *Petrus Romanus: The Final Pope Is Here* thoroughly and critically dissected this mystical prophecy and found widespread support for the document from Catholics and even evidence that, down through the years, cardinals elected popes who could somehow be viewed as fulfilling their line in this prophecy. As it involves Pope Francis, here is what the final line in the prophecy says:

In the extreme persecution of the Holy Roman Church, there will sit Peter the Roman [Pope #112, Petrus Romanus], who will pasture his sheep in many tribulations, and when these things are finished, the city of seven hills will be destroyed, and the dreadful judge will judge his people. The End.

When elected Pope #112, Jesuit Jorge Mario Bergoglio (Pope Francis) immediately did several fascinating things to wrap himself in his "Peter the Roman" title:

- First, he took as his namesake St. Francis of Assisi, an Italian (Roman) friar whose original name was Giovanni but that was later changed to Francesco di Pietro (Peter) di Bernardone—a name that can literally be translated "Peter the Roman" from the final line of the Prophecy of the Popes.
- Second, Pope Francis knows that Francis of Assisi was a prophet and that he predicted this final pope would "be raised to the Pontificate, who, by his cunning, will endeavor to draw many into error and death…for in those days Jesus Christ will send them not a true Pastor, but a destroyer." It is astonishing that Francis would pick as a namesake a man that foretold this of the final pope.
- Third, Pope Francis named Pietro Parolin as the Vatican's new secretary of state—a man who could sit on the throne of Peter if Pope Francis retires (like Benedict did), dies, or is killed, and whose name can also be viewed as "Peter the Roman." If Francis was not canonically elected, Pietro Parolin would actually become the real Pope #112 under that scenario.

And then there are those famous last words from the Prophecy of the Popes itself, which says: "When these things are finished, the city of seven hills will be destroyed, and the dreadful judge will judge his people." This idea, that the city of Rome will be destroyed during the reign of pope #112 (and just ahead of the Second Coming of Jesus Christ as Judge), is a vision repeated in numerous ancient prophecies from Greek,

Jewish, Catholic, and Muslim cultures. This includes what ISIS draws from their Hadith—that they will go to war against the army of Rome and destroy the Vatican's headquarters. As mentioned prior, ISIS has even produced a movie that depicts this apocalyptic event culminating in the destruction of Rome.[30] In tandem with the prediction, they have threatened to kill Pope Francis,[31] and the pontiff has responded by saying he is willing to be assassinated if that is God's will; he just hopes it doesn't hurt.[32] As this narrative continues unfolding toward the conflict I am predicting, it becomes increasingly clear that both Pope Francis and ISIS believe they are engaged in an end-times scenario, making some of what Francis has said and done since his "election" clearer within a larger oracular context.

For example, in addition to what the ISIS Hadith and the Prophecy of the Popes say about the destruction of Rome, shortly after he accepted the pontificate, Pope Francis consecrated the world to "Our Lady of Fatima" during Mass in St. Peter's Square.[33] Francis knows the prophecies and controversies connected to Fatima, including the vision of the "Holy Father" (pope) walking among a destroyed city (the Vatican) when ISIS-like fighters run in and kill him. Francis believes in this prophecy (obviously why he dedicated the world to precisely this Marian apparition), and ISIS vows to make it happen. In *Petrus Romanus*, we noted:

> The third part of the Secret of Fatima, which was supposedly released in total by the Vatican June 26, 2000, seems to echo the visions of Pius X. A section of the material reads:
>
> > …before reaching there the Holy Father passed through a big city half in ruins and half trembling with halting step, afflicted with pain and sorrow, he prayed for the souls of the corpses he met on his way…on his knees at the foot of the big Cross he was killed by a group of

soldiers who fired bullets and arrows at him, and in the same way there died one after another the other Bishops, Priests, men and women Religious, and various lay people of different ranks and positions.[34]

It's interesting, given the prediction from Fatima, that Pope Francis has also reached out to Kabbalist rabbis, whose Zohar (the most important work of the Jewish Kabbalah, which was written in medieval Aramaic over seven hundred years ago) also foretells this destruction of Rome (Vaera section, volume 3, section 34) in connection with "Messiah's" secret arrival in the year 2013 (is this why top rabbis in Israel are saying the Messiah's presentation to the world is imminent?). And, after this "Messiah" makes himself known to the international community, "the kings of the world will assemble in the great city of Rome, and the Holy One will shower on them fire and hail and meteoric stones until they are all destroyed."[35]

The depth to which Pope Francis can be thought of as a mystic and believer in such prophecy involving the coming destruction of Rome may also be connected to his knowledge of the Cumaean Sibyl, whose prophecy about the return of the god Apollo (identified in the New Testament as the spirit that will inhabit Antichrist) is encoded on the Great Seal of the United States,[36] as well as in Catholic art (from altars to illustrated books and even her appearance upon the ceiling of the Sistine Chapel, where four other Sibyls join her [Paul cast a demon out of one such prophetesses in the New Testament]), and the Old Testament prophets in places of sacred honor. Yet this Cumaean—who sits so prominently inside Catholicism's most celebrated chapel—gave forth other famous and forgotten prophecies, which we will examine later to show how she was quoted by early Church Fathers and actually connected the end-times Islamic Mahdi with a "Last Roman Emperor" (who arguably developed into the "Holy Pope" legend)—an eschatological figure whose time, and whose catastrophic war, may now have arrived.

Will Pope Francis be the one to play the role of the Last Roman Emperor? Or will it be another pontiff? Was there something strange about the conclave from which Pope Francis emerged to the pontificate? Something mentioned earlier in this chapter that suggests he was not actually "canonically elected?"

Even some Catholics think "illegitimate" activity may have gone on behind closed doors during the last conclave[37] and that, for reasons we do not yet understand, Francis was put in as a temporary "place-holder" until the *real* pope #112 (Petrus Romanus) could be installed. This, too, might echo the choice of St. Francis of Assisi as a namesake, as the ancient friar did predict, "a man, not canonically elected, will be raised to the pontificate." The mysterious reasons surrounding a "place-holder" pope—a *false* pope—is largely unknown to the public, but was foresaw by such mystics as Father Herman Bernard Kramer in his work, *The Book of Destiny*. During an unusual interpretation he made of the twelfth chapter of the book of Revelation concerning "the great wonder" mentioned in verse one, Father Kramer wrote:

> The "sign" in heaven is that of a woman with child crying out in her travail and anguish of delivery. In that travail, she gives birth to some definite "person" who is to RULE the Church with a rod of iron (verse 5). It then points to a conflict waged within the Church to elect one who was to "rule all nations" in the manner clearly stated. In accord with the text this is unmistakably a PAPAL ELECTION, for only Christ and his Vicar have the divine right to rule ALL NATIONS... But at this time the great powers may take a menacing attitude to hinder the election of the logical and expected candidate by threats of a general apostasy, assassination or imprisonment of this candidate if elected.[38]

Although we disagree with Kramer's interpretation of the book of Revelation, his fear that "great powers may take a menacing attitude to hinder the election of the logical and expected candidate" echoes the sentiment of priests mentioned elsewhere in our book *Petrus Romanus*, who see a crisis for the Church coming, and the Final Roman Emperor (Antichrist) rising as a result. As we move through 2016, Pope Francis is publically looking for a global political authority (such as the UN) to come alongside him to implement his religious and social agenda, President Barack Obama has just set his eyes on becoming the UN Secretary General following the US presidential election,[39] and Israeli President Benjamin Netanyahu is very concerned about the ramifications of both. Will the pope or ex-president step forward to fulfill the Cumaean Sibyl's prophecy…or are there others waiting in the wings? Either way, I predict that an ISIS WMD and a call by Rome to sanction war will soon result in both Muslims and Romans engaging in their own apocalyptica.

Oh…and as you will learn more extensively later in this book, nearly a decade ago, a major Islamic website set the date on which this war and it's Mahdi would unfold: "Based on our numerical analysis of the Quran and Hadith," they concluded, "the official beginning of the End of Time and the coming of the Imam Mahdi will most likely be in…2016."[40]

PREDICTION #2—On the Heels of War, a Great Awakening

Following the end of the Holocaust and people's awareness worldwide over what had happened to the Jews under Nazi Germany, a groundswell of support pressured member nations of the UN to assist the Zionist movement and declaration of a Jewish state. In the same way that I believe women will play a major role in the next Great Awakening, by January of 1948, via the efforts of people like Israel's Iron Lady Golda Meir, over twenty-five million dollars had been raised from American sympathizers of the Zionist movement (a number that continued to grow to 129 million by March of 1949). Shortly thereafter, the Haganah (Jewish paramilitary organization in the British Mandate of Palestine [1921–48], which became the core of the Israel Defense Forces or IDF) became a legitimate army on the offensive in the interest of reopening supply lines to Jerusalem and the surrounding settlements, adding infantry brigades, and drafting thousands upon thousands of Jewish men and women to support their cause.

On the morning of April 8, 1948 Palestinian Arab nationalist leader Abd al-Qadir al-Husayni fell in the battle of Al-Qastel (a village just outside Jerusalem). His death resulted in a significant interruption of organized Arab military in the Jerusalem area. More battles and sieges thundered upon the Jews, but the Arabic forces were losing their grip. After the Deir Yassin massacre (executed by radical Zionist groups, not the Haganah), the local press reported a great fear spreading through the Arab Liberation Army, and more of them fled. By this time, the Jews had obtained support from the US, as well as many other nations across the world, and the "Palestinian Arab military power was crushed."[41]

In the midst of this civil war, however, revisions had been made to Resolution 181(II) (the United Nations Partition Plan for Palestine, a proposal developed by the United Nations that recommended a partition with Economic Union of Mandatory Palestine to follow the termination of the British Mandate; on November 29, 1947, the UN General Assembly embraced a resolution recommending the adoption and implementation of the Plan as Resolution 181(II)). On May 12, 1948 (a little over a month after key Arab military leader al-Husayni was defeated), the *Minhelet HaAm* (Hebrew "People's Administration") assembled to vote on the last remaining issue: to declare independence, or to agree to a truce. The former was the prevailing vote, one that was endorsed by the then-current chairman of the World Zionist Organization.

Moetzet HaAm (Hebrew "People's Council") met two days later to hash out the final debates regarding borders, religion, the name of the state, and freedom of language, and finalize the Declaration of Independence document for Israel. The name of the state was voted six to three in favor of "Israel." The borders were not agreed upon, due to the ongoing clash of Arabic culture, and therefore, borders were not specified in the Declaration. Regarding the official faith and religion of the Jewish nation, the words "and placing our trust in the Rock of Israel" became the official lingo of the end of the document, allowing each individual the freedom to perceive said "Rock" as "*God* of Israel" or as the land of Israel, itself, as an independent state. The Hebrew language was agreed upon as the central language of the state, but because of the scattering of Jews throughout foreign lands, provisions were granted allowing freedom of language for the incoming Jewish settlers to still feel at home.

The Declaration ceremony took place on May 14, 1948, at the Tel Aviv Museum (today Independence Hall) only hours after Britain's rule over Palestinian territory expired. In fear that British authorities (or the whispered threat of another Arabic invasion) would prevent it, the ceremony was to be attended by only those two hundred and fifty who had received a hand-delivered invite by messenger, and all in attendance had been instructed to keep the event a secret. At 4 o'clock in the afternoon, executive head of the World Zionist Organization David Ben-Gurion brought his gavel down, and a silence fell upon the gathering in the hall. He then began to lead the people spontaneously in the singing of "The Hope" (Hebrew *Hatikva*, which later became Israel's national anthem) in front of a portrait of Theodor Herzl. The Israeli Declaration of Independence document was then read aloud, followed by the *Shehecheyanu* blessing (a Jewish prayer of blessing used on special occasions) by Rabbi Yehuda Leib Fishman.

After the blessing, the signatories made the document official. Literally overnight, the Palestinian lands transferred from British rule to the hands of the Jews. Israel was now a state, backed by international support (including the US), and the now established Jewish nation had a homeland. A Zion. The restoration of the Promised Land by God to Abraham.

According to Rabbi Yechiel Eckstein of the Jewish Virtual Library:

After the Holocaust, we Jews gazed dumbfounded at what had occurred. Was it possible to go on believing in a God of love after losing 6 million individuals, one third of the Jewish people, almost 2 million of whom were children? Was it possible to go on believing in God's covenant with Israel and their election?…

Like Ezekiel before us, we Jews stood amidst the ashes of [death camps] Auschwitz, Buchenwald, and Treblinka and [when] we looked down in the valley of Sheol we asked, "Can these dry dead bones again live [Ezekiel 37]?" Can we Jews possibly recover from this devastation? And behold, a miracle—God breathed life into those dry bones and they came together, sinew to sinew, bone to bone. They took on flesh and spirit. They arose and were reborn in Jerusalem. "For the Lord has comforted His people, He has redeemed Zion [Isaiah 52:9]."

What does Israel mean to the contemporary Jew? It means that God has not abandoned His people. It means that He is true to His Word! Israel's existence gives us our very will and determination to continue living…as Jews.[42]

The Jews were home.

The Age of Fire

Many adhere to the idea that there is only one earthly place that God has declared "holy," based on the words of the prophet Isaiah (24:23): "Then the moon shall be confounded, and the sun ashamed, when the Lord of hosts shall reign in mount Zion, and in Jerusalem, and before his ancients gloriously." Several other verses equally point to this (Deuteronomy 11:12; 33:13; Ezekiel 20:6). Likewise, the Jews, and Israel, are considered "God's chosen people" by many verse translations (Exodus 19:5; Deuteronomy 14:2; Deuteronomy 26:17–19; 2 Samuel 7:23–24; 1 Kings 8:53; 1 Kings 10:9; 1 Chronicles 17:20–21; Psalm 135:4; Isaiah 41:8; Isaiah 43:1–3; Isaiah 44:21; Jeremiah 31:1–4; Jeremiah 46:27–28; Ezekiel 36:24–28; Ezekiel 37:21–25; Joel 3:1–2; Amos 3:1–2; Romans 11:1–2). Again from the prophet Isaiah (51:16), we read, "And I have put my words in thy mouth, and I have covered thee in the shadow of mine hand, that I may plant the heavens, and lay the foundations of the earth, and say unto Zion, Thou art my people."

The relevance of understanding Israel as the Holy Land and the Jews as God's chosen people as it relates to the Great Awakening that followed the 1948 formation of a Jewish state (that particular spiritual awakening/revival lasted from the 1950s–1970s and is commonly called the "Age of Fire") lies in the Parable of the Budding Fig Tree (not to be confused with the Parable of the Barren Fig Tree). This parable appears in three New Testament Gospels locations (Matthew 24:32–35; Mark 13:28–31; Luke 21:29–33): "Now learn a parable of the fig tree; When his branch is yet tender, and putteth forth leaves, ye know that summer is nigh: So likewise ye, when ye shall see all these things, know that it is near, even at the doors. Verily I say unto you, This generation shall not pass, till all these things be fulfilled. Heaven and earth shall pass away, but my words shall not pass away."

The word "it" in Matthew 24:33 has been rendered also "He" or "the Kingdom of God." This passage, along with those that refer to the Holy Land and God's chosen people together make up the base Scriptures of what has become known as the "Fig Tree Prophecy."

The Fig Tree Prophecy

On the Mount of Olives, the disciples asked Jesus Christ about the end of the world (or "end of the age")—"And as he sat upon the mount of Olives, the disciples came unto him privately, saying, Tell us, when shall these things be? and what shall be the sign of thy coming, and of the end of the world?" (Matthew 24:3). After speaking for a moment about His Second Coming and the threat of the Antichrist, Christ tells His listeners that the first sign of the end of the age was when the fig tree "putteth forth leaves" (or "buds"). Because the fig tree is the last of the trees to flourish in the springtime, when it puts forth its leaves, it is an indication that "summer is nigh" (or "imminent").

Note that in Hosea 9:10a, Israel is referred to as a fig tree: "I found Israel like grapes in the wilderness; I saw *your fathers as the first ripe in the fig tree* at her first time" (emphasis added). Joel 1:6–7a makes the same comparison: "For *a nation* is come up upon my land, strong, and without number, whose teeth are the teeth of a lion, and he hath the cheek teeth of a great lion. He hath laid my vine waste, and barked *my fig tree*" (emphasis added). In addition to these references, nations have historically been typified by symbols and/or emblems (America: eagle; Russia: bear; Canada: beaver and maple leaf; Britain: lion; and so on), and for Israel, the emblem is a fig tree.

Jesus also spoke the following:

"I tell you, Nay: but, except ye repent, ye shall all likewise perish." He spake also this parable; "A certain man had a fig tree planted in his vineyard; and he came and sought fruit thereon, and found none. Then said he unto the dresser of his vineyard, Behold, these three years I come seeking fruit on this fig tree, and find none: cut it down; why cumbereth it the ground? And he answering said unto him, Lord, let it alone this year also, till I shall dig about it, and dung it: And if it bear fruit, well: and if not, then after that thou shalt cut it down." (Luke 13:5–9)

In Isaiah 5:7a, the "vineyard" is the property of God, and the "house of Israel" ("For the vineyard of the Lord of hosts *is* the house of Israel"; italics original). At the time Christ spoke the parable above in Luke 13:5–9, He had been three years into his public ministry. God's people (the vineyard) needed to "repent" or they would "likewise perish." Also note that Christ explicitly refers to the vineyard owner as "Lord" ("Lord, let it alone this year also"). So, in the parable, the "certain man" who owned the vineyard (God; "Lord") approached the "dresser" (Christ), and told him that for "three years" (Christ's public ministry up to that point) the vineyard owner had tried to find fruit from this fig tree (Israel). Because the tree would not produce fruit, the vineyard owner ordered the dresser to cut it down. (Translation: God told Jesus to cut Israel down.) But the dresser requests that the vineyard owner give the fig tree one more season of growth, during which the dresser will "dig about it" (make the ground around it healthy) and "dung it" (fertilize it). (Translation: Jesus requested more time to bring the nation of Israel to repentance.) If further efforts to see the fig tree produce fruit did not deliver, then the vineyard owner would cut it down.

Then, in AD 70, Israel was cut down by the Romans in the Siege of Jerusalem…

In Ezekiel, it is prophesied:

But ye, O mountains of Israel, ye shall shoot forth your branches [bud], and yield your fruit to my people of Israel; for they are at hand to come. For, behold, I am for you, and I will turn unto you, and ye shall be tilled and sown [made healthy again]: And I will multiply men upon you, all the house of Israel, even all of it: and the cities shall be inhabited, and the wastes shall be builded: And I will multiply upon you man and beast; and they shall increase and bring fruit: and I will settle you after your old estates, and will do better unto you than at your beginnings: and ye shall know that I am the Lord. Yea, I will cause men to walk upon you, even my people Israel; and they shall possess thee, and thou shalt be their inheritance, and thou shalt no more henceforth bereave them of men. (Ezekiel 36:8–12)

And in Amos, we are told of a replanting:

And I will bring again the captivity of my people of Israel, and they shall build the waste cities, and inhabit them; and they shall plant vineyards, and drink the wine thereof; they shall also make gardens, and eat the fruit of them. And I will plant them upon their land, and they shall no more be pulled up out of their land which I have given them, saith the Lord thy God. (Amos 9:14–15; emphasis added)

Then, in 1948, Israel was replanted…

We now arrive at an important conclusion: If Christ said the "end of days" was "even at the doors" when the fig tree "putteth forth leaves," and that "this generation shall not pass, till all these things be fulfilled," then the establishment of Israel as a nation marks the last generation before the end of days.

This is the core of the Fig Tree Prophecy.

The amount of time in a single generation is greatly varied from source to source. Some believe it to be forty years, some seventy, some eighty, some a hundred, and still others refer to when the last person within that generation passes away. When Christ told the disciples that "this generation shall not pass," He was telling them that Israel would be cut down before the end of their current generation. A generation in the Bible is typically forty years. If Christ was born in AD 1, as it is traditionally thought, then He would have prophesied the cutting down of the fig tree sometime during His public ministry in AD 30–33. Israel was destroyed in AD 70, about forty years later. Scholars in 1948 then presumed, if this forty-year timetable applied to Israel blossoming as a nation again in 1948, this suggested the last generation would end by 1988: 1948 + 40 = 1988. The '80s birthed a *great* number of date-setter ministers who claimed the world would end, or Christ would return, by the year 1988. And, obviously, they were wrong…

According to Psalm 90:10, "The days of our years are threescore years and ten, and if by reason of strength they be fourscore years" meaning *seventy or eighty* years, which brings us to the following equations: 1948 + 70 = 2018 and 1948 + 80 = 2028, two or twelve years from the time of this writing. Yet again, the account of Genesis 15:13–16 assigns one hundred years to a generation, when God warns Abraham of the coming slavery of his people: "Know of a surety that thy seed shall be a stranger in a land that is not theirs, and shall serve them; and they shall afflict them *four hundred years....* But *in the fourth generation* they shall come hither again" (emphasis added). This, of course, leads modern date-setters to assume the last days will arrive on or before 2048. Aside from all this math, in 2 Peter 3:8, we are instructed: "Be not ignorant of this one thing, that one day is with the Lord as a thousand years, and a thousand years as one day," which is why these authors do not subscribe to any particular dating methods. To strengthen this stance: "But of that day and hour knoweth no man, no, not the angels of heaven, but my Father only" (Matthew 24:36).

In any case, when Christendom was shaken by the notion that the world would end, or Christ would return, within forty years following the Israeli Declaration of Independence, preachers rose to alert the world of these "last days" with unadulterated fervor. The slumbering Church was also moved by the idea that prophecy was unfolding before their very eyes—that God was ushering in the literal "end times"—and this gave birth to a sense of evangelical urgency: that what was to be done had to be done *quickly*, resulting in an "awakening" that today we call the "Age of Fire." Billy Graham grew out of this awakening, as did Oral Roberts, Kathryn Kuhlman, Jack Coe, William Marrion Branham, Asa Alonso Allen (most often called A. A. Allen), and so many more. There is hardly any way of estimating the millions of souls that were saved and healed as a result of this mighty awakening, which itself led to what some consider even another awakening—the "Jesus Freaks" or "Jesus People" of the '60s–'70s counterculture movement.

Is the Next Great Awakening Right Around the Corner?

In the same way that the last Great Awakening(s) grew out of the tragedies of war and disillusionment over civil authorities, today we are witnessing the most amazing similarities between cultural phenomena (the threat of war, terror, an ISIS WMD, and the loss of faith in establishment politicians) that preceded many awakenings of the past, including the aforementioned "Age of Fire."

I predict these similarities are not by chance, but providence, and that at least one final Great Awakening awaits the immediate future. Indeed, the use of a WMD by ISIS will be the trigger event of not only Catholic and Muslim apocalypticism but a final Great Awakening! The forthcoming terrorist use of a weapon of mass destruction and the military conflict following it will—like the Holocaust did—partly provide the impetus for both the Church and society's awakening.

Not only do I predict a great revival of believers and awakening for salvation by the lost, but I'll take my prediction further and outline the following specific demarcations this awakening will be known for:

1. Women will be more involved than they were in any previous Great Awakening.

This will include women as prophets, teachers, and pulpit preachers.

Merely as one example of many female Church pioneers, let's consider Kathryn Kuhlman to further explain my inclusion of women in this prediction.

When Kathryn Kuhlman of the Age of Fire stepped forward to preach and heal multitudes in an era where women were expected to sit quietly in church, dress humbly, and leave all the theological interpretations to "the men," Kuhlman spoke confidently on the platform, dressed in flowing gowns and high heels, and interpreted Scripture. During a time that Pentecostalism was becoming prevalent but still hotly debated by more spiritually conservative Christian doctrines, Kuhlman, without shame or remorse, stood strong in her professions regarding the Holy Spirit and healing (which may have come across less brazen from a man as well). Understandably, these and other of her bold traits created quite the controversy.

Though Kuhlman's ministries have been ardently disputed over the years (some of the details of which will be discussed in a forthcoming book through Defender Publishing titled *Final Fire: Is the Next Great Awakening Right around the Corner?*), she was something the world had never experienced. During her day, a female preacher wasn't necessarily unheard of, but they typically only spoke to fellow women, and almost never to large groups at once. When Kuhlman's ministry resulted in miracles and crowds comparable to that of men like Oral Roberts, it propelled a category of mass followers no *man* would have ever had prior. It was a feminine and refreshing approach to the Gospel that had been so affected by decades of the "God's wrath" and "hellfire-and-brimstone" pulpit-pounding sermons by masculine church leaders (which also had their proper place and role in the awakening). It was the elegance behind her words. It was her tone of voice, the softer, gentler, "come to Christ" call that extended to lonely hearts even across denominational borders. It was, in its purest form, a tender revitalization of the Scriptures from an *affectionate* perspective.

When Christ came, He touched peoples' lives through *love*. Certainly, He had His moments of righteous anger (overturning tables, etc.), He said just as much about hell as He did heaven, and He railed against the Pharisees and Sadducees with a hot indignation…but it is within His *tenderness* that *both men and women alike* (as well as children, teens, and the elderly) find themselves continuously drawn. When Kuhlman preached, she brought this Christ into view as the kind Shepherd, the lover of mankind, the embracer of even the worst of sinners that He truly is, thereby primarily leaving sermons of the fears of hell and eternal torment to the other ministers who had for eons perfected such an oratory execution. And it was with this novel femininity and compassion that *a woman* led uncountable flocks to the Lord.

As a woman, Kuhlman was an evangelical Christian pioneer, and it was her graceful yet persistent response to the attacks against her teaching in church that paved the way for some of our modern paramount female ministers.

Today—thanks to the numerous evolutions of women's rights

and gradual incline of women's social, cultural, and political powers—those who would immediately dismiss the ministry of a woman simply because she is female have dwindled to a comparatively trivial minority. Women have influence more now than ever before, and their voices are as prominent within the Church as men. However, the world appears to be hungrier than ever before for the *affectionate* gospel of Christ. In fact, according to a study referenced by *USA Today*, the number of women preachers/pastors *doubled* between 1999 and 2009.[43]

Therefore, it stands to reason to predict here and now that women (*of all races!*) will not only play a larger role in the next Great Awakening than ever before, but that they will be *encouraged* to do so, and feel *equipped* to do so without the levels of opposition that applied in the past. Kuhlman is merely one example of the great women leaders who have risen from obscurity throughout religious history and into the archives of Christian headship. Many celebrated names are now making enormous strides in the Church, such as Joyce Meyer and Anne Graham Lotz.

2. Young people around the world will catch the vision and be drawn by deep, inextinguishable hunger to know the Word of God and to preach the Gospel of Jesus Christ.

People will also say it was because modern technology—which created social detachment in personal relationships—left them cold and hungry for something more, something *Divine*.

This part of my prediction is, of course, regarding how I have come to believe that young people will rise up as great leaders of the Church. However, I am *certainly* not the only one that has come to the conclusion that modern technology and social networking has led to the hindrance and impedance of true, deep connections to others within the human race.

One quick online search involving some equivalent to the words "social media and our young generation" will result in hundreds of thousands of results—articles, blogs, dissertations, speeches, online videos, and the like—all discussing the mindboggling, negative impact that technological social life has had on today's generation, as well as upon future generations. We spend more time today pouring into websites like Facebook, Twitter, and LinkedIn, subjecting ourselves to up to hundreds (and for some of us, thousands) of online friends each login whose one- or two-sentence interactions seems too often to be all we share between ourselves and our friends anymore. Baking cookies for a neighbor, stopping by Aunt Suzie's house, and visiting a sick acquaintance in person is preposterously inconvenient, when the same courtesy can (supposedly) be extended over a computer screen.

Through a recent social phenomenon called "trolling," we have evolved into a people who flippantly pass on the cruel comments of unaccountable and faceless musings, knowing we will not have to appear face-to-face and stand accountable for the horrible thing we said about Bill's weight gain, David's beard, or what we consider to be the outrageous amount of money our pastor just spent on his wife's anniversary gift.

To list yet another tragedy: social networking and media aren't just responsible for affecting the careless and vain interactions of society, one might even ask whether or not our children are actually being *raised* by these outlets. Like a character from the movie *The Matrix*, whose entire link to the world is through the virtual and misleading download-plug affixed to the back of their heads, some of our nation's youth spend so much time on computers and tablets that the only life they know how to function in is the one they are "plugged into." No more dinners around the family table. No more sitting down as a family to study the Bible, read a good book, or have a pretty picnic out in the sunshine. When their electronics are not accessible, instead of returning to yesteryear's imagination games or even visiting, they have been documented to become depressed, anxious, and bored, not knowing what to do with themselves now that "their world" has been taken away. It's wonderfully handy (isn't it?) that kids are operating and navigating electronic devices at younger and younger ages every day, as iPads and iPhones are excellent babysitters…or so I hear.

Add to all of this the fact that these networks and devices continue to run at the most inopportune times. Even the family that dines together and prays together can't get through a meal or a devotion without their smartphone beeping some kind of notification or other. (It would be nice to see more parents and guardians adopting a "zero-tolerance policy" for these devices during these gatherings, but sadly—as I, myself, on frequent occasions have witnessed—this is an idea that has not been implemented by many households. Often, it is even in the middle of a sentence, *or a prayer*, that I have observed someone hear a notification, drop what they're doing, and start fiddling with their device. Even if they do remember what they were saying or hearing prior to the interruption—and we all know that is *not* always the case—moments of true communication with another *human* or with *God* has been lost in the process. One of the best decisions I ever made was when I threw my cell phone in the garbage a couple of years ago. It's been amazing having my life back from that constant distraction. Now if I can just get the rest of my family to follow suit! But I digress…)

And, it is through this disconnect that a hunger and thirst will bubble up within the youth of the next Great Awakening—not only for a more acute bond with people, but with *God*.

When one studies the history of all previous revivals and Great Awakenings—from as far back as the Bohemian Reformation of the 1300s (which later triggered the Protestant Reformation) to as recent as the "Jesus People" movement (referred to by many scholars as the fourth Great Awakening)—the evidence is clear: the stirring began *so* often within the hearts of the *youth*, and toward the ministries of those sprightly hearts, adolescents were the first to respond. In fact, some of the most prominent names associated to these revivals and awakenings belonged to people whose epochs of passion and ministerial peaks occurred while they were still fledgling Christ-followers barely out of their teens or in their mid-twenties.

Just to name a few examples of this:

- Jonathan Edwards of the first Great Awakening chose to equip local elders within his surrounding communities to take his sermons out of the church and into home discipleship programs when he was *twenty nine years old*. The *children and teenagers* within his area were amongst the largest groups to stand up, take responsibility for their own actions, adopt an upright living code, and join the fires of revival.

- John and Charles Wesley (commonly "the Wesley brothers"), whose mission work highly influenced both the first and second Great Awakenings, formed an organization at Oxford in 1729 called the "Holy Club"—thus named "by their fellow collegians in mockery of their emphasis on devotions."[44] At this time, John was *twenty-six*, and Charles was *twenty-two*. The mission of the club was to meet for prayer and Bible study, participate in organized fasts, and carry out good deeds for the needy, including contributions of food to the poor, visitations to prisoners, and educational assistance to young children (primarily orphans). Membership throughout the years included such celebrated names as John Gambold, John Clayton, James Hervey, Benjamin Ingham, and Thomas Brougham, all eminent historical leaders within their religious domains. Many, including Charles W. Keysor, who authored *Our Methodist Heritage*, are of the opinion that today's Methodist Church holds its origins in this "Holy Club." Through John's personal ministry, as well as other evangelists he inspired, Methodists became central to many social matters, seeing to the needs of the poor and parentless and comforting prisoners, among a long list of other good deeds. John is now credited as the founder of Methodism. Charles remained an English leader of the evangelical Methodist movement alongside his brother; however, to this day, he is mostly remembered as the illustrious writer of over six thousand hymns, many of which allude to a personal indwelling of the Holy Spirit. The Wesley brothers *together* are credited with having played critical roles in the later development of Pentecostalism.

- Another young man heavily involved in the "Holy Club," alongside the Wesley brothers and only *fourteen* or *fifteen* at the time he joined, was George Whitefield, whose life was—through his experiences in the Holy Club and as an associate of the Wesley brothers—thereafter righteously affected to the point that he became one of the most illustrious preachers of the Great Awakenings this world has ever known. (He was active during the years of the first Great Awakening, but his published sermons continued to ignite revival for years afterward, and even directly inspired other Great Awakening frontrunners, such as Dwight Moody during the American Civil War.) When the Wesley brothers left Oxford for Georgia, Whitefield became the club's leader for a short time. After reading a book on the Northampton revival written by Jonathan Edwards, the inspired Whitefield took the Gospel outdoors to crowds reportedly as large as thirty thousand at any given time, and was documented to preach publicly on eighteen thousand occasions.[45]

- James McGready was the central figure behind the 1800 Kentucky Revival, which is considered by most mainstream scholars to be the trigger event behind the second Great Awakening. Although he was nearing the age of forty by the time his ministry launched the revival, its most profound effect was upon the youngest members of the camp meetings, including tiny children, through whose fervor the widespread enthusiasm for spiritual resuscitation reached all others around them, even the elderly. The events that transpired at this time have been repeatedly documented to have produced outpourings of the Holy Spirit only familiar within the Pentecostal denomination, even though the three leading denominations circa 1800 within the South states of that year were Presbyterian, Baptist, and Methodist. In one account from Richard McNemar, author of the 1808 documentation *The Kentucky Revival*, we read the following:

The general meeting at Indian creek, Harrison county…continued about five days and nights.… But there was very little appearance of that power which strikes conviction to the heart of the sinner, until the third day about two o'clock in the afternoon. A boy from appearance about twelve years old, retired from the stand-in time of preaching under a very extraordinary impression, and having mounted a log at some distance, and raising his voice in a very affecting manner, he attracted the main body of the people in a few minutes. With tears streaming from his eyes, he cried aloud to the wicked, warning them of their danger, denouncing their certain doom if they persisted in their sins, expressing his love to their souls, and desire that they would turn to the Lord and be saved. He was held up by two men, and spoke for about an hour, with that convincing eloquence that could be inspired only from above. When his strength seemed quite exhausted and language failed to describe the feelings of his soul, he raised his hand and dropping his handkerchief, wet from sweat from his little face, cried out, "Thus, O sinner! Shall you drop into hell, unless you forsake your sins and turn to the Lord." At that moment some fell like those who are shot in battle, and the work spread in a manner which human language cannot describe.[46]

- Dwight Lyman Moody (frequently D. L. Moody) was *in his early twenties* when he took the gospel to the streets of Chicago, to the poor, to the homeless, and most often to the *children*. By November of 1860 when he was about *twenty-five years old*, and when US President Abraham Lincoln came in person to visit Moody's ministry, the crowd of children and young teens in his circle had grown to fifteen hundred,[47] requiring the abandonment of the freight car in a urine-stained slum referred to by the locals as "Little Hell" that he had been using to preach. Early the following year, when the American Civil War was in full swing, Moody became a chaplain, ministered to thousands of soldiers on both sides of the political and slavery schism, and found solace in George Whitefield's published sermons. When the war was over, he had his own variation of a Pentecostal "upper room" experience, and took his gospel (which was centered on the *love* of God, not the *wrath* of God, which was so popular a theme within church walls at the time) to multitudes uncountable in the US and Europe, becoming the pivotal name behind the third Great Awakening. Not only was Moody, himself, incredibly young when he launched one of the most astonishing revivals our country has observed, but because of his emphasis on the important role that *children* and *teens* played within the Church, many of the changed boys and girls became integral religious leaders who rose from his influence.

- In the fourth Great Awakening, otherwise referred to by many as the "Jesus Freaks Movement" or "Jesus People Movement" (a national revival that did not, as the others mentioned prior, have a key minister who launched an awakening), crowds of teens and young hippies formed the primary core of the spiritual brushfire. They hailed from communes peppered all over the US (predominantly originating in the Haight-Ashbury district of San Francisco during the "Summer of Love" in 1967). By the mid-1960s—with the same tenacity of the counterculture's civil, liberal, and political demonstrations (minus the violence and riots)—came floods of Jesus Freaks (or Jesus People) throughout main cities, holding positive signs, preaching the Word, pooling resources to feed and house the hungry and homeless, singing hymns of praise outside shopping centers, and sharing everything they had in the interest of witnessing to others about this "Son of God." Jesus-centered magazines, pamphlets, and periodicals were printed and distributed by hand across all demographics without bias. With the same communal lifestyle as the flower children came opened doors to any and all to gather for scriptural study for days on end during meetings with no structured start or ending times, and before long, "churches" formed in the unlikeliest of places: personal homes, bus stations, coffee shops, restaurants, abandoned buildings, barns, parking lots, random fields, etc. Unlike some of the preceding religious eras: Their sermons were delivered in *joy*, not demands. They raised their voices to be heard with *smiles*, not angry fists. They sang with lyrics of *praise* and *love*, not with condescension, arrogance, pride, or hatred toward opposing opinion. Their meetings were met with *hugs*, not riots. The atmosphere surrounding them was one of *buoyancy*, not anxiety or agitation. Almost all of those who either led or helped spread the gospel during this Great Awakening were very young.

Because the key players in the previous Great Awakenings have so often been in their early twenties (and some even in their teens), and because their actions have time and again motivated crowds even as undeveloped as children, I predict that the next Great Awakening will see a rise in youthful involvement within the Church.

3. Orthodox Jews and Muslims will convert to Christianity in record numbers, becoming some of the most dynamic, unstoppable witnesses in the world.

On this aspect of the coming Great Awakening, our good friend and host of *Sid Roth's It's Supernatural* calls today's Church body *The Incomplete Church* in his 2008 thusly titled tome. Roth argues the Church cannot be truly complete until the Jewish people embrace Jesus as their Messiah; he believes Jews and Gentiles will converge, each having a unique role, into a complete Church for the Messiah's millennial reign from Jerusalem. We believe Roth's "convergence" may be what Paul (Romans 11:25–30) and Zechariah (12:10) both prophesied. Finally, Yahweh promises to restore the Jewish people again, with faith in Jesus, at this time. "And it shall come to pass in that day, That the Lord shall set his hand again the second time To recover the remnant of his people, Which shall be left, from Assyria, And from Egypt, and from Pathros, And from Cush, and from Elam, and from Shinar, And from Hamath, and from the islands of the sea" (Isaiah 11:11).

Roth wrote:

> While the Bible makes many promises to the Jewish people, the greater end-time call belongs to Gentile believers. They are called to lead the Jewish people to Jesus. "To provoke them [the Jew] to jealously, salvation has come to the Gentiles" (Rom 11:11b). When the Jew and the Gentile converge together… it will spark an end-time revival such as the world has never seen.[48]

4. Undeniable angelic manifestations will be worldwide.

Why do I say this? Because one cannot read the apocalyptic texts—including Daniel and especially the book of Revelation—and fail to note that everything that is happening in the endtimes suddenly involves angelic activity. Angels begin pouring out bowls of judgment, they sound trumpets to cue apocalyptic events, they hold back winds of judgment, and they even gather God's elect from the four corners of the world. But how many know that angels will also be preachers of the Gospel at the end!? "And I saw another angel fly in the midst of heaven, having the everlasting gospel to preach unto them that dwell on the earth, and to every nation, and kindred, and tongue, and people, Saying with a loud voice, Fear God, and give glory to him; for the hour of his judgment is come: and worship him that made heaven, and earth, and the sea, and the fountains of waters" (Revelation 14:6–7). Can you imagine how quickly the world will come to a halt at the sight of such an appearance?

Again, we plan to publish that entire vision of the next Great Awakening before the end of this year, Lord willing. And we will include the "signs and wonders" already unfolding, such as the following testimony from Cris Putnam.

A Special Note from Cris Putnam: A Precognitive Dream?

As I, Cris Putnam, write this out, there are empty boxes from the liquor store scattered about my office.

No, I haven't taken to the drink.

First, let me tell you about my dreams…

In late 2011, apocalyptic fervor was at a fever pitch, and I contacted Tom Horn about the Prophecy of the Popes, which, unknown to me, he had just entered his hotel room to make notations about. The result was beyond my wildest dreams: the best-selling book, *Petrus Romanus: The Final Pope Is Here.* The follow-up, *Exo-Vaticana: The Vatican's Plan for the Arrival of an Alien Savior,* even outsold the first, becoming a cultural meme of sorts. After that, I took some time to publish an apologetic treatise: *The Supernatural Worldview.*

Interestingly, in that book I demonstrated how God uses dreams and near-death experiences to communicate to His servants, and further, I confirmed that there is compelling scientific evidence that dreams sometimes forecast the future.[49] Horn and I followed up by discussing the immortal beings and interdimensional portals while tracing the ancient unseen world to the Western continent in *On the Path of the Immortals,* and the book now in your hands is the fourth and final (or is it?) investigation in that co-written series.

But before all of that, I had a couple of memorable dreams about the beginning of the end.

The first of these has occurred more than once and still disturbs me. It's really a *nightmare,* actually, about a nuclear explosion within the United States. In the nightmare, there are massive causalities and the country becomes a virtual police state as a result of this nuclear terrorism. I told my wife and a few of my friends about this back in 2012. (Within the last few months, the Islamic State has threatened to use its Mexican drug cartel connections to smuggle a nuclear bomb across the Southwestern border.)

The second dream was, and remains, even more interesting. A massive explosion had occurred in the Middle East but the "who, where, and when" details are fuzzy. Whatever this enormous detonation entailed, we—me and numerous co-workers in the dream—were celebrating; we believed the blast signified the beginning of the Tribulation. In other words, I believed the sixth seal had broken. There were many friends around as we talked about the event on television. But why would I be on TV? (At that point, I had only one published essay about transhumanism. I had no knowledge of Tom Horn's future intention to start SkyWatch TV. The dream made little sense to me.) I was working as a television commentator for Tom Horn in this dream, whom I barely knew through email at the time and had never met. While this may seem unremarkable to those of you who have seen me speaking at Strategic Perspectives 2015 or on GodTV or the History Channel, at that time I was a virtual unknown.

After *Petrus Romanus* exploded into the public's eye, I told Tom Horn about these nighttime images. We were sitting in a pickup truck parked outside of Southwest Radio Church where we were interviewed by the late Noah Hutchings. Tom laughed and said, "That is interesting, but I don't have a television show." Being somewhat indoctrinated with science, I eventually wrote it off as amusing, brain-manufactured nonsense. I only told two people about the concept when it occurred: my wife, Shelley Putnam, and Tom Horn. Both now verify that I told them about these night visions long before *SkyWatch TV* was ever mentioned, even as an idea.

Now, referring back to all of those empty liquor boxes: In North

Carolina, the ABC Store is one of the best places to get good-sized empty boxes for free. Oh…perhaps you haven't heard yet? *We are moving to Crane, Missouri*, where I accepted a job offer to be a staff writer for Defender Publishing and the developer of a new program for *SkyWatch TV*—Tom Horn's new television outlet and website.

It seems that *part* of this dream, the portion regarding my appearances on television that I originally couldn't make sense of, has already come to pass. Like the predictions found in this book, the rest remains to be experienced.

Are *you* ready?

2

Theories of War
Just, Jihad, and Crusade

"WAR IS HELL" is famously attributed to Union Gen. William Tecumseh Sherman.[50] He served as a general in the Union Army during the American Civil War (1861–1865), for which he not only received recognition for his brilliant military strategy, but a legacy of reproach for his "total-war" and "scorched-earth" stratagems used against the Confederate States. "Scorched earth" was a military strategy that entailed burning everything to the ground, and includes the annihilation of anything that might be useful to the enemy while moving through an area. Borrowing from the Crusade ethos, it prescribes the total destruction of all of the enemies' assets, including non-military goods such as food, transportation, information technology and communications infrastructure, industrial resources, and, in the case of the IS, gratuitous murders visited upon civilians in metropolitan areas like Paris and Rome. It is hard to imagine such a civil war today, but the IS' battlefield ethos makes them an existential threat.

Sherman's brutality earned him a formidable legacy, but his "total war" tactics do work. They work so well, in fact, that the US military has never really abandoned them. Sherman burned Atlanta down to hot cinders for the same reason we bombed Baghdad—to invite the ene-mies' submission. John Marszalek describes Sherman as setting the bar for modern psychological warfare.

> And so, in Atlanta, Sherman instituted tactics later generations of American war leaders would use in World War II, Korea, Vietnam, Iraq and Afghanistan. In these later conflicts, largely through the use of air power, Americans attempted to destroy enemy will and logistics (a doctrine colloquially known as "shock and awe" in Operation Iraqi Freedom). On the ground and on a much smaller scale, Sherman pioneered this process, becoming the first American to do so systematically. He is rightly called the American father of total warfare, a harbinger of the psychologi-cal tactics of the next century.[51]

The US employs Just War principles in order to deploy using a bor-rowed Crusade ethos (but without its divine justification). It seems as if the US wants to have its cake and eat it, too. War really *is* hell, and people will go to incredible ends when engaged in mortal combat. Sher-man is also widely *credited* for actually saving lives because he boldly seized the moment and *ended* the war decisively. If it had dragged on, many more men would have been killed on both sides.

As a seminarian, author Cris Putnam studied with Southeastern Baptist Theological Seminary ethics professor Daniel Heimbach.[52] Born to US missionary parents on Chinese soil, Heimbach was educated at the US Naval Academy, Trinity Evangelical Divinity School, and Drew University. Of particular relevance, he served on the White House domestic policy staff for George Herbert Walker Bush, even advising the first President Bush on "Just War" principles at the dawn of the first Gulf War to rescue Kuwait.[53] Heimbach writes that the Christian tradition "recognizes that the use of deadly force is sometimes a tragic but moral necessity because evil is ever present in a fallen world."[54] He characterizes the tradition as holding "war as a limited, morally necessary, short-term response to a specific violation of peace and order."[55] With that in mind, Heimbach addressed the IS directly back in September of 2014.

> Full application of just war principles does not only warrant air-strikes, but a far more vigorous level of engagement as well.... The reality we must not ignore is how responding to ISIS with too little will make matters a lot worse, and responding to ISIS too late will make success less likely and a lot more costly.[56]

We believe it is likely that a coalition force will attack the IS during or right after this book is being printed. Of course, Pope Francis has repeatedly articulated Just War terminology in his remarks addressing the IS to the UN. After the Paris attack, the rest of the free world (including Russia[57]) is in agreement. While it's easy to agree that the IS needs to be stopped, questions remain concerning why, given the ground intelligence we have shown, they were ever allowed to get so far. The intelligence community has been monitoring the IS for many years prior to 2014 and predicted our current situation, as did some of the media. We are not resting our overarching thesis on the current IS situation alone, but rather are pulling out to consider a more long-play perspective of history. The IS' documented acts of terrorism justify taking action; they provide just cause.

Just cause is amply supplied by the IS' 1) murder and displacement of Syrians and Iraqis; 2) known terrorist attacks (e.g., Paris, Russian airliner); and 3) documented threats against major cities including Istanbul, Rome, New York, Washington, DC, Jerusalem, and Saudi Arabia.

An academic text suggests that because some outcomes are worse than war, preventing them is justification in and of itself. "Just War theory postulates that war, while very terrible, is not always the worst option. There may be responsibilities so important, atrocities that can be prevented or outcomes so undesirable they justify war."[58] The history of

Just War theory begins with the biblical standards in Deuteronomy and Amos; it was developed in the ethical works of early Greek philosophers like Plato, who expounded on "just cause;" and it was modified later by the Romans. Ethically minded theologians like Ambrose, Augustine, and Aquinas combined and expanded on these works in an effort to develop an ethical grid by which one might guide a nation.

Unfortunately, tyrannical rulers can and will abuse saintly theories. St. Ambrose (AD340–397), a former Roman imperial officer, appropriated Christianity as his *jus bellum* ("right to war"). He justified all of the Roman Empire's wars as a means of "peacekeeping," harkening the *Pax Romana* ("Roman Peace"), which originally facilitated the proliferation of the gospel message across the empire in the hands of Paul and Timothy until AD 180.

Ambrose argued that the "peace of the church" ensued after Constantine issued the Edict of Milan decriminalizing Christian practice in AD 313. Even so, it is widely agreed that Constantine's rationale was self-serving, political, and represented the beginning of what grew over time to encapsulate the Church and state into a beast never intended by Christ (John 18:36) called "Christendom," comprising the area now known as Europe. As a result, the office of the papacy became a power grab for disingenuous royals, which led to the Crusades and indulgence profiteering. It took Henry VIII's cheekiness[59] and the Protestant Reformation led by Martin Luther and John Calvin to get the pope's full attention.

Thus, pre-Reformation theologians were still at the mercy of the Roman Empire, but more glaringly, we do not anywhere see a pope leading the entire Church. In fact, there is no evidence whatsoever for a centralized papacy based in Rome in the second through fifth centuries. The New Testament falsifies Rome's central claim on Peter. The Acts of the Apostles ends with Paul in a Roman prison, at a time when Catholics would have us believe Peter was sitting as pope, seemingly indifferent to Paul's case. In response to the Catholic revisionism, a Baptist apologist,

James White, makes the case from original source documents that the early Church of the Nicaean period did not:

1. Look to the Bishop of Rome as the Vicar of Christ, the head of the universal Church, the pastor of all Christians;
2. Believe in the Marian doctrines that set Rome apart, such as the Immaculate Conception of Mary and her Bodily Assumption;
3. Embrace such concepts as the *thesaurus meritorum*, purgatory, and indulgences;
4. Believe in the Roman concept of authority, replete with extra-biblical, revelatory or inspired "traditions" that add to the "deposit of faith" items and beliefs not found in Scripture:
5. Nor practice the necessary devotions to reserved, consecrated hosts that would substantiate the leap from a belief in "real presence" to the much later belief in "transubstantiation."[60]

White cogently argues and documents those five points in the footnoted debate. Applying the principle of Occam's razor, a simpler solution is that the Catholic tradition and the related claim to apostolic succession from the "peterine office" was a later concoction for justifying papal power. In other words, it was created ad-hoc from Matthew's Gospel (Matthew 16:18) and shoehorned into history, and that explains why it does not match the historical record written early by Luke in the New Testament. The primacy of Peter is a post-Luke invention. University of Notre Dame history professor, Thomas F. X. Noble, wrote, "Peter did not found the Roman community, and there is no good evidence that that community had a bishop—an 'overseer'—in the 1st century."[61] More conspicuously, Paul omits Peter from his extensive list naming *twenty-seven* Christians in Rome (Romans 16:3–16). The letter was composed at exactly the time the Vatican would have us believe Peter was bishop there (AD 42–67). If Peter were the sitting pope, it is not only difficult to explain Paul's ignorance, but it would be an unimaginable oversight in Luke's historiography (Luke 1:3–4).

Even conspiracy theorists err by tacitly accepting the Catholic version of history when accusing the papacy of crimes that were committed before it really existed (e.g., Catholics conspiring via the Council of Nicaea).[62] Despite an overabundance of allegations, the bishop of Rome didn't even bother to appear at the first Council of Nicaea. He sent an alternate in his place and, despite the elaborate fictions popularized by Alexander Hislop,[63] Constantine was personally indifferent concerning various complex theological debates. He depended on his advisors, as most royals do. For the most part, Constantine, the man, seems typical of the entitled pagan royalty, but he was baptized a Christian, actually only *one day* prior to his death.[64] However, it wasn't until AD 380 that Christianity became the state religion. Oxford historian Christopher Tyerman paints a more tarnished version of Church history than Rome's revision:

> Ambrose of Milan (d. 397), as befitted a former imperial official, consolidated this symbiosis of the Graeco-Roman and Christian: Rome and Christianity were indissolubly united, their fates inextricably linked. Thus the war of one was that of the other, all *Rome's wars were just in the same way that those of the Old Testament Israelites have been*; even heresy could be depicted as treason. Ambrose's version of the Christian empire and the wars to protect it which constituted perhaps the earliest formulation of Christian warfare was, therefore, *based on the union of church and state;* hatred of foreigners in the shape of barbarians and other external foes; and a sharp intolerance towards dissent and internal debate, religious and political (emphasis added).[65]

Augustine's *City of God* provides a primary foundation for Just War theory in Western literature. Augustine held to the belief that pacifity in the face of evil that could, in harsh reality, only be stopped by violence, is a sin. One also has a stewardship to protect one's family and to be a good neighbor. Defense of one's self or others, including killing one's adversary could, at times be deemed a moral necessity. That is, especially when authorized by a legitimate authority (like the state), as explained in *City of God* chapter 21:

OF THE CASES IN WHICH WE MAY PUT MEN TO DEATH WITHOUT INCURRING THE GUILT OF MURDER:

However, there are some exceptions made by the divine authority to its own law, that men may not be put to death. These exceptions are of two kinds, being justified either by a general law, or by a special commission granted for a time to some individual. And in this latter case, he to whom authority is delegated, and who is but the sword in the hand of him who uses it, is not himself responsible for the death he deals. And, accordingly, they who have waged war in obedience to the divine command, or in conformity with His laws, have represented in their persons the public justice or the wisdom of government, and in this capacity have put to death wicked men; such persons have by no means violated the commandment, "Thou shalt not kill."[66]

Nine hundred years later, Thomas Aquinas, the legendary theologian-polymath, codified Augustine's reflections into the distinct criteria that remain the basis of Just War theory as it is still used today. Aquinas used the authority of Augustine's arguments to specify the three conditions under which a war could be just:[67]

First, just war must be waged by a properly instituted authority such as the state. (Proper Authority is first: represents the common good: which is peace for the sake of man's true end—God.) Aquinas wrote, "First, the authority of the sovereign by whose command the war is to be waged."[68]

Pope Francis criticized Obama for finally bombing the IS. "One nation alone cannot judge how to stop an unjust aggressor. After the Second World War there was the idea of the United Nations."[69] Thus, the United Nations is precisely named as the properly instituted authority by the pope. As a related side note, perhaps Catholic US military officers are bound to follow the pope above their commander, according to Church doctrine.

Second, the theory requires that war must occur for a good and just purpose, to make right a wrong. Aquinas termed it "just cause." "Secondly, a just cause is required, namely that those who are attacked, should be attacked because they deserve it on account of some fault."[70] Pope Francis implied that the IS also meets this second condition. He identified the IS as an unjust aggressor, and added, "To stop the unjust aggressor is a right that humanity has, but it is also a right that the aggressor has to be stopped so that he does not do evil."[71] Of course, this criticism applies to nebulous cold-war constructs like "national security interest" as well. With the benefit of hindsight, many analysts doubt the 2003 invasion of Iraq met the "just cause" qualification.[72] Accordingly, national security interest was severely compromised rather than served. Rabid Mahdism is more widespread than ever, as the direct result of the US invasion of Iraq.

Third, the basic requirement is that peace is the ultimate motive. It addresses intent, and so, precise terminology is required. For instance, if some Muslims define "peace" to mean "a worldwide caliphate under Sharia law" when Western diplomats understand it in terms of "mutually assured total annihilation," then more specific syntax is obviously required. According to Aquinas, "Thirdly, it is necessary that the belligerents should have a rightful intention, so that they intend the advancement of good, or the avoidance of evil."[73] Aquinas implies that right-minded soldiers must fight for justice, not glory. He specifies that the response should be proportional to the injury and the motive justice rather than punishment or victory for victory's sake.

In the following statement about the IS, Pope Francis tipped his mitre to Aquinas: "The crime of aggression has to be taken to the UN to decide which are the best means to stop the aggressor. He made clear 'I do not say bomb.'"[74] He made the last distinction for a reason. "The Syrian Observatory for Human Rights has estimated that 181 civilians have been killed in the coalition airstrike campaign against the Islamic State, as of mid-August."[75] With millions of refugees flooding Europe, air strikes are a notoriously indiscriminate method of waging war.

What is a "proportional response" to IS' ever-rising death toll? In 2014, more than 4,325 Iraqi *civilians* were killed by IS alone, *not* including combatants.[76] "In the year since it declared itself a 'caliphate,' more than 3000 people in Syria, including over 1500 civilians, have died at the hands of Islamic State."[77] In 2014, the ongoing four-year Syrian civil war's death toll was estimated to be two hundred thousand. However, the *New York Times* qualified,

> The constant violence has forced more than four million to flee the country, fueling a refugee crisis in the Middle East and Europe. The country is so dangerous that a definitive tally of deaths is not possible, but several groups are trying to document how many Syrians have died, and what killed them.[78]

In November 2015, more than seven hundred thousand Syrian Christians are classified as displaced, but we know a significant number of those are dead.[79] If the trend has continued until now, as we predict from the rate of change before, those numbers could be, by the time this book is distributed in spring 2016, nearly double what is cited. While the IS' atrocities are well recognized, we question the right of the papacy to speak as a moral authority, given its institutional track record.

Drunk with the Blood of the Saints

Daniel A. Plainsted is a mathematician and computer science professor at the University of North Carolina at Chapel Hill (close enough for

Putnam to pay him a visit), and spends most of his time working on "instance-based theorem proving strategies,"[80] algorithms, and whatnot. He is an expert in handling data—in this case, a body count. Plainsted wrote a paper in 2006 that informs our present discussion: "Estimates of the Number Killed by the Papacy in the Middle Ages and Later."[81] If you haven't studied history, some of the following information might be surprising. We first expected he might challenge the reasonableness of some of the large numbers of martyrs cited in post-Reformation Protestant literature. For instance, the missionary pastor credited with founding Methodism, John Wesley, explained, "Partly by war, partly by the Inquisition, and a thousand other methods of Romish cruelty? No less within forty years, if the computation of an eminent writer be just, than five and forty millions!"[82] Other examples include Brownlee, who alleged that during the late medieval period to the early Reformation period, the Roman Catholic Church martyred more than fifty million Christians.[83]

What makes it all the more interesting is that these numbers were not considered controversial when published and were not challenged by Rome until much later. Plainsted noted:

> Some persons today are claiming that this figure of 50 million has no basis in fact and is an exaggeration based on anti-Catholic sentiment. Therefore it is of interest to find out how this figure was originally computed in order to evaluate its reliability. This study reveals some aspects of history that are being neglected today and also gives us an insight into the extent to which *the true history of religion is being lost.*[84] (emphasis added)

A proximate example is *Halley's Bible Handbook* (1965 edition), which stated, "Historians estimate that, in the Middle Ages and Early Reformation Era, more than 50,000,000 Martyrs perished."[85] Note that it specified "martyrs," so the fifty million included mostly Christians killed by the so-called "Holy Roman Empire," a political whorehouse of a Church and state monstrosity that led to the Thirty-Years War and the dungeon horrors of the Inquisition. Plainsted examines the sources and never discredits the high death tolls. In fact, he establishes their reasonableness given the associated historical context. Plainsted surmises:

> These quotations give us important clues about the origin of the figure of 50 million killed by the Papacy in Europe. Another individual recalled to the author that this figure of 50 million consisted mostly of those killed after the beginning of the reformation, suggesting that this 50 million figure contained the 45 million figure. Because Wesley quoted the figure of 15 million killed by war and the Inquisition, it is reasonable to conclude that this is part of the figure of 45 million, and that this figure of 45 million is part of the often quoted figure of 50 million. The figure of 30 million killed in 40 years probably refers to a period including the Thirty Years' War from 1618 to 1648. Thus the figure of 45 million is probably the sum of these two other figures of 15 million killed from 1518 to 1548 and 30 million killed in 40 years including the period from 1618 to 1648. It is interesting that even in 1714, such computations were being done.[86]

Fifty million martyrs seemed prohibitive at first glance, but it is supported (with room to spare) by independent historiography. Plainsted concluded that "the time and place of the major persecutions contributing to the 50 million figure have been determined with reasonable confidence"[87] and that "one can assign reasonable totals to these persecutions that do add up to 50 million."[88] Jesuit historical revisionists have infiltrated academia and have discredited as demonstrably absurd exaggerations of the body counts, but, all too often, the numbers are horrifically high enough that, in good conscience, I cannot politely stay silent. For example, Plainsted's analysis of the Protestant historian's "exaggerated" numbers against independently collected population data is cold hard mathematical, and damning of popery.

> Concerning the Irish rebellion, John Temple's *True Impartial History of the Irish Rebellion* of 1641, written in 1644, puts the number of victims at three hundred thousand, but other estimates are much smaller. Some estimates are larger:
> In addition to the Jesuit or Catholic atrocities of this century already enumerated with some particulars, they massacred 400 Protestants at Grossoto, in Lombardy, July 19th, 1620; are said to have destroyed 400,000 Protestants in Ireland, in 1641, by outright murder, and cold, and hunger, and drowning;…
> —Cushing B. Hassell, *History of the Church of God*, Chapter XVII
> In fact, the population of Ireland is estimated to have decreased from 2 million in 1640 to 1.7 million in 1672, according to R.F. Foster, Modern Ireland 1600–1972 (1988). However, this could have resulted from British reprisals to some extent and from emigration, forced or voluntary. The population should have increased by about 200,000 during this period, assuming a 30 percent growth rate per century. This implies that 500,000 people in excess of normal either died or left Ireland during this time, and is consistent with 300,000 or more Protestants being killed in 1641.[89]

The loss implied by the population figures given in Foster's *Modern Ireland*[90] is five hundred thousand in excess of normal spanning the thirty-two year period from 1640–1672, but, more specifically, it favors the actuality of the three hundred thousand to four hundred thousand deaths recorded by the older Protestant historians whose figures are, so often today, discredited by accusations of "anti-Catholic" bias and summarily dismissed. We think it is important to recognize and remember the millions of Protestant martyrs killed in terrorist assaults like the St. Bartholomew's Day massacre.[91] Above, a scientist draws from independently sourced population data, not the rabid imaginations of Protestant historicism. Another example centers on Spain just as Columbus sailed the ocean blue.

The notorious Spanish Inquisition was established at Seville in 1480 by the blind religious zeal of Queen Isabella and the unscrupulous avarice of King Ferdinand and of Pope Sixtus IV.—the grand object of this infamous institution being to make money by the confiscation of the property of wealthy "heretics." In 1481, the first year of its operation, two thousand persons were burned. In the sixteen years of the generalship of Thomas de Torquemada (1483–1498), it is said that 8,800 were condemned to the flames, 6,500 burned in effigy, and 90,000 subjected to imprisonment, confiscation and other penalties. Llorente, the secretary and official historian of the Spanish Inquisition, estimates that that the institution, during the whole period of its existence, burned about 30,000 persons alive, and condemned about 300,000 to punishments less severe than death. In 1492, persecution was begun against the Jews, of whom 500,000 were expelled from Spain and their wealth confiscated. In seventy years the population of Spain was reduced from 10,000,000 to 6,000,000 by the banishment of Jews, Moors and Morescoes ("Christianized" Moors), the most wealthy and intelligent of the inhabitants of that country.
—Cushing B. Hassell, *History of the Church of God,* 470.[92]

Plainsted verified the plausibility of Hassell's claim against independent population data. "In fact, the population of Spain had at one time been twenty million higher."[93] Again, independent historical research confirms the veracity of Hassell's estimate. We are forced to conclude that the numbers given should be given the benefit of a doubt, no matter how fantastic they first seem. Separated by centuries of time and widespread ignorance, Rome has largely succeeded in obscurantism and accusing Protestant historians of bias. Who else other than fellow Protestants would care to record the deaths of such martyrs? The truth is that everyone has a bias, but the brute fact that someone has a strong opinion does not prove that the numbers he or she uses are skewed. Falsification requires contrary population data in a contemporary source, which the Catholic revisionists cannot produce.

Catholic apologists who simply invoke absurdity without accounting for the historical events and known population data are not addressing the question from a data-driven perspective, but from a subjective emotional one. The Reformers were certainly right about salvation and, as we have shown, the Protestant historians preserved an accurate record of Rome's deplorable hostility, on all fronts. Of course, this tension has been the norm ever since, but we challenge the reader to skim over the *The Canons and Decrees of the Sacred and Ecumenical Council of Trent*, taking note of the vehement language of hatred spewing forth.

Plainsted confirms the Roman Catholic Church's distinction as one of the world's greatest mega-murdering institutions, right behind the USSR and just ahead of Nazi Germany, revising Western history toward its favor. As we first argued in *Petrus Romanus*, the Church in Rome used fraudulent documents to claim Constantine had deeded the land surrounding Rome to the sovereignty of the Church. In so doing, they changed from a spiritual office to a geopolitical entity with all of the power and corruption characteristic. As a result of the power-lust inherent in the incestuous Church-state marriage, the Church in Rome has been the greatest institutional enemy that the true gospel will ever face. Primarily, it is because it replaces the true gospel with a man-made system of works-based religion. While ever so close and even more cleverly guised in "high-Church" proto-Latin piety, the sacramental system pits salvation as a prize the pope can *indulge* upon one who meets his approval. Claiming the role of "Vicar of Christ" while claiming to decide mankind's fate is the very definition of ἀντίχριστος ("antichrists") as it appears in 1 John "even now are there many *antichrists;* whereby we know that it is the last time" (1 John 2:18). The term is used in the sense of "one who is opposed to Christ, in the sense of usurping the role of Christ."[94] The juxtaposition of a singular, final, Antichrist and many antichrists, plural, suggests the coherence of the charges by Luther and Calvin. They were correct that the office of the papacy was the kingdom of Antichrist. We believe it could play out with the pope as the second Beast and the Roman Catholic Church as the "Great Harlot" the Beast rides. Rome's death toll adds weight to the association. "And I saw the woman drunken with the blood of the saints, and with the blood of the martyrs of Jesus: and when I saw her, I wondered with great admiration" (Revelation 17:6).

Accordingly, it seems proportional that papal Rome belongs beside the USSR with sixty-two million killed by government, China with thirty-five million, and Nazi Germany with twenty-one million.[95] Given that the Ottoman Empire is only credited with a total of two million,[96] one marvels at the pope's bravado in criticizing the West while employing Just War terms against the IS. While we agree the IS must be stopped, we are still wondering if Rome ever has. With a death toll hovering around fifty million, one ponders a proportionate response to the damage inflicted by the papacy? They certainly have never measured up to the criteria established by the theologians responsible for the development of Just War tradition.

Augustine was not a pacifist, but held Christian soldiers to a high moral standard, based on Jesus' Sermon on the Mount and a worldview that acknowledges man's natural tendency to escalate a defensive response rather than seek proportionality.

"An eye for an eye, a tooth for a tooth," and what the Lord says, "But I say unto you, that ye resist not evil; but if any one smiteth thee on thy right cheek, turn to him the other also," and so on. The old precept as well as the new is intended to check the vehemence of hatred, and to curb the impetuosity of angry passion. For who will of his own accord be satisfied with a revenge equal to the injury? Do we not see men, only slightly hurt, eager for slaughter, thirsting for blood, as if they could never make their enemy suffer enough? If a man receives a blow, does he not summon his assailant, that he may be condemned in the court of law? Or if he prefers to return the blow, does he not fall upon the man with hand and heel, or perhaps with a weapon, if he can get hold of one?[97]

Accordingly, a soldier may fight for a just cause but with the wrong motives. In other words, the ethical foundation that justifies the war does not amount to a "get of jail free card" for the behavior of individual politicians, popes, prelates, and soldiers.

Of course, the papacy has its hands covered in the blood of countless medieval Crusaders and the Muslims and Jews they battled. The original "just cause" behind the Crusades was to protect Christians who make pilgrimage to Jerusalem (another way to earn away years in purgatory). The Crusaders were conned by the disingenuous promise of a papal plenary indulgence, a fraudulent document that allegedly absolves the Crusader of all sinand negates punishment in purgatory, thus gaining the martyr a straight shot to paradise. (Doesn't this seem like the same false promise offered to suicide bombers?) Consequently, one could lead an amoral lifestyle, but sidestep all accountability by dying in a papal Crusade. As reprehensible as the above history seems, the ongoing issu-ance of papal indulgences reveals Luther was ignored. Largely in Latin America and developing areas, indulgence practices still victimize the laity at their weakest moments of life. The issuance of indulgences on behalf of the dead not only victimizes the mourners, it undermines the gospel. The status of the deceased is unaffected by the pope's conjuring; justification is sealed by one's beliefs about Jesus.

As a theological construct, the indulgence empowers the pope at the expense of Christ's suffering on the cross. In no uncertain terms, *Luther was correct*. The popes are selling salvation for personal gain. They are antichrists by accepting the papal appointment. Even an elementary reading of Scripture makes the sufficiency of the cross for past, present, and future sin very clear, "for then he [Jesus] would have had to suffer repeatedly since the foundation of the world. But as it is, he has appeared *once for all* at the end of the ages to put away sin by the sacrifice of himself" (Hebrews 9:26, emphasis added). The Catholic Mass claims to do just what that passage denies. The Catholic doctrine, *Unam Sanctum,* states, "Now, therefore, we declare, say, determine and pronounce that for every human creature *it is necessary for salvation to be subject to the authority of the Roman pontiff*" (emphasis added).[98] In light of scriptural clarity, the "benefit of a doubt" is absurd and undeserved. *The papal indulgence is the worst kind of manipulative lie.*

However, Pope Francis rightfully desires to stop the IS, and he well enough knows who he is dealing with—radical Mahdists. Airstrikes alone are not working. The pope is not calling for a ceasefire or negotiations. Instead, he is asking for an armed response, a Just War by the United Nations against the Islamic State. But isn't this playing into the globalist dialectic of which we have been warning in our previous books? What if the *real* problem is not with flesh and blood (Ephesians 6:11), but is the long game (spanning several human lifetimes) of the powers and principalities and luciferian globalists?

Popes, Jesuits, Hegelian Dialectics, and the UN

Because people rarely make radical changes from the status quo, dialectic technique offers an exaggerated antithesis of one's opponent (like the IS is an antithesis of Western society) and then suggest an equally exaggerated counter position (like popes' global socialism). In the end, the two sides agree to meet somewhere in the middle—a synthesis—but by clever design, the process itself moves the original instigator a step closer toward his goal. In this case, if a United Nations peacekeeping force can take down the IS, then by all means, do so.

However, when the Vatican wrote the "State of Palestine," on official diplomatic paperwork, it was suggesting a dialectic thesis to see what sort of antithesis was offered. Nevertheless, it was a bold diplomatic move, and it seems to have been staged for our benefit, as the news media propagated the story with uncommon speed.[99] Although the Vatican did not punt Palestine through the goalposts of statehood, they moved them a bit closer to that goal, as their policy does influence Roman Catholics worldwide. Perhaps it is time for Catholic laity to ask why Pope Francis is advocating global Marxism if he believes Jesus will return.

It seems to us that something along the lines of the infamous "Pike to Mazzini letter" *is true*. It makes the Third World War seem almost inevitable. If so, then even the seemingly *just causes* for wars increasingly run the risk of being manufactured provocations designed to lead to the kingdom of Antichrist, or, as Pope Francis is fond of labeling it, "a true world political authority,"[100] which is the same New World Order Pope Benedict XVI described "as a world authority to manage the economy," end poverty by managing "food security and peace," and bring about "timely disarmament" in order that "the concept of the family of nations can *acquire real teeth*" (emphasis added).[101] The globalist push has been *on* ever since the parallel enthronement of Lucifer with Pope Paul VI.

Also speaking to the UN, Paul VI described "a world authority, able to act efficaciously on the juridical and political levels."[102] Christians need to be aware that the United Nations has been carefully crafted by occultists and the extraterrestrial, "true believer" and pantheistic monist, the Jesuit—Omega Point—mystic, Pierre Teilhard de Chardin. Marilyn Ferguson wrote in *The Aquarian Conspiracy* that a survey of New Agers showed that the leading influence on their spiritual "awakening" was the Roman Catholic mystic, Pierre Teilhard de Chardin. In her *Aquarius Now: Radical Common Sense and Reclaiming Our Personal Sovereignty*, she praised "the Jesuit philosopher Pierre Teilhard de Cardin [who] wrote 'ever new eyes with, ever more to see.'"[103] Ferguson goes on to explain the Omega Point in terms of Chardinian christology:

Through science, research, technology communications and virtually every other area of human activity, we are weaving a delicate membrane of consciousness, what Teilhard called the "noosphere" or the thinking layer of Earth that is embracing and drawing into itself the entire planet. It will infuse the whole of humanity with a feeling of relationship and resonance. He called this potential experience "the Christification of the Earth."[104]

In Chardinian terms, the Second Coming marks the maximum level of complexity and consciousness evolutionarily possible also called the Omega Point.

Barbara Marx Hubbard, an avowed New Age enemy of biblical Christianity,[105] wrote of Chardin as defining her understanding of God and theistic evolution: "For me, the most vital source of meaning of conscious evolution is the Catholic understanding of God and Christ as the source of evolution, as its driving force as well as its direction."[106]

Known as the father of global education, Robert Muller created a "World Core Curriculum"[107] that earned him the UNESCO Prize for Peace Education in 1989. He represents the International Peace Research Association (IPRA), a group of scholarly constatives to the Economic and Social Council of the United Nations (ECOSOC). Muller wrote "Teilhard [de Chardin] had always viewed the United Nations as the progressive institutional embodiment of his philosophy."[108] Pope Francis wrote a letter to UN Secretary General Ban Ki-moon stating:

In renewing my urgent appeal to the international community to take action to end the humanitarian tragedy now underway, I encourage all the competent organs of the United Nations, in particular those responsible for security, peace, humanitarian law and assistance to refugees, to continue their efforts in accordance with the Preamble and relevant Articles of the United Nations Charter.[109]

When we consider globalism is being simultaneously promoted by the Roman Catholic Church, the United Nations, the Islamic State, the Freemasons, the Bilderbergs, the Council on Foreign Relations, and the Trilateral Commission, it seems a bit shortsighted to dismiss it being identified with end-time prophecy as mere "newspaper exegesis." Former president of Dallas Theological Seminary, John Walvoord, explains:

> Revelation 13, however, gives much insight into the character of the Great Tribulation. It will be a time of one world government and one world religion, with one world economic system. Those who will resist the ruler and refuse to worship him will be subject to execution, and the martyrs may outnumber the believers who survive. It will be Satan's final and ultimate attempt to cause the world to worship him and to turn them from the worship of the true God and Jesus Christ as their Savior.[110]

When dispensationalists connect Jesus' birth pains to the unprecedentedly constant state of world war, they are not being sensationalists. Globalists *require* war, so they can offer the solution. What the average educated American overlooks is that there is, and always has been, a *long game* in play. The elites are running an agenda right up the middle of the ideological divide, and it inevitably settles closer and closer toward the idea of world government. David Rockefeller wrote in his *Memoires*:

> Some even believe we [Rockefeller family] are part of a secret cabal working against the best interests of the United States, characterizing my family and me as "internationalists" and of conspiring with others around the world to build a more inte-

grated global political and economic structure—One World, if you will. If that's the charge, I stand guilty, and I am proud of it.[111]

Admittedly, we also struggle to understand how this Beast's many tentacles got tangled in the United States. The America we once knew blew away almost like a vapor. When a US Naval Academy graduate like Chuck Missler, who rose to branch chief of the Department of Guided Missiles in the United States Air Force, publicly renounces his former patriotism as "a strange form of idolatry," we know the America we were taught to love as kids is a distant memory(that is, if it ever really existed at all).

Consider that no matter who wins a war, any war, the military industrial complex always *profits* (which to them, means "winning").Even the stated US policy seems incoherent unless one understands that the real objective is *not* to spread peace and democracy, but rather to keep the Middle East in a constant state of instability. The great British-American historian of oriental studies, Bernard Lewis,[112] wrote:

> Since the collapse of the Soviet Union, a new American policy has emerged in the Middle East, concerned with different objectives. Its main aim is to prevent the emergence of a regional hegemony—of a single regional power that could dominate the area and thus establish monopolistic control of Middle Eastern oil. This has been the basic concern underlying successive American policies toward Iran, Iraq, or to any other perceived future threat within the region.[113]

Ever since the gas lines of the 1973 oil embargo, the executive branch and intelligence community have defined the United States' "national interest" in the Middle East as "political unrest and instability." Because this is the case, we empathize with majority world peoples, who criticize the Western world led by the United States for merely pretending to be a defender of human rights, democracy, and so-called Just War. In truth, it is more often justified in terms of national security interest or, frankly, greed. There is an ethical disconnect between rhetoric and practice as well. For example, depleted uranium doesn't merely stop an aggressor, but rather poisons the land, inevitably impacting innocent civilians and wildlife. How can America claim moral ground by invoking Just War principles while leaving behind spent ammunition made with depleted uranium shell casings? I (Cris Putnam) doubt that the ten-year-old girl dying from leukemia acquired via depleted uranium poisoning (and her family, neighbors, and friends) think of the United States as their liberators.[114] In the Middle East, our duplicity is obvious, because, all the while, the US is offering almost unlimited support to the biggest human-rights abuser on the planet, Saudi Arabia. For example, President Obama claims to be the champion of homosexuals, yet bows to the Saudi King Abdullah.[115] And yes, it has everything to do with Islam. Saudi Arabia is the home of *Wahhabism* (ultraconservative Sunnism), and he is a Wahhabi king who enforces the death penalty for homosexuality—but that doesn't keep the president up at night. William McCants, an authority on Islam, revealed:

> The Islamic State's theology and method of engaging with scripture is nearly identical to Wahhabism, the ultraconservative form of Islam found in Saudi Arabia. It's very different from the kind of Islam you find in other parts of the world. In Wahhabism, religious innovation is bad; medieval scholarly authorities are respected but disregarded if need be; outside cultural influences should be expunged; and the definition of a good believer is very narrow.[116]

While belligerently refusing to implicate Islam, the president is only postmodern as it suits him. Even so, the cognitive dissonance involved in bowing to a leader of Wahhabism while holding such liberal positions on domestic issues like same-sex marriage would cripple an objective thinker. We are forced to conclude that he betrays his own "principles" very easily—that is, when it serves another of his interests. Of course, Republicans are culpably no better, as the Bush family oil dynasty's affairs with the Nazis and the bin Laden family are virtually like the new Americana and should require no citation.[117] Craig Unger pointed it out this way:

> America, the beacon of democracy, was to arm and protect a brutal theocratic monarchy. The United States, sworn defender of Israel, was also the guarantor of security to the guardians of Wahhabi Islam, the fundamentalist religious sect that was one Israel's and America's mortal enemies. Astoundingly, this fragile relationship had not only endured but in many ways had been spectacularly successful. In nearly three decades since the oil embargo of 1973, the United States had bought hundreds of billions of dollars of oil at reasonable prices. During that same period, this Saudis had purchased hundreds of billions of dollars of weapons from the United States.[118]

We can see only two alternatives: Either the Saudis entranced US leaders, or it's a Faustian bargain along the lines of, "We do not criticize Saudi culture in exchange for reasonable oil prices." Or perhaps it is the former? *Istikhara* is a form of Muslim occultism entailing the ritualistic chanting of the Qur'an for some magical result. An encyclopedia developed by former Muslims reveals, "Today, this Islamic Black Magic is very much alive among the devout Muslims. If a Muslim is serious about protection from harmful slander, he just recites verses 36:65–66."[119] Accordingly, the Saudis have either mesmerized our Ivy-League-educated government officials into some sort of Qur'anic trance, *or maybe it really is about the oil.*

Jihad

While translating from Arabic literally to "strive" or "struggle" in English, modern scholars seem to agree that *jihad* has two meanings: an inner spiritual struggle or the "greater jihad," and an outer physical struggle against the enemies of Islam or the "lesser jihad."[120] In the context of the Qur'an, it plays out in both realms, but is depicted primarily as a military effort. According to Middle East historian Bernard Lewis, "In the Quran and still more in the Traditions commonly though not invariably followed by the words 'in the path of God,' it has usually been understood as meaning 'to wage war.'"[121] Lewis qualified this was not his own idea but rather that "the overwhelming majority of classical theologians, jurists," and Hadith scholars "understood the obligation of jihad in a military sense."[122] In other words, the majority believed jihad usually entailed the military struggle to spread Islam, just as Muhammad did in his day.

The idea of "divine license" in warfare is extremely dangerous, but giving a teenage social media IS recruits a new Humvee and a MI6A4 is to summon demons. The French scholar Laurent Murawiec, a former RAND defense analyst, explained the jihadi as "elite amoral supermen" in his salient *The Mind of Jihad.*

> The conviction that one knows God's will is heady stuff that often leads to shedding torrents of blood in the name of one's mission. Living in a "second reality" deemed superior to the "real" reality shared by the rest of mankind is a recipe for mass murder.[123]

With such a jihadi mindset as ground zero, the twenty-first century Mahdist is able to summon more adrenalin behind his millenarian apocalypticism. Graeme Wood, a journalist heralded for his *Atlantic* essay, "What ISIS Really Wants," explains the IS's allure is in its Mahdism.

They believe they are personally involved in struggles beyond their own lives, and that merely to be swept up in the drama, on the side of righteousness, is a privilege and a pleasure—especially when it is also a burden.…That ISIS holds the imminent fulfillment of prophecy as a matter of dogma at least tells us the mettle of our opponent. It is ready to cheer its own near-obliteration, and to remain confident, even when surrounded, that it will receive divine succor if it stays true to the Prophetic model.[124]

Before arguing that Mahdism eclipses the jihadi ideology of hate groups like Hamas, we are compelled to concede that as "a means to an end," all radical jihadism is properly labeled a death cult. Murawiec observed this generalized veneration of death amongst Islamic radicals.

The slaying is not instrumental: it is an act in itself; it is human sacrifice. The blood of the enemy renews the identity of the lynch mob: To be a Palestinian is to spill the blood of Israelis. Death is not an instrumentality—like the death of the enemy on the battlefield—it has become an end in itself. How else may we fathom the signs on the walls of Hamas kindergarten in Gaza, "The Children Are the Holy Martyrs of Tomorrow" Death is a source of unalloyed joy: "We love death."[125]

While the above statement is horrific, it comes from Hamas—a terrorist group formed to "liberate Palestine" from alleged Jewish "occupation" and to establish an Islamic state in modern-day Israel, the West Bank, and the Gaza Strip. Hamas members are terrorists, but not necessarily *mujahideen*. The term was originally used for the US-backed Taliban soldiers who defeated the communist government of Afghanistan during the Afghan War (1979–92), but has been subsequently used more freely to refer to any Muslim groups engaged in militantjihad with non-Muslims. However, the lack of precision in terminology allows for too much equivocation in Western threat analysis. In this case, ignorance doesn't merely lead to embarrassment; it literally can get you killed.

The similarities between jihadists like Hamas and the Taliban mujahideen who fought the Soviets are superficial at best. In contrast, Hamas routinely utilizes pusillanimous strategies like firing rockets at Israeli soldiers from UN-sponsored "safe zones" (like school playgrounds)with the purpose of later accusing Israel of war crimes, that is, if Israel responds to protect their own citizens. For example, in what has been labeled the "al-Fakhura school incident," rockets flew into Israel from Gaza in 2009 and several eyewitnesses in Gaza saw "terrorists firing mortar rounds from a street close to the school."[126] The IDF responded, resulting in civilian casualties, and it took a lot of heat in the press internationally for shooting at a school. A spokesperson for the IDF stated, "The initial examination conducted with forces operating in the area shows that mortar shells were fired from within the school at IDF forces."[127] Muslims need to take ownership of events like this; it was Hamas rather than the IDF who endangered the school. Hamas uses women and children as human shields, and because of such tactics, they are not by any means to be confused with actual *soldiers*.

IS members are far more dangerous than a mujahedeen death cult like Al-Qaeda, because they are true *Mahdists*—an apocalyptic death cult. The transformation from militant-jihadist to Mahdist occurred when the IS declared themselves to be the new worldwide caliphate of Islam. The significance of such a move is not sufficiently understood by most folks, because it is rooted in medieval history. Historically, the caliph was the political and religious successor to the prophet Muhammad and the leader of the entire Muslim community. According to Muslim prophecy in the Hadith, there are five stages of world history. The fifth (and final) stage begins with the return of the caliphate responsible for ushering in the Mahdi—the final successor of the prophet Muhammad and leader of the entire Muslim world. The IS claims to be that very one.

Jihad is often translated as "holy war," but Muslims never apply "holy" to anything other than Allah.[128] Even so, it is fair to say the IS and most all Muslim fundamentalists operate under a Crusade war ethic, and Mahdism adds more fuel to that already raging fire.

Crusade as a War Ethic

Crusade, as a theory of war, treats mortal combat as the only truly effective means for destroying persistent evil and imposing ultimate good. Seen as morally *unconditional*, within the Crusade ethos, the ends *do* justify the means. The purpose of war is to destroy evil and impose a perceived "ideal" social order by force. Led by an individual like the leader of the Russian Orthodox Church, the Roman Pontiff, or a Muslim caliph, "Crusade" as an ethical system treats war as a religious matter involving *divine* (not human) authority. It is in the truest sense a "holy war." That's why the world cringed at the language used by the head of the Russian Orthodox Church's Public Affairs Department, Vsevolod Chaplin, when he said, "The fight with terrorism is a *holy battle* and today our country is perhaps the most active force in the world fighting it" (emphasis added)[129] We realize that not everyone has studied ethics as an academic discipline. If the "holy battle" quote doesn't disturb you yet, it's about to make you squirm.

Concerning the crusade ethical system, Heimbach noted its feigned amorality is allegedly justified by divine transcendence.

> Because war is fought for the sake of that which defines the ultimate meaning of good and evil, crusade has no place for restraining actions taken against enemies. The conduct of war functions above civil law and otherwise applicable norms of morality because it is waged for the sake of that which defines right and wrong on a cosmic scale and is the source of all valid law and morality. Of necessity, therefore, wars of crusade are fought as "total war." The struggle is "all out," with "no holds barred;" and "no quarter given."[130]

Perhaps that explains the IS' hanging the unborn babies of Christian mothers from trees? Probably not... Such an atrocity is internally coherent with Muhammad's war ethic, but *completely dependent* on one external factor. Is the call to "holy war" actually holy? Is the total war commanded by the transcendent creator of the universe, a man-made contrivance, or the Prince of Darkness? We are not arrogant enough to think we've solved the puzzle or unraveled all of Satan's tricks. The motives for such wars may also overlap in unanticipated combinations, for reasons we are not capable of imagining, at least not yet (1 Corinthians 15:52, 1 John 3:2). Considering the brutality of the IS, we agree with Clinton Arnold, a New Testament scholar and Dean at the Talbot School of Theology, who observed, "Purely naturalistic explanations are not adequate for describing many forms of evil in the world."[131] Using sex slaves and gratuitous, slasher-style violence as recruiting tools, the IS is certainly demonically inspired.[132]

According to Crusade War theory, good can *never* find middle ground with evil, which explains why, no matter how well intended Secretary of State John Kerry might be concerning the "two-state solution" in Palestine, it is doomed to fail. Since Crusade requires "total war," there is no place for surrender. Because they all employ a true Crusade theory of war, the real crusaders in the Middle East today are the Muslim jihadists. To put it in terms of biblical theology, the IS believes it has the same sort of mandate God gave Joshua when the Israelites first crossed the Jordan to eliminate the Nephilim and Canaanite hordes. Now think about the Israelites walking around Jericho blowing shofars (it's not considered a practical strategy at West Point).

The Crusade War Ethic in the Hebrew Bible

Christians must concede Yahweh's war ethic toward the Canaanites represents a textbook *Crusade* theory of war. However, in Scripture, "It has to come through a prophet. It is not a democratic thing where the nation can get together and take a vote and agree that we are going to battle or any tribe can decide or majority of tribes."[133] In the ancient world, war was necessarily more brutal, man-to man-type combat requiring athletic speed and well developed skills with various bows, spears, and swords rather than GPS-guided drones controlled from a distance. We believe the IS will be quickly overwhelmed by a technologically superior army like the United States. Of course, such an assault by Western "crusaders" is exactly what the Mahdists want.

A common way of parsing a Crusade in the Torah is "devote to destruction," as explained in a standard modern lexicon:

> **charam** (355c); a prim. root; *to ban, devote, exterminate*:—annihilate(1), covet(1), destroy them utterly(1), destroy utterly(1), destroyed them utterly(1), destroying(1), destroying them completely(2), destruction(2), devote(2), forfeited(1), set apart(1), sets apart(1), utterly destroy(11), utterly destroyed(22), utterly destroying(3).[134]

The *Theological Wordbook of the Old Testament* explains why the translation "devoted to destruction" is probably the most accurate English rendering:

> The idea first appears in Num 21:2–3, where the Israelites vowed that, if God would enable them to defeat a southern Canaanite king, they would "utterly destroy" (i.e. consider as devoted and accordingly utterly destroy) his cities. This word is used regarding almost all the cities which Joshua's troops destroyed (e.g. Jericho, Josh 6:21; Ai, Josh 8:26; Makkedah, Josh 10:28; Hazor, Josh 11:11), thus indicating the rationale for their destruction. In Deut 7:2–6, the command for this manner of destruction is given, with the explanation following that, otherwise, these

cities would lure the Israelites away from the Lord (cf. Deut 20:17–18). Any Israelite city that harbored idolators was to be "utterly destroyed" (Deut 13:12–15; cf. Ex 22:19).[135]

The key distinction that justifies Israelite Crusade versus something like the Muslim jihad against Jews and Christians is that the Hebrew Bible is a true revelation from God. If Yahweh is really God, then His command is justified by who He is: the Great I AM. Alternately, if Allah is God, then Muhammad's medieval war crimes are justified by Allah's authority. The question is ironically the same one that Joshua, one of the spies, faced when commanded to slay the giant clans who had every physical advantage.

> And if it seem evil unto you to serve the Lord, choose you this day whom ye will serve; whether the gods which your fathers served that were on the other side of the flood, or the gods of the Amorites, in whose land ye dwell: but as for me and my house, we will serve the Lord. (Joshua 24:15)

Indeed, Jews, Christians, and Muslims have both adopted the same Crusade War ethic, but the only legitimate claimant belongs to Joshua and the Israelites born to parents who wandered the Sinai desert for thirty-eight years for fear of the Nephilim (Numbers 13:31). As we have discussed briefly in this chapter and more rigorously in *Petrus Romanus: The Final Pope Is Here*, the papal Crusades were based on unbiblical theology involving purgatory, pilgrimage, and the false promise of indulgences. These were wars commanded by popes, not God, and we cannot call them "holy." The same line of reasoning applies to Muslim jihad.

Allah is either a concocted idol by Muhammad and his followers, or perhaps the revelation of an immortal Paul identified in the Ephesian epistle (6:12) as an *archon*, a Greek term for "a supernatural power having some particular role in controlling the destiny and activities of human beings."[136] If so, Muhammad and his followers justify jihad with the Crusade ethic for personal or preternatural reasons, and *neither is holy*. A Sharia law manual defines jihad simply as "war against non-Muslims."[137] Yahweh's Crusade is actually His, for the benefit of the Israelites, not for their own desires, as Muhammad and the popes commanded.

> If the biblical presentation of this subject were couched in language implying that such "devotion" was practiced because the Israelites only thought the Lord wanted it (but God nowhere asked them to do it), the idea would still be disturbing. But it is stated several times explicitly that Joshua acted "as the Lord God of Israel commanded" or "as Moses the servant of the Lord had commanded" (10:40; 11:12; cf. Deut. 7:24).[138]

Holy war presented in the Old Testament is especially brutal. However, we are arguing a somewhat different case than the standard apologetic. The war ethic against the Canaanite giant clans in the Promised Land seems "inhuman" because *it actually was*. In fact, it is never even hinted at that it was a human strategy. If your worldview allows the existence of Yahweh, the angel of the Lord, angels, fallen angels, demons, evil spirits, ghosts, seraphim, cherubim, Nephilim, sorcerers, mediums, diviners, seers, astrologers, and 'little-g' gods, then it is probably consistent with the worldview of the inspired biblical authors. If these are novel and strange subjects, then, as a result, you can read and even memorize an English translation and miss the author's point entirely, and, possibly, even come to the opposite conclusion.

When Jesus told His twelve disciples, "But these things have I told you, that when the time shall come, ye may remember that I told you of them. And these things I said not unto you at the beginning, because I was with you," (John 16:4) it reads like Jesus is preparing them for the divine inspiration that will lead to composing the New Testament. He speaks of the Third Person of the Trinity: "Howbeit when he, the Spirit of truth, is come, he will guide you into all truth: for he shall not speak of himself; but whatsoever he shall hear, that shall he speak: and he will shew you things to come" (John 16:13). Jesus is assuring the disciples that the "Spirit of truth" will assist them in getting the Gospels and epistles into the New Testament canon. Jesus was speaking to His apostles on what He intended for them (the twelve) to do after He left. The idea that the Holy Spirit would bestow the hard-earned expertise required to interpret ancient Near-Eastern texts upon uneducated minds remains a common but vacuous interpretation of this passage. We have to be informed to understand the context.

The Holy Spirit convicts us that we need the expertise of other believers, but in this case, Christians who understand ancient Near-East languages, including idioms, figures of speech, slang, grammar, and apocalyptic symbolism. Recently discovered tablets of clay have taught us much about the ancient context of the Bible. We ask, "How many readers know that Baal the Canaanite god was called the 'cloud rider' and how that deepens the meaning of the biblical text?"[139] (For the answer, follow the endnoted article.)

Yahweh chose ancient prophets like Isaiah, who possessed the background knowledge along with a literary penchant for sarcasm, to tease the Canaanite gods. A great deal of humor and biblical theology in the Old Testament is simply lost in the three-thousand-year-old cultural divide, but the recovery of Ugaritic literature has deepened the context of Scripture.

Archaeology (a relatively recent academic endeavor) and the resulting decipherment of previously unknown ancient languages (like Ugaritic) over the last century or so have proven to be helpful in deciphering the Hebrew Bible in its original Sinai context. The problem is that only the nerds who can read Ugaritic are aware of what is affected, but Christians are super-critical of new ideas (often rightfully so). All the more, Christian teachers and theologians have an intellectual duty to keep up with new data and how it informs the Bible's context and offers nuances or even challenges long-held assumptions.

Within the conservative Christian community, many top of the top biblical scholars are afraid to even talk about some issues, because they also want to keep their jobs. One of the best conservative Old Testament scholars, Bruce Waltke, resigned from a teaching position at Reformed Theological Seminary for the crime of publicly recognizing that there are legitimate readings of Genesis that call young-earth creationism into serious question.[140] Interestingly, some of the same folks who criticize scholars like Waltke also attempt to demythologize the Nephilim out of the Bible, but at great cost.

A proper understanding of Genesis 6 clarifies why such total destruction was prescribed. With this in mind, we now revisit Yahweh's commands to Joshua: "Now therefore kill every male among the little ones, and kill every woman that hath known man by lying with him"(Numbers 31:17). It seems fair to label this as an "ethnic cleansing" and connect it to Genesis 6.

The Nephilim Apologetic

Remember, God had promised enmity between the seed of the woman (all of mankind, coming to ultimate fruition in Christ) and the seed of the Nachash, the serpentine entity who deceived Eve and lured Adam. Given the "war of the seed" declared in Genesis 3:15, it seems reasonable to think a genetic cleansing was necessary to extricate the Watchers' giant traits, intermixed with generations of Canaanites and giants of various races. It didn't concern the Israelites, because they knew the call to holy war was from Yahweh. The historical record and archaeological evidence is enough to justify the ancient Hebrew accounts above all others.

Douglas Stuart, the chair of Biblical Studies and Old Testament professor at Gordon-Conwell Theological Seminary,[141] pleads for intellectual honestly—when it comes to extermination of particular ancient Near-Eastern peoples:

> This is what seems hardest for most people to get—the idea of the total annihilation of the enemy. This seems very brutal. When you read the descriptions, you know, "Spare not a one of them, destroy them all, destroy their animals, burn everything." You say, "Wow, what kind of vicious behavior is this?" You must remember a couple of things. One, it is a war of judgment. God who knows right and wrong quite well has said, "I want to eliminate this Amorite culture." He does not say none of the children can go to heaven under two-years-old. None of that is said. We do not know anything about God's fairness in dealing with those people at that time, under those conditions, but he does say, "Gotta eliminate the culture."[142]

As believers in the divine inspiration of Scripture, we believe these "devotion to destruction" commands really do come from the Creator of the Universe. Thus, we trust God had a really good reason for ordering what would otherwise seem to be genocide, a great evil. We trust that God's character is upright and know that He is longsuffering and faithful. Nephilim genetics were like an ancient antediluvian curse, and it seems compelling that the Lord commanded the Israelite invaders to cleanse the land of them. It makes for an interesting apologetic rejoinder when facing a skeptic who uses these passages to paint God as a "malevolent bully."[143]

We believe God had good reasons for ordering the extermination of particular people groups. Michael Heiser has noted that the tribes "devoted to destruction" are the same giant clans associated with the Rephaim and Nephilim giants.[144]

There is no doubt the Scriptures describe organized tribes or groups of giants living in the great walled cities of Canaan (Numbers 13).

These tribes include: Amalekites, Amorites, Anakims, Ashdothites, Avi-ums, Avites, Caphtorims, Ekronites, Emins, Eshkalonites, Gazathites, Geshurites, Gibeonites, Giblites, Girgashites, Gittites, Hittites, Hivites, Horims, Horites, Jebusites, Kadmonites, Kenites, Kenizzites, Maacha-thites, Manassites, Nephilim, Perizzites, Philistines. Rephaim, Sidonians, Zamzummins, Zebusites, and Zuzims.

We are still astounded by the seemingly well-intended but embar-rassingly misguided interpreters who do not correlate Crusade Wars and Just War theory against such cursed persons and who attempt to censor the giants out of the Bible. Giants are integral to understanding the con-text of the desert-wandering curse, during which Moses composed the Torah under divine inspiration. Interpreters who deny that the super-natural sons of God mated with the "daughters of men" in Genesis 6 have an even harder time with all of the giants in the Promised Land, and some skeptics try to dismiss them as cowardly fictions.

A common but easily refuted example maintains that the spies' report, "And there we saw the giants, the sons of Anak, which come of the giants: and we were in our own sight as grasshoppers, and so we were in their sight" (Numbers 13:33), was necessarily untrue because it is labeled as "an evil report of the land" (Numbers 13:32) by Moses, in the narrator's voice. However, they were not all liars. The group of spies included Caleb, the son of Jephunneh, and Joshua, who not only did not denounce the presence of giants as a lie, but argued that God would supernaturally help the Israelites fulfill the Just War crusade and defeat them(Numbers 13:30). Finally, it doesn't make sense that the spies (pos-sessing first-hand knowledge) would wander the desert for thirty-eight years to protect a known lie.

In the end, the fear of giants causes the majority of the Exodus escapees to die pitifully wandering the Sinai in circles. By design, the sole survivors were also "evil-report" witnesses, Joshua and Caleb, who did not originally fear the giants: "But Joshua the son of Nun, and Caleb the son of Jephunneh, which were of the men that went to search the land, lived still" (Numbers 14:38). Finally, Moses acknowledged "the descendants of Anak, were there" as *the narrator*, not from within the spies' evil report (Numbers 13:22), and he later connected them to "the sons of Anak, which come of the giants" (Numbers 13:33), whereas the Hebrew beneath the English word "giants" was actually *nephilim*—an Aramaic term for "giants": סִילְפַּן

Thus, we conclude the "evil report" rejoinder as an alternative to the presence of real giants in the Promised Land, is incoherent with the inspired author's intention for his original readers. In theology, it's labeled "demythologization," but in layman's terms, "unbelief" is a good synonym.

It is important to note that, Crusade War ethic aside, Yahweh takes most of the credit for Israel's victories (Joshua 24:5–13). We don't imagine Joshua beheading Canaanite journalists on social media like the IS' psychological warfare videos. *Do not watch the beheading videos unless it is absolutely necessary.* The purpose is known as fear propaganda; they want to infiltrate your mind with irrational fear. However, the IS should fear a more sophisticated response than drones and air strikes, likely at the hands of an international coalition force as prescribed by the pope and predicted by these authors.

A passage from the same periscope gives us pause. "And I sent the *hornet* before you, which drave them out from before you, even the two kings of the Amorites; but not with thy sword, nor with thy bow" (Joshua 24:12, emphasis added). The Hebrew term *tsirah,* rendered "hornet," is used in the same way in other books (Exodus 23:28; Deuteronomy 7:20).Because it also was an idiom for panic, some scholars believe the context is better served by the "fear-panic" meaning.[145] The King James Version reads, "God will send the hornet among them, until they that are left, and hide themselves from thee, be destroyed" (Deuteronomy 7:20). More recent renderings have the advantage of older source material found in the Dead Sea Scrolls. The Lexham English Bible translation leaves out all of the unoriginal commas and gives a more sinister impression of the supposed insects, "Yahweh your God will send the hornets [*tsirah*] among them until both the survivors and the fugitives are destroyed before you" (Deuteronomy 7:20, LEB). If the enemy combatants are destroyed "before you," the grammar implies that you are a spectator and the so-called hornets are doing all the work. We get the impression these are deadly entities more akin to the genetic-hybrid monstrosities that emerge during the trumpet judgments rather than common insects (Revelation 9:10; 9:19).

The Book of First Enoch, "The Book of the Watchers," is seemingly verified as being written by "Enoch, the seventh from Adam," by Jesus' brother Jude, who cites it in the New Testament (Jude 14). Within, God tells Enoch:

> And now, the giants, who are produced from the spirits and flesh, shall be called evil spirits upon the earth, and on the earth shall be their dwelling. Evil spirits have proceeded from their bodies; because they are born from men, and from the holy Watchers is their beginning and primal origin; they shall be evil spirits on earth, and evil spirits shall they be called. As for the spirits of heaven, in heaven shall be their dwelling, but as for the spirits of the earth which were born upon the earth, on the earth shall be their dwelling. And the spirits of the giants afflict, oppress, destroy, attack, do battle, and work destruction on the earth, and cause trouble: they take no food, but nevertheless hunger and thirst, and cause offences. And these spirits shall rise up against the children of men and against the women, because they have proceeded from them. (Enoch 15:1–12)

According to ancient texts, the deceased human-hybrid giants are now evil spirits upon the earth. Furthermore, the biblical text testifies that God had warned the demon-worshipping inhabitants in the land of Cana: "But in the fourth generation they shall come hither again: for the iniquity of the Amorites is not yet full" (Genesis 15:16). Clearly, there is a particular level of depravity that Yahweh will not abide. Yet, this passage implies Yahweh's perseverance over four generations, with the very people He later ordered annihilated by holy war. The text of Numbers connects it to the progeny of the Watchers, the previously listed giant clans.

Interestingly, when the Israelites crossed the Jordon to claim land, they reported encountering Nephilim giants (Numbers 13:33; cf. Genesis 6:4).[146] In fact, it was the peoples' fear of the Nephilim that resulted in their being punished by wandering about the Sinai desert. After that generation died in the desert, Yahweh's immortal soldiers (Hebrew *tsaba*[147]) fought the Battle of Jericho, led by the divine "captain of the host of the Lord" (Joshua 5:14, 15), while the Israelites marched around in a circle blowing *shofar* ("horns") (Joshua 6:1–27). In truth, the unseen army of Yahweh (2 Kings 6:17) was slaughtering the Nephilim within the falling walls around Jericho.

This immortal "captain of the hosts" is described as a "theophanic angel" in the standard Hebrew lexicon, *Brown-Driver-Briggs Hebrew and English Lexicon*.[148] We agree with Chuck Missler that this passage concerning Joshua's encounter with the immortal "captain of the host of the Lord am I now come. And Joshua fell on his face to the earth, and did worship, and said unto him, What saith my lord unto his servant?" (Joshua 5:14) indicates a *theophany* ("an Old Testament appearance of God") by a preincarnate Jesus Christ. In his *Joshua Commentary*, Missler notes:

> Angels are not to be worshiped! John does twice in Revelation and the angel does not allow it, also note the appellation: "Lord." He is the "captain of our salvation" (Hebrews 2:10). This "angel" permits (*commands*) worship (cf. Revelation 19:10; 22:8,9); and uses the same language given to Moses and Joshua forty years earlier (Exodus 3:5).[149]

For these reasons, Missler believes that Jesus Christ was the real commander of Yahweh's army. His opinion is also based on a passage by Zechariah, "Then shall the Lord go forth, and fight against those nations, *as when he fought in the day of battle*" (Zechariah 14:3, emphasis added). Missler then asks, "When was this past 'day of battle' being compared to Armageddon?" and answers "Here!'"[150] If this is so, then Joshua *really* met Jesus Christ, as commander.

Scholars have noted that "the material in Joshua, particularly chapters 5–7, possesses the quality of an eyewitness account."[151] Incidentally, the latest evidence from archaeology has overthrown years of skepticism resulting from Katherine Kenyon's previous work that challenged the Bible's historicity. Recently, even *The New York Times* conceded, "After years of doubt among archeologists, a new analysis of excavations has yielded a wide range of evidence supporting the biblical account about the fall of Jericho."[152] As the Bible's historicity continues to be confirmed and the events of end-time prophecy seem to align in the Middle East (Amos 9:14–15), the growing concern over the described end-time judgments is illustrated by former nuclear silos being converted into disaster bunkers for the affluent.[153] Intriguingly, they seem to fulfill prophecy as well (Revelation 6:15).

Later, suggesting a cryptic reference to a lost ancient scroll Moses called "the book of the wars of the Lord" might also describe the battles of the One the book of Revelation prophesies will return in fury as the "Lion of the tribe of Judah" (Numbers 21:13b–14 cf.; Zechariah; Revelation 5:5, 16:19).[154] In addition, Heiser has done a great deal of scholarly work showing that pre-Christian-era rabbinic thought recognized "two Yahwehs" as "two Powers in Heaven."[155] For example, "Then the Lord rained upon Sodom and upon Gomorrah brimstone and fire from the Lord out of heaven" (Genesis 19:24). How does the Lord (physically present in the city) rain fire on Sodom *from* the Lord in heaven, without *two* Lords, one on earth and one in heaven?

The term "theophany" is defined as "an appearance of Jesus Christ in the Old Testament."[156] A standard academic source provides a more rigorous definition, including the *Koine Greek* etymology:

> Theophany, the self-disclosure of God, is a widely attested phenomenon in the literature of ancient Israel, recorded by its historians, prophets, sages, and psalmists. The word "theophany" itself is a Greek term, from *theos,* "god," and *phainein,* "to appear," a classical example of which in Greece was a festival at Delphi at which the statues of Apollo and other gods were shown to the people. Though the term is not a Hebrew one, and though divine images were not a part of Israelite ritual, "theophany" and related terms—"epiphany," "appearance," and "hierophany," "appearance of the sacred"—have come to be used among scholars for descriptions of the appearance of God in the Hebrew Scriptures[157]

Many scholars believe that appearances of the "Angel of the Lord" represent such supernatural events. A Logos Bible Software search of the Old Testament returns 220 results for the term "Angel of the Lord." Moses ascribed extrasensory telepathic abilities to Him. Robert Alter noted how the "angel of Yahweh" read Sarah's mind.

> The angel of the Lord, with the advantage of the auditory equivalent of clairvoyance, hears these unvoiced words, but this is how he repeats them to Abraham: "Why is it that Sarah laughed, saying: Will I really give birth, I being old?" The angel, with divine tact, has clearly tempered the vehemence of Sarah's interior monologue.[158]

Considered to be a theophany, a manifestation of Yahweh, this immortal killed an army of 185,000 men in one night (2 Kings 19:35). Theologian Millard Erickson offers three possibilities:

(1) he is merely an angel with a special commission; (2) he is God himself temporarily visible in a humanlike form; (3) he is the Logos, a temporary preincarnate visit by the second person of the Trinity. While none of these interpretations is fully satisfactory, in light of the clear statements of identity either the second or the third seems more adequate than the first.[159]

The angel of the Lord sounds much like the captain of the army of hosts in Joshua.

The Crusades, Purgatory and Indulgences

A medieval crusade was summoned by the pope, and combined the developing theologies concerning holy war and pilgrimage. Crusade is a holy war in the sense that it is fought on behalf of a God. In the original case, the Crusade was called to protect Catholic pilgrims who were being abused by the reigning Muslims in Jerusalem. The Crusaders who died in battle were martyrs; their willingness to die, often horribly, atoned for their sins and merited their salvation. Of course, the very idea of such an indulgence contradicts Paul's contention that one is justified, "Not of works, lest any man should boast" (Ephesians 2:9).

A Crusade was a pilgrimage in the sense that Crusaders went on long journeys after making a public vow, earning all of the mythological spiritual benefits that pilgrims otherwise enjoyed. The Crusader popes sweetened the deal beyond measure with the wholesale manufacture of plenary indulgences, that is, the remission of all temporal penalties and punishment due to sin by papal mandate. Secular historians have made sport of the practice:

A sizable carrot was presented in the form of remission of all the penalties of confessed sins. In a divinely ordered world, where everyone believed in God and was terrified of purgatory, war had hitherto been seen as a sinful deed that required penance. Now, for those "took the Cross," or who vowed to become crusaders, it was sanctified slaughter, a penitential act in itself. Crusaders were told that if they died in the service of the Cross they would vault over purgatory "as if in one leap they pass into heaven."[160]

That sort of false hope also helped to drive the unbiblical doctrine of purgatory deep into the Roman Catholic sacramental system. It is the "safety net" that keeps the never-ending treadmill of works based salvation grinding away. In this case, a Crusader could earn his way out of any sin imaginable by martyrdom. But such a practice reeks of humanness.

Papal profiteering on indulgences was the impetus of Luther's protest "Disputation on the Power and Efficacy of Indulgences," also known as "The 95 Theses," a list of questions and propositions for debate, nailed to the wooden front door of the Wittenberg Castle church on the blustery evening of October 31, 1517. Committed to the idea that salvation is by grace through faith alone, Luther boldly defied the corrupt papacy, "Those who believe that they can be certain of their salvation because they have indulgence letters will be eternally damned, together with their teachers."[161] One surely cannot accuse the German biblical scholar of being intellectually or theologically timid. Luther rescued the biblical gospel from the clutches of an evil papacy bent on obscuring it.

In Thesis 16, Luther observed, "Hell, purgatory, and heaven seem to differ the same as despair, fear, and assurance of salvation."[162] In case the respective nature of Luther's grammar is neglected, "hell" is despair, "purgatory" is fear, and "heaven" is assurance of salvation. Johann Tetzel famously coined the phrase, "As soon as the coin in the coffer rings, The soul from Purgatory springs."[163] It's not surprising that this evil rises from the stench of war and conquest.

Roman Catholic theologians manufactured purgatorial fires for those justified by Christ (Romans 8:1) in order to incite wars and exploit the faithful at their weakest moments. Philip Daileader, a scholar and history professor at William and Mary, connects the Crusades with the development of the doctrine of purgatory.

> During the 12th and 13th centuries, as crusading became more commonplace, theologians further developed the doctrine of purgatory. They spoke of it as a place not just for those who committed minor sins but for those who had committed major sins, confessed them, and then for some reason—such as sudden death—failed to do sufficient penance to atone for those sins. They also spoke of purgatory as a place through which many, perhaps most, souls would pass before entering heaven.[164]

The elaborate building and artistic adornment of St. Peter's Basilica was largely financed by such spiritual extortion. By the time of the Protestant Reformation, the Roman Catholic Church was literally selling tickets to heaven like it was a corporate theme park under their own exclusive purview.

Pope Francis has not only offered plenary indulgences for following him on Twitter,[165] he is spreading the wealth by allowing the office of local priest the power to forgive abortion, an indulgence usually reserved for the office of bishop. But, after all, it is a Jubilee year! The pope harkens the Middle Ages in his call to war as well. Reporter Max Fisher of VOX made an allusion to the original Crusades in an article titled "News from 1096 AD: Pope Discusses Military Force against Middle Eastern Caliphate."[166] Fisher was tongue-in-cheek implying that the "Pope Calls for New Crusade," but, technically, it is more correct to write, the Pope called for a "Just War" to stop an ongoing "Crusade" by the Islamic State.

The Twelfth Crusade

US President George W. Bush actually labeled his War on Terrorism a "crusade" in a speech delivered on the heels of the Twin Towers (and Building 7) crashing into dust. The president misappropriated the term "crusade," sending shivers of horror up the spines of folks educated in ethical theories of war.

> This crusade, this war on terrorism, is going to take a while. And the American people must be patient. I'm going to be patient. But I can assure the American people I am determined, I'm not going to be distracted, I will keep my focus to make sure that not only are these brought to justice, but anybody who's been associated will be brought to justice. Those who harbor terrorists will be brought to justice. It is time for us to win the first war of the 21st century decisively, so that our children and our grandchildren can live peacefully into the 21st century.[167]

Columnist Alexander Cockburn called the War on Terrorism "the Tenth Crusade" (ignoring that there had already been *eleven*)—but, even so, predicted the outcome accurately:

> But does anyone doubt that if the Bush administration does indeed topple Saddam Hussein and occupy Baghdad, this will be truly a plunge into the unknown, one that would *fan once more the embers of Islamic radicalism that peaked as long ago* as the end of the 1980s? (emphasis added)[168]

Allowing Cockburn's allusion while correcting his math, the *twelfth* Crusade is ongoing, but the enemy has morphed into a monster (the Islamic State). A beast that is a worse threat to global security than the one Bush originally declared the crusade to eliminate (Saddam Hussein).

Writing in 2002, Cockburn predicted it would "fan once more the embers of Islamic radicalism," which is exactly what we are now facing with the IS and Mahdism. The Paris attack has galvanized the world toward an armed response. In other words, the Islamic State looms dark on the horizon as an intentional antithesis to freedom and values, pulling the West along a dialectic trajectory, a hook in the jaw towards globalism.

3

Petrus Romanus, Albert Pike, the Islamic State, and Armageddon

Most of us are not competitors… We are the stakes. For the competition is about who will establish the first one-world system of government.
—Malachi Martin, *The Keys of this Blood*[169]

LAST SUMMER, Pope Francis expressed his belief that a fragmentary world war was already underway: "Even today, after the second failure of another world war, perhaps one can speak of a third war, one fought piecemeal, with crimes, massacres, destruction."[170] In another press conference, he said, "Today we are in a world at war, everywhere."[171] Of course, many prophecy watchers were intrigued because a Third World War is assumed to culminate with Armageddon and the return of Jesus Christ. Joseph De Courcey, editor of *Intelligence Brief,* wrote:

If something is not done to reverse these current developments, the result is likely to be a final, catastrophic was between the Arabs and the Jews, possibly pitting superpower against superpower and possibly including nuclear and other weapons of mass destruction.[172]

Lyndon H. LaRouche wrote in 1992, "You might say that World War III has already begun. We have a spreading war in the Balkans; we have a war in Transcaucuses, involving the Turkish population against the Armenians, and the Georgians against the Abkhazians, and so forth and so on; we have a war in Central Asia. We can say, in general, World War III is spreading rapidly in the form of these local wars. It's like a forest fire, threatening to engulf whole continents, and perhaps the world as a whole."[173] LaRouche connected all of this to the intentional design for world government by Scottish Rite Freemason Albert Pike in the same end-noted speech.

The trend of recent references to World War Three have captivated readers familiar with Pike, who allegedly wrote a letter to Giuseppe Mazzini dated August 15, 1871, proposing a diabolic strategy involving three world wars as a means of creating a one world order. The source that originally popularized the letter was *Pawns in the Game* by William Guy Carr, a former intelligence officer in the Royal Canadian Navy. According to Carr:

> Pike's plan was as simple as it has proved effective. He required that Communism, Naziism, Political Zionism, and other International movements be organized and used to foment the three global wars and three major revolutions. The First World War was to be fought so as to enable the Illuminati to overthrow the powers of the Tzars in Russia and turn that country into the stronghold of Atheistic-Communism. The differences stirred up by agentur of the Illuminati between the British and German Empires were to be used to foment this war. After the war ended, Communism was to be built up and used to destroy other governments and weaken religions.
>
> World War Two was to be fomented by using the differences between Fascists and Political Zionists. This war was to be fought so that Naziism would be destroyed and the power of Political Zionism increased so that the sovereign state of Israel could be

established in Palestine. During World War Two, International Communism was to be built up until it equalled in strength that of united Christendom. At this point it was to be contained and kept in check until required for the final social cataclysm. Can any informed person deny Roosevelt and Churchill did not put this policy into effect?

World War Three is to be fomented by using the differences the agentur of the Illuminati stir up between Political Zionists and the leaders of the Moslem world. The war is to be directed in such a manner that *Islam (the Arab World including Moham-medanism) and Political Zionism (including the State of Israel) will destroy themselves* while at the same time the remaining nations, once more divided against each other on this issue, will be forced to fight themselves into a state of complete exhaustion physically, mentally, spiritually and economically. Can any unbiased and reasoning person deny that the intrigue now going on in the Near, Middle, and Far East isn't designed to accomplish this devilish purpose? (Emphasis added)[174]

Carr claimed he was shown the letter by Cardinal Rodriguez of Santiago, Chile, who wrote about the letter, documented to be published prior to the Second World War, in his book *The Mystery of Freemasonry Unveiled* (1925).

Authentic or not, the letter had been published long enough before the events, not to be an invention accommodated *post factum*. Its publication is catalogued in the British Museum of London and the plan attributed to Pike is also in part in *Le Pal-ladisme* Of Margiotta, p. 186 published in 1895. It is a plan to destroy Catholicism, to throw the Pope out of Italy and force him to seek refuge in Russia; and then, when the autocratic empire had become the citadel of Papal Christianity, "we," continues the author of the letter, "shall unleash the Nihilists and

Atheists, and we shall provoke a formidable social cataclysm which in all its horror will show clearly to the nations the effect of absolute atheism, origin of savagery and of the most bloody turmoil. Then everywhere, the citizens, obliged to defend themselves against the world minority of revolutionaries, will exterminate those destroyers of civilization, and the multitude, disillusioned with Christianity, whose deistic spirits will be from that moment without compass, anxious for an ideal, but without knowing where to render its adoration, will receive the *true light* through the universal manifestation of the pure doctrine of Lucifer brought finally out in the public view, a manifestation which will result from the general reactionary movement which will follow the destruction of Christianity and atheism, both conquered and exterminated at the same time.[175]

Even the existence of the Pike-to-Mazzini letter is controversial, mostly due to Carr's popular style but poor scholarship; he didn't document the source material carefully enough, and the letter's veracity (and possible sources) will be discussed later. Even so, if the alleged letter (or a similar document) so accurately described even one of the first two world wars *before* it occurred and, while remaining skeptical, everyone must acknowledge that Cardinal Rodriguez' book discussing this plot by Pike was in print decades before the second world war began,[176] one must take its prediction of a Third and *final* World War pitting the West, and especially Israel, against the Muslim world, very seriously...that is *especially*, if one maintains a supernatural worldview.

All three world wars were allegedly engineered with one goal in mind: a one-world government ostensibly ruled by Scottish Rite Freemasons and their luciferian cronies. If there is any truth to it all, we believe this plan describes the coming kingdom of Antichrist and battle of Armageddon. While a few competent debunkings of the "letter to Mazzini" exist on the Internet, this seems more indicative of pro-Rome tricksters feeding Carr information.[177] Overall, the "Three World War" plan seems plausible and does have supporting evidence. The record of history falls very neatly in place. The conflict with the Islamic world is obviously ongoing. Carr wasn't wrong, but likely fell for a Jesuit prank that ironically (diabolically) *came true*. The letter will probably never see the light of day…that is, if it ever did exist.

Carr also wrote that Satan has his "agentur within the hierarchy of Roman Catholicism just as they had Judas amongst Christ's own apostles."[178] Of course, we dealt with this very real satanic group that the former Jesuit scholar, Malachi Martin, dubbed the "Roman Phalanx" in our books *Petrus Romanus* and *Exo-Vaticana* and pointed to evidence suggesting Benedict XVI was under pressure to resign in order to make way for a "Final Pope" who had been dedicated since youth to Satan for his purposes. As we go to press, a controversial biography of Belgian cardinal Godfried Danneels and Catholic journalist Edward Pentin confirms we were on the right track:

> At the launch of the book in Brussels this week, the cardinal said he was part of a secret club of cardinals opposed to Pope Benedict XVI.
>
> He called it a "mafia" club that bore the name of St. Gallen. The group wanted a drastic reform of the Church, to make it "much more modern", and for Cardinal Jorge Bergoglio to head it. The group, which also comprised Cardinal Walter Kasper and the late Jesuit Cardinal Carlo Maria Martini, has been documented in Austen Ivereigh's biography of *Pope Francis, The Great Reformer.*[179]

Thus, we have the identities of three high-ranking churchmen: Danneels, Kasper, and Martini, the former shamelessly admitting to participating in the sedition, and capitalize on the conspiracy, as a means of promoting his "cloak and dagger" style Vatican-insider "tell-all" autobiography. In other words, he is "cashing in" by bragging about what a joke *Unam Sanctum* and the utter ridiculousness of a human being the vicarious Christ, as if any man but Jesus can assume His role. It shows the utter contempt these cardinals have for the Peterine doctrine of apostolic succession, because they so easily conspire but even portray the unmitigated gall to brag about forcing Pope Benedict to retire in favor of a more progressive choice.

Bergoglio's papal namesake, St. Francis of Assisi, warned shortly before he died seven prophetic travails centering on a pope who is labeled *a destroyer*:

1. The time is fast approaching in which there will be great trials and afflictions; perplexities and dissensions, both spiritual and temporal, will abound; the charity of many will grow cold, and the malice of the wicked will increase.

2. The devils will have unusual power, the immaculate purity of our Order, and of others, will be so much obscured that there will be very few Christians who will obey the true Sovereign Pontiff and the Roman Church with loyal hearts and perfect charity. At the time of this tribulation a man, *not canonically elected*, will be raised to the Pontificate, who, by his cunning, will endeavor to draw many into error and death. [The recent anti-Benedict conspiracy revelation by Belgian Cardinal Danneels arguably qualify Pope Francis as one *not canonically elected.*[180]]

3. Then scandals will be multiplied, our Order will be divided, and many others will be entirely destroyed, because they will consent to error instead of opposing it.

4. There will be such diversity of opinions and schisms among the people, the religious and the clergy, that, except those days were shortened, according to the words of the Gospel, even the elect would be led into error, were they not specially guided, amid such great confusion, by the immense mercy of God.

5. Then our Rule and manner of life will be violently opposed by some, and terrible trials will come upon us. Those who are found faithful will receive the crown of life; but woe to those who, trusting solely in their Order, shall fall into tepidity, for they will not be able to support the temptations permitted for the proving of the elect.

6. Those who preserve in their fervor and adhere to virtue with love and zeal for the truth, will suffer injuries and, persecutions as rebels and schismatics; for their persecutors, urged on by the evil spirits, will say they are rendering a great service to God by destroying such pestilent men from the face of the earth. but the Lord will be the refuge of the afflicted, and will save all who trust in Him. And in order to be like their Head, [Christ] these, the elect, will act with confidence, and by their death will purchase for themselves eternal life; choosing to obey God rather than man, they will fear nothing, and they will prefer to perish rather than consent to falsehood and perfidy.

7. Some preachers will keep silence about the truth, and others will trample it under foot and deny it. Sanctity of life will be held in derision even by those who outwardly profess it, for in those days JESUS CHRIST WILL SEND THEM NOT A TRUE PASTOR, BUT A DESTROYER.[181]

Recall that Malachi Martin warned us about a cabal of high-ranking Jesuits, whose goal was to transform the papacy into an instrument of the devil, in our previous work *Petrus Romanus*. We also wrote about a secret parallel enthronement ceremony in Rome and Charleston, South Carolina (interestingly, also connected to Albert Pike):

Martin stated publicly on more than one occasion that this enthronement of Lucifer in Rome was based on fact, and that to facilitate the black magic, a parallel ceremony was conducted simultaneously in the United States in Charleston, South Carolina. The reason this location was selected has remained obscure to many, but given what Malachi said about the Masonic connection, it makes sense that South Carolina was chosen: It is the site of the first Supreme Council of the Scottish Rite Freemasonry in the United States, called "the Mother Lodge of the World," where in 1859, champion of luciferian dogma for the Masonic-Illuminatus, Albert Pike became Grand Commander of the Supreme Council, where he served the Order of the Quest until his death in Washington DC on April 2, 1892. Pike was known as a Satanist in his adopted state of Arkansas and loved to sit naked in the woods astride a phallic throne while participating for days in drunkenness and debauchery. Today, his body is proudly entombed at the House of the Temple, headquarters of the Southern Jurisdiction of the Scottish Rite Freemasonry in Washington DC.[182]

If Malachi Martin, a former Jesuit and advisor to three popes, was correct, then that satanic influence, only hinted at by Carr, has now been exposed as having completely overtaken the Vatican and the papacy. The purpose of the Charleston, South Carolina, ritual was described by Martin in no uncertain terms. "No longer was the Petrine Office [the papacy] to be an instrument of the "Nameless Weakling" [Jesus]. It was to be fashioned into a willing instrument of the Prince, and a living model for "the New Age of Man."[183] This Jesuit luciferianism seems preternaturally similar to the words of Albert Pike.

Pike is infamous as the author of *Morals and Dogma of the Ancient and Accepted Scottish Rite of Freemasonry* in which he wrote concerning the book of Revelation:

Seven trumpets to sound, and Seven cups to empty. The Apocalypse is, to those who receive the nineteenth Degree, the

Apothesis of that Sublime Faith which aspires to God alone, and despises all the pomps and works of Lucifer. LUCIFER, the Light-bearer! Strange and mysterious name to give to the Spirit of Darkness! Lucifer, the Son of the Morning! Is it he who bears the Light, and with its splendors intolerable blinds feeble, sensual or selfish Souls? Doubt it not![184]

Recalling Martin's thesis in his first nonfiction best seller, *The Jesuits*: "A state of war exists between the papacy and The Religious Order of the Jesuits—the Society of Jesus, to give the order its official name. That war signals the most lethal change to take place within the ranks of professional Roman clergy over the last thousand years."[185] With Pope Francis as the first sitting Jesuit Pope, it seems the diabolic champion of Martin's theological/ideological war is now obvious. With horns like a lamb, Pope Francis allowed Islamic Prayer services to be conducted in the Vatican, while meeting "Israeli President Shimon Peres and Palestinian Authority President Mahmoud Abbas in Vatican City, a gathering designed to pray for Middle Eastern peace."[186] Following the overt denial of Jesus as the Christ (Islamic prayer) being officially condoned, Pope Francis called Mahmoud Abbas, "an angel of peace."[187] It's a smack to the face of the families who know Abbas was instrumental in the terrorist plot that killed Olympic athletes in Munich.

Abbas is a terrorist who proudly wrote his doctoral dissertation on the idea the Zionists collaborated with the Nazis and the Holocaust killed less than one million Jews. We are not joking; apparently, he actually believes it. The thrust of the thesis is that the Holocaust was a Zionist ruse to take Palestine from the Arabs.[188] Abbas still argues that the Zionists and Nazis collaborated. In 2013 he offered a dare, "I challenge anyone to deny the relationship between Zionism and Nazism before World War II."[189] We must refer our present readers to chapter 15, "The Woman Clothed with the Sun and the Red Dragon," and chapter 16, "The Burdensome Stone" of our book *Petrus Romanus* for essential background. Abbas claims the UN (1948) and eventually the Vatican's

(1992) "recognition of a Palestine state is a ploy to bounce it into virtual existence by getting the world to agree it exists. The sole reason it does not in reality exist is that, resting on a wholesale denial of Jewish history in the land, the purpose of such a state is to create the platform for a devastating war on Israel."[190] At best he is a revisionist, but Abbas is not likely that innocent. Labeled by *Newsweek* as "the most famous rabbi in America," Rabbi Shmuley Boteach wrote:

> Abbas's career as a merchant of death rather than an angel of peace stretches all the way back to the early 1970s. According to Abu Daoud, the Mastermind of the 1972 Munich Olympic Massacre that left 11 Israeli athletes murdered, Abbas funded the operation. And when Abu Daoud died in 2010, Abbas wrote a letter of condolence to the infamous terrorist's family saying "He is missed. He was one of the leading figures of Fatah and spent his life in resistance and sincere work as well as physical sacrifice for his people's just causes."[191]

Abbas is also guilty of stealing from the people he claims to represent. At a House subcommittee hearing on the Middle East entitled "Chronic Kleptocracy: Corruption Within the Palestinian Political Establishment,"[192] committee chairman, Rep. Steve Chabot (R-OH), claimed that Mahmoud Abbas has used his position "to line his own pockets as well as those of his cohort of cronies, including his sons, Yasser and Tareq…allegedly receiving hundreds of thousands of dollars in USAID contracts."[193] The deep-seated corruption of the Palestinian Authority is the principal reason that Palestinians continue to suffer economically. The so-called refugees are largely pawns in a chess match used by Israel's Arab neighbors who will not accept them into their own lands.

This also explains why many traditionalist Catholics are today called *Sedevacantists*, a title representing their belief that the present occupant of the papacy is not a true pope, and that, for lack of a valid pope, the

Papal See has been vacant since the death of Pope Pius XII in 1958. The enthronement ceremony that Malachi Martin wrote about and Vatican II were the dawn of the final stage of apostasy about to reach its ultimate fruition.

The Rise of the Islamic State

As mentioned near the beginning of this book, the Islamic State of Iraq and Syria (ISIS), also known as the Islamic State of Iraq and the Levant (ISIL), or, as their pop-savvy branding experts now prefer, simply the Islamic State (IS), is a Muslim terrorist group governing large portions of territory in Iraq and Syria, with growing territories in Libya, Nigeria, and cells within Pakistan, Algeria, Egypt, Philippines, Lebanon, Indonesia, Jordan and Israel.[194, 195]

On June 29, 2014, the terrorist army renamed itself the "Islamic State" (IS), implying its sovereignty over all Muslims rather than merely the region of Iraq and Syria they now control.[196] For that reason, we will refer to them as the Islamic State (IS) as they do themselves. More significantly, the group proclaimed itself to be the worldwide caliphate of prophecy, with Abu Bakr al-Baghdadi (aka Abu Du'a) being named its leader. Baghdadi is now being referred to as "khalifah Ibrahim." *Khalifa* is an Arabic title that means "leader" and *Ibrahim* is the Arabic transliteration of the prophet and patriarch "Abraham." Like the biblical Abraham, in the minds of the IS, Abu Du'ais God's messenger. A short excerpt from the IS's announcement follows:

> We clarify to the Muslims that with this declaration of khilāfah, it is incumbent upon all Muslims to pledge allegiance to the khalīfah Ibrāhīm and support him (may Allah preserve him). The legality of all emirates, groups, states, and organizations, becomes null by the expansion of the khilāfah's authority and

111

arrival of its troops to their areas. Imam Ahmad (may Allah have mercy upon him) said, as reported by ʿAbdūs Ibn Mālik al-ʿAttār, "It is not permissible for anyone who believes in Allah to sleep without considering as his leader whoever conquers them by the sword until he becomes khalīfah and is called Amīrul-Muʾminīn (the leader of the believers), whether this leader is righteous or sinful."[197]

IS really believes it has reestablished the *final* caliphate, and their caliph, Abu Bakr al-Baghdadi, they believe, will reign over the global Muslim community until the arrival of the Mahdi, a messianic figure who precedes the arrival of Jesus.

In the aftermath of September 11, 2001, many Christian prophecy authors have tackled Islamic eschatology, but usually from the perspective of Iran and Shia Islam. We find it a bit odd. In 2009, Shia Muslims constituted around 10 percent of the world's Muslim population, but, in contrast, Sunni Muslims comprise 90 percent of the world's Muslim population.[198] Given the Western media is largely a propaganda tool, mass media-instilled fear involving a nuclear showdown with Iran seems to likely be a distraction. While Iran has made direct threats against the United States and Israel, it seems to us that an inordinate amount of time has been invested in the end-time beliefs of the 10 percent Shia while the 90 percent Sunni[199] has been virtually overlooked in Bible prophecy teaching. Of course, we are horrified by Iran's ambition to continue enriching uranium for the manufacture of nuclear weapons. However, there are compelling reasons to believe the Iranian threat is designed to lead prophecy watchers to ignore a different, but currently more plausible, Armageddon scenario.

The IS is at odds with Iran and hates Shia Muslims as much as Jews and Christians. In fact, Hamas—a terrorist organization supported by Iran controlling Gaza—is fighting for Assad against IS. What if popular scenarios involving a nuclear Iran are averting the intelligence community and most prophecy teachers from the true instigators of the time of Jacob's trouble? What if the Sunni radicals are actually more dangerous than the legendary Shia eschatology of the Twelfth Imam emerging from the chaos of war—as the story goes—created by a nuclear-armed Iran?

Fueled by billions of petrol dollars, expanding rapidly through social media recruitment, and driven by psychotic atrocities, the IS has immense eschatological significance to many Muslims. Both houses of Islam agree that the Mahdi will reestablish the universal caliphate just prior to the return of Jesus (Isa). Not surprisingly, the declaration of a caliphate has been heavily criticized by Middle Eastern governments, Sunni theologians, and rival jihadist groups.[200] With such delusions of grandeur providing a perceived divine mandate, left unchecked, IS will continue its military expansion until it defeats Rome, conquers Istanbul (former Constantinople), and achieves global dominance. This new self-declared Islamic superpower is committed to bringing the Muslim end-time scenario to pass or die trying. How did we get here?

It is a documented fact that Western intelligence agencies knowingly sat on their hands and watched the IS seize power. While it is certainly true that Obama's incompetent Iraq exit strategy paved the way, the formation of a new Middle-Eastern nation claiming to establish a modern-day Islamic caliphate was not the unfortunate result of President Obama's negligent inaction, but, more disturbingly, it was the direct result of US *action*.

First, by intentionally creating a power vacuum in Iraq by leaving an untrustworthy leader and an untrained, unprepared Iraq defense force, the IS rose from ashes of the Iraqi military and al-Qaeda when the US-backed Shia administration turned on the Sunnis. President Obama had left Prime Minister Nouri Kamil Mohammed Hasan al-Maliki and his Shiite cronies to their own devices. After superficially agreeing to work peacefully with Sunni leaders when the US troops withdrew, Prime Minister Maliki began his first unsupervised day by arresting most of the Sunni Muslims within the government and throwing them into prison. Many of those frightened Sunnis who escaped—especially Saddam Hussein's military leadership—went south to Syria and joined the new IS to fight Assad, and transformed from mere *mujahideen* (from Arabic mujāhidūn, "those engaged in jihad")to the even more determined version of Muslim terrorists known as *Mahdists*.

As an ideology, Mahdism is more extreme than run of the mill, militant jihadism. Mahdism entails the belief that Islam's prophesized messiah, the Mahdi, is returning in one's lifetime. According to an expert on Islamic eschatology, Timothy Furnish, PhD, "The central messianic figure in Islam is al-Mahdi, 'the rightly guided one,' who will come near the end of historical time in order to usher in a worldwide Islamic state with the help of the returned prophet Jesus."[201] The "lateness of the hour" is behind the IS' decision to declare the caliphate prior to building the State. According to Sunni eschatology, the final caliphate has nothing to do with the legendary occulted twelfth imam of Shia fame—literally a hilarious belief amongst the Sunnis, who control Mecca, the holiest site in Islam. Abdulrahman Kelani, a published Sunni Muslim eschatology expert, explains:

> Al-Mahdi will be an ordinary man, born to an ordinary woman, raised by ordinary people and living an ordinary life among the people of his time. He has not been living in caves, as the Shiites believe. In reality, al-Mahdi will be an *imam* and a caliph, among other caliphs who rule Muslims with justice. However, what differentiates al-Mahdi from other caliphs is that he will meet Jesus, son of Mary, who will pray behind al-Mahdi.[202]

According to the increasingly annoyed military intelligence community, the IS is *not* weakening as propaganda agents/elected officials, including Secretary of State John Kerry, retired Marine Gen. John Allen, and President Obama himself have stated. Over fifty professional military and high-level strategic scholars went on record, signing an official complaint, that intelligence reports from the field concerning the IS were altered and entire sections were intentionally removed by officials in Washington to put a misleadingly positive spin on the largely negative analysis presented by professionals actually in Syria and Iraq.[203] Even worse, the IS is demonstrably gaining territory and recruiting fresh but fiercely loyal battle-hardened soldiers.[204]

Wood wrote, "One difference between ISIL and other Islamist and jihadist movements is its emphasis on eschatology and apocalypticism, and its belief that the arrival of the Mahdi is imminent. ISIL believes it will defeat the army of 'Rome' at the town of Dabiq in fulfilment of prophecy."[205] He refers to a prophecy attributed to Muhammad that will be examined in detail in a later chapter:

> The Last Hour would not come until the Romans would land atal-A'maq or in Dabiq. An army consisting of the best (soldiers) of the people of the earth at that time will come from Medina (to counter act them).[206]

According to Islamic scholar Farzana Hassan Shahid, "Scholars and commentators of hadith suggest 'Romans' stands for Christians, the Roman Catholic Church being the symbol of the largest division within Christianity."[207] When the IS took control of Dabiq in Northern Syria, it was to begin the process of fulfilling this prophecy. Jessica Stern and J. M. Berger explain:

> Why is ISIS's obsession with the end of the world so important for us to understand? For one thing, violent apocalyptic groups tend to see themselves as participating in a cosmic war between good and evil, in which ordinary moral rules do not apply. Most terrorist groups worry about offending their human audience with acts of violence that are too extreme. This was true even for bin Laden and al Qaeda Central, who withdrew their

support for the Algerian terrorist group GIA and admonished AQI for their violence against Muslims, as we have seen. But violent apocalyptic groups are not inhibited by the possibility of offending their political constituents because they see themselves as participating in the ultimate battle. Apocalyptic groups are the most likely terrorist groups to engage in acts of barbarism, and to attempt to use rudimentary weapons of mass destruction. Their actions are also significantly harder to predict than the actions of politically motivated groups. The logic of ISIS is heavily influenced by its understanding of prophecy. The military strategic value of Dabiq has little to do with ISIS's desire for a confrontation there.[208]

The IS even named its propaganda magazine *Dabiq*. It then used that same periodical to provoke the Roman Catholic Church, predict the overthrow of Rome, and topped it off by threatening to set off a nuclear device on US soil with the assistance of its Mexican drug cartel connections and detonate another nuke somewhere in India through its Pakistani Taliban friends.

Islamic eschatology must be studied seriously by the military in order to determine appropriate defense and strategy. Furnish maintains the website MahdiWatch.org, to track modern Mahdists' movements. He wrote concerning recent events:

> Mahdism is active in Syria, as the jihadist opposition group Jabhat al-Nusra claims to be fighting to prepare the way for his coming; and in the new "Islamic State/caliphate" spanning Syrian and Iraqi territory, as its leadership promotes the upcoming apocalyptic battle with the West at Dabiq, Syria.[209]

While feared as a brutal terrorist group and a major force in that region, the IS threats against the United States are seemingly still not taken seriously by President Obama. IS boasted about purchasing a nuclear device from Pakistan to detonate within the continental United States. Along with the majority of the intelligence community, we believe such an atomic tragedy is more a matter of "when" than "if." Furnish, who also works as an advisor to the US military on Mahdism, explained:

> Islamic messianic insurrections are qualitatively different from mere fundamentalist ones such as bedevil the world today, despite their surface similarities. In fact, Muslim messianic movements are to fundamentalist uprisings what nuclear weapons are to conventional ones: triggered by the same detonating agents, but far more powerful in scope and effect.[210]

In other words, if Al-Qaeda is like dynamite, then the IS is an atomic bomb. As July of 2015 drew to a close, Sara A. Carter, a journalist for the American Media Institute, obtained a secret recruitment document from an unnamed (but verified) Pakistani source connected with the Taliban.

> An apparent Islamic State recruitment document found in Pakistan's lawless tribal lands reveals that the extremist group has grand ambitions of building a new terrorist army in Afghanistan and Pakistan, and triggering a war in India to provoke an Armageddon-like "end of the world."[211]

US intelligence officials believe the document is authentic. It boasts about an attack on India designed to provoke US intervention. "Even if the U.S tries to attack with all its allies, which undoubtedly it will, the ummah (the global Muslim community) will be united, resulting in the final battle."[212] Muslims also believe in a final battle, *Malhama*, corresponding to the Christian prophecy concerning the Battle of

Armageddon but usually centering on Constantinople (today's Istanbul) rather than Jerusalem. President Obama's failed military strategy places US citizens under a threat greater than the danger formerly posed by Saddam Hussein (the stated *jus ad bellum* or "just cause" for the original Iraq war). We now face a situation in which our own weapons are being used against us…again!

In the 1980s, the US equipped the Taliban against the Soviet Union, only to be attacked by some of the same US-trained guerilla fighters using those very same weapons a couple of decades later. A former CIA counterterrorism analyst, Aki Peritz, observed that when you give away valuable weapons in an impoverished area like Afghanistan or Iraq, they are guaranteed to disappear.[213] It seems obvious to us that hungry people will trade weapons for necessities when the threat of an immediate war ends. Thus, we are not surprised that the IS seized tons of US weapons supplied to Iraq and is currently using them to kill Americans. More than two-thirds of the US Humvees supplied to Iraq were taken when IS took Mosul in 2014 and are now, as of this writing, still in their possession.[214] Given the Obama administration's criminal altering of crucial intelligence, even an internal conspiracy to arm the IS seems unthinkable, yet strangely plausible. Nonetheless, it grows much more serious than weapons and vehicles.

The Obama administration was informed concerning the creation of a rogue state led by Iraq's displaced al-Qaida. The warning was seemingly ignored. Furnish sounded a dire warning at the fourth International Conference of Mahdism Doctrine held in 2008, but the IS was given a pass by the US before pulling the troops. If the following comment had been taken seriously then the events in Paris on Friday, November 13, 2015, need never have occurred.

Since the end result of the Mahdi's plans would be, they believe, a global caliphate, nothing he asked would be beyond his followers: detonating a nuke in Vegas or Manhattan, intentionally infecting oneself with plague or smallpox and then crisscrossing American airports [or] suicide-bombing Christian day care centers in the Midwest. Helping the Mahdi restore Islam to planetary predominance would obtain one even more glory than the promised 72 *huris* in Paradise.[215]

Celestial virgin concubines aside, the IS' triumphal announcement of a global caliphate coupled with a few obligatory beheading videos of Western journalists for psychological warfare purposes, a slick recruitment/propaganda magazine self-published in English and several other languages (named after a prophesied defeat of the Romans in Dabiq) distributed via social media to the World Wide Web makes the IS an existential threat to the entire civilized world. Individuals or small cells can incite havoc at anytime, anywhere. The danger is palatable.

The President's incompetence around all this is a matter of public record. Graeme Wood explained, "In the past year, President Obama has referred to the Islamic State, variously, as 'not Islamic' and as al-Qaeda's 'jayvee team,' statements that reflected confusion about the group, and may have contributed to significant strategic errors."[216] Evidence has surfaced proving that Obama was warned, in no uncertain terms, ahead of time about the formation of IS. Yet despite the analysis for the president, the commander-in-chief not only ignored it, but had it altered. Ostensibly, it was to fulfill ill-informed campaign promises to bring the troops home. The reality is that the US left the Middle East in far worse shape than it was with Hussein in Iraq.

Judicial Watch obtained a US Defense Intelligence Agency (DIA) document dated August 12, 2012, that reveals the Obama administration knew the anti-Assad rebels would likely form a new Islamic state and, despite warnings, continually supplied and funded the rising caliphate. The top-secret DIA document states that al-Qaeda in Iraq (AQI), the precursor to the "Islamic State in Iraq" (ISI), which became the "Islamic State in Iraq and Syria," "supported the Syrian opposition from the beginning, both ideologically and through the media."[217]

Ideological lines were drawn with the West, Gulf countries and Turkey, who supported ISIS against Assad, allied with Russia, China, and Iran. Before pulling US troops, Judicial Watch warned Obama:

THIS CREATES THE IDEAL ATMOSPHERE FOR AQI TO RETURN TO ITS OLD POCKETS IN MOSUL AND RAMADI, AND WILL PROVIDE A RENEWED MOMEN- TUM UNDER THE PRESUMPTION OF UNIFYING THE JIHAD AMONG SUNNI IRAQ AND SYRIA, AND THE REST OF THE SUNNIS IN THE ARAB WORLD AGAINST WHAT IT CONSIDERS ONE ENEMY, THE DISSENT- ERS. ISI COULD ALSO DECLARE AN ISLAMIC STATE THROUGH ITS UNION WITH OTHER TERRORIST ORGANIZATIONS IN IRAQ AND SYRIA, WHICH WILL CREATE GRAVE DANGER IN REGARDS TO UNIFYING IRAQ AND THE PROTECTION OF ITS TERRITORY.[218]

Obama and his administration knew the formation of a new radical IS was a likely outcome of their policies. The report damningly and explicitly forecast the probable declaration of "an *Islamic State* through its union with other terrorist organizations in Iraq and Syria" (emphasis added).[219] We offer three possibilities that explain Obama's strategy: 1) incompetence; 2) collaboration; 3) Obama is a pawn in a larger global conspiracy.

If the rise of the IS was due to incompetence, then it is likely due to the error of "mirror imaging" among Westerners—the tendency to assume that the other "thinks like me." When the IS, or al-Qa`idah, states that they are waging "holy war in the path of Allah," incredulous Westerners attempt to explain it as really being motivated by political angst, unemployment, or Western interference in the Middle East. Because it is difficult to imagine that the president of the United States is so woefully ignorant, many otherwise rational people believe Obama is *intentionally* bungling US Mideast strategy. Obama's seeming ineptitude could be a subterfuge and many in the truth movement are crying foul. For example, a discussion thread at Prison Planet.com reads:

> ISIS has been created by and backed by the United States, where the hypocrisy of the United States is almost beyond belief—where the US is creating the war to keep the public in a state of fear and manipulation by terror.[220]

A conspiracy theory that either Mossad or the CIA are funding and advising the IS, in order to marginalize Muslims, is gaining traction in Arab circles. For example, Saudi government official Saleh Al-Fawzan, known for his extremist views, claims that IS is the creation of "Zionists, Crusaders and Safavids."[221] Yasmina Haifi of the Dutch Justice Ministry offered, "[Islamic State] has nothing to do with Islam. It's part of a plan by Zionists, who are deliberately trying to blacken Islam's name."[222] The original rumor appears to have started via social media:

> Content from external source
> Urgent and very serious: has social media important subject the Iranian side was able to detect the identity of the leader of the Islamic State (daash).
> Where the subject matter that the real name of Abu Bakr Al-Baghdadi was "Simon Elliott" from father and mother Jewish.
> The so-called "Eliot" was recruited in the Israeli Mossad for a year during which he fought many trials and tests and field to be eligible to lead a devastating thought of Arabic and Islamic.
> This and the leaks allegedly attributed to the roles of Snowden, and published by newspapers and news websites, the leader of the "Islamic State," Abu Bakr Al-Baghdadi Al-cooperation with us and British intelligence and to create a terrorist organization capable of attracting extremists from all over the world in one place. (Translated by Bing)

James H. Fetzer, publisher of an anti-Semitic conspiracy website *Veterans Today*, reported that the IS leader al-Baghdadi is actually an Israeli Mossad agent named Simon Elliot.[223] The site claims that NSA documents leaked by Edward Snowden reveal this connection. "Abu Bakr al-Baghdadi, so-called "Caliph," the head of ISIL (Islamic State in Iraq and the Levant) is, according to sources reputed to originate from Edward Snowden, an actor named Elliot Shimon, a Mossad trained operative."[224] It is also claimed that photographs prove Baghdadi really is Elliot.

Nous vous proposons ci-dessous trois traductions qui se veulent affirmer que le Khalife Al-Baghdadi est un agent intégral du Mossad et qu'il serait né de père et de mère juifs :

Alleged proof that Baghdadi is a Zionist Agent

Source: http://www.veteranstoday.com/2014/08/04/

french-report-isil-leader-mossad/

The photos do look like the same person, but it is a weak claim without even going into who Simon Elliot is and whether or not he is a Mossad agent. It depends entirely on people accepting pictures (which are always suspect in the digital age) and the Zionist conspiracy narrative that comes along with them at face value. Of course, the claim seems rather absurd. Steeped in anti-Semitic conspiracy lore, the above scenario seems more like an attempt by more moderate Sunni Muslims (like the Saudis) to distance themselves from the new "more Islamic" Islamic State...and for obvious reasons.

In June 2015, the Pentagon confirmed that the IS "had acquired a sufficient amount of radioactive materials to be incorporated in conventional weapons, such as artillery, to spread harmful radiation."[225] This is the news we are getting *with the spin*, so the truth could be much worse. While the use of radioactive ammunition has immediate consequences for those on the fronts in Syria and Iraq, it also poses a threat to Southwestern US. Apparently, the IS can make a "dirty bomb" (conventional explosives with radioactive materials) that could kill or harm US citizens and poison US soil and farmland, far into the future.

The IS has explicitly threatened such an attack. Boasting about its relationship with the Mexican drug cartels, the terrorists claim to have enough money from oil sales to purchase a nuclear bomb from Pakistan in order to smuggle it over the southern border of the United States.[226] Even at his worst, Saddam Hussein never made such an explicit threat against the continental US. After spending billions of dollars on Iraq, the US finds itself in a deeper hole than when it started. The powers of this present darkness tickled President Obama's Muslim sympathies to serve a larger global agenda—*the New World Order promoted by Rome and the United Nations.*

Pope Francis has seemed a bit limp-wristed at times, once remarking, "Who am I to judge?" when asked about homosexual priests and implying that atheists please God by obeying their conscience. When asked if he approved of the US airstrikes against the Islamic State, Pope Francis responded:

In these cases where there is an unjust aggression, I can only say this: it is licit to stop the unjust aggressor. I underline the verb: stop. I do not say bomb, make war, I say stop by some means. With what means can they be stopped? These have to be evaluated. To stop the unjust aggressor is licit.

But we must also have memory. How many times under this excuse of stopping an unjust aggressor the powers [that intervened] have taken control of peoples, and have made a true war of conquest.

One nation alone cannot judge how to stop an unjust aggressor. After the Second World War there was the idea of the United Nations. It is there that this should be discussed. Is there an unjust aggressor? It would seem there is. How do we stop him? Only that, nothing more.[227]

Pope Francis' use of terminology like "unjust aggressor"[228] invoked "Just War theory" in the academic disciplines of political science and ethics or the "Just War tradition" based on its origination in the writings of Christian thinkers like Augustine and Aquinas. According to this longstanding tradition, there must be a "just reason" to go to war (*jus ad bellum*),[229] and a soldier's warfare conduct should be just (*jus in bello*).[230] Three important points are implied within the pope's statement: 1) IS is an unjust aggressor and it is legal to stop them. 2) The Roman pontiff and Vatican diplomats are increasingly advocating the use of deadly military force. 3) The pope emphasizes it is a global responsibility under the exclusive prevue of the United Nations.[231] Let's examine these three clear points in light of *jus ad bellum* (going to war) and *jus in bello* (waging war).

First, Christian persecution reached historic levels in 2014, with approximately one hundred million Christians around the world living in fear for their lives.[232] Archbishop Silvano Maria Tomasi, the Vatican's top diplomat at the UN, called it genocide. "We have to stop this kind of genocide," she said. "Otherwise we'll be crying out in the future about why we didn't so something, why we allowed such a terrible tragedy to happen."[233] In response, rather than firing missiles from an elementary school or beheading journalists, we have a truly genocide level event underway with Syria's 1.1 million Christian population reduced to under 250,000.[234] It is easy to agree with the pope on this first point that the IS is an unjust aggressor.

Second, a superior ground force is needed to "stop" the IS, and the Iraqi military has not measured up. Historically, stopping an army like ISIS entails American "boots on the ground," but senior Vatican UN diplomat Tomasi and the pope both emphasize that any such military coalition must be led by the UN.[235] Archbishop Warda, the Chaldean Catholic prelate of Erbil, in northern Iraq, pleaded with Britain to send troops to Iraq back in February of 2015. "It is very hard for me as a Catholic bishop to say I have to advocate military action but there is no other option. These people have no other way to be dealt with but with military action."[236] We agree and we are convinced there are indeed circumstances when the first and most urgent moral obligation of governments is to stop evil despots by waging war. We are not Christian pacifists, but respectfully acknowledge our brothers and sisters in Christ who hold that view. War is a great evil but, while the Lord tarries, it is a necessary one. Theologian and research fellow at the Center for Ethics and Culture, Notre Dame University, Thomas D. Williams, PhD, surmised the current situation in a somber but realistic tone:

> Recent years have seen an increasing reluctance on the part of the Vatican to speak of the traditional "Just War Doctrine," as Church officials have urged the exhaustion of diplomatic solutions before even considering the use of force. This reluctance seems now to be giving way to a grittier realism in the face of a relentless enemy with whom constructive, rational dialogue is impossible.[237]

The call for military action is, indeed, remarkable, considering that the Vatican has recently opposed all Middle Eastern military intervention, especially the two American-led Gulf Wars. It builds, however, on specific Catholic buzzwords recently employed by Pope Francis that the use of force is "legitimate… to stop an unjust aggressor."[238] On July 10, 2015, Pope Francis—*Petrus Romanus,* according to St. Malachy's prophecy of the popes—boldly declared an ongoing Third World War:

> Today we are dismayed to see how in the Middle East and elsewhere in the world many of our brothers and sisters are persecuted, tortured and killed for their faith in Jesus, in this third world war, waged piecemeal, which we are now experiencing, a form of genocide is taking place, and it must end.

Again in 2015 the pope spoke of a Third World War.

> On several occasions, I called this time a time of war, a third world war "in pieces," in which we see daily in heinous crimes, with massacres and bloody madness of the destruction. Unfortunately, even today, we hear the muffled cry and overlooked by so many of our brothers and sisters, helpless, who because of their faith in Christ or of their ethnicity are publicly and atrociously killed, beheaded, crucified, burned alive, or forced to leave their land.[239]

The pontiff's remarks were a call for justice for the Christians who have been mercilessly beheaded and unthinkable atrocities characteristic of the Islamic State, including hanging unborn babies with Christian parents from trees and crucifying the teenagers (literally).[240] The genocide is ongoing. There are credible reports that IS[241] and Assad[242] are both using chemical weapons. Of course, President Obama drew a red line in the sand that was quickly dyed yellow. It appears that 2015 will be even worse, leading some Catholic pundits to call for a new crusade.[243] Theodore Shoebat enthusiastically writes, "The Crusades are coming back, and that means a strong Church—which is the true Church—is going to arise from the weak and crumbling ruins of the decayed church of the masses."[244]

Third, the pope qualified his "just cause" by arguing that it would be unjust for the United States to intervene once again. Unfortunately, the facts about American intervention support his point. "One nation alone cannot judge how to stop an unjust aggressor. After the Second World War there was the idea of the United Nations."[245] The papacy has been endorsing world government for decades. The pope's recent remarks are consistent with this little-known speech by Pope Paul VI to the United Nations on October 4, 1965. In his address, Paul VI also called for an expanded UN role in global affairs:

> Your Charter goes further than this, and Our message advances with it. You exist and operate to unite the Nations, to bind States together. Let Us use this second formula: to bring the ones together with the others. You are an association. You are a bridge between peoples. You are a network of relations between States. We would almost say that your chief characteristic is a reflection, as it were, in the temporal field, of what our Catholic Church aspires to be in the spiritual field: unique and universal. In the ideological construction of mankind, there is on the natural level nothing superior to this. Your vocation is to make brothers not only of some, but of all peoples. A difficult undertaking, indeed; but this is it, your most noble undertaking. Is there anyone who does not see the necessity of coming thus progressively to the establishment of a world authority, able to act efficaciously on the juridical and political levels?[246]

The Globalist Hegelian Dialectic

In order to move the rival nation states toward globalism, the power elite, or *illumined ones*, deploy a global scale Hegelian dialectic. Georg Friedrich Hegel was a nineteenth-century German philosopher who devised a method for resolving disagreements, a *dialectic*. In 1847 the London Communist League led by Karl Marx and Frederick Engels used Hegel's theory of the dialectic to back up their communist economic theory. Through the global elites, the Hegelian-Marxist thinking affects our entire social and political structure. The Hegelian dialectic is the framework for guiding our thoughts and actions into conflicts that lead us to a predetermined solution that is primarily global governance. President Obama uses Islam to this end.

For those reasons, we favor the third possibility for why the US allowed the formation of the new Islamic State: that Obama is a pawn in a larger globalist conspiracy. Because the military-industrial complex is the only real winner when war breaks out, the IS is likely a mere a pawn used as the antithesis of a geopolitical dialectic. World events are guided by an invisible hand, and the IS has a hook in its jaw to bait the United States by attacking European cities like Paris and perhaps Rome. Wahhabi Islam makes a perfect antithesis of Western liberalism. It's so neatly opposite, it betrays intelligent design. For this among other reasons discussed throughout this book, we believe something along the lines of Albert Pike's legendary three-world-war letter—whether that document is authentic or not. We suggest something rather simple like:

Thesis: Removal US Forces from Iraq/Middle East;

Anti-thesis: The resulting unrest results in a new radical Islamic State declares a world caliphate;

Synthesis: United Nations Peacekeeping Force (a step toward global governance).

A state of affairs that advances biblical prophecy significantly toward its ultimate fulfillment. Next, we examine the origins of the IS and discover that the events of 2014–2015 were actually no surprise to analysts in the field no matter how exasperated the president pretends to be.

4

The Origin of the Islamic State

We declare Fallujah as an Islamic state, and we call on you to be on our side! We are here to defend you from the army of Maliki and the Iranian Safavids!
—Islamic State fighter (then Islamic State of Iraq and Syria) on the podium at the declaration of statehood in Fallujah, January 3, 2014[247]

ALTHOUGH OUR overarching thesis transcends mere flesh and blood (Ephesians 6:12), this chapter delves into a "this worldly" geopolitical, strategic analysis of the IS' formation and prosperity. While the main stream media originally reported that the IS appeared out of nowhere when Obama pulled the troops from Iraq, most now link the group's formation to Jordanian criminal al-Zarqawi. Zarqawi converted to Islam and moved to Afghanistan to engage in jihad. In 1999, he started a group called *Jamaat al-Tahwidwa-i-Jihad* (JTWJ), focused on effecting regime change in Jordan.[248] Along the way, he became increasingly convinced that the end times were upon us and that the Mahdi would soon appear. Zarqawi's early aspirations are why many accounts trace today's IS back to 1999. For example:

ISIS was founded in 1999 by the Jordanian extremist Abu Musab al-Zarqawi. Within five years, al-Zarqawi's new group chose to associate themselves with Osama bin Laden and Al-Qaeda. They are considered to be Islamic extremists, Islamists or Jihadists, closely linked to the concept of Jihad or "struggle." Various similar groups, such as the Taliban, Boko Haram, Al-Qaeda, Hamas and Hezbollah have also made the news for decades, but ISIS appears to be in a league of its own.[249]

Notice that it misses the key distinction, Mahdism. While Zarqawi is accurately traced, the origin of the new state and caliphate is not fully accounted for. Other accounts in non-Arabic media are similarly incomplete. "A leading scholar of militant Islamism,"[250] William McCants documented that a new state and caliphate was much more Mahdist than that of Al-Qaeda and was not exclusively Zarqawi's vision. The disagreement was described in a recent fact book:

> However, one account that has gained popularity and is supported by a large number of scholars and observers is that ISIS began in 2004. It can be attributed to what was originally called Alqaeda in Iraq. Owing to the fallout with the mother organization, which it was named after; Al-Qaeda, it rebranded in 2006. The cause for the fallout is attributed to the short and long term goals. Although both were opposed to Western values and influence, ISIS wanted to focus its energies to activities in Iraq and Syria. It was and is still preoccupied with establishing an independent Islamic state. Alqaeda on the other hand was predominantly occupied with fighting the west, particularly the USA.[251]

Sayf al-Adl was Zarqawi's Al-Qaeda contact in Qandahar, Iraq. Zarqawi was sent to form a new training camp in the mountains. His mission was to resist the United States invasion, and Obama played right into his hands. McCants cited an early quote from Adl already speaking of a "state" and "caliphate," reflecting his Mahdism and the brain-seed of the IS.

> Sayf recalled. "This is our historical opportunity…to establish the state of Islam, which would play the greatest role in lifting injustice and bringing truth to this world, by God's permission. I was in agreement with brother Abu Mus'ab [al-Zarqawi] in this analysis." For Sayf and presumably for Zarqawi, the "state of Islam" was the caliphate itself.[252]

Zarqawi's Mahdism was reinforced by Sayf Adl and in 2004, Zarqawi wrote that the group would establish the "caliphate according to the prophetic method."[253] After many successful raids, Zarqawi became a folk hero to Iraqi Sunnis. Although it has been argued that the IS was a product of the Arab Spring,[254] it is more accurate to credit their genesis to the US troop pullout in Iraq. In that sense, the US is responsible for the IS' formation. From 2004 forward, we track four stages of development.

Stage One: Mahdism (1999–2006)

In 2004, JTWJ formally became an Al-Qaeda affiliate with the establishment of the branch of Al-Qaeda in Iraq led by Zarqawi and called "Al-Qaeda in Mesopotamia (Iraq)." While not personally a member of Al-Qaeda, Zarqawi teamed up with them in Iraq, where his Mahdism was fueled by associates who, convinced of the Mahdi's soon arrival, later became the leadership of the IS. Zarqawi led a terrorist-guerilla war against the American and coalition forces and against the Shi'ite population. The first stage ended when Zarqawi was killed in an American targeted attack in June 2006.

Stage Two: ISI to ISIS(2006–2014)

ISI served as an umbrella network for several jihadi organizations waging a guerilla campaign against the United States' Coalition Forces. After the American army withdrew from Iraq, the Obama administration's puppet Prime Minister Nouri al-Malik betrayed prominent Sunni leaders that had been arrested, which only deepened the divide and strengthened the IS. Following the escalation of the Syrian civil war…they declared the Islamic State in Iraq and Greater Syria (ISIS).

Stage Three: ISIL to the IS (June 2014–November 2015)

This stage is characterized by dramatic ISIS military achievements. The most important was the takeover of Mosul in June 2014, the second-largest city in Iraq. At the same time, ISIS established its control in eastern Syria, where it set up a governmental center (its "capital city") in Al-Raqqah and conquered the prophetically important Dabiq. In the wake of its success, ISIS declared the establishment of a caliphate headed by a recently released US detainee, vetted by the IS theologians to match Hadith qualifications, Abu Bakr al-Baghdadi, an intellectual with a legitimate PhD in Islamic studies. Baghdadi was handpicked as the future of the IS, but he had nothing to do with its creation.

Stage Four: The IS to Da'esh (November 13, 2015–Present)

The Paris bombing changed the landscape, and there is enormous global pressure to completely eradicate the IS but increasing conciliation that it is indeed a state. Putin and the entire international community are calling for a new crusade. We believe the IS has attracted too much international attention to survive much longer. After deploying a weapon of mass destruction, we believe a global campaign will make an example out of the US fulfilling a dialectic. The IS' sectarianism and gratuitous violence make it a unlikely candidate for mass appeal. Sectarianism is poorly understood.

For example, Middle East reporter, Hana Levi Julian, suggests that Sunni and Shia might work together against Israel. She fails to recognize the depth of the sectarian divide.

A cataclysmic clash of civilizations is taking place in Syria, one that a number of nations have patiently awaited for decades.

Turkey, so deeply invested in the glorious history of its Ottoman Empire period, would find great satisfaction in stretching its influence with a modern-day "Turkish Islamic Union" that might embrace like-minded nations in the region and perhaps also beyond.

Da'esh, as it is known in the Middle East and which in English calls itself the "Islamic State" (known by others as ISIS or ISIL) is rapidly stretching its influence to build a worldwide Sunni caliphate. It began as a splinter group from the Al Qaeda terrorist organization, and then morphed into the Islamic State in Iraq and Syria (hence "ISIS")—but at last count had successfully recruited more than 41 other regional Muslim terrorist organizations to its cause from around the world on nearly every continent.[255]

Despite a bitter hatred of each other that surpasses even anti-Semitism, Sunni and Shia will eventually cooperate against the Second Coming, but only after demonic allurement (Revelation 16:13–14). In regard to Armageddon, Israel's Muslim neighbors are demonically compelled to Jerusalem as the sixth angel pours out his vial or bowl of wrath by the three "frog" spirits. For the IS' narrative to be coherent with its theology and recruitment literature, they have to attack Istanbul next to take "Constantinople" and then Rome and then Jerusalem, at least that is how the most trusted Hadith reads. The Mahdi appears in Constantinople, which is now called Istanbul after being taken by the Ottoman Empire in 1453.

> Cerantonio notes that the Ottomans, who defeated the Byzantines, accepted the mantle of "Rome" explicitly: The sultan called himself the "Caesar of Rome" and believed he was establishing a third Roman Empire. And when the Ottoman line ended in 1924—leaving the world without a caliph—their successors were the secular republicans of Mustafa Kemal Ataturk. Those successors still reign in Istanbul and Ankara, and the Islamic State considers them apostates, even though the most recent of them, Recep Tayyip Erdogan, is generally counted as an Islamist by those who aren't members of ISIS.[256]

However, for the IS' Dabiq prophecy interpretation to remain coherent, from Dabiq they must go to Constantinople. The Sahih Muslim, Hadith, recorded the alleged prophecy.

> Abu Huraira reported Allah's Messenger (may peace be upon him) as saying: The Last Hour would not come until the Romans would land at al-A'maq or in Dabiq. An army consisting of the best (soldiers) of the people of the earth at that time will come from Medina (to counteract them). When they will arrange themselves in ranks, the Romans would say: Do not stand between us and those (Muslims) who took prisoners from amongst us. Let us fight with them; and the Muslims would say: Nay, by Allah, we would never get aside from you and from our brethren that you may fight them. They will then fight and a third (part) of the army would run away, whom Allah will never forgive. A third (part of the army) which would be constituted

of excellent martyrs in Allah's eye, would be killed and the third who would never be put to trial would win and they would be conquerors of Constantinople.[257]

Given that the IS places itself as the defeaters of the crusaders, the Ottoman conquest of Constantinople cannot fulfill the prophecy and they must defeat Istanbul, and only then do they attack Rome. However, logical inconsistencies have not stopped the IS from attacking Paris, so anything goes. As they build a fledgling state, we wonder how many years must pass before their interpretation is discredited. Also note the glaring absence of the Mahdi in the Dabiq prophecy. Interestingly, we cannot find a single truly ancient source with Muhammad prophesying a Mahdi. All are found in eighth- and ninth-century *Hadiths* published after the *Apocalypse of Psuedo-Methodius,* which is now classified as Christian pseudapigrapha. Apparently, the Mahdi was created as a Muslim alternative to the Great Roman Emperor Topos of medieval Christian eschatology.

Even so, it is not at all likely that Sunni and Shia will "team up" against Israel anytime soon because of the war in Syria. The IS has killed more Muslims than it has Christians, and even attacked a Shia funeral.[258] The IShas attacked Hamas, a Palestinian Sunni-Islamic fundamentalist organization, who attacks Israel.[259] The divide is deeper than non-Muslims comprehend and it stifles Muslim expansionism. Dietrich Jung, a political scientist, writes, "Sunnis have not forgotten that during the Muslim Brothers' confrontation with the Syrian regime, Iran made a tactical decision and supported the Syrian authorities not the Muslim Brothers."[260] We do not believe Iran will ever cooperate with the IS, or vice versa.

The IS Responds to Petrus Romanus

The pope's call for a "Just War" has not escaped the IS. Sheikh Abu Muhammad al-Adnani responded to the pope and the Vatican diplomats:

And so we promise you [O crusaders] by Allah's permission that this campaign will be your final campaign. It will be broken and defeated, just as all your previous campaigns were broken and defeated, except that this time we will raid you thereafter, and you will never raid us. We will conquer your Rome, break your crosses, and enslave your women. If we do not reach that time, then our children and grandchildren will reach it, and they will sell your sons as slaves at the slave market.[261]

The IS published a fabricated image with the black IS flag flying above the obelisk in St. Peter's Square, on the cover of IS' official magazine *Dabiq*. Also see the cover of this book for our version.

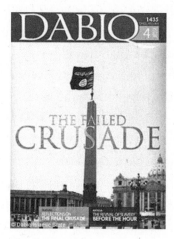

Dabiq Magazine 4

Habeeb Al-Sadr, the Iraqi ambassador to the Vatican since 2010, warned, "What has been declared by the self-proclaimed Islamic State is clear—they want to kill the Pope, the threats against the Pope are credible."[262] After the Paris incident, Italian Interior Minister Angelino Alfano banned all drones from the St. Peter's Square as the Year of Mercy is due to attract millions of tourists to the Vatican. Alfano stressed, "Particular attention has been dedicated to the risk of an attack from the air, using drones."[263]

The UN and Vatican are undoubtedly working together. Following his promotion of the UN to stop unjust aggressors, Pope Francis asked, "Is there an unjust aggressor? It would seem there is."[264] By way of implication, it seems at minimum a Just War—or perhaps something more akin to the Last Crusade—has already been called for by *Petrus Romanus*. Addressing the Italian Parliament, Mr. Alfano said that security would be tightened around any potential target, particularly around St. Peter's Square. "Particular attention has been dedicated to the risk of an attack from the air, using drones."[265] It seems Rome anticipates an attack on the city, as many of their own prophecies, the occult Sibylline and Zohar predictions, and the book of Revelation agree.

Gog of Magog?

Obama administration officials conceded on October 1, 2015, that there was little they could do in Syria to protect the CIA trained anti-Assad rebels who were taking airstrikes from the highly trained Russian Air Force (as this book goes to press). According to *The Daily Beast*:

> The rebels attacked by Russian forces on Wednesday and Thursday were in western Syria, alongside al Qaeda affiliates and far from any ISIS positions. That suggests the rebels were not there to fight the self-proclaimed Islamic State, as the Obama administration called the top priority. Instead, they were battling the Assad regime as part of a still-active CIA program for rebels which has run in tandem with the disastrous and now-defunct train and equip Pentagon program.[266]

Army Col. Steven Warren said, "We don't believe that [Russia] struck [ISIS] targets. So that is a problem." This was confirmed by Lt. Gen. Robert Otto, the Air Force's deputy chief of staff for intelligence, surveillance, and reconnaissance, who reiterated, "Where those strikes occurred, those were not anti-ISIS strikes."[267] Other than the obvious potential for World War III between the nuclear superpowers, Russia's elimination of the CIA-supported rebel groups fighting Assad is so troublesome because it strengthens the Islamic State by eliminating their enemies. Russia is defending the Assad government. Apparently, there is a proxy war underway between Russia and the United States.

Senate Foreign Relations Committee Chairman Bob Corker was almost speechless: "I don't even know what to say, we are getting to a place where there are very little, if any, options left."[268] Oklahoma Senator Jim Inhofe, the former top Republican on the Senate Armed Services Committee, added, "The answer is not 'Go after Russia and start World War III.' I just don't know what the [solution is]—that's what we're working on now."[269] But what if Russia (or the IS) leaves us no choice? Over 750,000 of the world's most ancient Christian population has already been displaced or brutally murdered. How many more Syrian Christians must die before the US—or as suggested by Pope Francis, a United Nations Force—does intervene?

However, seemingly in response to the US criticism, a few days later, Putin nailed nine important Islamic State targets. As this book goes to press, we read, "Soviet jets pounded terrorist targets in Syria overnight using bunker busting bombs to blow up an ISIS command outpost, potentially killing dozens of fighters." Even so, the Russian strategy emphasizes bombing American supported rebels more than the IS.

> Russian diplomats and military officials contend the air attacks are aimed at Islamic State extremists, but that claim is widely disputed by the US and others, who say the Russians have too often bombed Syrian opposition fighters who have no connection with, or allegiance to, the Islamic State militants.[270]

The raids come after a senior British military expert said the West has been totally outflanked by Putin on the Syria crisis because its policymaking has been dominated by "wishful thinking."[271] Where does this place Vladimir Putin in the long-game, preternatural dialectic of the powers and principalities? As one might expect, many prophecy watchers believe Putin is a likely candidate for Gog of Magog, the leader who comes against Israel from the North in the famous prophetic battle of Ezekiel 38–39.

Doug Woodward explains the Islamocentric view of Mystery Babylon as "an ascendant empire in the Middle East (usually Turkey, Saudi Arabia, possibly Iran or now, ISIS) will become the power base of Antichrist, when he claims to be the Mahdi."[272] For example, my [Putnam's] former seminary professor, Michael Heiser, once wrote, "We need not twist such prophecies to target modern political villains, like the former Soviet Union. The Israeli-Muslim feud is both more rational, and more biblical."[273] Heiser explained:

> The book of Revelation prophesies the revival of the now defunct eastern Roman Empire ("mystery Babylon"; Rev. 17) in the future—a kingdom with which the beast/Antichrist is somehow associated. This revived Babylonian empire, the revived eastern Roman Empire, encompasses all of today's modern Muslim nations, as did the original eastern (Byzantine) Roman Empire.[274]

Heiser's view stands in sharp relief to the *Scofield Reference Bible*, which explicitly identified Russia and was actually published long before the Marxist revolution and formation of the militantly atheistic Soviet Union. In a sense, Islam is a more modern enemy in that Mahdism, as expressed by the IS, is a relatively late phenomenon resulting from the US invasion of Iraq and Afghanistan. Woodward predicts that the "Islamic-centric view will prove incorrect within a few short years. Many will object, but I will continue to advance the much more conventional position that Gog is not just a Turk."[275]

Defending the Scofield view, Woodward notes, "The conventional view has held for over a century that the 'revived Roman Empire' (inferred from Daniel 9:24–27), from which Antichrist draws his earthly power, will arise from Western Europe (the 'merchants of Tarshish') or its 'young lions' (their colonies in the Western Hemisphere—See Ezekiel 38:13). Alongside this conclusion, the traditional view sees Russia leading the alliance of Islamic nations (Iran, aka Persia)."[276] He believes that Putin might indeed be the infamous Gog, at least the humanly visible side of an unseen "power" driving his ideology.[277] Gog does not seem to be Muslim because its "evil purpose" (Ezekiel 38:10) is about securing financial gain (Ezekiel 38:12–13). He does not attack Israel to gain the holy land (Ezekiel 5:5; 38:12–13). He has no interest in the Temple Mount or its sanctuaries. "Gog's battle is not launched against Israel because of who Israel is in relation to God, nor because of the spiritual significance that Jerusalem holds to Christians, Jews, or Muslims."[278] If Gog were the Mahdi or any Muslim, a religious motivation for invading Israel would be present.

When it comes to Russia as Magog or Turkey, rather than an "either/or" situation, this could be a case of "both/and"—especially because of both Turkey and Russia's continuing political alliance with Muslim nations like the Assad regime and Iran. A Messianic teacher, Benni Kleynhans, identified: "Russia, Moscow, Tobolsk, Iran, Iraq, Afghanistan, Ethiopia and Sudan, Lybia, Austria and Germany, Eastern Europe, Southern Europe and Russian allies are respectively identified with the following names from Ezekiel: Gog and Magog, Mesech and Tubal, Persia, Ethiopia, Lybia, Askenaz, Gomer, Togarmah and many nations with you."[279] One is not bound to an exclusively Muslim confederation, much like Israel's political enemies in the UN; the Magog war very well could entail Russia leading a group of Islamic nations.

The Russian Orthodox Christian Church has described the Putin administration's fight against the IS as a "holy battle" [crusade]. Head of the Church's Public Affairs Department, Vsevolod Chaplin, told Interfax news agency:

The fight with terrorism is a *holy battle* and today our country is perhaps the most active force in the world fighting it. The Russian Federation has made a responsible decision on the use of armed forces to defend the People of Syria from the sorrows caused by the arbitrariness of terrorists. Christians are suffering in the region with the kidnapping of clerics and the destruction of churches. Muslims are suffering no less (emphasis added).[280]

He also said that an interfaith council representing Russia's main religions—Orthodox Christianity, Islam, Judaism, and Buddhism—*will* release a joint statement supporting the crusade against ISIS. In early 2012, Putin met with church representatives who described the horrific treatment of Christians around the world, especially the Muslim world:

The head of External Church Relations, Metropolitan Illarion, said that every five minutes one Christian was dying for his or her faith in some part of the world, specifying that he was talking about such countries as Iraq, Egypt, Pakistan and India. The cleric asked Putin to make the protection of Christians one of the foreign policy directions in future.

"This is how it will be, have no doubt," Putin answered.[281]

The Muslim rebels were quick to respond. Syrian opposition member, Bassam-Jaara said:

The Orthodox Church's call for a holy war in Syria warrants a declaration of jihad. The Orthodox Church described Putin's battle in Syria as 'holy', meaning a crusade war.... A "holy" war requires a call for jihad.[282]

The stage is set for World War III and, perhaps, the final battle occurring at "a place called in the Hebrew tongue Armageddon" (Revelation 16:16).

5

Pope Francis: Destroyer

Our Lord Jesus Christ will send them not a true Pastor, but a
destroyer.
—St. Francis of Assisi

And I beheld another beast coming up out of the earth; and he
had two horns like a lamb, and he spake as a dragon.
—Revelation 13:11

ONE MORNING in late September of 2015, the headline "Pope Francis
Wants to Be President of the World" was right in front of me in bold
titling. Sheer astonishment at *The Huffington Post* byline almost caused
me to blow coffee out of my nose. Howard Fineman was basically
documenting the fulfillment of what Tom Horn and I warned about
prior to Jorge Mario Bergoglio's election to the Petrine Office, now confessed to be no election at all, but rather through an under-the-table
anti-Benedict conspiracy.[283] As I was beginning to wake up, the *Huffington Post's* global editorial director waxed eloquent about the new pope
negotiating the geopolitical scene "shrewdly, methodically and with a
showman's flair, the soft-spoken, 78-year-old Argentinian Jesuit priest

named Jorge Mario Bergoglio—Pope Francis—showed Thursday that he is running to become president of the planet."[284] President Obama might have something to say about his ambition because CNN already declared that Obama was "President of the World" when he was elected in 2008.[285] But who are Obama and Bergoglio fooling? Apparently, most of the unbelieving world.

To us and the majority of Christians we know personally, this pope seems so puerile when claiming that atheists please God by obeying their conscience. "Sin, even for those who have no faith, exists when people disobey their conscience."[286] The Bible teaches the exact opposite: "But without faith *it is impossible to please him*: for he that cometh to God must believe that he is, and that he is a rewarder of them that diligently seek him" (Hebrews 11:6, emphasis added). The biblical analysis only gets worse: "Unto the pure all things are pure: but unto them that are defiled and *unbelieving* is nothing pure; but even their mind and *conscience is defiled*" (Titus 1:15, emphasis added). It places Roman Catholics who attempt to follow biblical theology in the uncomfortable position of defending the pope's ignorance, or perhaps the reflection of rebellion? Sometimes, Pope Francis must just be embarrassing to his staff apologists.

For example, while visiting Harlem, New York City, in 2015, Pope Francis commented on an eight-year-old student's iPad video of a rat dragging a slice of pizza down a staircase in the projects as being comparable to the Savior bearing mankind's burden for all past, present, and future sin—in our opinion, a blasphemous allusion. Yes, that's right, the pope effectively *christologized* a rodent. "The little creature embodies the very struggles and daily toils shared by you and me, and the heavy burden taken on by our Lord and Savior Jesus Christ. May God bless the Pizza Rat on his universal journey."[287] Of course, most folks who heard the pope's remarks to the young African-American girl likely already understood the term "rat" as a synonym for "betrayer,"[288] suggesting that a Judas Iscariot allusion would have been more appropriate. Even so, by the end of this chapter you will see that high-ranking Roman Catholic officials are already crediting Pope Francis with supernatural miracles. With that in mind, his worldly status as a "destroyer" predicted by St. Francis of Assisi is examined in the context of the false-prophet hypothesis we presented in 2012 prior to Bergoglio's election.

In this chapter, we strive to convince the reader that the pope's actions, since we wrote *Petrus Romanus,* have not only confirmed our own hypothesis, but have realized Vatican insider Malachi Martin's worst suspicions. Martin worked for the Jesuit Cardinal Augustin Bea and the pope as both a scholar and geopolitical adviser from 1958 until 1964 when the liberalism codified at the Second Vatican Council burdened him to make a strange request to be released of his Jesuit status. Martin revealed that Cardinal Bea was shown the "real" Third Secret of Fatima and that Pope John XXIII was *not* going to reveal the Third Secret to the world. He implied the content of the Third Secret involved the apostate "Superforce" and the failure of the uncorrupted leadership to adequately put it to rest. William H. Kennedy, an author who assisted Martin, wrote:

> What Martin called Lucifer's Lodge or the Superforce refers to a…cabal within the Vatican that controls certain aspects of church policy and has set guidelines allowing for wide-scale sexual abuse by Catholic clerics—a small number of whom are involved in satanic ritual abuse. This faction is merely a component of a greater conspiracy that operates within and outside of the Roman Catholic Church…. Suddenly it became inarguable that now, during this papacy, the Roman Catholic organization carried a permanent presence of clerics who worshipped Satan and liked it; of bishops and priests who sodomized boys and each other; of nuns who performed the "Black Rites" of Wicca, and who lived in lesbian relationships…every day, including Sundays and Holy Days, acts of heresy and blasphemy and

outrage and indifference were committed and permitted at holy Altars by men who had been called to be priests.[289]

While remaining a priest, Martin was released from his Jesuit vows of silence, poverty, and obedience. Free to expose the satanist-infiltrated Society of Jesus, he moved to New York and became a best-selling writer and Coast to Coast AM regular.[290] In 1999 he wrote, "Anybody who is acquainted with the state of affairs in the Vatican in the last 35 years is well aware that the prince of darkness has had and still has his surrogates in the court of St. Peter in Rome."[291] He died while working on a book, *Primacy: How the Institutional Roman Catholic Church Became a Creature of the New World Order*, which never saw the light of day.[292] Perhaps that unpublished exposé is *why* Malachi died.

We think it is essential to reiterate that Malachi Martin warned us about *two* wars: One has already been decided and the other is *ongoing*. First, the former Vatican-insider warned about an internal war between the papacy and Jesuits in *The Jesuits: The Society of Jesus and the Betrayal of the Roman Catholic Church* back in 1987. Second, in his nonfiction dynamo, *Keys of this Blood: Pope John Paul II Versus Russia and the West for Control of the New World Order*, he warned of a three-way war between the Roman Catholic Church, Marxists, and business elites (like David Rockefeller and the Trilateral Commission, the Bilderberger group, and the Bohemian grove attendees) to control the burgeoning New World Order, *the utopian dream of all globalists beginning with Nimrod:*[293] "Come on, let us build ourselves a city and a tower, the top of which may reach to the heavens; and let us make ourselves a name, lest we be scattered over the face of the whole earth" (Genesis 11:4). With the technological undoing of the Babel dispersion via the global Internet (Chardin's noosphere as detailed in our book *Exo-Vaticana*), Nimrod's dream can finally be realized.

Through a vision of Jesus delivered by an angel (Revelation 1:1), the apostle John prophesied that the Antichrist will be given "authority over every tribe, and people, and tongue, and nation" (Revelation 13:7). Martin's first war was decided in favor of the Jesuit cabal and is bringing about the kingdom of Antichrist. Martin did not mince words either when he wrote concerning the internal war's global influence; this is Martin's description of the scope of war number one—Jesuits vs. Papacy—which has ended by *the former taking over the latter.*

> As both papacy and Jesuits know, the effects of their policies go far beyond the confines of the Roman Catholic Church; even beyond the nearly one billion Catholic men and women around the world. Almost everything that happens in this war [papacy vs. Jesuits] bears directly and immediately on the major dissensions that wrack every nation and people in the world. It is involved in the very heart of the rivalry between the United States and the Soviet Union, for example, it bears right now on the fate in misery or happiness of 350 million people in Latin America, It affects deeply the changing public moral code and national consensus of the American people, the imminent preponderance in human affairs of the People's Republic of China; the tangible persistence of a free Western Europe; the security of Israel; the still rickety promise of a viable black Africa just adorning. All of these things, separate and unconnected as they may seem, are not only interwoven with one another, but are and will be profoundly influenced by the tides and outcome of the global collision between the papacy and the Society of Jesus.[294]

As the first Jesuit pontiff, Cardinal Jorge Mario Bergoglio was the existential victor of that internal war between traditionalists and modernists. Now the first Jesuit pope has revealed himself to be a shameless Marxist, one of Martin's worst fears.

Concerning the second, external war between Marxism, the global elite, and the Roman Catholic Church, Martin wrote, "The competition began and remains a three way affair because that is the number of rivals with sufficient resources to establish and maintain a new world order."[295] Interesting as a Jesuit steeped in Marxism, Pope Francis represents the remarkable combination of two of Martin's three competitors to the New World Order throne. Of course, we might add a fourth. Martin's over seven-hundred-page epic, *Keys of this Blood*, prescient as it was in 1990, was written before Islam reasserted itself as a player on the world stage. Martin probably never envisioned oil-financed Mahdists like today's IS with the finances and willpower to actually obtain and detonate nuclear weapons. The Associated Press reports that local authorities from the small land-locked Eastern European nation known as the Republic of Moldova (post USSR), working alongside the FBI, have interrupted four attempts to buy nuclear materials from Moldovan gangs with deep Russian connections. That means four attempts, including the most recent case involving a deal with a representative of the IS,[296] that *they know about*, it cannot be ruled out that the IS succeeded in a yet undiscovered nuclear "buy." Even so, we believe Islam is the antithesis in the supernatural powers' and principalities' long-play dialectic—the synthesis and prize for the victor being control of the New World Order.

Thesis: Western Capitalism, Democratic Republic.

Antithesis: Sharia law, Islamic theocracy.

Synthesis: Technocratic socialism, a Marxist New World Order with authority to redistribute wealth.

Because he viewed Pope John Paul II as a staunch enemy of communism, Martin was also under the false impression that the three players in war number two were mutually exclusive.[297] Nevertheless, Pope Francis also marks the merging of Marxism and Vatican II Catholicism—two of Martin's three. This adds new relevance to the prophecies we have discussed previously. Principally, what we call the "destroyer prophecy" based on the improbable "coincidence" that Bergoglio's papal namesake, St. Francis of Assisi, is documented as having warned his followers concerning seven prophetic travails centering on a non-canonically elected pope who during the Tribulation is labeled *a destroyer.*[298]

The edition of St. Francis' prophecies we are citing footnotes the prophecy, saying, "Mark of Lisbon and others think that this prophecy received its accomplishment in the great schism which desolated the Church after the election of Urban VI, in the year 1378. But it may also partially refer to other calamities which have befallen the Church in the latter ages."[299] Francis of Assisi died October 3, 1226, but Mark of Lisbon's opinion aside, the "great" schism of 1336 wasn't really all that great; it was for the most part a boring internal Roman Catholic affair. According to the *Catholic Encyclopedia*:

> Meanwhile, in the name of the pope, the aforesaid cardinals proposed two expedients to settle the differences, a general council or a compromise. Both these means were made use of at the time of the Western Schism. But the opponents of Urban resolved on violent measures and declared their intentions in a letter of the utmost impertinence. On 2 August this letter was followed by the famous "Declaration," a document more passionate than exact, which assumed at once the parts of historian, jurist, and accuser. Seven days later they published an encyclical letter, repeating false and injurious accusations against Urban, and on 27 August left Anagni for Fondi, where they enjoyed the protection of its lord (Urban's arch-enemy), and were near Joanna of Naples; the latter at first had shown great interest in Urban, but was soon disappointed by his capricious ways. On 15 September the three Italian cardinals joined their colleagues, influenced, perhaps, by the hope of becoming pope themselves, or perhaps frightened by the news that Urban was about to create twenty-nine cardinals in order to supply the vacancies left by the thirteen French ones. Charles V of France, more and more doubtful of the lawfulness of Urban's election, encouraged the

Fondi faction to choose a rightful pope and one more agreeable to France. A letter from him arrived on 18 September, and hastened a violent solution. On 20 September Robert of Geneva was chosen pope, and on this day the Western Schism began.[300]

It doesn't particularly match Francis' description, which sounds more like what one should expect in the Great Tribulation described by Daniel and Jesus (Daniel 12:1; Matthew 24:21). Francis parallels these classic end-time texts.

> There will be great trials and afflictions; perplexities and dissensions, both spiritual and temporal, will abound; the charity of many will grow cold, and the malice of the wicked will increase. The devils will have unusual power, the immaculate purity of our Order, and of others, will be so much obscured that there will be very few Christians who will obey the true Sovereign Pontiff and the Roman Church with loyal hearts and perfect charity.[301]

The wording is clearly patterned after Jesus' life: "And because iniquity shall abound, the love of many shall wax cold" (Matthew 24:12). We think this implies that St. Francis' wanted us to understand it as an *end-time* vision rather than some internal dissension. We first connected the dots in *Petrus Romanus* (2012):

> Further speculation about the Masonic plot originally spelled out in the Alta Vendita does seem related to what went on in the 1958 and 1963 conclaves because it was under these secret meetings when the popes were "elected" that would implement the Second Vatican Council and its Vendita-like heretical decrees. Of course we could cite once again a plethora of Church Fathers, Marian apparitions, and Catholic seers down through

time that had forecast these events as a pre-game for the arrival of Petrus Romanus. Even St. Francis of Assisi—one of the most venerated religious figures in history—gathered his devotees shortly before his death and prophesied that: "At the time of this tribulation a man, not canonically elected, will be raised to the Pontificate, who, by his cunning, will endeavor to draw many into error and death.... Some preachers will keep silence about the truth, and others will trample it under foot and deny it...for in those days Jesus Christ will send them not a true Pastor, but a destroyer.[302]

Doesn't Bergoglio's election by anti-Benedict conspiracy[303] qualify as "non-canonical"? Originally, we connected St. Francis' destroyer prophecy to St. Malachy's Prophecy of the Popes, because both predicted the judgment of Rome. Published at least by the late sixteenth century, the Prophecy of the Popes predicts the following during Francis' reign:

In the extreme persecution of the Holy Roman Church, there will sit Peter the Roman, who will nourish the sheep in many tribulations; when they are finished, the City of Seven Hills will be destroyed, and the dreadful judge will judge his people. The End.[304]

That is the English translation of the Latin text in Arnold de Wion's *Lignum Vitae* (Tree of Life), which was originally published in 1595.[305] If this prophecy holds, and so far it has, Pope Francis is necessarily *Petrus Romanus* (that is UNLESS he was not canonically elected as suggested in the first chapter of this book), because he is the final pope on the successive list attributed to the Irish saint. In 2013, Tom Horn and Cris Putnam were paired off against Roman Catholic apologists who label it a hoax in the WND documentary: *The Last Pope?* But no one was willing to answer the question Putnam posed, "If it's a hoax, then why have so many of your 'infallible' popes endorsed it?" One could almost hear crickets chirping.

We are not claiming that our False-Prophet hypothesis is *proven,* but rather that it's still on the table, and still on track as we originally proposed. Even though we discuss many confirmations in this chapter, we understand that these do not *prove* our hypothesis, but we do argue that nothing has falsified it yet, either.[306] Thus, we see no compelling reason to diverge from our original idea that the sitting pope very well may be the second Beast rising up from the earth. "It had two horns like a lamb, and he spake as a dragon" (Revelation 13:11).

Our rationale is not merely circumstantial. We are likely to be accused of so-called newspaper exegesis by Catholic and amillennial apologists, but it is truly based on scholarly exegetical research of ancient apocalyptic symbolism. New Testament scholar Craig Keener writes, "The 'horned lamb' probably parodies Christ (Revelation 5:6)"[307] and the False Prophet's "fire from heaven parodies and so apparently relativizes the miraculous power of God's witnesses" (Revelation 11:5)"[308] The ESV Study Bible notes that the "horns of an animal, which it uses both for defensive and offensive fighting, are frequently found in Scripture as a symbol of the military power of a nation"[309]—hence, a powerful leader who appears Christ-like, yet speaks for the dragon. Given the historical situation, we believe there is simply no better candidate than the Vicar ("instead of") of Christ, the supreme Roman Pontiff Francis. Accordingly, we stand by our 2012 exegesis that "two horns, like a lamb who speaks like a dragon" seems to forecast a powerful (horns) Christian (lamb-like) leader, clandestinely doing the bidding of Satan (the dragon).

Now this pope has called for a "boots-on-the-ground" war against a group of Mahdists who are, in response to Islamic eschatology, challenging to overthrow Rome. They plan to fly a black flag on top of the infamous imported Egyptian obelisk, the one in St. Peter's square with a global grid wind rose compass pointing to the Dome of the Rock and

Constantinople's Dome of Hagia St. Sophia church,[310] connecting them to "one of the most powerful star gates in the world"[311] as argued by Tom Horn in *Zenith 2016* and *On the Path of the Immortals*. While they are a genuine threat, the swagger exhibited by the IS shows real resolve, they might be insane but they *are* serious.

There is nothing vague about Pope Francis' world government agenda. This chapter will document several sobering concerns that should trouble any true Christian. First, Pope Francis is clearly a Marxist, at least in terms of a socialist redistribution of wealth. Marxism addresses the problem on a superficial level that does not account for man's fall. It assumes man's heart is basically good and does not account for human sinfulness. We understand the sentiment. It is estimated that the annual income of the richest one hundred people is enough to end global poverty four times over.[312] But we believe the Christian worldview identifies poverty and oppression as primarily spiritual problems, not socioeconomic ones (Mark 10:21, Luke 6:24, James 5:1–6). What follows is a short excerpt from his May 9, 2014, address to the United Nations, "Address of Pope Francis to the UN System Chief Executives Board for Coordination."

> Today, in concrete terms, an awareness of the dignity of each of our brothers and sisters whose life is sacred and inviolable from conception to natural death must lead us to share with complete freedom the goods which God's providence has placed in our hands, material goods but also intellectual and spiritual ones, and to give back generously and lavishly whatever we may have earlier unjustly refused to others.
>
> The account of Jesus and Zacchaeus teaches us that above and beyond economic and social systems and theories, there will always be a need to promote generous, effective and practical openness to the needs of others. Jesus does not ask Zacchaeus to change jobs nor does he condemn his financial activity; he

simply inspires him to put everything, freely yet immediately and indisputably, at the service of others.

Consequently, I do not hesitate to state, as did my predecessors (cf. JOHN PAUL II, *Sollicitudo Rei Socialis*, 42–43; *Centesimus Annus*, 43; BENEDICT XVI, *Caritas in Veritate*, 6; 24–40), that equitable economic and social progress can only be attained by joining scientific and technical abilities with an unfailing commitment to solidarity accompanied by a generous and disinterested spirit of gratuitousness at every level. A contribution to this equitable development will also be made both by international activity aimed at the integral human development of all the world's peoples and by the *legitimate redistribution of economic benefits by the State*, as well as indispensable cooperation between the private sector and civil society.[313]

This is an unambiguous endorsement of the Marxist dream: *the redistribution of wealth by the state.* As a young Argentinian Jesuit priest, Bergoglio was steeped in the Marxist ideology of liberation theology. Atheistic by definition, Marxism condemns religion for supporting the status quo and legitimating the power of the oppressor.

Richard Wurmbrand, a Romanian Christian who spent over three decades in prison for his faith and later founded Voice of the Martyrs, wrote a book demonstrating from Marx's poetry featuring lines like, "I wish to avenge myself against the One who rules above"[314] that Marx was not really an atheist after all, but rather an active Satanist. Wurmbrand cites many such lines.

Marx dreamt about ruining the world created by God. He said in another poem:

Then I will be able to walk triumphantly, Like a god, through the ruins of their kingdom. Every word of mine is fire and action. My breast is equal to that of the Creator.[315]

The words "I shall build my throne high overhead" and the confession that from the one sitting on this throne will emanate only dread and agony remind us of Lucifer's proud boast, "I will ascend into heaven, I will exalt my throne above the stars of God" (Isaiah 14:13).[316]

It seems that Marx's advocacy of atheism was more from spite than unbelief. According to Wurmbrand, Marx believed in God and Satan, but chose the latter.

Dave Hunt pointed out that while virtually all of our attention is directed on the ongoing apostasy and soon coming of Antichrist (2 Thessalonians 2:3)—the "Man of Sin" or "Man of Lawlessness" (a distinction based on one's preference in Greek manuscript traditions) is still only half the story—the other half is the False Prophet: a man who has "two horns like to a lamb, and spake as a dragon" (Revelation 13:11) leading a one-world religion symbolized by "a woman who rides the beast," arguably (according to many Catholic scholars[317]) the apostate Roman Catholic Church leading a one-world religion—the great harlot, in appropriately Catholic robes of "purple and scarlet"[318] (Revelation 17:3). Hunt wrote, "Liberation Theology was spawned in Latin America by radical Catholic priests and nuns whose aroused consciences could no longer justify the oppression of the masses by both Church and state."[319] Communism and liberation theology have the same basic goals, but liberation theology turns to the Christian faith rather than atheism to rationalize its confiscation of private property, allegedly to benefit the less fortunate. Latin American liberation theologians contend, most often correctly, that, in addition to the sins of the past like European imperialism, their continent is still being victimized by multinational corporations (e.g., the Amazon rain forest saw a 28 percent rise in the rate of deforestation from August of 2012 to July of 2013[320]).

The leading proponents of Latin American liberation theology include Peruvian Jesuit Priest Gustavo Gutiérrez S. J. Leonardo Boff, a philosophy of religion professor at the Rio de Janeiro State University in Brazil, and Juan Luis Segundo of Uruguay. As a group they are philosophically indebted to the perspectives of Kant, Hegel, and Marx. Martin wrote that Gutierrez, a Peruvian Jesuit priest, "analyzed 'theology' in light of the Marxist theory of class struggle."[321] He promoted the idea that the gospel burdens the Church with liberating the world from poverty and oppression. Growing up impoverished, it isn't difficult to be charitable concerning Gutiérrez's sincere desire to help the poor. But, intentions aside, liberation theology really *was* a communist conspiracy. According to a Romanian defector, Gutierrez was under the spell of the Soviet KGB.

The head of the Russian Orthodox Church, Patriarch Kirill, was working for the Soviet secret police Komitet Gosudarstvennoy Bezopasnost (KGB)[322] under the code name "Mikhailov." Pacepa bluntly asserts, "Liberation Theology was not invented by Latin American Catholics, but rather it was developed by the KGB."[323] Liberation theology was concocted by the KGB and the Patriarch Kirill promoted it. Thus, Kirill was instrumental in spreading Marxism into the Western hemisphere, an existential threat to US soil. Kirill appears to be a rather sinister character. According to investigative journalist Stephenson Billings:

> The man in question is named Patriarch Kirill, a genuinely ruthless figure in the harsh world of Soviet politics. A former KGB agent and now a close associate of Vladimir Putin, he has called his leader "a god." He has been widely condemned for spreading Stalinism and atheism to the Ukraine in a cruel bid to expand his empire. Evidence unearthed in Soviet archives has revealed that the Russian Orthodox Church has long been infiltrated and managed by the KGB as a tool of population control. This is one of the many reasons that the CIA has kept a very close watch on the secretive kingpin Kirill for decades.[324]

Apparently, the KGB pays well, because "Archbishop Kirill's personal wealth was estimated at $4 billion by the Moscow News."[325] Of course, this information has concerning implications in regard to the Russian

Orthodox Church's recent "holy war" declaration as well. Kirill also profited heavily from importing cigarettes duty free through church channels.

The *Evangelical Dictionary of Theology* emphasizes that liberation theology "is for the most part a Roman Catholic theological movement."[326] It follows naturally that, as a former Argentine Cardinal, the Pope was profoundly influenced by this communist-inspired Latin American movement. In fact, his socialism is impossible for American Catholics to simply explain away. Especially with widespread reporting of statements like the following concerning the European refugee problem:

> These poor people are fleeing war, hunger, but that is the tip of the iceberg. Because underneath that is the cause; and the cause is a bad and unjust socioeconomic system, in everything, in the world—speaking of the environmental problem—in the socioeconomic society, in politics, the person always has to be in the centre. That is the dominant economic system nowadays, it has removed the person from the centre, placing the god money in its place, the idol of fashion. There are statistics, I don't remember precisely, (I might have this wrong), but that 17% of the world's population has 80% of the wealth.[327]

According to the pope, the world's problem is no longer sinful man's rebellion against a holy God, but rather a "bad and unjust socioeconomic system." The pope's theme is reminiscent of the Marx-popularized catchphrase, "From each according to his ability, to each according to his need."[328] A British Library description of the class struggle between the proletariat and the capitalist from *The Communist Manifesto* contextualizes wealth redistribution as the big idea behind Marxism:

> Following the proletariat's defeat of capitalism, a new classless society would emerge based on the idea: "from each according to his abilities, to each according to his needs." In such a society,

land, industry, labour and *wealth would be shared between all people*. All people would have the right to an education, and class structures would disappear. Harmony would reign, and the state would simply "wither away." (emphasis added)[329]

On a superficial level, it seems obvious enough that liberation theologians were deceived into a communist ideology—a conspiracy "theory" which moved into the category "fact" after having been confirmed by high-ranking communist defectors.[330]

The call for Christians to be champions for social justice and good stewards of the environment is valid, but it entirely misses the Bible's description of human depravity (Romans 3:10–18) and, as a result, excludes the real point of evangelism and missions: the true gospel message that "Christ died for our sins" (1 Corinthians 15:3–8). Theologian D. D. Webster critiques liberation theology as a postmodern construct. Actually, it is quite an alien solution to the world's problems according to biblical theology.

A Christian understands sin and alienation from God as a dilemma confronting both the oppressor and the oppressed. Liberation theology's emphasis on the poor gives the impression that the poor are not only the object of God's concern but the salvific and revelatory subject.[331]

In relation to the pervasiveness of Zionist conspiracy theories, Barry Segal explained the human condition in the following way:

Man leans more toward the evil than the good; fear and power have more control over him than reason.... All men seek power, and there is none who would not be an oppressor if he could; all, or nearly all, are ready to sacrifice the rights of others to their own interests.[332]

Socialism ignores man's fallen nature and, naively, assumes the opposite. Ideologically it is at war with the gospel. In other words, in their zeal for the oppressed, many Latino priests (like Bergoglio) lost sight of the actual gospel. Recall Jesus' response when Judas Iscariot, another son of perdition, offered his own first-century version of the liberation theology.

> But Judas Iscariot, one of his disciples (he who was about to betray him), said, "Why was this ointment not sold for three hundred denarii and given to the poor?" He said this, not because he cared about the poor, but because he was a thief, and having charge of the moneybag he used to help himself to what was put into it. Jesus said, "Leave her alone, so that she may keep it for the day of my burial. For the poor you always have with you, but you do not always have me." (John 12:4–8)

The liberation-theology movement was partly inspired by the Second Vatican Council that was called by Pope John XXIII[333]—the famous patriarch of Venice, a city famous for its streets of water, that the Malachy prophecy foretold as a *Pastor &nauta* ("pastor and sailor"). It is rumored that in response to studying Malachy's Prophecy of the Popes and to show himself as the fulfillment of his line in the prophecy, "he hired a boat, filled it with sheep and sailed up and down the Tiber River in full view of the conclave."[334] He codified Rome's curse of "saved by faith alone" by confirming that the precepts of the Council of Trent continue to the modern day, a position that was confirmed by his successor.[335] The first post-Lucifer enthronement pope—John XXII—famously advocated a "public authority with power," and the means co-extensive with these problems, and "a world-wide sphere of activity" in his 1963 encyclical Pacem in Terris.[336]

His successor Pope Paul VI was the pope installed during the luciferians' parallel enthronement ceremony in 1963. Calling the satanic cabal a "superforce," Martin wrote:

> Most frighteningly for [Pope] John Paul [II], he had come up against the irremovable presence of a malign strength in his own Vatican and in certain bishops' chanceries. It was what knowledgeable Churchmen called the "superforce." Rumors, always difficult to verify, tied its installation to the beginning of Pope Paul VI's reign in 1963. Indeed Paul had alluded somberly to "the smoke of Satan which has entered the Sanctuary"...an oblique reference to an enthronement ceremony by Satanists in the Vatican. Besides, the incidence of Satanic pedophilia—rites and practices— was already documented among certain bishops and priests as widely dispersed as Turin, in Italy, and South Carolina, in the United States. The cultic acts of satanic pedophilia are considered by professionals to be the culmination of the Fallen Archangel's rites.[337]

By this time, Vatican II was being praised in Latin America and, rather than criticize the fledgling liberation theology movement, Paul VI, in his encyclical *Octogesima Adveniens,* equivocated socioeconomic ideologies as unilaterally weak.

> Today moreover the weaknesses of the ideologies are better perceived through the concrete systems in which they are trying to affirm themselves. Bureaucratic socialism, technocratic capitalism and authoritarian democracy are showing how difficult it is to solve the great human problem of living together in justice and equality.[338]

He should have condemned socialism as being derived from an atheistic Marxist ideology. Instead, the penultimate-parallel-enthronement pope advised one to discern between various overlapping "levels" of socialism:

> Distinctions must be made to guide concrete choices between the various levels of expression of socialism: a generous aspiration and a seeking for a more just society, historical movements with a political organization and aim, and an ideology which claims to give a complete and self-sufficient picture of man. Nevertheless, these distinctions must not lead one to consider such levels as completely separate and independent. The concrete link which, according to circumstances, exists between them must be clearly marked out.[339]

Socialism fails because it naively gives mankind too much credit. While social justice is a noble pursuit, one does not achieve it through redistribution of wealth. People are not basically good and there is no authority but Jesus Christ who can decide what is equitable. While socialism is an idea foreign to Scripture, social justice is a prominent *eschatological* theme. Jesus said, "Blessed be ye poor: for yours is the kingdom of God" (Luke 6:20b). Considering He also said, "It is easier for a camel to go through the eye of a needle, than for a rich man to enter into the kingdom of God" (Matthew 19:24), a brief life of earthly poverty may turn out to be an immortal blessing in the value system of God's Kingdom (Matthew 6:20). In other words, chances are strong that being rich now will turn out to have not been worth it from an afterlife perspective (James 5:1). Nevertheless, more by what he failed to say, than what he actually said, Paul VI encouraged Latin American liberation theology. During his papacy, a Frenchman named Vicomte de Poncins may have put two and two together as to who the real players in the game of words were, and in so doing exposed a Masonic cabal.

There is at present in Catholic circles a constant, subtle and determined campaign in favor of Freemasonry. It is directed by the progressive element which is currently enjoying a great influence in French and American Church circles and beginning to show its hand in England too.... This element consists of a number of priests, including a Jesuit, Editors of Catholic newspapers and several writers of note.[340]

It's likely no coincidence that the next pope, John Paul I, was allegedly murdered only thirty-three days after taking office (33 is an occult Masonic marker) just prior to exposing a conspiracy led by cardinals, bishops, and high-ranking prelates that were also Freemasons.[341] Likely, it was the same group Malachi Martin labeled "Lucifer's Lodge"[342] or the "Superforce."[343] Shortly after his election, John Paul I ordered an investigation of the Vatican's banking practices. As a result, Cardinal Egidio Vagnozzi warned the pope about the cabal. David Yallop revealed:

> The information that Vagnozzi had obtained over decades insured that a highly detailed dossier was soon in the Pope's hands. Immediately after the discovery of the pope's body the Vagnozzi report along with the papers covering the various changes were removed by Cardinal Villot, whose deputy Caprio was most certainly aware of the contents of the report. An indication of just how explosive the contents were can be gauged by the fact that Roberto Calvi subsequently became aware of the Vagnozzi report and its contents and after being offered a copy by a Vatican contact for three million dollars haggled the price down to one point two million dollars then kept the copy close to himself for the rest of his life.[344]

The pope's replacement, John Paul II, was, by all appearance, an avowed enemy of the Soviet Union, but still leaned hard left in his politics. John Paul II wrote, "It is necessary to state once more the characteristic principle of Christian social doctrine: *the goods of this world are originally meant for all humanity*" (emphasis added).[345] Allowing the pope's statement to be true, for the sake of argument, it begs the question of how to equitably divvy up the goods and a discussion about who gets to decide. John Paul II answered that humanity "needs a greater degree of international ordering, at the service of the societies, economies and cultures of the whole world."[346] In other words, he was a globalist. In all fairness, John Paul II had a reputation of opposing the Soviet Union and objected to the Latin American Jesuit endorsement of Marxist ideas, their support for revolutionary movements, and their criticism of traditional Church institutions. Malachi Martin idolized him as a determined enemy of communism, but, as we have shown, globalist Marxist ideas ran deep in post-parallel-enthronement Catholicism, and his papacy was no exception.

Pope Benedict XVI openly advocated world government as well. On the day before his meeting with US President Obama and the G-8 summit in Italy, Pope Benedict promulgated the encyclical titled *Caritas in Veritate,* or "Charity in Truth," from which we exposed his call for a "world political authority" with "*real teeth*" in our first book, *Petrus Romanus.*[347] Next, in *Exo-Vaticana,* we uncovered Benedict XVI's status as "a Chardinian mystic of the highest order"[348] and documented how he interpreted the "doctrine of the Second Coming of Christ to advance Chardin's 'Omega Point,' in which a 'new kind' of God, man, and mind will emerge."[349] We have now covered every pope from the enthronement of Lucifer in 1963 to where we stand today, and all, without exception, have advocated Marxist views akin to liberation theology. This is important, because we believe feigned socialism will be behind the False Prophet's role in implementing a global financial control mechanism (Revelation 13:16).

Others in the Roman Catholic Church (like former Jesuit Malachi Martin) exposed liberation theology and Marxism. For instance, Martin railed against the Latin American Jesuit Lupe Carney, who wrote that the new socialism would be "a brotherhood and sisterhood of all humanity,"[350] as being "drunk on the ignorance-laden idealism of Liberation Theology."[351] Carney taught that Christianity and Marxism were ideologically identical and Roman Catholics ought to "get rid of any unfair and un-Christian prejudices you have against armed revolution, socialism, Marxism, and communism.... There is no third way between being a Christian and being a revolutionary."[352] In spite of his prescient warnings, all of Martin's worst fears have come about in the first Jesuit Pope. In addition, journalist Cliff Kincaid wondered why "the leader of the worldwide Catholic Church, considered by Catholics the personal representative of Jesus Christ, has become an advocate for one of the most corrupt organizations on the face of the earth—the United Nations."[353] A very intriguing question that the book in your hands intends to answer.

A recent book about the Vatican outlines how very real, physical underground tunnels in Italy were used to help many Nazi's escape post-war justice by relocating them to Latin American countries like Argentina and Venezuela (incidentally liberation theology strongholds). Writing anonymously under an apparent pen name "Maury," the author connects the Jesuits not only to communism but also pre-Nazi Labor Zionism, the socialist left-wing of the Zionist movement in pre-Holocaust Germany. Maury contends:

> The Jesuits pushed the idea of communism based on their experience with the communes in South America. They joined with the apostate Jews Karl Marx and Frederick Engels to further this goal, which later gave rise to Bolshevism in Eastern Europe. By 1933 only Labour Zionism was allowed to represent the Jews in Germany. German Jews were first indoctrinated into Bolshevism in Labour Zionist camps and then transferred to Palestine, to work on a kibbutz (commune), with British approval. The Jesuit inspired communism was atheistic (which reduced the influence of the Orthodox Church in Eastern Europe and of

Judaism.) The only explanation of why the fascist Germany would support and work with communist Labour Zionism was because it was a Jesuit idea, and they had plans for the Jews.[354]

Similar to the quest by Marx, Engels, and the Jesuits of the 1930s, the current pope's encyclical on "climate change," *Sulla Cura Della Casa Comune*, not only advocates dubious "climate change" science, it contains an astonishingly blatant demand for world government and calls for lifestyle changes and energy conservation to avert the "unprecedented destruction of the ecosystem" before the end of this century. But more importantly, the pope calls for a *world authority* to manage the global economy, disarmament, peacekeeping, and poverty, as well as enforcing various carbon emission standards to protect the environment. Asking for people to have an "open heart" as they read his encyclical dedicated to the environment, Pope Francis concluded:

> To manage the global economy; to revive economies hit by the crisis; to avoid any deterioration of the present crisis and the greater imbalances that would result; to bring about integral and timely disarmament, food security and peace; to guarantee the protection of the environment and to regulate migration: for all this, there is urgent need of a *true world political authority*, as my predecessor Blessed John XXIII indicated some years ago, (emphasis added).[355]

Similar to Marx, the pope unambiguously calls for a supranational "global authority" to move the world toward Utopia. It sounds eerily like *The Communist Manifesto*. Ecumenical Patriarch of Constantinople Bartholomew I, the author of several environmentalist books, quickly expressed his approval.[356] Advocating a "world economic authority" is certainly a significant step in the direction that will "require everyone, who wishes to buy and sell, to be marked on the right hand or the forehead" (Revelation 13:16–17). The "mark of the beast" seems like a perfectly logical development and, in fact, *necessary* technology for tracking income, to realize the redistribution of wealth the pope is openly advocating.

Political cartoon featuring Karl Marx, Friedrich Engels, and Pope Francis

Our last major confirmation is that Pope Francis is laying the groundwork for a *one-world religion* by merging pluralist/inclusivist branches of Judaism, Islam, and Christianity. Allowing Islamic prayer to be conducted within the Vatican and labeling PLO terrorist Mahmoud Abbas as an "angel of peace" were mentioned previously. A Muslim journalist, Khwaja Khusro Tariq, reminded us how Pope Francis has consistently recognized Islam's holy days, "On Maundy Thursday (the day before Good Friday) in 2013 he kissed the feet of a Muslim female prisoner during a pre-Easter ritual that symbolizes the Pope's willingness to serve God through humanity. On Maundy Thursday in 2014 he kissed the feet of a disabled Muslim man."[357] In 2016, the pope offered an especially emotional message during the Hajj pilgrimage to Mecca, Saudi Arabia.

The "stoning of the devil" is part of the annual Islamic Hajj pilgrimage to the holy city of Mecca in Saudi Arabia. The stoning is one of a series of ritualized acts that must be performed in the pilgrimage. Unfortunately, in 2015, more than 1,470 people were killed[358] and nearly 900 others were injured during the stoning ritual.[359] In 2006, a similar stampede killed at least 363 people. During a speech at St. Patrick's

Cathedral in New York City, the Roman Catholic pontiff offered prayers in response to the deadly stampede in the Mina valley, outside the Islamic holy city of Mecca.

> I would like to express two sentiments for my Muslim brothers and sisters: Firstly, my greetings as they celebrate the feast of sacrifice. I would have wished my greeting to be warmer. My sentiments of closeness, my sentiments of closeness in the face of tragedy. The tragedy that they suffered in Mecca. In this moment, I give assurances of my prayers. I unite myself with you all. A prayer to almighty god, all merciful.[360]

An enthusiastic Muslim seemed swayed by the "Francis effect," almost gushing, "It is hard to imagine more heartfelt and clear messages that under his Papacy the Church also extends its benediction to those of faiths other than Catholicism, including Islam."[361] So, apparently, some Muslims understand the Church extends its benediction to Islam. This merging of religions is what we identified as an important part of the Antichrist's agenda.

While logically incoherent, Pope Francis' Muslim position isn't that radical in a post-Vatican II, luciferian-parallel-enthronement world. *The Catechism of the Catholic Church*, paragraph 841, reads,

> The Church's relationship with the Muslims. "The plan of salvation also includes those who acknowledge the Creator, in the first place amongst whom are the Muslims; these profess to hold the faith of Abraham, and together with us they adore the one, merciful God, mankind's judge on the last day."[362]

Because of the Qur'anic revisionism concerning Jesus, Muslims deny that Jesus was even crucified, so they, necessarily, are forced into a position that cannot allow them to believe *He died* for their sins, nor was He resurrected. In effect, the Qur'an seeks to vaccinate them against the gospel.

> And their saying: Surely we have killed the Messiah, Isa son of Marium, the messenger of Allah; and *they did not kill him nor did they crucify him,* but it appeared to them so (like Isa) and most surely those who differ therein are only in a doubt about it; they have no knowledge respecting it, but only follow a conjecture, and they killed him not for sure. Nay! Allah took him up to Himself; and Allah is Mighty, Wise (Surah 4:157–158, emphasis added).[363]

That is a Muslim claim in which one must invoke the law of the excluded middle. In philosophy, it entails the idea that a truth claim is binary, true or false, and that it must be one or the other, with no third way. It's an "either/or" situation; it is not logically coherent to assert "both/and." According to the New Testament, belief in Jesus' death, burial, and resurrection are not optional for salvation (1 Corinthians 15:3–8). An accomplished apologist who formally debates the best Muslim scholars, James White, explains why these are non-negotiables:

> For Christians, the deity of Jesus, the eternal relationship of the Father and the Son, and the personality and deity of the Spirit are not side issues that can be relegated to the realm of "excesses." These *define* the object of our worship; they *define* our relationship to God.[364]

After defining the gospel, the apostle Paul also appealed to the excluded middle, "And if Christ be not raised, your faith is vain; ye are yet in your sins" (1 Corinthians 15:17). If Paul is right, then the Catholic Catechism is wrong and we must logically conclude that Muslims will die in their sins.

Pope Francis has been credited with ending the Great Schism of 1054 that created the Eastern Orthodox Church. CNN reported, "Francis and Patriarch Bartholomew I—the spiritual leader of some 300 million Orthodox Christians worldwide—signed a declaration on Sunday committing to unity between the two churches."[365] Now, if he could just convince those pesky Muslims to co-exist. At the beginning of his papacy in 2013, Pope Francis was already implying that the Muslim and Jewish spiritual teachings are just two paths to the same God that Roman Catholics also worship—an absurdity in light of blatant contradiction between them.[366] While it seems polite, such ecumenism is irrational because one religion (Christianity) contradicts the other two (Judaism, Islam) concerning the divinity of Jesus, who is revealed as the God-Man in the New Testament (Romans 9:5, John 8:58; 10:30). They also disagree concerning the resurrection, and "if Christ be not raised, your faith is vain; ye are yet in your sins" (1 Corinthians 15:17).

Nevertheless, ecumenical naiveté—oneism disguised in Christian terminology—rules the standing pontiff's epistemology (theory of knowledge). He seems oblivious to the blatant contradiction between his claimed authority of apostolic succession, which has always derived from the famous praise by Jesus "that thou art Peter, and upon this rock I will build my church;" (Matthew 16:18) and the Qur'anic contention "the Christians say: The Messiah is the son of Allah.... How perverse are they!"(Surah 9:30).[367] Recall that Jesus was responding to Peter's confession: "Thou art the Christ, the *Son of the living God*" (Matthew 16:16, emphasis added) and ask yourself if the pope can really be that *oblivious* to the contradiction? It seems doubtful.

More likely, this is another Hegelian dialectic, employed by "long game" globalists and immortals, aimed at synthesizing a one-world religion. We offer it as an alternative, because he is not that stupid. Even a first-year undergraduate philosophy student can see that the pope's actual position amounts to both Islam and Roman Catholicism being flawed revelations. It's not logically possible, in this or any other world, that both religions are *correct* concerning Jesus' status as the "Son of God" (Matthew 26:63–64, Mark 3:11, Luke 1:35, John 3:18). It is an "either/or" situation entailing that both Jesus and Muhammad can be wrong, or *one can be right and the other wrong*, but in no circumstance can they *co-exist* as both being correct. Again, we invoked the "law of the excluded middle"—and yes, people do read about it in Introduction to Philosophy 101 undergraduate courses.[368] That's why we think the pope must have *another* agenda.

6

The Last Crusade Agenda

IN ORDER TO realize true world authority, the pope knows the Middle East crisis needs to be solved. While the Vatican delayed doing so until 1993, the UN recognized Israel in 1948. But now, under Francis, the Vatican has officially, for the first time, recognized Palestine as a state. Palestinian Foreign Minister Riyad al-Maliki called the agreement with the Vatican "historic"[369] because of the Vatican's novel use of language referring to Palestine as an actual nation-state (proven to be an absurd revision of history). Al-Maliki gleamed:

> For the first time, the agreement includes an official recognition by the Holy See of Palestine as a state, in recognition of the right of the Palestinian people to self-determination, freedom and dignity in an independent state of their own, free from the shackles of occupation.[370]

But as we have demonstrated, Palestinian children are routinely indoctrinated with the idea that a two-state solution is a travesty since, in their revision of history, the Israelis are characterized as colonialist thugs. Furthermore, biblical prophecy promises that Yahweh will judge the nations based on how they have divided *His* land. The Hebrew prophet, Joel, spoke for God:

> I will also gather all nations, And will bring them down into the valley of Jehoshaphat, And will plead with them there for my people and for my heritage Israel, Whom they have scattered among the nations, and *parted my land* (Joel 3:2, emphasis added).

Because scholars recognize that "there is no valley with this name known in Israel from the Bible or from other sources, or even from tradition,"[371] most conservatives agree that "Valley of Jehoshaphat" refers to the place where the final judgment occurs rather than a known geographical location.[372] It means "Yahweh judges" in Hebrew and is probably one of the valleys surrounding Jerusalem.[373] Walvoord pointed out that "some scholars suggest it is a yet-future valley, to be formed by the splitting of the Mount of Olives at the Messiah's return" (Zechariah 14:4).[374]

The expression in verse 1, "in those days and at that time" (Joel 3:1), is found through Jeremiah's end-time oracles:

> For, lo, the days come, saith the Lord, that I will bring again the captivity of my people Israel and Judah, saith the Lord: and I will cause them to return to the land that I gave to their fathers, and they shall possess it. (Jeremiah 30:3)

> In those days, and at that time, will I cause the Branch of righteousness to grow up unto David; and he shall execute judgment and righteousness in the land. (Jeremiah 33:15)

> In those days, and in that time, saith the Lord, The children of Israel shall come, They and the children of Judah together, Going and weeping: they shall go, And seek the Lord their God. (Jeremiah 50:4)

In those days, and in that time, saith the Lord, The iniquity of Israel shall be sought for, and there shall be none; And the sins of Judah, and they shall not be found: For I will pardon them whom I reserve. (Jeremiah 50:20)

Like Jeremiah, Joel's language is coherent with those layers of prophetic tradition that are dominated by the theme "Israel and the nations," which have as their goal the final restoration of Judah and Jerusalem.[375] Now Pope Francis is meeting with Shimon Peres and Mahmoud Abbas at the Vatican. Why? We went out on limb in 2012 by suggesting that Pope Francis is necessarily *Petrus Romanus* according to St. Malachy's Prophecy of the Popes. But everything we wrote about seems to be falling in place. Also consider that, a decade prior, Dr. Michael Heiser wrote concerning the fact that both the Qur'an and Hebrew Bible predict the Jews return:

> I further believe that the Antichrist will be the leader who seizes upon these predictions and this theology to unite Israel and her Arabian (and hence Muslim) siblings in an unprecedented peace-making event, all (unfortunately) to serve his own end of world domination.[376]

Intriguingly, Obama and Pope Francis' actions are in lockstep with Heiser's speculation that the final Antichrist agenda, will be to unite Jews and Muslims. As we go to press, President Obama is allegedly making a bid to be UN secretary general. James Lewis has criticized this ambition to be "messianic"[377] and too naïve to take the threats made by terrorists like the IS seriously.

> President Obama is basically a Marxist of the "Third World" variety, which means that he lives in the faith that some elite political minority can rule first the United States and Europe, and then the world.... Like all grandiose narcissists with uncontrollable

ambitions, Obama figures he can somehow resolve all the inter-
necine warfare between Shi'ites and Sunnis, between Persians and
Arabs, Turks and Kurds, Copts and Salafists, and finally get all
"the fifty-seven states"[378]—57 is the number of Muslim states in
the UN—to vote for him as a messianic UN Secretary General.

Later, Lewis adds a bit more criticism concerning Israel and Islam,
this time in relation to one of President Obama's longest serving advisers
and confidantes, Valerie Jarret.[379]

Obama and Jarrett—they are a classic *"folie a deux,"* a two-
person cult—started the surrender to Iran at the start of this
administration, while lying endless times about never permit-
ting the mullahs to have nuclear weapons. But since 1979 the
mullahs have been screaming every single day "Death to Israel!
Death to America!" Liberals are cursed with a delusional inabil-
ity to believe such threats, no matter how serious they are. Hitler
made such threats. Tojo made such threats. Lenin and Stalin
did. But history has no impact on liberal minds. Realists understand world-conquering threats all too well.[380]

It follows that Obama is a threat to Israel. Since signing the nuclear
deal with America, Iran was pleased to show off its ballistic missiles
"capable of hitting a variety of targets in the Middle East."[381] It makes
Obama an increasingly interesting candidate for the "Man of Sin," especially if he becomes the UN secretary general—arguably the leader of a
revived Roman Empire. *American Thinker* published an applicable piece
titled, "To Become UN Sec General Obama Must 'Solve' the Existence
of Israel," exactly the Antichrist's agenda briefly cited from Heiser's *Islam
and Armageddon*, Heiser continued:

I further believe that the Antichrist will be the leader who seizes
upon these predictions and this theology to unite Israel and her

Arabian (and hence Muslim) siblings in an unprecedented peace-making event, all (unfortunately) to serve his own end of world domination. The Old Testament makes clear that not every Muslim will embrace the truce. Those whose national boundaries lie outside the parameters of the Abrahamic covenant and those who have no ethnic affinity with Abraham will have little to gain by the fulfillment of the Jewish and Qur'anic prophecies. As we shall see, biblical prophecy is clear that certain Muslim nations will side with the Antichrist when he breaks covenant with the children of Abraham, defying "the God of his fathers." This choice will propel the world toward Armageddon.[382]

Obama's post-presidential UN ambitions aside, Pope Francis makes a very likely candidate for the False Prophet with "horns like a lamb"—we argue a symbol for a Christian leader with power (represented by horns),"highlighting the second beast's imitative role with respect to the true Lamb in the rest of the book (e.g., Revelation 5:6–6:1–17; 13:8; 14:1)"[383]—working hand in hand with Obama's policy of avoidance when it comes to criticizing Islam while making himself a "cult of personality." This influence elicited by Obama and Pope Francis was described by philosopher Max Weber as "charismatic authority."

> There is the authority of the extraordinary and personal gift of grace (charisma), the absolutely personal devotion and personal confidence in revelation, heroism, or other qualities of individual leadership. This is 'charismatic' domination, as exercised by the prophet or—in the field of politics—by the elected war lord, the plebiscitarian ruler, the great demagogue, or the political party leader.[384]

Presenting himself with an air of charismatic authority is a talent that Pope Francis has mastered according to *The Washington Post*, who dubbed it the "Francis effect."

The new pope's influence has been dubbed the "Francis effect"; he's been compared to Princess Diana and called "the people's pope." Early polls indicate that Francis is unusually popular, and in the months since his election, Catholics and non-Catholics alike can be found buzzing about his latest sermon or act of humility. Did you hear, the pope isn't living in the papal apartment? Did you see, Pope Francis paid his own hotel bill after becoming the leader of the Catholic Church? Did you notice, the leader of the world's 1.2 billion Catholics carried his own bag onto the plane for his trip to World Youth Day?[385]

The "like a lamb" simile seems to flawlessly describe Pope Francis' humble public persona, but under his leadership, the speech of the dragon is now resounding.

The Vatican recently instructed that Catholics should *not* undertake organized efforts to convert Jews. The document, titled, "The Gifts and Calling of God are Irrevocable" was released on December 10, 2015, by the Vatican's Commission for Religious Relations with the Jews and adopts so-called "dual covenant" theology. It is a clever piece of sophistry misapplying the biblical text that since God's covenant with the Jews is still valid, then they don't need the New Covenant in order to be saved. In its most explicit commentary on evangelization regarding Jews, the document said Catholics should take a different approach to Judaism than to other religions. The document clearly takes an antichrist position.

The Church is therefore obliged to view evangelisation to Jews, who believe in the one God, in a different manner from that to people of other religions and world views. In concrete terms this means that the Catholic Church neither conducts nor supports any specific institutional mission work directed towards Jews.[386]

Imagine Paul's horror! "We who are Jews by nature, and not sinners of the Gentiles, Knowing that a man is not justified by the works of the law, but by the faith of Jesus Christ, even we have believed in Jesus Christ, that we might be justified by the faith of Christ, and not by the works of the law: for by the works of the law shall no flesh be justified" (Galatians 2:15–16). Paul would never agree with how the Jesuits have twisted his words: "As concerning the gospel, they are enemies for your sakes: but as touching the election, they are beloved for the fathers' sakes. For the gifts and calling of God are without repentance" (Romans 11:28–29).

Craig Keener is a scholar (PhD, Duke University) and a New Testament professor at Asbury Theological Seminary.[387] He is famous for his work as a New Testament scholar on Bible backgrounds and contextual commentaries on the New Testament in its early Jewish and Greco-Roman surroundings. Keener's comment on Romans 11:28–29 reveals Rome's contextual error.

> Unlike some interpreters today, Paul does not regard God's promises to ethnic Israel as cancelled—only deferred (cf. Deut. 4:25–31); God still had a covenant with the fathers (Deut. 7:8). Most readers today subscribe to one of two systems: Israel and the church are separate and irreconcilable entities, and Israel will be restored; or Christians become the true Israel and ethnic Israel has no more purpose in God's plan. Paul would have rejected both extremes, believing that ethnic Israel as a whole would return to the covenant in the end time, joining the Gentiles and Jewish remnant that already participate in it.[388]

We agree with Keener and point out that an honest reading of Galatians suggests Paul would have certainly repudiated the Vatican's position as heresy. In Romans Paul makes it clear that because all are under sin, *only* the gospel is sufficient (Romans 3:9–10; cf. Galatians 2:15–16; Ephesians 2:15–16). When compared with the informed biblical scholarship, the *Commission for Religious Relations with the Jews'* document is a monstrous justification of heresy. *The Dictionary of Paul and His Letters* characterizes Paul's Jewishness.

While Paul was "an apostle to the Gentiles" (Rom. 11:13), he cannot forget his own people. Indeed, the turning of the Gentiles to Christ causes the Jews to become jealous: "Inasmuch then as I am an apostle to the Gentiles, I magnify my ministry in order to make my fellow Jews jealous, and thus save some of them" (Rom. 11:13–14). The very vigor with which Paul pursued his Gentile apostolate has suggested to some interpreters that Paul thought he was entering into the very eschatological purpose of God in saving all Israel. Paul not only had "unceasing anguish" for his "kinsmen by race," but he gave himself for their salvation, a side effect of his Gentile mission being *the conversion of Jews* (emphasis added).[389]

The Vatican also claimed "The New Covenant can never replace the Old,"[390] which is directly refuted by the author of Hebrews. "In that he saith, A new covenant, he hath made the first old. Now that which decayeth and waxeth old is ready to vanish away" (Hebrews 8:13). The force of the argument presented in Hebrews 8 is impossible to reconcile with Vatican's position. Like so many of Rome's doctrines, this latest Catholic spin of dual-covenant theology trades on biblical ignorance to promote an Antichrist agenda. Jesus is the Messiah predicted in the Hebrew Bible (Isaiah 53, Zechariah 12), and Jews do need to reconcile with their Messiah for salvation (John 14:6–7).

Jesus lamented, "O Jerusalem, Jerusalem, thou that killest the prophets, and stonest them which are sent unto thee, how often would I have gathered thy children together, even as a hen gathereth her chickens under her wings, and ye would not! Behold, your house is left unto you desolate. For I say unto you, Ye shall not see me henceforth, till ye shall say, Blessed is he that cometh in the name of the Lord" (Matthew 23:37–39). Upon His return, Jesus will stand as the prosecutor in Rome's anti-evangelism apostasy. Malachy's Prophecy of the Popes predicted, "The dreadful judge will judge his people and the city of seven hills will be destroyed."[391]

Miraculous Signs and Lying Wonders?

While it's beyond question that he is *a* false prophet, the decisive test of Pope Francis' status as *the* False Prophet is whether he ever calls down fire from heaven. The False Prophet is said to do so and uses miracles or "miraculous signs" (*sēmeion*) to deceive people into following the first Beast (Revelation 13:13). Believe it or not, Pope Francis has already been credited with such signs. The archbishop of Naples, Cardinal Crescenzio Sepe, credited Pope Francis with a miracle entailing the morbid veneration of human blood. Pope Francis allegedly transformed the dry, two-thousand-year-old blood powder of St. Gennaro, an early Christian beheaded during the persecution by the brutal Roman Emperor Diocletian, back into liquid form. Of course, it begs the embarrassing question of "why was he handling powdered blood in the first place?"

In *Petrus Romanus*, we first revealed that Pope John Paul II's vial of blood was on a worship tour of Latin America.[392] We called it "macabre practice," citing a standard academic source, *The Gale Encyclopedia of Religion*:

> Relics may loosely be defined as the venerated remains of venerable persons. This should be taken to include not only the bodies, bones, or ashes of saints, heroes, martyrs, founders of religious traditions, and other holy men and women but also objects that they once owned and, by extension, things that were once in physical contact with them.
>
> According to the principles of contagious magic, any personal possession or part of a person's body can be thought of as equivalent to his whole self, no matter how minute it may be, or how detached in time and space. Thus a bone, a hair, a tooth, a garment, a footprint can carry the power or saintliness of the person with whom they were once associated and make him or her "present" once again.[393]

When we labeled it "necromantic," we had no way of guessing that, only a few months later, the first Jesuit Pope—a purveyor of liberation theology—would choose the papal name "Francis," borrowed from a saint credited with many prophecies and miracles, and would be credited with making dry blood whole and other miracles. Benge Nsenduluka reported for the *Christian Post*:

> During a visit to Naples Cathedral, the pontiff venerated a vial of blood belonging to the Neapolitan patron St. Gennaro, who was once the bishop of Naples until he was martyred in 305, and it began to liquify. The dry blood turned to liquid after the pontiff prayed the "Our Father" over it and kissed the relic, prompting the Archbishop of Naples, Crescenzio Sepe, to declare the rare phenomenon a miracle.[394]

The pope has also been credited with causing a paralyzed girl to rise up from a wheelchair and walk,[395] and, just a few days before this writing, healing a female Down-syndrome infant's heart defects. The second case, astounded cardiologist in tow, has medical documentation. After the papal healing, the baby's mother, Lynn Cassidy, seemed convinced that "God can act through the pope's blessings in miraculous ways."[396] She described when her husband passed the baby over a barricade in St Peter's Square via a security guard to the eager Pope Francis, passing by in the popemobile. According to Mrs. Cassidy, the pope kissed her baby and asked for her name. The pope is now being credited with causing the infant's damaged heart to spontaneously heal.

> The Pope asked my husband, "How old is she? What's her name?" He told (the Pope) she has two holes in her heart. When we got home in May, we went back to the cardiologist for a check-up. One of the holes was completely closed and one was half the size.[397]

Are these the beginning of the "miraculous signs" (*sēmeion*) that John associated with the False Prophet? Paul wrote that the Antichrist's coming was also "after the working of Satan with all power and signs and lying wonders" (2 Thessalonians 2:9). In *Petrus Romanus*, we documented several popes, who openly practiced the occult, especially pope Sylvester II who learned the dark arts in Spain studying with Moorish Muslim sorcerers:

> Pope Sylvester II (r. 999–1003), born Gerbert d'Aurillac, was reputed to have studied occult lore while a young man in Seville, then under the control of the Muslims. He was the first French Pope and undoubtedly a very gifted man in science and math, having studied under the Moors in Spain. As the legend goes he had lived there with a practitioner of the black arts who possessed a grimoire which could subdue the devil to its masters will. As the account goes, he stole the book and made a pact with the devil, trading his soul to become pope. The bargain entailed that he was to enjoy the opulence of the papacy as long as he refrained from conducting high mass in Jerusalem. Cambridge scholar E. M. Butler reveals, "Gerbert was believed to have carnal intercourse with the devil and to be accompanied by a familiar spirit in the form of a shaggy black dog. He was supposed to be able to blind his adversaries and to divine hidden treasure by the much-execrated practice of necromancy."[398]

The current pope's first miracle centered on the macabre veneration of human blood. Old Testament laws like, "Ye shall not eat anything with the blood: neither shall ye use enchantment, nor observe times [interpret signs]" (Leviticus 19:26), and Jesus' description of the scribes and Pharisees as "whited sepulchres, which indeed appear beautiful outward, but are within full of dead men's bones, and of all uncleanness" (Matthew 23:27) seem to strongly dissuade such a practice. The

Roman Catholic veneration of dead men's bones[399] as demonstrated in the image of John Paul II venerating two skulls of new saints he beatified in Mexico. Critics pointed out that the two receiving beatification, were outlaws, "Juan Bautista and Jacinto de los Angeles were little more than snitches who betrayed their fellow townspeople after years of armed persecution by the Spanish and forced conversions to Catholicism."[400]

Pope John Paul II venerates snitch skulls

Malachi Martin was correct in connecting such supernaturalism and occultist behavior as being behind the Jesuit conspiracy against the papacy and Antichrist-hatching global politics.

For while the war they have chosen to fight takes place on the plane of geopolitics, it is also and more fundamentally a war over the question of the very existence of the Spirit as the basic dimension of the world of men and women. It is about the supernatural as the element that makes each of us human and that defines our existence and our world.[401]

Recall that Martin requested and was granted a release from his Jesuit vow of silence so he could expose what he believed was a satanic communist conspiracy transforming the papacy to where it is today in Pope Francis. Michael W. Cuneo, a professor of sociology and anthropology at Fordham University, who studies the belief in exorcism and demons, writes:

In June 1964 Martin resigned his position at the Pontifical Institute, and eight months later he asked to be released from the Society of Jesus. He was granted provisional release in May 1965, and under the terms of an agreement that was approved by Pope Paul VI on June 30, 1965, he was dispensed from his priestly vows of poverty and obedience (but not, significantly, from the vow of celibacy) and returned to the lay state. Martin left Rome in July 1965, and after a brief sojourn in Paris he moved to New York City, where he drove a cab and worked in an East Side doughnut shop before settling into a new career as a writer of bestselling religious potboilers.[402]

It was the Second Vatican Council's codification of radical inclusivism ("all spirituality leads to salvation") that disheartened traditionalist Catholics like Martin, who objected by taking Jesus at His word (Matthew 7:13–14, John 14:6). Vatican II was also the impetus for the political radicalism and liberation theology movement that, shortly thereafter, dominated the Latin Jesuit Order. Radical inclusivism amounts to a form of *oneism*—defined in Putnam's *The Supernatural Worldview* as being nearly identical to "the pantheistic monism asserting "Nirvana" or "Brahman" found in Eastern religions, the "Omega Point" of Jesuit mystic Pierre Teilhard de Chardin, extraterrestrial disclosure for the UFO community, and the technological singularity of transhumanism. "All is one," labeled oneism and explained as "an esoteric read on reality" by New Testament scholar, Peter Jones, is the prevailing spiritual idea of our age.[403] We are burdened to point how unlikely it is that these diverse philosophies all converge on this oneism by chance. In *The Supernatural Worldview*, Putnam offered a theory concerning the popular embrace of oneism: "I contend it is by design and leading toward the *sine qua non* of cosmic history—the return of Jesus Christ to judge the world—described in the book of Revelation."[404] Pope Francis is determined to promote oneism and Chardinian occult doctrines about the Omega Point.

Relic worship is also indulged by other pantheistic monists, like Hindus and Buddhists. Less than a year ago, the pope visited the South Asian Island Sri Lanka to canonize a new Saint: Blessed Joseph Vaz, a seventeenth-century Oratorian priest and missionary to Sri Lanka, then known as the *Island of Ceylon*.[405] This completed the beatification process initiated by Pope John Paul II in 1995. Known as the Apostle of Ceylon, Vaz arrived on the island following the Dutch defeat of the Portuguese called the Dutch occupation. During this period, the Calvinist Netherlanders were imposing Reformed theology on the island's Catholics as an alternative to being charged with heresy. According to island legend, St. Vaz surreptiously trekked throughout the isle pretending to be a Hindu, all the while bringing the Eucharist and the sacraments to clandestine groups of Catholics, at a time when they were legally outlawed. Of course, by completing the beatification process John Paul II began, Pope Francis, already known as a champion of the poor, is now a hero to most Sri Lankan Catholics.

While he is still far from calling down fire from heaven, nothing about Pope Francis rules out the original False Prophet hypothesis we presented in *Petrus Romanus* (2012), that is, before we knew of his rigged "election" and many details concerning his Marxism, globalism, and heresy, which now seem to confirm it. With each new development, it becomes harder to deny that the current pope really is *Petrus Romanus*, the pope who will nourish the sheep during many tribulations until the City of Seven Hills is destroyed and the dreadful judge judges his people—*and* the conspiratorially elected pontiff his namesake, St. Francis of Assisi, warned us about: "at the time of this tribulation a man, not canonically elected, will be raised to the Pontificate."[406] The saint's prophecy closes dramatically with, "for in those days Our Lord Jesus Christ will send them not a true Pastor, but a destroyer."[407]

250   *Works of St. Francis of Assisi.*

who outwardly profess it, for in those days Our Lord Jesus Christ will send them not a true Pastor, but a destroyer.*

St. Francis' Destroyer Prophecy

7

Anti-Zionism Leading to Armageddon

Pray for the peace of Jerusalem: They shall prosper that love thee.
—Psalm 122:6

I believe I am working in accordance with the Almighty Creator: by defending myself against the JEW, I am fighting for the work of the Lord.[408]
—Adolf Hitler

The last hour would not come unless the Muslims will fight against the Jews and the Muslims would kill them until the Jews would hide themselves behind a stone or a tree and a stone or a tree would say: Muslim, or the servant of Allah, there is a Jew behind me; come and kill him; but the tree Gharqad would not say, for it is the tree of the Jews.[409]
—Muhammad (Sahih Muslim)

For thus saith the Lord of hosts; After the glory hath he sent me unto the nations which spoiled you: For he that toucheth you toucheth the *apple of his eye*.
—Zechariah 2:8, emphasis added

AN ANONYMOUS Gaza-based Muslim cleric brandished a knife during a sermon calling for Palestinians to continue visiting brutal attacks against unarmed Israeli civilians.[410] The violence is escalating, as the *Chicago Tribune* reported, "The attacks in Jerusalem, including a deadly shooting and knifing spree on a bus and a violent hacking attack caught on video, escalated the month-long unrest and raised the pressure on Prime Minister Benjamin Netanyahu to take action."[411] The latest attacks on the Temple Mount are of an especially brutal nature.

> Palestinians were conspiring to attack Jews visiting the site during the holiday. The night before, security forces found a pipe bomb being smuggled into the Temple Mount and arrested several young Palestinians on suspicion of conspiring to commit violence. The arrest led to clashes on the Temple Mount between Palestinians pouring out of Al-Aqsa Mosque and the Israeli police, who were subjected to a barrage of rocks and fireworks. In the end, the mosque was closed, and hundreds of Jewish visitors were allowed to visit the Temple Mount.[412]

How is it that both claim Jerusalem? Why are the Jews hated? The identity of the chosen seed, Isaac or Ishmael, is unavoidably related to which religion, Judaism or Islam, has the rightful claim to the Promised Land and Temple Mount.

It's no secret that Jew-Arab conflict can be traced all the way back to Abraham's unfaithful decision to procreate with his consort Hagar, at the suggestion of his wife Sarah (Genesis 16:1). As a result, Abraham, the Jewish patriarch, and Hagar, an Egyptian servant, became the parents of Ishmael (Genesis 16:15) and, via his twelve sons, the twelve tribes of the Arab peoples:

> Now these are the generations of Ishmael, Abraham's son, whom Hagar the Egyptian, Sarah's handmaid, bare unto Abraham: and

these are the names of the sons of Ishmael, by their names, according to their generations: the firstborn of Ishmael, Nebajoth; and Kedar, and Adbeel, and Mibsam, and Mishma, and Dumah, and Massa, Hadar, and Tema, Jetur, Naphish, and Kedemah: these are the sons of Ishmael, and these are their names, by their towns, and by their castles; twelve princes according to their nations. And these are the years of the life of Ishmael, an hundred and thirty and seven years: and he gave up the ghost and died; and was gathered unto his people. And they dwelt from Havilah unto Shur, that is before Egypt, as thou goest towards Assyria: and he died in the presence of all his brethren. (Genesis 25:12–18)

While God did promise to make Ishmael into a nation—"Behold, I have blessed him, and will make him fruitful, and will multiply him exceedingly; twelve princes shall he beget, and I will make him a great nation" (Genesis 17:20)—the son of promise, Isaac (Genesis 17:19), was necessarily the one born *miraculously* to Abraham's elderly wife, Sarah, who had laughed out loud at the idea she was still fertile in her nineties (Genesis 17:17). The Angel of the Lord seems to be able to read Sarah's thoughts while she "laughed to herself" (Genesis 25:12–15). Anticipating the future controversy, Yahweh explained the situation to Isaac:

Sojourn in this land, and I will be with thee, and will bless thee; *for unto thee, and unto thy seed, I will give all these countries*, and I will perform the oath which I sware unto Abraham thy father (Genesis 26:3, emphasis added).

In contrast, the Qur'an teaches that Ishmael is the son of promise.

My Lord! Vouchsafe me of the righteous. So We gave him tidings of a gentle son. And when (his son) was old enough to walk with him, (Abraham) said: O my dear son, I have seen in a dream that I must sacrifice thee. So look, what thinkest thou? He said: O my father! Do that which thou art commanded. Allah willing, thou shalt find me of the steadfast. Then, when they had both surrendered (to Allah), and he had flung him down upon his face, We called unto him: O Abraham! Thou hast already fulfilled the vision. Lo! thus do We reward the good. Lo! that verily was a clear test. Then We ransomed him with a tremendous victim. And We left for him among the later folk (the salutation): Peace be unto Abraham! Thus do We reward the good. Lo! he is one of Our believing slaves. And we gave him tidings of the birth of Isaac, a prophet of the righteous. And We blessed him and Isaac. And of their seed are some who do good, and some who plainly wrong themselves. (Surah 37:100–113)

Two arguments are offered in this passage. One, because Ishmael was born before Isaac, he could not be the son spoken of since God is recorded as commanding Abraham to sacrifice his "only son" (Genesis 22:2, 12), and this could only have been Ishmael at a time before Isaac was born, when Ishmael was Abraham's only son. But intellectually honest Muslims admit it isn't so. "The Qur'an did not mention the name of the sacrificial son, and hence Muslim historians disagree in this regard."[413] In contrast, the positive identification as "your only son Isaac" (Genesis 22:2) implies that God viewed Isaac as the son of promise. Muslims respond that this is Jewish corruption of the original revelation. According to Heiser, "What is certain, however, is that this issue will be resolved, and that Jew and Arab Muslims will come together during the time of the Antichrist. Both the Hebrew Bible and the Qur'an foresee this day."[414]

Accordingly, the elephant in the room when the Pope negotiates is that Jews and Muslims fundamentally disagree as to which son the promise was given: Isaac or Ishmael. We believe this disagreement will only be sorted out at the Lord's return. A growing number of Americans are anti-Semitic. According to surveys by the Anti-Defamation League, "15 percent of Americans hold anti-Semitic views, 3% more than in results of a similar poll carried out in 2009."[415] Worse yet, 19 percent of Americans admitted to believing the conspiratorial canard, ala the "Protocols of Zion," entailing that the Jews co-control Wall Street.[416] A co-belief is that the Jews control Hollywood as well.

The Zionist conspiracy to control the world has earned the status of a modern mythology. It's nothing new. "The myth of Jews as children of the Devil, mysterious, uncanny and possessed of sinister powers, has persisted since the second century, when they were accused of killing Christian children, torturing the consecrated wafer and poisoning wells."[417] First published in Russia in 1907, *The Protocols of the Learned Elders of Zion* was revealed to be plagiarized from an 1864 novel, *Dialogues in Hell*, by Maurice Joly.[418] Adolf Hitler was a major proponent and the hoax was studied, as if factual, in German classrooms after the Nazis came to power in 1933 and "German propaganda agencies distributed the book to Latin America."[419] Stephen Eric Bronner, a noted philosopher, prolific author, and Rutgers University political science professor, contended that the notorious forgery had as much to do with negative reactions against postmodernism, liberalism, and democracy as it did with anti-Semitism. If true, it explains why it resonates so well with fundamentalist Muslims, who also reject modernity. Bronner argued that the popularity of the *Protocols* stems from "political anti-Semitism"[420] linking Jews to the evils of the Enlightenment and proposed that "the repeal of modernity is possible only with the eradication of the Jewish Spirit."[421] He also wrote:

> The image of the Jew constructed in the *Protocols* reminds the anti-Semitic audience of fears and longings in their own hearts. Contempt for the masses in a burgeoning mass society is the key to the new anti-Semitic perspective on mass politics in the modern

era. Since only an elite few can really understand the urgency of the situation—given the supposed Jewish control over the press, public sphere as well as all financial and political institutions— anti-Semites long for an authoritarian state in which they can press their message without criticism of opposition.[422]

In one fell swoop, the *Protocols* blamed the Jews for everything from Marxism to world poverty. Most unfortunately, the Christian Church has demonized the Jews, as an ethnic group, for thousands of years as well.[423]

Associate professor of religious studies at Rice University, Dr. David Cook, another of the world's foremost experts on Muslim eschatological Hadiths, reveals that in modern Muslim apocalyptic literature, the *Al-Dajjal*—the Muslim Antichrist—is always a Jew.

In general, these writers perceived the Jews as being part of a Communist world conspiracy and sought to discern a Jewish hidden hand behind the numerous revolutions, the social tur-moil, and antireligious agitation of the first half of the twentieth century. It is not unusual for pictures on the covers of apocalyp-tic books in Arabic to have the characteristics of anti-Semitic portrayals of Jews. Jews are perceived as the eternal enemy of Christianity, subverting it at every level and controlling its his-tory for their nefarious purposes, and driving ultimately toward the rule of the Jewish Antichrist.[424]

Rejecting both the Qur'anic revision of history and the more plau-sible, ancient tradition preserved in the Hebrew Bible, Muslim radicals typically deny modern Israel's right to exist in their historic homeland. For example, the Palestinian Liberation Organization's concession, "The struggle with the Zionist enemy is not a struggle about Israel's borders, but about Israel's existence."[425] Right from the beginning, the

IS threatened the "real Zionist holocaust" using Twitter.[426] We now face computer-savvy anti-Semitic mujahedeen?

The Qur'an is noticeably anti-Jewish but not terribly original. A central claim of Islam is that the Jews and Christians had a true revelation but allowed it to be corrupted—we argue elsewhere in this book that the similarities are more reflective of Muslim plagiarism than divine correction. The Qur'an says,

> And verily We gave unto Moses the Scripture and We caused a train of messengers to follow after him, and We gave unto Jesus, son of Mary, clear proofs (of Allah's sovereignty), and We supported him with the Holy spirit. Is it ever so, that, when there cometh unto you a messenger (from Allah) with that which ye yourselves desire not, ye grow arrogant, and some ye disbelieve and some ye slay? And they say: Our hearts are hardened. Nay, but Allah hath cursed them for their unbelief. Little is that which they believe. (Surah 2:87–88)[427]

The rhetorical question, "Which of the prophets have not your fathers persecuted? and they have slain them which shewed before of the coming of the Just One; of whom ye have been now the betrayers and murderers" (Acts 7:52) is overtly plagiarized from Stephen's testimony to the Sanhedrin (Acts 7:1–53), the same historical narrative that promptly reported Stephen being executed as the first Christian martyr, a victim of the very brutal Jewish tradition of death by stoning. All the while, a pre-Christian Saul (who became the apostle Paul) laid Stephen's garments at the feet of his rock-pummeled corpse (Acts 7:58). According to Paul's biographer, the biblical scholar, F. F. Bruce:

> According to this testimony, he associated himself with Stephen's accusers, guarding the outer garments of the witnesses as, in conformity with the ancient law, they threw the first stones at

his execution (Deuteronomy 17:7). "Then he took part enthusiastically in the campaign of repression against the church of Jerusalem, 'breathing threats and murder against the disciples of the Lord'" (Acts 9:1), arresting and imprisoning men and women, endeavouring to make them renounce their faith when they were brought before synagogue courts, and pursuing refugees beyond the frontiers of Judaea in an attempt to bring them back to face trial and punishment.[428]

Today's fundamentalist Jews and Muslims remind us of Saul's preconversion hatred of Christians. Today in Syria, where Saul had his Damascus Road visitation of a post-resurrection Jesus resulting in his being renamed Paul, the Christian population has been *literally* decimated by the IS. George J. Marlin, chairman of Aid to the Church in Need USA, wrote hopefully of the pope's (then upcoming) September 2015 address to the UN:

> The pope *should* state that tens of thousands are being persecuted, deprived of their fundamental human rights, discriminated against and killed simply because they are Christians. He should point out that persecution of Christians by radical Islamists means second-class citizenship; job and education discrimination; abduction and murdering of clerics; destruction of Christian churches, homes and businesses by mobs; being kidnapped and sold into slavery—and it means being jailed or executed for practicing one's faith.[429]

Unfortunately, Marlin was necessarily disappointed. The pope only mentioned Syria once, in passing, during his September 28, 2015, address. "Not only in cases of religious or cultural persecution, but in every situation of conflict, as in Ukraine, Syria, Iraq, Libya, South Sudan and the Great Lakes region, real human beings take precedence over partisan interests, however legitimate the latter may be."[430] As far as persecution, that was about it…the martyrs and millions of displaced Syrian Christians were effectively abandoned by the Pope. However, Francis made sure to reiterate the need to protect "the natural environment and the vast ranks of the excluded. These sectors are closely interconnected and made increasingly fragile by dominant political and economic relationships. That is why their rights must be forcefully affirmed, by working to protect the environment and by putting an end to exclusion."[431] Of course, he means the "world authority"[432] prescribed in his environmental encyclical *Sulla Cura Della Casa Comune*. So environmentalism with an obvious spin toward the dubious science behind climate change, and the Marist emphasis on the class war against the oppressed majority world took precedence. The Islamic State or Islam was never mentioned. The existential threat posed to Israel by a nuclear Iran also was not mentioned. He did call for global disarmament, labeling the United States' sadly realistic policy of deterrence by threat of mutual destruction, as morally incoherent and an insult to the UN.

> An ethics and a law based on the threat of mutual destruction—and possibly the destruction of all mankind—are self-contradictory and an affront to the entire framework of the United Nations, which would end up as "nations united by fear and distrust." There is urgent need to work for a world free of nuclear weapons, in full application of the non-proliferation Treaty, in letter and spirit, with the goal of a complete prohibition of these weapons.[433]

Instead of defending the apple of God's eye (Deuteronomy 32:10), the pope expressed approval over the recent Iran nuclear deal. "The recent agreement reached on the nuclear question in a sensitive region of Asia and the Middle East is proof of the potential of political good will and of law, exercised with sincerity, patience and constancy."[434] Seriously?

The Vatican has officially recognized the "State of Palestine"[435] in an official treaty, and to top it off, Pope Francis met with the terrorist and Holocaust denier, Mahmoud Abbas, and described him as "an angel of peace"[436]—all the while commending and participating in Islamic and Talmudic prayer—implying these religions are all equal paths to the same God.[437] The pope commented, "It is my hope that this meeting will mark the beginning of a new journey where we seek the things that unite, so as to overcome the things that divide."[438] Did the deity of Christ, or perhaps the fact that "Christ died for our sins" (1 Corinthians 15:3), ever bother the alleged Vicar of Christ as he waxed poetic about religious unity amongst belief systems with blatantly contradictory theologies? Let's be real: We really doubt it, especially since this pope is already on record as saying that "proselytism is solemn nonsense, it makes no sense."[439] So, dear reader, as the one with "two horns like a lamb" would have us believe, spread the word: The Great Commission has been officially cancelled by the President of the World.

While the Qur'an and the Torah have both been used to justify atrocities, neither supports denying the Jews right to Jerusalem and the land of Israel. Honest Muslims acknowledge the teachings of their main sacred text, the Qur'an. Abdul Hadi Palazzi wrote, "Using Islam as a basis for preventing Arabs from recognizing any sovereign right of Jews over the Land of Israel is new. Such beliefs are not found in classical Islamic sources. Concluding that anti-Zionism is the logical outgrowth of Islamic faith is wrong. This conclusion represents the false transformation of Islam from a religion into a secularized ideology."[440] This malevolently secular ideology drives all of radical Islam including the IS. For example, Yassar Arafat's position: "I'll never compromise. I cannot and I will not. I am a revolutionary. I have dedicated my whole life to the Palestinian cause and the destruction of Israel."[441] The textbooks used to educated Palestinian high school seniors teach that the Jewish nation has no right to exist whatsoever.

Palestine's war ended with a catastrophe that is unprecedented in history, when the Zionist gangs stole Palestine and expelled its people from their cities, their villages, their lands and their houses, and established the State of Israel.[442]

Unlike the wishful thinking extended by the Vatican and the Obama administration, Palestinian schoolbooks make no attempt to educate for peace and coexistence with Israel. We would like to ask the pope, "How can there be a *two*-state solution when Palestine repeatedly states that there can be only one?" Palestine is obviously not interested in a two-state solution. Who do liberals think they are fooling? Certainly not Benjamin Netanyahu, who has stated that there would never be a Palestinian state while he is in control.[443]

Former senior international policy analyst with the RAND Corporation, Laurent Murawiec, a French Jew, served in the French army, advised the French Ministry of Defense, and taught history and economics after earning a BA and MA in philosophy from Sorbonne University.[444] He was an associate of Lyndon LaRouche (who believed Pike's influence was driving a Third World War) and wrote for his *Executive Intelligence Review* in the 1980s.[445] Using impeccable scholarship, he traced the origins of modern jihad ideology to the Bolsheviks, the Russian terrorists who ultimately became the Communist Party of the Soviet Union (USSR). Murawiec demonstrates how violent Bolshevik political strategies were appropriated by radical Islam through various channels of communication. The French scholar explained:

Modern jihad erupted in full force with the Islamic Revolution in Iran in 1979 in both the Shiite and the Sunni world. It was a reflection, a result, and a concentrate of all the main political pathologies of the twentieth century, led by the parade of motley totalitarian ideologies, but transformed by its absorption into the Islamic cultural matrix. What a striking historical paradox

197

this was: The world of Islam was falling behind the fast-paced progress made by the modern world and those areas of the world that had taken up the challenges of modernity. It was falling behind not only because it did not invent modernity or espouse it, but because it actively rejected it. On the other hand, it avidly absorbed the dark shadow of modernity, its evil side—the totalitarian ideologies that sprung up as the corruption of modernity, Bolshevism, fascism, Nazism, postmodernism.[446]

Writing as a scholar of religion and as a geopolitical analyst, Murawiec labels radical jihadi philosophy as *gnostic* because its adherents believe they are divinely appointed agents operating above the rest of mankind. This implies that they operate under a Crusade War ethic (explained earlier in this book). Murawiec compares modern jihadi to medieval sectarians.

Likewise, modern jihad, which massively drew on the modern sectarians, has its roots in traditional jihad, and has stirred the tidal messianic hopes of disoriented Islamic masses, their dislocated lives, and their incensed ruminations and is twice promising them the Gnostic Paradise, in Allah's kingdom erected on earth, and in Paradise as martyrs. Modern jihad is the modern form of Mahdism. It is Islamic in its cultural idiom, form, and content. There is no firewall between Mahdism and mainstream Islam, since it is all "in the Book," in the Quran, in the vast hadith literature.[447]

William McCants writes, "The early Islamic apocalyptic prophecies are intrinsically sectarian because they arose from similar sectarian conflicts waged at the time in Iraq and the Levant."[448] However, jihadi politics fundamentally contradict passages "in the Book," which acknowledge that Allah gave the Land of Israel to the Jews.

O Children of Israel! Remember My favour wherewith I favoured you, and fulfil your (part of the) covenant, I shall fulfil My (part of the) covenant, and fear Me. (Surah 2:40)[449]

And (remember) when Moses said unto his people: O my people! Remember Allah's favour unto you, how He placed among you prophets, and He made you kings, and gave you that (which) He gave not to any (other) of (His) creatures. O my people! Go into *the holy land which Allah hath ordained for you.* Turn not in flight, for surely ye turn back as losers. (Surah 5:20–21, emphasis added)[450]

Because the Qur'an is so heavily derivative of the Hebrew Bible, some truths are preserved alongside the heavily revised Islamized-version of history. Even so, the Qur'an also predicts Allah will restore the Holy Land to the Jews during the end times:

And We [Allah] said unto the Children of Israel after him: Dwell in the land; but when the promise of the Hereafter cometh to pass We [Allah] shall bring you as a crowd gathered out of various nations" (Surah 17:104).[451]

It explicitly promises the Jews will come together in the Holy Land, "when the promise of the Hereafter comes to pass." This being a well-known fact amongst the educated, how can Muslim apologists remain intellectually honest while fighting so hard against Zionism when Quranic and biblical prophecy *both* promise to gather the ethnic Jewish people, fellow Semites,[452] in the historic land described in the Qur'an and Hebrew Bible?

The biblical prophets were covenant enforcers who spoke for Yahweh. It is a common misconception to assume they were akin to modern psychics, mediums, or fortune tellers. Biblical scholars Gordon Fee and

Douglas Stuart argue that less than 5 percent of Old Testament prophecy describes events still future.[453] The prophets did predict the future, but it was usually the immediate future of Israel and their enemies. It dovetails with Ezekiel's description of the watchman's role (Ezekiel 33), as the prophets were warning of coming judgment due to Old Covenant violations. Even so, many prophecies have a double reference, as explained by theologian John Walvoord:

> It is not unusual in Scripture for a prophecy to be partially fulfilled early and then later have a complete fulfillment. Accordingly, what seems to be a partial fulfillment of a prophecy should not be assumed to be the final answer as the future may record a more complete fulfillment.[454]

It is fair to say that the Hebrew prophets speak more to the heart, to inspire moral conviction, than to logic and reason. They appeal more to emotion in order to confront and convict people about their sinful lifestyles. Hence, the prophets speak more in poetic forms, called oracles of various types: lawsuit (Hosea 3:3–17), woe (Habakkuk 2:6–8), promise (Amos 9:11–15), enactment prophecy (Isaiah 20), and messenger speech (Isaiah 38:1–8; Jeremiah 35:17–19; Amos 1:3–2:16; Malachi 1:2–5).[455] Accordingly, one must determine what type of oracle is being delivered and interpret it according to its proper genre, rather than simply assuming it is always literal, like the genre: historical narrative that dominates the Torah. In contrast, the prophets more often use figures of speech, metaphors, word pictures, and symbols.

Often, characters and circumstances recognizable to Israel's ancient neighbors are employed to this end. One favorite technique was to adopt a myth about Baal, but supplant the false god with Yahweh within the story. Heiser demonstrates that Jesus' claim to return by "coming in the clouds of heaven" (Mark 14:62) is a reference to the "cloud rider" described in Daniel 7:13 and is ultimately a polemic against Baal, who is described in Canaanite literature as the "cloud rider."[456] Without scholars' recently acquired knowledge of Ugaritic literature, this Old Testament background would remain obscure. Sometimes, our understanding of the biblical context changes as new archaeological discoveries are made. Accordingly, the prophets are prone to hyperbole, and must be interpreted in their proper literary genre and context. Above all, the context is paramount.

Isaiah 1:1–14 is described as a vision that is a form of divine revelation not based on real physical sight, but on word pictures and symbols.[457] We know the context is prior to the exile in 605 BC and sacking of Jerusalem in 586 BC, as chapter 6 reveals that Isaiah's commissioning was in the last year of King Uzziah, about 640 BC.[458] It is a lawsuit-type oracle. This is made evident as the heavens and earth are called as witnesses to the indictment being brought. The charges being brought are rebellion (v. 2), sinfulness (v. 4), and hypocrisy (v. 11). The nature theme runs throughout as the people are contrasted with nature as a stubborn ox and a mule who seem to believe they know their place better than God's people (v.3). In verses 5–8, their wayward spiritual condition is depicted as a badly beaten body, a burned-out city, and an abandoned tent in a harvested field. These visions all seem to speak to what will be left in 586 BC after Nebuchadnezzar sacks the city, leaving it like Sodom. Verses 10–15 describe the Israelites' vain attempts to placate God with hypocritical religion, that He promises to ignore (v. 15). The message is clear: If the Israelites' hearts are no different from the unrepentant in Sodom, their fate will be no different.

Although we are not under the Old Covenant, in many ways, modern American Christians mirror Isaiah's charges. As a body, we have abandoned biblical theology. In a recent Pew Forum surveying the evangelical church, 57 percent agreed that "many religions lead to eternal life," and 53 percent agreed that "there is more than one true way to interpret the teachings of my religion."[459] Verses 10–15 of Isaiah's lawsuit oracle (Isaiah 1:1–14) are still applicable because New Covenant believers can still fall into the trap of using religious ritual as a means of manipulating God for our own benefit. The teachings of reciting the rosary, obtaining an indulgence, making a pilgrimage, or repeating "Hail Mary" are similar errors, inherent in the Roman Catholic sacramental system. Luther connected the fact the Hebrew prophet Habakkuk's statement, "the righteous shall live by his faith" (Habakuk 2:4b), was quoted by Paul (Galatians 3:11, Romans 1:17) and arguably was also stated in Hebrews (10:38). He recovered the biblical teaching that *salvation was by faith alone*, not the power of Church. Luther, Calvin, and the heroes of the Reformation were barely able to restore the gospel, and did not have time to rework Christian eschatology, a process that started with historicism but was displaced by dispensationalism in the early nineteenth century.[460] According to Darby, the Antichrist is a satanic figure who would tyrannize the world for seven years, unleashing his fury especially against the Jews and the state of Israel. Darby called that seven-year period "the Tribulation"—a heptad of years ending when the forces of Antichrist would gather from all corners of the world in one last attempt to destroy the Jewish people in the great, cataclysmic Battle of Armageddon. God still has designs for the Jewish nation, the purpose of the Tribulation is to force Israel's hand concerning Jesus.

Israel's literal national restoration is not captured any more explicitly than in Amos 9:11–15. Verses 11–12 speak of the political revival under the Davidic Messiah (cf. Ezekiel 34). "In that day will I raise up the tabernacle of David that is fallen, And close up the breaches thereof; And I will raise up his ruins, And I will build it as in the days of old: That they may possess the remnant of Edom, and of all the heathen, Which are called by my name, Saith the Lord that doeth this" (Amos 9:11–12). This is the fulfillment of the Davidic Covenant and of the angel Gabriel's promise to Mary that Jesus would sit on David's throne forever, which did not even exist during the First Advent (Luke 1:32–33). Verses 13–15 turn to the restoration of the fertility of the land and the return of the people. "Behold, the days come, saith the Lord, That the plowman shall overtake the reaper, And the treader of grapes him that soweth seed; And the mountains shall drop sweet wine, And all the hills shall melt. And I will bring again the captivity of my people of Israel, And they shall build the waste cities, and inhabit them; And they shall plant vineyards, and drink the wine thereof; They shall also make gardens, and eat the fruit of them. And I will plant them upon their land, And they shall no more be pulled up out of their land which I have given them, Saith the Lord thy God" (Amos 9:13–15). While this passage was a message of hope for the exiles, it is necessarily a case of "already but not yet" as well. God states categorically that they will return to "never again be uprooted" (v.15). Isaiah foretold:

> And it shall come to pass in that day, That the Lord shall set his hand again *the second time* to recover the remnant of his people, Which shall be left from *Assyria*, And from Egypt, and from Pathros, And from Cush, and from Elam, and from *Shinar*, And from Hamath, and from the islands of the sea. (Isaiah 11:11, emphasis added)

We live in a time of active prophetic fulfillment because this began in 1948, when national Israel was reestablished and Jews returned from far and wide to the land. This is ongoing and, is reflected in the present-day turmoil in the Middle East over Jerusalem (Zechariah 12:2–3). Notice that the territory currently held by the IS is mentioned specifically as the ancient Near Eastern regions *Assyria* (spans modern Syria and Iraq) and *Shinar* (Iraq).

8

The Christian Roots
of Anti-Zionism

THE BIBLE does not teach that the church has *replaced* Israel. Theologies akin to Roman Catholic teachings are still popular in many otherwise Reformed denominations like Presbyterianism. It creates a lot of confusion about God's promises, especially amongst new believers. When theological constructs seem to undermine God's integrity, they should be re-examined. Alan Kurschner of Eschatos Ministries holds an MA in biblical languages from Gordon-Conwell Theological Seminary and is a PhD candidate in Greek linguistics at McMaster Divinity College. Blogging regularly in support of premillennial eschatology, he recently highlighted the cognitive dissonance created by simultaneously embracing the strong assurance offered by Reformed theology and necessary belief in the namby-pamby nature of God's promises to the Jewish people. That is, God seems wishy-washy, according to the inescapable salvific implications inherent in supercessionism. Worse yet, Kurschner cogently contends that "replacement theology" is closer to Muslim belief than classical Christianity:

> It is a fundamental tenet of the Koran that both Israel and the Church failed. Moses was a prophet. Jesus was a prophet. But

Muhammad was the seal of the prophets, the messenger of the final revelation. The Jews are not the people of God—they failed! The Christians are not the people of God—they failed! It is the Muslims who are the people of God. Of course this is preposterous. But, in the event that you are still uncertain about the calling of Israel, consider this simple truth: If God could *forsake* Israel, in spite of His unconditional, everlasting promise, then He could forsake the Church! If God could *replace* Israel, in spite of His unconditional, everlasting promises, then He could replace the Church!"[461]

In fact, we have pointed out before that Jesus had the perfect opportunity to clarify Israel's destiny, but He did *not* teach replacement theology. Just before His ascension, the disciples asked Jesus, "Lord, wilt thou at this time restore again the kingdom to Israel?" (Acts 1:6). What Jesus did not say is as important as what He did say. He did not say, "Sorry guys, it's never going to happen; Israel forfeited." Rather than a mere argument from silence, notice what Jesus *does* say: "It is not for you to know the times or the seasons, which the Father hath put in his own power" (Acts 1:7). His answer implies a future time that God has fixed by His authority when He *will* restore the Kingdom to Israel.

We have always believed a careful reading of Romans 9–11 should settle the matter for a Bible-believing Christian. Paul warned the Gentiles in no uncertain terms of adopting the attitude expressed by Rome:

Boast not against the branches. But if thou boast, thou bearest not the root, but the root thee. Thou wilt say then, The branches were broken off, that I might be graffed in. Well; because of unbelief they were broken off, and thou standest by faith. Be not highminded, but fear: For if God spared not the natural branches, take heed lest he also spare not thee. Behold therefore the goodness and severity of God: on them which fell, severity;

but toward thee, goodness, if thou continue in his goodness: otherwise thou also shalt be cut off. (Romans 11:18–22)

In *When A Jew Rules the World: What the Bible Really Says about Israel in the Plan of God* by Joel Richardson, the author reflects on Paul's warning to the original Church in Rome (which, according to Paul's letter, was not led by Peter, *at the very time Rome places him there*):

Today, as we look back two thousand years to Paul's warning, a terrifying reality immediately grips us. When we take an honest look at the Gentile-dominated Christian Church throughout its history, right up to this present day, most believers have utterly failed to heed Paul's warnings. The vast majority of the Church from very early on, from the top down, fell headlong into wrong ideas and arrogance toward unbelieving Israel. How quickly they forgot about the promises of God and Israel's ongoing role in His plan! And the results have been horrific.

One of the results of the Church's ignorance of Israel's role in the plan of God is the profound blindness of much of the Church concerning unfolding prophecy. Many Christians have heard of "the sons of Issachar," mentioned in 1 Chronicles 12:32. We are told that they were "men who understood the times, with knowledge of what Israel should do." Today the Church is in desperate need of understanding concerning the times and the ability to properly respond. The Jewish prophets, apostles, and Jesus Himself have given us such a profound gift in that their words contain a tremendous amount of information concerning what we will witness in the days ahead. Throughout the pages of Scripture, the future, like the past, is laid out in great detail on a divinely revealed timeline. Understanding the times and recognizing where we are on this timeline is of tremendous strategic benefit to the Church as it seeks to fulfill its divine mandate. But when the Church fails to acknowledge and recognize the consistent thread of the people and the land of Israel that runs through the entire timeline, it quickly becomes distorted beyond understanding, resulting in a thick fog of confusion settling over the vision of the Church. Such is the state of the Church today. This timeline, the great strategic blueprint that the Lord has given to His people, has essentially been scribbled over, defaced with the errant doctrines of a Gentile-dominated Church. Not only are vast segments of the Church fundamentally unaware of where they presently sit on God's prophetic timeline; many reject the idea that such a clear timeline even exists. If the Church is to ever truly blow the fog away, if it is to ever regain the clarity and prophetic spirit it needs to navigate the dark days ahead, then it must both identify and thoroughly reject those false doctrines and wrong ideas that crept into the Church early on. This process of cleansing must begin by acknowledging Israel as the essential thread that runs throughout the Lord's unfolding promise-plan of redemption.[462]

Arnold Fruchtenbaum, a Messianic scholar and dispensational theologian, has pointed out that Israel is eschatologically regathered in two stages. "The first regathering is the one in unbelief prior to the Great Tribulation in preparation for judgment."[463] But the second gathering is after they recognize Jesus as Messiah in preparation for the millennial reign from Jerusalem (Isaiah 11:11). This second regathering is not merely from Babylon or the Middle East, but from all over the world (v. 12).[464]

We believe that the prophetically crucial regathering "in unbelief" process ensued with the reformation of Israel as a nation state in 1948. Many amillennial Christians are ignorant about the two-stage regathering described in the Jewish prophets and assume that dispensational premillennialists blindly support the secular state of modern Israel. Barry E. Horner writes:

No premillennialist perceives the present "geopolitical re-establishment of the State of Israel" in a consummate sense. It is a precursor of that "restoration" (Acts 3:21) and "redemption" of the created order (Rom. 8:22–23) in which saved national Israel will gloriously participate. However, this does not mean that we walk blindly through this world as if historic events have little significance. Surely not only the continued increasing material and military strength of national Israel obtained in the face of seemingly insuperable opposition, but particularly in possession of Old Jerusalem after a hiatus of over 1,900 years, has troubled those of Reformed Augustinian constrictions.[465]

We well enough know that modern Israel is fertile with technological development, arguably more than any other nation in the world.[466] We believe this thriving economic development drives the "gathering in unbelief" ongoing to the ultimate satisfaction of the Ezekiel 36 dry-bones prophecy, representing the return of Jesus, when Israel will recognize Him as Messiah. At this time in history, "every knee will bow to Jesus, and every tongue will praise God" (Romans 14:11). Laying the fanatical boasting of the Islamic State aside, the lateness of the hour does not bode well for modern Israel's enemies. The King James text of Ezekiel reads:

> Also, thou son of man, prophesy unto the mountains of Israel, and say, Ye mountains of Israel, hear the word of the Lord: Thus saith the Lord God; Because the enemy hath said against you, Aha, even the ancient high places are ours in possession: Therefore prophesy and say, Thus saith the Lord God; Because they have made you desolate, and swallowed you up on every side, that ye might be a possession unto the residue of the heathen, and ye are taken up in the lips of talkers, and are an infamy of the people: Therefore, ye mountains of Israel, hear the word

of the Lord God; Thus saith the Lord God to the mountains, and to the hills, to the rivers, and to the valleys, to the desolate wastes, and to the cities that are forsaken, which became a prey and derision to the residue of the heathen that are round about; Therefore thus saith the Lord God; Surely in the fire of my jealousy have I spoken against the residue of the heathen, and against all Idumea, which have appointed my land into their possession with the joy of all their heart, with despiteful minds, to cast it out for a prey. Prophesy therefore concerning the land of Israel, and say unto the mountains, and to the hills, to the rivers, and to the valleys, Thus saith the Lord God; Behold, I have spoken in my jealousy and in my fury, because ye have borne the shame of the heathen: Therefore thus saith the Lord God; I have lifted up mine hand, Surely the heathen that are about you, they shall bear their shame.

But ye, O mountains of Israel, ye shall shoot forth your branches, and yield your fruit to my people of Israel; for they are at hand to come. For, behold, I am for you, and I will turn unto you, and ye shall be tilled and sown: And I will multiply men upon you, all the house of Israel, even all of it: and the cities shall be inhabited, and the wastes shall be builded: And I will multiply upon you man and beast; and they shall increase and bring fruit: and I will settle you after your old estates, and will do better unto you than at your beginnings: and ye shall know that I am the Lord. (Ezekiel 36:1–11)

Then, the famous dried-up bones (representing Israel's present spiritual state) acquire new flesh and sinews and come back to life, a horror-movie style metaphor from a three-thousand-year-old text that describes Israel's national restoration and eventual repentance.

The hand of the Lord was upon me, and carried me out in the spirit of the Lord, and set me down in the midst of the valley which was full of bones, And caused me to pass by them round about: and, behold, there were very many in the open valley; and, lo, they were very dry. And he said unto me, Son of man, can these bones live? And I answered, O Lord God, thou knowest. Again he said unto me, Prophesy upon these bones, and say unto them, O ye dry bones, hear the word of the Lord. Thus saith the Lord God unto these bones; Behold, I will cause breath to enter into you, and ye shall live. (Ezekiel 37:1–5)

A good reason *not* to relegate Ezekiel 36–37 exclusively to the post-Babylonian captivity era, as many modern scholars do, is that the Messiah necessarily appears prior to the described eschatological regathering. Fruchtenbaum commented:

The key passage for this characteristic is found in the vision of the valley of dry bones of Ezekiel 37:1–23. Ezekiel is first commanded to prophesy over the dry bones scattered all over the valley (vv. 1–6). When he does, the bones all come together with sinews and skin, and then the breath of life is given to them so they become alive again (vv. 7–10). As God interprets the vision of the valley of dry bones (vv. 11–17), these bones are said to represent the whole House of Israel which has become spiritually dead and dispersed (v. 11). Yet God will regather them, and they will again possess the land (vv. 12–13). At the time of the regathering and possession of the land, Israel will be regenerated by the Spirit of God so as to have a living and right relationship (v. 14).[467]

In Joel C. Rosenberg's *The Ezekiel Option*, the author argues that the dry-bones prophecies have largely come true in this generation. Rosenberg then asks if prophecies such as the rebirth of the State of Israel came to pass in the late nineteenth and early twentieth centuries, then why shouldn't we expect the next prophecies to occur? We've heard a similar rhetorical question based on the spiritual degradation and darkness over the land: "If the Bible is not true, then why does it seem like all of its worst enemies—especially those Jesuits on the left-hand path—are going out of their way to make it *seem* like prophecy is being fulfilled?" God has a way of turning evil on its heels and using it for good, as in the case of Jesus' death by crucifixion and unexpected triumphal resurrection: "And having spoiled principalities and powers, he made a shew of them openly, triumphing over them in it" (Colossians 2:15).

Rosenberg's version aside, taken at face value, Ezekiel's dry-bones prophecy is necessarily yet to be *fully* fulfilled because Israel will not be spiritually regenerated until "they shall look upon me whom they have pierced," Jesus the Messiah (Zechariah 12:10). This term "pierced" stems from a primitive Hebrew root *daqar,* meaning to "pierce, run through as retributive act,"[468] and finds its equivalent in the New Testament Greek term, *ekkeneteo* ("to pierce,"[469]) in John's Gospel with "and again another scripture saith, they shall look on him whom they pierced" (John 19:37). David, Jesus, and Paul explained that until this event occurs, Jews are spiritually hardened or metaphorically "blinded" to the reality of Jesus' Messiahship (Psalm 69:22, 23; Matthew 13:14; Romans 11:25).

Of course, modern religious Jews of various stripes are still expecting a different Messiah, likely the one evangelicals label the Antichrist. Louis Jacobs, a distinguished rabbi at the New London Synagogue, wrote the "Jewish State is the 'beginning of the redemption,' that is, it is paving the way for the advent of the Messiah."[470] Thus, it is not terribly controversial to interpret the famous dry-bones prophecy (Ezekiel 36–37) as an ongoing event.

Ezekiel could even be describing recent horrors committed by the IS in Asshur, an area of the ancient Near East corresponding to a region of modern Syria and Iraq, classical Assyria.[471] The IS boasted about destroying a fifth-century Assyrian Christian monastery in the southeastern Syrian town of Qaryatain, and has made sport of beheading Christians in a manner eerily described in the book of Revelation.

Shortly after writing to Timothy, Paul was beheaded and immediately brought safely to the presence of the Lord where he would be rewarded heavenly treasures (Matthew 19:21) and freedom from all the questions, limitations, and burdens of this life.

> The strong among the mighty shall speak to him out of the midst of hell with them that help him: they are gone down, they lie uncircumcised, slain by the sword. Asshur is there and all her company: his graves are about him: all of them slain, fallen by the sword: Whose graves are set in the sides of the pit, and her company is round about her grave: all of them slain, fallen by the sword, which caused terror in the land of the living. (Ezekiel 32:21–23)

Many Bible readers seem to glance over the impact of what is being declared by Yahweh. The Jews are not God's chosen people because they are somehow superior, more sophisticated. or more fortunate. The Lord gave two reasons for restoring the "house of Israel": first, for the sake of His holy name, *not because the Jews deserve it* (vv. 21–22); and, second, it serves notice to the surrounding Muslim nations that Yahweh, *the God of Israel*, is still in full control of His creation (v. 23). Jesus lamented the Jews' hardened hearts were blinding their eyes: "Saying, If thou hadst known, even thou, at least in this thy day, the things which belong unto thy peace! but now they are hid from thine eyes" (Luke 19:42). From that point forward in the Gospel narrative, "these things" [e.g., the gospel, the arrival of the Kingdom] were hidden from his contemporary Israelite's eyes, Jesus teaches they are temporarily blinded. While Jesus opens the mission field to include the entire world (Matthew 28:19), He does not teach that the Jews were replaced as God's chosen nation.

Replacement Theology (Supercessionism) Refuted

Supercessionism is the idea that the Christian church has superseded Israel and, as a result, all unfulfilled prophecy concerning the Jewish people now applies to the invisible Church, i.e., "the Israel of God" (Galatians 6:16). However, this is a juxtaposition to "Jerusalem which now is, and is in bondage with her children" (4:25), analogous to Abraham's slave Hagar contrasted with the true people of God, the believing children of Abraham (3:7, 29), the sons of Abraham's wife, Sarah, who belong to the "Jerusalem which is above is free, which is the mother of us all" (4:26). This passage is most likely describing Messianic Jews as a subset of the invisible Church. One need not embrace supercessionism to explain "the Israel of God."

Jesus reiterates a prophecy in Luke much like the "hidden from their eyes" passage, a prediction that simply cannot coherently apply to the Church: "And they [the Jews] shall fall by the edge of the sword, and shall be led away captive into all nations: and Jerusalem shall be trodden down of the Gentiles, until the times of the Gentiles be fulfilled" (Luke 21:24). Three important points in Jesus' prophecy stand out. First, it is a prophecy of the *diaspora* (from Greek διασπορά, "scattering, dispersion"), which occurred when the Romans spread the Jews all over the known world, selling many into slavery. The Jews revolted against the Roman Empire in AD 66 during the period known as the *First Jewish–Roman War,* which culminated in the destruction of Jerusalem in AD 70. During the siege, the Romans destroyed the Second Temple and most of Jerusalem.[472] This event marked the beginning of the Roman exile, also called Edom exile. Jewish leaders and elite were exiled, killed, or sold into slavery. In his work, *Antiquities of the Jews,* Flavius Josephus included a number of official Roman documents that testify to the Jewish communities in the diaspora.[473]

Second, When Jesus uses the term "until" (Greek *achri:* "until, as far as"[474]) in predicting that Jerusalem would be in Gentile hands "*until* the times of the Gentiles be fulfilled," it implies that one day Jerusalem *will be* back in Jewish hands. Third, for those reasons, Luke 21:24 is a prophecy predicting the reformation of Israel in 1948 and the reclamation of Jerusalem in 1967. Jerusalem certainly was under Gentile control until 1967, and, because the Temple Mount is still under Jordanian control today, it seems to involve a process more than a one-time event. The fact that most of Jerusalem is now under Jewish sovereignty is a sign that the times of the Gentiles are nearly fulfilled.

Perhaps even more clearly, the apostle Paul, a first-century trained rabbi and educated scholar, spelled it out in his original letter to the Roman Church:

> For I would not, brethren, that ye should be ignorant of this mystery, lest ye should be wise in your own conceits; that blindness in part is happened to Israel, until the fulness of the Gentiles be come in. And so all Israel shall be saved: as it is written, There shall come out of Sion the Deliverer, and shall turn away ungodliness from Jacob: For this is my covenant unto them, when I shall take away their sins. As concerning the gospel, they are enemies for your sakes: but as touching the election, they are beloved for the fathers' sakes. For the gifts and calling of God are without repentance. For as ye in times past have not believed God, yet have now obtained mercy through their unbelief. (Romans 11:25–30)

Paul's belief in the restoration and eventual renewal of a Jewish remnant was in accordance with his classical education as a Roman citizen and Hebrew Bible scholarship as a Jewish rabbi. Before encountering the resurrected Jesus on the road to Damascus (Acts 9), Saul most likely "came to Jerusalem at about the age of twelve to study under the famous rabbi Gamaliel."[475] After his conversion, Paul's intimate knowledge of Hebrew Bible prophecy led him to teach a glorious future for national Israel.

Surely Paul was pointing directly to the prophecy delivered by Zechariah, a priest and the son of Berechiah, a prominent priestly family who had returned from Babylon with Zerubbabel around 538 BC (Nehemiah 12:4). Zechariah prophesied, about as explicitly as possible, concerning the crucifixion of Yeshua, the Messiah, upon His First

Coming. Through Zechariah, God seems to describe the future day the Jewish people nationally recognize that Jesus really (was) and still *is* the Christ whom they pierced.

> And I will pour upon the house of David, and upon the inhabitants of Jerusalem, The spirit of grace and of supplications: And they shall look upon me whom they have pierced, And they shall mourn for him, as one mourneth for his only son, And shall be in bitterness for him, as one that is in bitterness for his firstborn. In that day shall there be a great mourning in Jerusalem. (Zechariah 12:10–11)

A Messianic Jew and Semitic language scholar, Michael Brown, PhD, writes concerning the Jewish prophecy:

> Although there are ambiguities in the Hebrew text, this passage clearly speaks of a time of national mourning in Israel over one slain, resulting in the spiritual cleansing of the nation (Zech. 12:10–13:1). One of the oldest Jewish interpretations of this passage, found in the Talmud, refers Zechariah 12:10 to the death of Messiah ben Joseph, the suffering Messiah of Jewish tradition. Why then should it surprise you that the New Testament interprets Zechariah 12:10 with reference to Yeshua?[476]

Recall that John's Apocalypse (the book of Revelation), specifically connects this prophecy (Zechariah 12:10) to Jesus: "Behold, He cometh with clouds; and every eye shall see him, and *they also which pierced him: and all kindreds of the earth shall wail because of him.* Even so, Amen" (Revelation 1:7).

Our good friend and host of *Sid Roth's It's Supernatural*, calls today's Church body *The Incomplete Church* in his 2008 thusly titled tome. He argues that the Church cannot be truly complete until the Jewish people embrace Jesus as their Messiah. He explains his Jewish evangelism focus on the supernatural as being based on: "For the Jews require a sign, and the Greeks seek after wisdom" (1 Corinthians 1:22). Roth believes Jews and Gentiles will converge, each having a unique role, into a complete Church for Messiah's millennial reign from Jerusalem. We believe Roth's "convergence" is what Paul (Romans 11:25–30) and Zechariah (12:10) both prophesied. Finally, Yahweh promises to restore the Jewish people again, with faith in Jesus, at this time.

> And it shall come to pass in that day, That the Lord shall set his hand again the second time To recover the remnant of his people, Which shall be left, from Assyria, And from Egypt, and from Pathros, And from Cush, and from Elam, and from Shinar, And from Hamath, and from the islands of the sea (Isaiah 11:11).

Roth's book makes a compelling case for the eschatological convergence of Jew and Gentile into the complete Church; what Paul described as One New Man: "Having abolished in his flesh the enmity, even the law of commandments contained in ordinances; for to make in himself of twain *one new man*, so making peace; And that he might reconcile both [Jew and Gentile] unto God in *one body* by the cross, having slain the enmity thereby" (Ephesians 2:15–16, emphasis added). Roth wrote:

> While the Bible makes many promises to the Jewish people, the *greater end-time call belongs to Gentile believers*. They are called to lead the Jewish people to Jesus. "*To provoke them [the Jew] to jealously, salvation has come to the Gentiles*" (Rom. 11:11b). When the Jew and the Gentile converge together as One New Man, it will spark an end-time revival such as the world has never seen.[477]

We believe this reflects that during Millennium, Israel will possess her land as God promised (Genesis 12:1–7; 13:14–17; 15:7–21; 17:7–8), and Jesus the Messiah will reign over the entire world with a rod of iron as Israel's promised Davidic king (2 Samuel 7:16; Psalm 89:3–4; Isaiah 9:6–7; Daniel 7:27; Zephaniah 3:15; Revelation 2:27). Rather than blending into a homogenous whole, several passages indicate that the ethnic Jews are held in high regard. First, Matthew records an interesting promise to the twelve.

> And Jesus said unto them, Verily I say unto you, That ye which have followed me, in the regeneration when the Son of man shall sit in the throne of his glory, ye also shall sit upon twelve thrones, judging the twelve tribes of Israel. (Matthew 19:28)

Jesus taught the apostles that tribal identity is still important, even after He returns in judgment and the One New Man is complete. Zechariah explains that Gentiles will know the Israelites are God's people.

> Thus saith the Lord of hosts; In those days it shall come to pass, that ten men shall take hold out of all languages of the nations, Even shall take hold of the skirt of him that is a Jew, saying, We will go with you: for we have heard that God is with you. (Zechariah 8:23)

Apparently, everyone will know that the God of Israel really is the one true God and the Jews still are His people (v. 8). Consequently, the nations will come to Jerusalem for worship during the Millennium, keeping the Feast of Booths (Zechariah 14:16–19; Isaiah 2:3, 66:23). Finally, even the promised New Jerusalem at the end of the Bible mentions the twelve tribes of Israel, terminology that was never applied to the Gentile Church.

> And had a wall great and high, and had twelve gates, and at the gates twelve angels, and names written thereon, which are the names of the twelve tribes of the children of Israel. (Revelation 21:12)

If the names of the gates corresponding to the millennial New Jerusalem are what are being described by Ezekiel (48:31–34), then the north side from east to west would have the gates named Levi, Judah, and Reuben. On the south side from east to west: Simeon, Issachar, and Zebulun. On the east and west sides the gates run from north to south: Joseph, Benjamin, and Dan, as well as Naphtali, Asher, and Gad, respectively. Oddly, Ezekiel mentions Dan, but not Manasseh; Revelation omits Dan, substituting Joseph and Manasseh. These odd discrepancies and Dan's apostate tribal history are two of a host of reasons leading interpreters to believe the Antichrist might be a Jew from the tribe of Dan posing as the expected Messiah (Genesis 49:17; cf. Genesis 3:15).

Many confuse Messianic Judaism—a movement that combines the Christian belief that Jesus is the Messiah, with elements of Judaism and Jewish traditions (e.g. Feasts, Hanukah, etc.)—with the so-called Hebrew Roots Movement (HRM). The two are often hard to tell apart superficially, but "roots-movement" devotees are usually *not* ethnic Jews. Although the two belief systems seem similar, two simple theological tests separate the wheat from the chaff.

First, HRMers typically deny the Pauline teaching: "For by grace are ye saved through faith; and that not of yourselves: it is the gift of God: Not of works, lest any man should boast" (Ephesians 2:8–9). A good tactic is to ask the person to explain the role of the law in salvation. Put the burden on the perspective believer to defend his or her beliefs. If the person promotes the law, citing passages like Matthew 5:17–18 while avoiding Paul's teaching that "by the deeds of the law there shall no flesh be justified in his sight: for by the law is the knowledge of sin" (Romans 3:20), then the person is probably a HRM cultist, who is truly on the same level theologically as a Jehovah's Witness or Mormon, and is not a Messianic Jew—a Christian who happens to be Jewish, and so keeping Hebrew traditions as a matter of ethnicity and culture, not as a requirement of the law.

The second HRM heresy is rejecting the doctrine of the Trinity. The Trinity is admittedly hard to understand and developed in early (pre-papal) Christianity, over centuries, through rigorous written theological debate. HRMers ignorantly label the Trinity "pagan" (usually based on debunked scholarship by Alexander Hislop[478]) by emphasizing, like Muslims, the oneness of God over the triune nature revealed in the New Testament. In a formal debate moderated by Derek Gilbert, Cris Putnam debated Russ Houck, the author of *Epidemic Examining the Infected Roots of Judaism and Christianity* on the idea that Constantine forced the trinity into the Bible.[479] The Church Father Tertullian actually wrote about the Trinity a century prior to Constantine's birth,[480] so the outcome of the "debate" speaks for itself. Suffice it for now to say, God's triune nature is explicitly iterated in Jesus' Great Commission baptismal formula, "Go ye therefore, and teach all nations, baptizing them in the name of the Father, and of the Son, and of the Holy Ghost" (Matthew 28:19). To deny this passage is to deny the Great Commission and, in effect, the Christian faith as we understand it.

While by asking probing questions concerning "saved by grace" and the Trinity, one can identify heretical HRMers, much more in the movement is rotten. Eight years ago, Roth sat as a watchman on the wall:

> Some will take the revelation of Jewish roots and create a legalistic system based on a works mentality. Eventually, these Judaizers will evolve into a denomination and fossilize. A religious spirit will settle on them. Their identity will be in their Jewish culture and not the Jewish Messiah. They will cause much disunity in the Body. Many in the Church will fight this Jewish roots movement because of the legalists.[481]

In closing, Paul seems to have well anticipated such Judaizers in his letter to the Galatians. The best apologetic against HRM heresy is to learn as much as possible about the epistle to the Galatians and the New Covenant (Jeremiah 31:31–37) as explained by the letter to the Hebrews (chapters 8–11). Don't let the roots-movement cultists discourage genuine Jewish evangelism or let them dissuade you from learning more about the Jewish background of the Bible.

The Qur'an Refutes Replacement Theology and Anti-Zionism

Even the Qur'an recorded that the Jews faced Jerusalem as "their direction,"—opposed to the Muslims, who faced Mecca, described as "your direction,"—when engaged in prayer: "Even if you were to bring to those who were given the Book every proof, they [Jews] would not follow *your direction*, nor are you to follow *their direction*, nor do they follow the direction of one another" (Surah 2:145, emphasis added).[482] Islamic scholar Palazzi agrees, "Whoever claims that Jewish sovereignty over the Land of Israel is something new and rooted in human politics denies divine revelation and divine prophecy as explicitly expressed in our Holy Books (the Bible and Koran)."[483] Semitic language scholar Michael Heiser commented, "In effect, the Qur'an treats Jerusalem as playing the same role for Jews as Mecca does for Muslims."[484] Many Muslim scholars agree that the Jews faced Jerusalem. The Jewish practice of facing Jerusalem is further supported by Daniel's prayer room in Babylon, described as an "upper chamber open toward Jerusalem" (Daniel 6:10).

While it might sound like an argument from silence, Jerusalem is not mentioned once in the Qur'an. In sharp relief, Jerusalem is mentioned more than six hundred times in the Hebrew Bible. Heiser does not sugar-coat the PLO's revisionism: "There is no Qur'anic or historical requirement that the Dome of the Rock (the al-Aqsa mosque on the Jewish Temple Mount) must remain under Muslim control, or that Jerusalem rightfully belongs to the Muslims. These beliefs are very recent in origin, and stem from the political hatred of the Jew, not the religion of Islam."[485]

On November 10, 2014, the IS announced in *Dabiq* issue 5 that it had received pledges of allegiance from jihadists in Egypt's Sinai to prepare for the final assault to retake Jerusalem from the Jews. "Sinai is also a front against the Jews, an important step towards the liberation of Baytul-Maqdis [the Al-Aqsa mosque on the Temple Mount]. This expansion brings the battle where the Jews hide behind their gharqad trees closer to the Muslims."[486] The IS' call for the Egyptians to take Jerusalem is in accordance with the following Hadith prophecy.

> Abu Huraira reported Allah's Messenger (may peace be upon him) as saying: The last hour would not come unless the Muslims will fight against the Jews and the Muslims would kill them until the Jews would hide themselves behind a stone or a tree and a stone or a tree would say: Muslim, or the servant of Allah, there is a Jew behind me; come and kill him; but the tree Gharqad would not say, for it is the tree of the Jews.[487]

The problem is that the Qur'an, Islam's ultimate authority, doesn't seem to agree with the Hadith prescribing an Islamic crusade against Jews or any of the popular anti-Semitic conspiracy theories.

Reiterating Surah 17:104, a passage clearly directed at the Jewish people, "but when the promise of the Hereafter cometh to pass We shall bring you [the Jews] as a crowd gathered out of various nations"[488] The text implies that, perhaps very soon, more reasonable Muslims will take the pope's hand and allow for Israel's national existence in their historic Levant homeland and then perhaps they will erect some sort of new universal temple preaching the popular "coexist" message, theologically codified by Vatican II's inclusivism, on the mount of assembly, Mount Zion. Our Islamic eschatology chapter interprets a Hadith that uses remarkably similar language about portents: "the final is that a Fire would spread from Yemen and drive the people to their place of gathering (Assembly)." (Sahi Muslim, Tirmidhi, Abu Dawud).[489] "The

Muslims' place of assembly on the day of the Great Battle will be in Ghouta near a city called Damascus, one of the best cities in al-Sham."[490]

Later in this book, we will demonstrate the case that the infamous Battle of Armageddon has more to do with "the Mount of Assembly" than the plains of Megiddo, but the Qur'anic parallel is noted.

The Qur'anic regathering of the "children of Israel" is a reiteration of the Hebrew Bible's identical promise to regather the Israelites in their historic homeland just prior to the resurrection and judgment. We believe this simply reflects that most of the Qur'an is simply plagiarized from the Hebrew Bible and given a Muslim slant. Even so, it contains enough of its source material to support the Jews regathering in Palestine and, as a result, makes Muslim anti-Zionism a defiance of its teaching.

In summation, biblical theology dictates conditions for the ultimate eschatological restoration of Israel and then the nations are judged based on how they treated the Jews, in accordance with "and I will bless them that bless thee, and curse him that curseth thee: and in thee shall all families of the earth be blessed" (Genesis 12:3)—part of the formal Abrahamic Covenant.[491]

9

Islamic Eschatology

ESCHATOLOGY (Greek *eschaton:* "last") refers to the study of last things, but it also extends to a broader perspective of a particular religion's purpose and direction for history. Thus, in Christian eschatology, it covers items like the rise of Antichrist, the *parousia* ("return of Christ") at the Battle of Armageddon, and the resurrection of the dead for final judgment. In the New Testament, the ultimate purpose of history is to glorify God, right all wrongs, and for Christians to rule and reign with Jesus in a New Jerusalem (Revelation 20:6). Because God may have a purpose for allowing evil to reign for a limited time, eschatological hope is the ultimate theodicy (answer to evil) because final justice is delivered, every tear is dried, and death and pain are vanquished (Revelation 21:4).

Because Islam has garnered so much attention since September 11, 2001, many folks are noticing that the minor and major signs of Islamic eschatology seem to uncannily match most of what is commonly known about the Christian end-time sequence. Since both are falling in place, as written centuries ago, it seems to add weight to the sense of urgency. However, a major premise of this book is that these correspondences are no accident. The primary difference in our thesis and that of various Islamic Antichrist theories (which we feel give too much credit to

Muslim prophecies) is that we think it's demonstrable that those correspondences are largely due to plagiarizing rather than supernatural inspiration. A plethora of competent scholars agree after comparing the Muslim and Christian texts in their original languages, concluding that the Hadith collectors simply borrowed from the popular eschatological literature of eighth-century AD, and this is reflected on an overreliance on Catholic and Eastern Orthodox legends (e.g., *The Apocalypse of PseudoMethodius*) that stray far from the canonical literature. Even so, the Christian prophecies and signs are genuine, so, no matter Muslim revisions, in their original form, they are indicative that the *end is near*.

For many folks, the year 2012 demarcated an end-time event horizon, and it is demonstrable that apocalyptic tension has grown considerably worldwide since. *The Washington Times* reports that "54 percent of Protestants agreed with that statement—and 77 percent of evangelicals" believe we are currently living in the end times.[492] In this chapter, we will examine the Islamic perspective through a critical Christian lens. We agree many of the signs have come to fruition but, of course, we disagree with the veracity of Muslim revelation. We have written quite a few pages explaining why we believe the Tribulation and Armageddon are near. Why? In a nutshell, the sheer existence of modern Israel speaks volumes about the veracity of the Hebrew Scriptures and New Testament. Addressing the British Society for Propagation of the Gospel in 1864, the legendary "prince of preachers," Baptist pastor, Charles Haddon Spurgeon, elaborated on Ezekiel's prophecy (Ezekiel 37).

> If there be anything clear and plain, the literal sense and meaning of this passage—a meaning not to be spirited or spiritualize— must be evident that both the two and the ten tribes of Israel are to be restored on their own land, and that a king is to rule over them.[493]

Keep in mind that Spurgeon was writing nearly one hundred years *prior* to Israel's reformation based on the biblical text. We believe his reading of the Bible was prescient and inspired. Accordingly, the rebirth of National Israel on May 15, 1948, is a foreboding portent and a potent apologetic. The late Christian apologist Grant Jeffrey and all dispensationalists agree that it "is one of the greatest fulfillments of Bible prophecy in history."[494] Jeffrey makes a strong case that this exact date can be derived from the biblical text based upon the biblical precedent of multiplying a punishment by seven, resulting in the year 1948.4, which corresponds neatly with history (for exact mathematical explanation, follow footnoted link).[495]

Needless to say, recent events in the Middle East only confirm the lateness of the prophetic hour. Like the War on Terror sparked a Mahdist revival, the West is expressing apocalyptic tension as well. Since September 11, 2001, current events morally and politically *do seem to match what is described by Jesus in biblical prophecy*. Dispensationalists have been pointing out how recent events uncannily and increasingly correspond to the birth pains Jesus forecast just prior to His return, and perhaps the seals of Revelation as well. We make special note of how these biblical portents correspond on the minor signs recorded in various Islamic sources seven hundred years after the New Testament. These parallels fuel various theories concerning Islam's true role in the end-time scenario.

The primary difficulty with the study of Islamic eschatology is that so little of it comes from reliable sources. There are two main sources—the Qur'an, viewed as infallible, and the Sunna (Arabic "habitual practice")—that are viewed more critically. The Sunna is "the body of traditional social and legal custom and practice of the Islamic community."[496] It is from the Sunna that Sharia law is derived. Richardson emphasized, "What must be understood regarding the Sunna is that it is equally important to the Muslim as the Quran. This is because it is the Sunna that interprets the Quran. *Without the Sunna, the Quran cannot be properly understood*" (emphasis original).[497]

Most of the specific predictions in Islam are thus derived from voluminous *Hadiths* ("recorded sayings of the prophet Muhammad"). An academic *Encyclopedia of Religion* explains that most of the main characters are drawn from the Hadiths. "Key figures include al-Dajjal, the false savior or 'Antichrist,' and the Mahdi, the divinely guided one. Al-Dajjal, who appears in the *Hadith* but not in the Quran, will emerge toward the end of time after a long period of social and natural disintegration, and he will conquer the earth until he is killed either by the returned Jesus or the Mahdi, another non-Quranic figure."[498]

All of the Hadiths are composed of the *isnad* ("chain of transmitters") and the *matn* ("the sayings or actions of Muhammad"). Consider the IS' trademark prophecy about Dabiq.

> Abu Huraira reported Allah's Messenger (may peace be upon him) as saying: The Last Hour would not come until the Romans would land at al-A'maq or in Dabiq. An army consisting of the best (soldiers) of the people of the earth at that time will come from Medina (to counteract them).[499]

The *isnad* is "Abu Huraira reported Allah's Messenger (may peace be upon him) as saying" and the *matn* is the actual prophecy that he related: "The Last Hour would not come until the Romans would land at al-A'maq or in Dabiq." But this paragraph adopted by the IS is applied to current events. When is this predicted to occur specifically? Didn't Muhammad know that the Turks of the Ottoman Empire would conquer Constantinople and call it Istanbul? The "elephant in the room" with all of the Hadiths is that they are short, one-sentence-to-paragraph-length snippets lacking a real context. This is a problem that led Hadith eschatology scholar, David Cook, to concede that even within Islamic scholarship, "it is hardly surprising to find that there has been considerable disagreement as to the order in which events are to take place before the end of the world."[500] The Hadiths are a guessing game at best.

Since the time of Muhammad, many other prophets, like Joseph Smith, the founder of Mormonism, have risen to fame with the same idea that they were sent by God to correct the Bible. Chris White is a Christian apologist who takes issue with the idea that the real Antichrist is Muslim. He critiques the Islamic Antichrist theory by comparing Islam to other "corrective" cults.

> The first way that Islamic eschatology developed is by hadith writers looking at what the Bible said about the end times and changing certain details to make Islam appear to be victorious in the end times. This, of course, required them to make the heroes all Muslim and the bad guys Jews and Christians. There is nothing about this process that should make us think their version of the end times, where they differ from the Bible, is going to come to pass any more than we should expect the Mormon or Jehovah's Witness's versions of the end times to come to pass.[501]

The Day of Judgment

Islamic eschatology is centered on *Yawm ad-Dīn* ("the Day of Judgment") or *Yawm al-Qiyāmah* ("the Day of Resurrection"), or found in Surah 75 of the Qur'an that borrowed from the ultimate divine judgment of the dead from Daniel 12:2 and Revelation 20:12 in the Old and New Testaments, respectively. Thus, it is accepted in all three alleged "Abrahamic" religions: Judaism, Christianity, and Islam. The seventy-fifth Sura of the Qur'an, *al-Qiyama*, has as its main subject the resurrection.

> Nay, I swear by the Day of Resurrection; Nay, I swear by the accusing soul (that this Scripture is true). Thinketh man that We shall not assemble his bones? Yea, verily. We are Able to restore his very fingers! But man would fain deny what is before him. He asketh: When will be this Day of Resurrection? But when sight is confounded, And the moon is eclipsed. And sun and moon

are united, On that day man will cry: Whither to flee! Alas! No refuge! Unto thy Lord is the recourse that day. (Sura 75:1–12).[502]

Reflecting its dependence on the Christian and Jewish "Day of the Lord" Scriptures, Islam also teaches a final tribulation, resurrection of the dead, and eternal division of the righteous and wicked. Islamic apocalyptic literature describes a final battle, like Armageddon, known as *fitnah, malāḥim* ("bloody fights," "massacres"), or *ghaybah* in Shī'a Islam.[503]

For Muslims, it is a singular, final assessment of humanity by Allah, consisting of the annihilation of all life, a general resurrection of the dead, and weighing on the scales of judgment based on ones works in life (Surah 101). The righteous people are rewarded with pleasures of *Jannah* (paradise), while the unrighteous folks are tormented in *Jahannam* (hell). It is another doctrine borrowed from the New Testament with some minimal revisionism (or a plagiarists' confusion).

In contrast, the book of Revelation describes *two* resurrections. Christians are raised for the Millennium: "But the rest of the dead lived not again until the thousand years were finished. This is the first resurrection" (Revelation 20:5). The second resurrection is the judgment of non-Christians (including Muslims) according to the Old Testament law, and the New Testament is clear that "therefore by the deeds of the law there shall no flesh be justified in his sight: for by the law is the knowledge of sin" (Romans 3:20). For this reason, we believe Islam is a false hope. Only by confessing "Jesus is Lord" and "I am a sinner" while believing that He died for your sins and rose from the dead is sufficient (1 Corinthians 15:3–7). That gospel fundamentally disagrees with the Qur'an.

Belief in the Day of Judgment is one of the six *aqīdah* ("articles of faith") in Sunni Islam. This is seen in the Qur'an: "It is not righteousness that you turn your faces towards the East and the West, but righteousness is this that one should believe in Allah and the last day."[504] In fact, belief in the last day is the second of the five pillars of Islam, making eschatology more central to Islam than Christianity and Judaism.

The Qur'an is quite limited in its discussion of the "day of judgment" and, as a result, the majority of eschatological details come from the more questionable Hadith literature.[505] Complicating matters, the Hadiths are hearsay statements reported from those who allegedly overheard Muhammad say "such and so," and would probably not even be admitted into a US court of law. A scholar of the Islamic religion who has written an authoritative comparison of Christian and Muslim eschatology, Dr. Samuel Shahid, wrote concerning the Hadith, "There is no assurance or guarantee that all the information cited here is accurate or trustworthy. Muslim scholars admit that a sizable volume of the hadith is spurious."[506] Some Hadith traditions are rather easily debunked.

For instance, Shahid makes sport of a wacky Hadith that claims actually the Jews conquer Constantinople by walking around it like the Israelites were instructed to do at the fall of Jericho in the Hebrew Bible (Joshua 5:13–6:27).

On the authority of Abu Huraya related that the hour would not come until seventy thousands of the children of Isaac (the Jews) invade Constantinople without employing any type of arms. All of its fortified walls would fall by praises and the call of "God is greater." Based on the historical account, Constantinople was conquered by the Ottoman dynasty (Turks) in the fifteenth century and not by Arabs. Secondly, the contradiction between the two traditions is obvious since the Children of Isaac has nothing to do with the conquest of Constantinople. Thirdly, it seems more that the narrator of this tradition was historically confused that he failed to differentiate between the episodes of the fall of Jericho as it is recorded in chapter six of the book of Joshua and the myth of the conquest of Constantinople. Such contradiction and confusion suggest that this tradition was a late fabrication by the narrators who sought to amaze their audience. Most probably, they heard the biblical story from some Jewish friends and weaved it into the fabric of their tradition.[507]

We believe that critique explains the majority of Islamic eschatology coming from the Hadith. From the ever-dubious Hadith, the Islamic portents of the end-times are derived.

There are many signs that are said to precede the Day of Judgment. Muslim scholars divide these in the minor (lesser) signs and the major (greater) signs.[508] The minor signs are "are moral, cultural, political, religious, and natural events designed to warn humanity that the end is near and to bring people into a state of repentance."[509] They are nearly universal, and it is relatively easy to find "fulfillments" of these so-called omens. Muslims believe many of them are already fulfilled, while qualifying that some have begun but not yet concluded. The major signs comprise a more precise template by which the discerning student may supposedly derive the lateness of the hour on the end-time clock. Cook explains, "They detail a series of events of ever-increasing severity that will precede the end of the world, at which time the damned will be judged and the blessed will begin to taste the pleasures God has in store for them in heaven."[510] We will briefly review the excess of minor signs and then we'll look at the ten, more specific, major signs.

The Minor Signs

Minor signs can be bifurcated into normal events that seem to plague most modernizing cultures and truly extraordinary events that are said to be heralds of the apocalypse.[511] The formula for all the minor signs listed begins with "the last hour will not occur until…". Accordingly, number 4 below reads, "The last hour will not occur until earthquakes increase." Thus, one should assume that phrase for each numbered sign.

The normal signs include: 1) the increase of ignorance of Islam and betrayal of Muslim daily religious rituals; 2) the pervasiveness of alcohol consumption; 3) an increase in apostasy as many are deceived by the Muslim "antichrist" known as the *Dajjal;* 4) an increase in earthquakes;[512] 5) a population in which women will outnumber men; 6) corruption of political leaders; 7) the building of lavish mosques; 8) the desire of death for many people; 9) Muslim countries imitating the actions of non-Islamic nations (e.g., Turkey's bid for the EU status); 10) a large number of casualties resulting from a major internal war within Islam (e.g., the Sunni/Shia conflict); 11) the appearance of a man from Qahtan appears, who may be the Mahdi (in some South Arabian traditions); 12) the appearance of thirty to forty false prophets, four of whom are women; 13) instances of some Muslims murdering their leader (many caliphs have been assassinated throughout history); 14) many Muslims questioning their faith; 15) the rise of the final caliphate (the claim of the IS) and its establishment in Jerusalem; 16) the destruction of many of the Arabs; 17) the expansion of *Ihab* to *Yahab* (ancient locations in the suburbs of Medina; people reject the Divine Decree of destiny (the Islamic doctrine of predestination, e.g.,Qur'an 22:70); 18) the defeat of the crusaders at Allepo or Dabiq, Syria (The IS's trademark prophecy, e.g., *Sahih Muslim*, 6924);[513] 19) the conquering of Constantinople (a seeming absurdity, given that today's Istanbul is already Muslim); 20) the peaceful death of Muslim believers, leaving only the wicked on earth (seems to parallel the Rapture); 21) the destruction of the city of Mecca and the plundering of the Ka'ba'. It's interesting that IS has threatened to bring this to pass as well.[514]

The extraordinary signs are *much* stranger, and, if they were to occur, such events would draw many to believe in Islamic prophecy. The signs classified as extraordinary include: 1) the appearance of people who eat with their tongues like cows[515] (no explanation is given, but they seem to be different sort of entity than a regular human); 2) the contraction of time: a year is like a month, a month like a week, a week like a day, and a day like an hour[516] (Shahid contends this clumsily borrows from Matthew 24:22);[517] 3) wild beasts speaking to men;[518] 4) the Euphrates River uncovering a mountain of gold and people fighting over it.[519] Shahid points out how this parallels the drying-up of the Euphrates in this passage in the biblical Apocalypse: "And the sixth angel poured out his vial upon the great river Euphrates; and the water thereof was dried up, that the way of the kings of the east might be prepared" (Revelation 16:12). Running for approximately 1,728 miles from the northwest to the southeast, the Euphrates was classically viewed as a dividing line between East and West.[520] As this suggests, many of these signs are borrowed from the much-older Christian prophecies, especially the "beginning of sorrows" listed by Jesus in the KJV or called the "birth pains" in modern versions (Matthew 24:8). The following table compares the birth pains to some of the minor signs.

Christian Birth Pains	Muslim Minor Signs
"And ye shall hear of wars and rumours of wars: see that ye be not troubled: for all these things must come to pass, but the end is not yet" (Matthew 24:6).	Muslims assassinate their leader, fight amongst themselves, etc. 'Alim, *Sunnan of al-Tirmdhi*, #1435. Many wars are listed as signs: Dabiq, Constantinople, Jerusalem, Saudi Arabia, Rome, etc.
Famine: "For nation shall rise against nation, and kingdom against kingdom: and there shall be famines, and pestilences, and earthquakes, in divers places" (Matthew 24:7).	"stricken with famine, calamity, and the oppression of rulers" *Sunan Ibn Maajah*, # 4019
Pestilence: "For nation shall rise against nation, and kingdom against kingdom: and there shall be famines, and pestilences, and earthquakes, in divers places" (Matthew 24:7).	"afflicted by plagues and diseases unknown to their forefathers" *Sunan Ibn Maajah*, # 4019

Christian Birth Pains	Muslim Minor Signs
Earthquakes: "For nation shall rise against nation, and kingdom against kingdom: and there shall be famines, and pestilences, and earthquakes, in divers places" (Matthew 24:7).	"Abundance of earthquakes" Sahih Bukhari Volume 9, Book 88, # 237
"And then shall many be offended, and shall betray one another, and shall hate one another" (Matthew 24:10).	"The liar is believed, the truthful is called a liar and the honest is called a traitor." *Sunan At-Tirmidhi,* # 2209
"And many false prophets shall rise, and shall deceive many" (Matthew 24: 11).	"coming of 30 dajjals" 'Alim, *Sunnan of Abi Dawud,* Book 37, # 4319
"And because iniquity shall abound, the love of many shall wax cold" (Matthew 24:12).	"honourable people will perish and dishonourable people would prevail" Mujamma'uz-Zawaa'id, Book 7, # 327
"And this gospel of the kingdom shall be preached in all the world for a witness unto all nations; and then shall the end come" (Matthew 24:14).	The arrival of the Dajjal

The parallels to the biblical text are ubiquitous, but they demonstrably reflect borrowing rather than a true supernatural correspondence as some Islamic Antichrist theorists assert. Muslims apply the same flawed Qur'anic methodology applied to the Hebrew Bible's chosen seed when Isaac is swapped for Ishmael. Creative Hadith cobblers reversed roles in the Olivet Discourse (Mark 13) and the book of Revelation while redacting and condensing the original material heavily. In a literary sense, the

Dajjal corresponds to Jesus' prediction, "And many false prophets shall rise, and shall deceive many" (Matthew 24:11). Of course, we Christians believe Islam is false. Naturally, Islamic Antichrist proponents are fond of the Muslim's *Dajjal* being the *actual* Jesus Christ—our Messiah and returning King.

That near direct borrowing by the Hadith composers supports our plagiarism explanation for the correspondences. However, it does seem ironic that, if realized, it must be the case that their *false* messiah could be a friend to Christians *but not necessarily.* Joel Richardson offers the idea the Muslims will label the real Jesus the Dajjal when he does not confirm Islam as expected, making him a perfect deceiver in Muslim eyes.[521] But it's more likely the case of the Hadith being spurious Islamic pseudepigrapha. It seems more likely that the bitter Sunni/Shia split will prompt many inevitable Dajjal claims. Our opinion carries weight in that Mahdists require a Dajjal for their narrative to be coherent. It follows that his appearance is necessary for the current Mahdism (like the IS) to survive. We believe the Iraqi military with Western air support could eliminate the IS, but Mahdism will survive. It suggests a reasonable explanation for why Israel's neighbors attack Jerusalem at Armageddon.

In Islamic eschatology, a messianic figure known as the Mahdi will appear before the arrival of Jesus and the Day of Judgment to rid the world of corruption and establish Islam as the global religion. Some place the Mahdi's arrival as the middle point between the minor and major signs, but many assert him as the first major sign. Chris White explains, "The Mahdi is said to unite the Muslim world to fight several battles, including the conquest of Constantinople. He shares the wealth that he acquires through conquest with the people. He rules the world for five, seven, eight, nine, or nineteen years (Islamic sources differ) before Isa returns."[522] As we have documented, Mahdism fuels the IS and other such apocalyptic death cults, but there is disagreement as to exactly where the Mahdi falls in the sign classification theology. The

Hadith we studied list ten major signs and do not mention the Mahdi, a dubious fact that suggests the major sign narrative preceded knowledge of any such "rightly guided one." Furthermore, there is a profound incoherence with the minor sign, "The last day shall not arrive until the Muslim believers die peacefully leaving only the wicked on earth"[523] and "Mecca is turned into ruins"[524] (both minor signs) with the idea that the Mahdi makes the whole world Muslim. The signs seem to exclude each other. Of course, this reflects the dubious scholarship inherent to the Hadith.

Imminence of the Mahdi

According to Islamic tradition, the Mahdi's tenure will coincide with the Second Coming of Jesus Christ, who is to assists the Mahdi against the Dajjal (Antichrist). Some sources list the Mahidi as the first of the major signs and others leave him out. For example, in a modern book, *The Signs before the Day of Judgement,* Ibn Kathir wrote:

> After the lesser signs of the Hour appear and increase, mankind will have reached a stage of great suffering. Then the awaited Mahdee will appear; *he is the first of the greater, and clear, signs of the Hour.* There will be no doubt about his existence, but this will only be clear to the knowledgeable people. The Mahdee will rule until the False Messiah (al-Maseeh ad-Dajjaal) appears, who will spread oppression and corruption. The only ones who will know him well and avoid his evil will be those who have great knowledge and *Eemaan* (Arabic "faith").[525] (emphasis added)

It's not very surprising that Middle Easterners believe the Mahdi's arrival is imminent. In Iraq and Syria, most Christians are experiencing tribulation and many gruesome abominations that make what was once holy, desolate. Increasingly, Muslims of both houses are claiming the fulfillment of Islamic beliefs about the end times. The Pew Forum surmised, "In nine of the 23 nations where the question was asked, half or more of Muslim adults say they believe the return of the Mahdi will occur in their lifetime, including at least two-thirds who express this view in Afghanistan (83%), Iraq (72%), Turkey (68%) and Tunisia (67%)."[526] From this data, Furnish argues, "Mahdism must be taken seriously as an intellectual, sociological and even political strain within the entire Islamic world—not dismissed as archaic, mystical nonsense. In addition, the good, the bad and the ugly faces of Mahdism throughout history need to be considered—political correctness be damned."[527] It seems fair to say that well over half of the Middle East is preparing for the apocalypse in one form or another (is this merely coincidence?); the question then becomes which eschatological scenario one subscribes to.

Interestingly, the Pew Forum also employed Professor Emeritus of Near Eastern Studies at Princeton University, Bernard Lewis, to conduct research on American perceptions of Islam. Lewis has often been described as the West's greatest historian and interpreter of Islam. Lewis writes:

> Surveys we have done with the Pew Research Center find that only 4 out of ten Americans have a favorable view of Islam, and unfavorable views in this country are driven by what many perceive to be a close association between Islam and violence. It is a sobering fact, as our survey from last summer revealed, that more than half of the American public now believes the terrorist attacks over the last few years are, or soon will be, part of a major civilizational conflict between Islam and the West.[528]

It seems like Armageddon is written into humanity's collective consciousness. While most readers likely recall Harold Camping's failed Rapture date, a major Sunni website has already set dates: "Based on our numerical analysis of the Quran and Hadith, the official beginning of the End of Time and the coming of the Imam Mahdi will most likely be in…2016 and Jesus Christ (p) will come down from Heaven to Earth in 2022, in-sha Allah (if Allah is willing)."[529] While date setting has a 100 percent failure rate so far, we find it indicative of the rise in Sunni Mahdism now under examination. Eschatological hope is in the air in all so-called "Abrahamic" religions.

Major Signs

While lacking the contextual specificity necessary to construct a viable sequence, the Hadith describes the end-time events leading up to the Day of Judgment through ten major (greater) signs known as *alamatu's-sa'ah al- kubra* ("the major signs of the end"). Islamic scholars are in wide agreement that none of these major signs has yet happened.

> The Prophet said, "The last hour will not arrive till you have seen ten signs. He then mentioned the Smoke, Dajjal, Beast, Rising of the Sun from the place of its setting, the Descent of Isa, Ya'juj Ma'juj, Three Landslides: one in the East , one in the West and one in the Arabian Peninsula, after that a Fire would spread from Yemen and drive the people to their place of gathering." (Muslim)

This comes from a collection of Hadīths compiled by Imām Muslim ibn al-Hajjāj al-Naysāburi (rahimahullāh). His collection is considered to be one of the most authentic collections of the Sunnah of the Prophet.[530] Another, more obscure, Hadith contains remarkably similar major signs:

> Major signs are events of extraordinary nature prophesied by our Prophet (PBUH) to take place before Qiyamah like all the events mentioned in the following Hadith narrated by Hudhaifa ibn Usayd that the Prophet (PBUH) said, "The last hour will not

arrive till you have seen ten signs." The Prophet (PBUH) then mentioned the Smoke; Dajjal, Beast, Rising of the Sun from the West, the Descent of Isa, Yajuj Majuj (Gog and Magog), Three sinking of the earth where an earthquake swallows an entire city, earthquake sinking in the East, one earthquake sinking in the West and one earthquake sinking in Saudi Arabia between Madina and Mecca. Let me clarify the East and West earthquake. This prediction was given in the time of our Beloved Prophet (PBUH) so West here means to the West of Mecca, Saudi Arabia and East means to the East of Mecca, Saudi Arabia and the final is that a Fire would spread from Yemen and drive the people to their place of gathering (Assembly). (Sahi Muslim, Tirmidhi, Abu Dawud).[531]

Sunnis rank this collection of Hadiths by Abu Dawudas fourth in veracity out of their six major Hadith collections.[532] But its correspondence with the Imam Muslim collection gains it theological weight amongst Muslim scholars. Interestingly, neither mentions the Mahid. Thus, the ten major signs are:

1. The Dajjal will appear as a one-eyed man. He displays supernatural signs and will claim to be God and to hold keys to heaven and hell. He will lead many astray, although believers will not be deceived. The Dajjal would be followed by seventy thousand Jews.
2. The return of Isa (Jesus) from the sky to kill the Dajjal.
3. *Ya'jooj* and *Ma'jooj* (Gog and Magog), two tribes of vicious beings which had been imprisoned by *Dhul-Qarnayn,* will break out. They will ravage the earth, drink all the water of Lake Tiberias, and kill all believers in their way (or see). Isa, the Mahdi, and the believers with them will go to a mountaintop to pray for the destruction of Gog and Magog. Allah will eventually send disease and worms to destroy them.
4. A huge black smoke cloud will cover the earth.

5. *Dabbat al-ard* ("the Beast") will come out of the ground to talk to people.
6. The sun rises from the west.
7. Three massive sink holes open up in the earth: one in the east,
8. One in the west,
9. And one in Arabia.
10. The last trumpet will be sounded, the dead will return to life, and a fire will start in Yemen that will force everyone to gather all to *Mahshar Al Qiyamah* ("The Gathering for Judgment").

It seems strange that the Mahdi is not listed as a major sign, but we explain in the next chapter why *The Last Roman Emperor Becomes the Muslim's Mahdi* (we believe the Mahdi is based on a later Christian pseudepigraphal work, and that such a belief was foreign in Muhammad's day). A popular explanation is that the Mahdi appears just prior to the arrival of the Dajjal (the first of the ten major signs).

According to Furnish, "Contra conventional wisdom in the field, belief in the Mahdi, is as vital in Sunni as in Shi'i Islam."[533] Much attention has been focused on Iran, likely because of former President Mahmoud Ahmadinejad's frequent statements to the news media indicating his personal belief in the Mahdi's imminent return. While such certainly plays well with young males in the Iranian voter demographic, this has led to an overemphasis of Shi'ite belief in an occulted twelfth Imam when it is actually radicalized Sunnis (like the IS) who are actively attempting to bring end-time prophecy to pass. Furnish argues, "I would maintain that IS atrocities like the beheading of James Foley and the mass murders of Shi`is and Yazidis are, in effect, 'bizarre rituals intended to bring about the end of the world'—or at least to spark the Mahdi's coming. I truly think that IS has passed into the realm of trying to hotwire the apocalypse."[534] Furnish makes a compelling case.

Shia and Sunni Mahdism

Very good

Joel C. Rosenberg is the author of many bestsellers featuring Islam in an apocalyptic setting: *The Last Jihad, The Last Days, The Ezekiel Option, The Copper Scroll, Dead Heat, The Twelfth Imam, The Tehran Initiative, Damascus Countdown, The Auschwitz Escape,* and *The Third Target.* Don't confuse Rosenberg with Joel Richardson, author of *The Islamic Antichrist,* a nonfiction eschatological argument that connects Islamic and biblical prophecy. In contrast, Rosenberg writes mostly fiction based on real current events. A sample of his latest novel, *The First Hostage,* features the Islamic State:

> With these words, *New York Times* journalist J. B. Collins, reporting from the scene of a devastating attack by ISIS terrorists in Amman, Jordan, puts the entire world on high alert. The leaders of Israel and Palestine are critically injured, Jordan's king is fighting for his life, and the US president is missing and presumed captured.
>
> As the US government faces a constitutional crisis and Jordan battles for its very existence, Collins must do his best to keep the world informed while working to convince the FBI that his stories are not responsible for the terror attack on the Jordanian capital. And ISIS still has chemical weapons.[535]

Of course, Rosenberg's work incorporates the latest Middle-East news in a captivating style that has resonated with American readers. In the past, his books focused on Iran and Shia Islam, so it is of note to read that he has now incorporated the more mouth-foamingly rabid, Sunni Mahdism of the IS.

Shia is a branch of Islam that holds that Muhammad's proper successor was his son-in-law and cousin Ali ibn Abi Talib, who ruled over the Islamic caliphate from AD 656 to 661.[536] While Sunnis consider Ali the fourth and final of the rightly guided caliphs, Shias regard Ali as the first Imam after Muhammad. Shias also believe that Ali and the other Shia Imams (all of whom are members of the Ahl al-Bayt, Muhammad's household) are the rightful successors to Muhammad. This disagreement split the Muslim community into the Sunni and Shi'i branches.

The term "Twelver" refers to Shia's belief in twelve divinely appointed Imams (leaders of Islam), and their belief that the last Imam, Muhammad al-Mahdi, was occulted (mysteriously disappeared) and will reappear as the prophesized Mahdi. Shia only consists of around 10 percent of the world's Muslim population.[537] Since the overthrow of Iran's secular government in 1979, Shiite Ayatollah Ruhollah Khomeini has held control. He is credited with planning the first suicide bomb attacks in 1982, which inspired Hezbollah in Lebanon to cite Surah 9:111 and to promote the mythological martyrs paradise staffed with seventy-two celestial virgins as a distinctly Persian eschatology. Like the papal indulgence, the perverse promise has led uncounted thousands of starry-eyed adolescents into hell. In 2012, 85 percent of Shias were estimated to be Twelvers.[538]

In contrast, most Sunnis believe that Muhammad's father-in-law, Abu Bakr, was his proper successor. Until the United States invaded Iraq, the Sunnis looked down their noses at enthusiastic apocalypticism as being a predominately Shia error. Jean-Pierre Filiu has argued that most modern Sunni Muslims viewed apocalyptic thinking with suspicion before the United States invaded Iraq, but the 2003 "new crusade," War on Terror, changed everything. William McCants, a Brookings Institute scholar of Near Eastern Studies,[539] wrote:

> The US invasion of Iraq and the stupendous violence that followed dramatically increased the Sunni public's appetite for apocalyptic explanations of a world turned upside down. A spate of bestsellers put the United States at the center of the End-Times drama, a new "Rome" careering throughout the region

in a murderous stampede to prevent violence on its own shores. The main antagonists of the End of Days, the Jews, were now merely supporting actors. Even conservative Sunni clerics who had previously tried to tamp down messianic fervor couldn't help but conclude that "the triple union constituted by the Antichrist, the Jews, and the new Crusaders"[540] had joined forces "to destroy the Muslims."[541]

The Iraq war also changed apocalyptic discourse in the global jihadist movement. The languid apocalypticism of Osama bin Laden and Ayman al-Zawahiri now had to contend with the urgent apocalypticism of Abu Mus'ab al-Zarqawi, the founder of al-Qaeda in Iraq, and his immediate successors. Iraq, the site of a prophesied bloodbath between true Muslims and false, was engulfed in a sectarian civil war. As Zarqawi saw it, the Shi'a had united with the Jews and Christians under the banner of the Antichrist to fight against the Sunnis. The Final Hour must be approaching, to be heralded by the rebirth of the caliphate, the Islamic empire that had disappeared and whose return was prophesied.[542]

Of course the War on Terror did not end when President Obama kept his necessarily uninformed campaign promise to bring home the troops. In fact, US national interest in the Middle East is far worse now than it was in 2003. Of course, it depends on what one believes our national interest actually is; as Bernard Lewis pointed out, it was defined as the "prevention of the emergence of a regional hegemony—of a single regional power that could dominate the area and thus establish monopolistic control of Middle Eastern oil"[543] and not the spread of democracy and Western values. Bush and Obama's revisionism aside, it is *inextricably* related to Islam. The success of the IS is a byproduct of Shia/Sunni tensions and the Mahdist uprising amongst Sunnis in response to the US invasion of Iraq and Afghanistan and a bungled exit strategy.

Recalling the recent scientific survey by the Pew Research Center that revealed that at least half of all Muslims in the Middle East, North Africa, and South Asia expect the imminent appearance of the Mahdi, groups like the IS should not surprise us.[544] The Mahdi—whom they believe is alive today—is a Muslim political leader who Islamifies the world. In accepting that belief, almost anything goes to pave the way. Hence, the recent horrors in Jerusalem involving meat-cleaver attacks are absolved by definition.[545] The original founder of the IS believed the Mahdi's return was so soon, he ordered the infrastructure necessary for his global inauguration. McCants pointed out that as far back as 2006 (!), "Masri ordered his men to build pulpits for the Mahdi to ascend in the Prophet's mosque in Medina, the Umayyad Mosque in Damascus, and the Aqsa Mosque in Jerusalem."[546] Whether Islamic prophecy truly predicts the future or not, does not change the fact that millions of passionate believers and jihadi turned Mahdists (like Abu Musab al-Zarqawi) are desperately trying to bring it to pass—a state of affairs that seems apocalyptic, in and of itself, given today's geopolitics. Sahid has pointed out an outside influence from Persia.

> In Yatrib, city of the Prophet, Muhammad was more exposed to the Jews, the Christians, the Zoroastrians, or former adherents of these religions who were converted to Islam. But the impact of Christianity and Zoroastrianism on the Islamic eschatology was far more dominant than Judaism. In the eschatological realm the Jews, and the person of the Antichrist, manifested the forces of evil.[547]

Sunni's distinguish themselves from Persian (Shias), but Persian Zoroastrian influence also led to the myth of seventy-two virgins for the carnal indulgence suicide bombers in Paradise, leading many popular reference books to deny it.[548]

While both houses of Islam expect the Mahdi's arrival, Sunni and Shi'ite Islam have different beliefs concerning his identity. The Shi'ite "Twelvers" continue the line through other descendants of Ali to Muhammad al-Mahdi, the twelfth imam. Furnish disabuses a popular misconception that the Shi'ites dominate the field,

Even among scholars there is a stereotype that Mahdism is chiefly a Shi'i phenomenon, whereas in reality throughout Islamic history most Mahdist movements have sprung from the brows of charismatic Sunni holy men with an axe to grind against a usually Islamic regime. [549]

Furnish sounds an ominous warning, "Mahdism is much more likely to occur, and as the province of freelancers in Sunnism—and this is exactly what history demonstrates." [550]

And make no mistake: Mahdists would have even fewer constraints on their behaviour than do jihadis. Since the end result of the Mahdi's plans would be, they believe, a global caliphate nothing he asked would be beyond his followers: detonating a nuke in Vegas or Manhattan, intentionally infecting oneself with plague or smallpox and then criss-crossing American aiports, suicide-bombing Christian day care centers in the Midwest. Helping the Mahdi restore Islam to planetary predominance would obtain one even more glory than the promised 72 huris in Paradise. [551]

Historically, Sunni Islam has derived religious authority from the caliphate, who was in turn appointed by the companions of Muhammad at his death. The Sunnis view the Mahdi as the successor of Mohammad, the Mahdi is expected to arrive and establish global Sharia law.

Mahdists of both houses believe his arrival to be imminent. The arrival of the Mahdi is the first sign of the third and final period of Islamic eschatology. One of the leading Muslim scholars of the fourteenth century. Ismail Abu Al-Fadl' Umar ibn Kathir, was educated chiefly in Damascus, initially specializing in the study of Hadith. As a Syrian scholar, he would have been very familiar with extrabiblical Christian apocalyptic texts like the *Apocalypse of Pseudo-Methodius*. Even in Islam, the Mahdi does not really replace Jesus, he paves the way for Him. The next chapter will examine the origins of the Mahdi legend from Syrian Christian pseudepigrapha.

10

The Last Roman Emperor
Becomes the Muslims' Mahdi

MAHDISM HAS CHANGED the landscape of geopolitics by providing an outlet for disenfranchised Sunnis in Iraq and Syria. The dramatic declaration of the worldwide caliphate following the US withdrawal in 2014 under Abu Bakr al-Baghdadi, a public persona adopted by Ibrahim Awwad Ibrahim Al-Badri an Islamic religious scholar who turned Mahdist when the US invaded Iraq, was staged for propaganda purposes. We believe this to be so because they had actually declared statehood in 2006,[552] but, back then, they were not taken very seriously.

Sayf al-Adl, and Jordanian hooligan, Abu Mus'ab al-Zarqawi wrote of his plan to create the end of days, "caliphate according to the prophetic method."[553]

> After the United States killed Zarqawi on June 7, 2006, al-Qaeda in Iraq carried out its leader's dying wish. Rather than wait to establish the Islamic state until after the Americans withdrew and the Sunni masses backed the project, as Bin Laden and Zawahiri wanted, the Islamic State was proclaimed on October 15, 2006.[554]

Abu Ayyub al-Masri took over al-Qaeda in Iraq after Zarqawi died in June 2006, only to dissolve the group a few months later when the Islamic State was declared. According to the Islamic State's chief judge, Masri rushed to establish the State because he believed the Mahdi, the Muslim savior, would come within the year. To his thinking, the caliphate needed to be in place to help the Mahdi fight the final battles of the Apocalypse. Anticipating the imminent conquest of major Islamic cities as foretold in the prophecies, Masri ordered his men to build pulpits for the Mahdi to ascend in the prophet's mosque in Medina, the Umayyad Mosque in Damascus, and the Aqsa Mosque in Jerusalem.[555]

It is beyond dispute that Islam—especially in light of recent atrocities to the Holy Land—is a major factor in analyzing the Middle East, geopolitically and prophetically. The world awakened to the existential threat as the recent synchronized attacks in Paris and the IS' suicide bomber planted on a Russian Airliner in retaliation to recent airstrikes by the Russian Air Force illustrated. "Metrojet Flight 9268 crashed Saturday in Egypt's Sinai Peninsula after breaking apart in midair, killing all 224 people on board."[556] The IS claimed responsibility for the crash via twitter within hours of what now appears to be a suicide bombing.[557]

A few hasty analysts dismissed the IS' claim, but they overlooked the possibility that a "can bomb" was the IS' means. Reliable sources have confirmed the IS' culpability. At the end of 2015, "The latest US intelligence suggests that the crash was most likely caused by a bomb planted on the plane by ISIS or an affiliate, according to multiple US officials who spoke with CNN."[558]

Two-thirds of the Afghan and Iraqi populations self-identify as such Mahdists and envision the rise of a medieval-style caliphate, enforcing worldwide Sharia law—and the IS claims to be that caliphate. Mahdists are willing to martyr themselves, and Russia is offering no quarter. The latest reports state; "Russia has reportedly refused to rule out using nuclear weapons in its fight against ISIS."[559] Given the ongoing proxy war between the US and Russia over Assad in Syria, a palatable chance exists that World War Three could very well be the net result of today's policies. While chances are slim that the exegetical historiography that follows will dissuade the committed Mahdist, we sincerely hope it will put a "stone in the shoe" of those who ascribe preternatural prescience to dubious Hadith-based eschatology. Our position is quite simple: Early associates of Muhammad and their adherents plagiarized the eschatology of the day, a period of time when Damascus and Constantinople were centers of world religion and before the Ottoman Empire conquered Constantinople, transforming into it into a premiere Muslim civilization in regard to peaceful trade.

Islamic eschatology becomes terribly ironic once one faces the evidence that the "rightly guided one" Muslims revere as the Mahdi is nothing but a plagiarized character from Syrian pseudapigrapha—a legend of seventh-century Syrian Christianity, which is a mainstay in Roman Catholicism to this day. The story of Mahdi is not really from Muhammad; he is borrowed from a Syrian apocalypse. In fact, the evidence that the Mahdi is a fictional pilferage is strong enough to have inspired scholarly monographs.[560] This chapter will show why in all probability the Mahdi is a Muslim version of the popular "Last Roman Emperor"(who arguably developed into the "Holy Pope" legend) who had become legendary in medieval eschatology. It all stemmed from the *Apocalypse of Methodius*, an alleged last-days prophecy attributed to the late third-century Christian Church Father and St. Methodius of Olympus (died c. 311) bishop, biblical scholar-theologian, and martyr.

The Syriac Apocalypse of Pseudo-Methodius

The Syriac *Apocalypse of Pseudo-Methodius* is honored as the crown of Eastern Christian apocalyptic literature, but it is falsely attributed.[561] The real Methodius was an active Christian apologist and churchman who was martyred in the early fourth century (ca. 313). During his day, he was primarily concerned with the hotly debated theological controversies of his time, like the nature of Christ and the Trinity. Methodius was especially repulsed by the heresies of Origen. Even though today there is little doubt the Apocalypse was falsely attributed to him, it was widely accepted as authentic for centuries.

In *History of Apocalypse*, self-described agnostic sceptic,[562] Catalin Negru, describes the last Roman emperor:

> The reign of this emperor is characterized by great wealth, victory over the enemies of Christendom, the end of paganism and the conversion of the Jews. After he will defeat Gog and Magog "he will come to Jerusalem, and, taking off the tiara from his head and all the imperial clothes off his body, he will let the empire of the Christians to God the Father and to Jesus Christ His Son."[563]

In this way, the emperor will give free passage to the Antichrist:

> At that time the prince of injustice, who will be called the "Antichrist," will rise from the tribe of Dan. He will be the Son of Perdition and the culmination of pride, the master of great wonders and signs made through lies, He will deceive many through the art of magic so that he will appear [to] call fire from the sky.... When the Roman Empire will fall, then the Antichrist will show himself and he will sit in the House of God in Jerusalem.[564]
>
> The prophecy says that the Antichrist will be challenged by the two witnesses of the Apocalypse, Elijah and Enoch, but he will destroy them and he will begin a final persecution against Christians, until "he will be killed through the power of the Lord by Michael the Archangel on the Mount of Olives."[565] The pseudo-prophecy of the Tiburtine Sibyl was a source of inspiration for the Apocalypse of Pseudo-Methodius. This was written

in Syriac toward the end of the 7th century as a reaction to the Islamic conquests in the Near East, and it was falsely assigned to Methodius of Olympus in order to gain credibility.[566]

Scholars attribute the introduction of the Last Roman Emperor to the *Sibylline Oracles*. For example, *OrthodoxWiki*, a web-based encyclopaedia for Orthodox Christianity, notes: "The Tiburtine Sibyl, was a Roman sibyl (meaning "prophetess"), whose seat was the ancient Etruscan town of Tibur (modern Tivoli). An apocalyptic pseudo-prophecy exists among the Sibylline Oracles, attributed to the Tiburtine Sibyl, written ca. 380 AD, but with revisions and interpolations added at later dates. It purports to prophesy the advent in the world's ninth age of a final Emperor vanquishing the foes of Christianity."[567] The anonymous author of the *Apocalypse* likely borrowed from this popular Sibylline prophetic literature.

As the following citation demonstrates, the cobbled-together prophecy does have some uncanny descriptions of end-time culture that seem ripped right from today's headlines, and Islam is certainly the major geopolitical source of conflict facing the modern world. It was an extremely influential book and the messianic emperor is ubiquitous in Roman Catholic writings. After the canonical books Daniel and Revelation, it was among the most accepted medieval apocalyptic texts. Setting the issue of provenance aside, the following passage is rather chilling.

The Muslim Crisis

In the final seventh millennium the Persian Empire will be wiped out. In this seventh millennium the seed of Ishmael will begin to go forth from the desert of Ethribus. When they have gone forth, they will all assemble at the great Gaboath and there will be completed the saying of Ezekiel the prophet: "Son of man," he said, "call the beasts of the field and the birds of the air and exhort them saying, 'Gather yourselves together and come since I will give you a great sacrifice, to eat the flesh of strong men and drink the blood of the mighty'" (Ezek. 39:17)... And so the Lord God will give them (i.e. the sons of Ishmael) the power to conquer the land of the Christians, not because he loves them, but because of the sin and iniquity committed by the Christians. Such sins have not nor shall be committed for all generations. Men will get themselves up as false women wearing prostitutes' clothes. Standing in the streets and squares of the cities openly before all they will be adorned like women; they will exchange natural sex for that which is against nature. As the blessed and holy Apostle says, "men have acted like women" (Rom. 1:26–7). A father, his son, his brothers, and all the relatives will be seen to unite with one woman....

For this reason they will be given over by God into the hands of the barbarians from whom they will sink into all uncleanness and stink of pollution. Their women will be contaminated by filthy barbarians and the sons of Ishmael will cast lots for their sons and daughters. The land of the Persians is handed over to corruption and destruction, its inhabitants led away to captivity and death. They also attack Armenia and those who dwell there fall into captivity by the sword... *The land of Syria will be empty and reduced; those dwelling in her will perish by the sword....Egypt and the East and Syria will be under the yoke and hemmed in by great tribulations.* They will be constrained without mercy; weight of gold and silver beyond their strength will be eagerly desired of them. *The inhabitants of Egypt and Syria will be in trouble and affliction, seven times the greater for those in captivity.* The Land of Promise will be filled with men from the four winds under heaven. (Translated from E. Sackur, *Sibyllinische Texte*, pp. 80–83, emphasis added.)[568]

One is initially taken aback by the correspondence to the current moral climate, but upon reflection, it is just as prescient spiritually and geopolitically. It seems fair to suggest that the seventh-century author was describing a genuine end-time vision. We will not rigorously argue the case that it is a divine revelation, but something more akin to a precognitive dream. Of course, such moral preaching applies more today than ever, and this text laments the flaunting and acceptance of homosexuality as the primary injunction against God's people, describing the failure in modern morality, which undermines the nuclear family unit as the building block of society.

If one were to accept Methodius as the actual author, his fretting over Muslims—who would not exist for several more centuries—is extremely suspicious. It also recounts Muslim history from the decades just prior to the best estimate of its province, a dead giveaway of the real authors' historical context. The answer is easy enough when we understand that not one single copy predates the seventh-century Syriac version. Prescience aside, Methodius of Olympus did not write this revelation, but rather an anonymous but clever medieval author composed it. Methodius, the fourth-century Christian, was still blissfully ignorant concerning the "sons of Ishmael." For this reason, scholars are in agreement that it is an anonymous seventh-century Syrian pseudepigriphal (falsely attributed) work.

Prophecy of the Last World Emperor

It is often assumed that Catholic eschatology follows the biblical outline presented in Daniel and Revelation. However, there are significant differences due to their necessary emphasis on ongoing revelation. One such development is the "Last World Emperor" or "Great Catholic Monarch." Also called the "Last Roman Emperor," he is a figure of medieval European legend, who developed as an aspect of early apocalyptic literature. He first appears in the *Apocalypse of Pseudo-Methodius*.

255

The Last World Emperor

Then suddenly tribulation and distress will arise against them. The king of the Greeks, i.e. the Romans, will come out against them in great anger, roused as from a drunken stupor like one whom men had thought dead and worthless (Ps. 77:65). He will go forth against them from the Ethiopian sea and will send the sword and desolation into Ethribus their homeland, capturing their women and children living in the Land of Promise. The sons of the king will come down with the sword and cut them off from the earth. Fear and trembling will rush upon them and their wives and their children from all sides. They will mourn their offspring, weeping over them and all the villages in the lands of their fathers. By the sword they will be given over into the hands of the king of the Romans—to captivity, death, and decay.

The king of the Romans will impose his yoke upon them seven times as much as their yoke weighed upon the earth. Great distress will seize them; tribulation will bring them hunger and thirst. They, their wives, and their children will be slaves and serve those who used to serve them, and their slavery will be a hundred times more bitter and hard. The earth which they destitute will then be at peace; each man will return to his own land and to the inheritance of his fathers—Armenia, Cilicia, Isauria, Africa, Greece, Sicily. Every man who was left captive will return to the things that were his and his fathers', and men will multiply upon the once desolated earth like locusts. Egypt will be desolated, Arabia burned with fire, the land of Ausania burned, and the sea provinces pacified. The whole indignation and fury of the king of the Romans will blaze forth against those who deny the Lord Jesus Christ. Then the earth will sit in peace and there will be great peace and tranquility upon the earth such as has never been nor ever will be anymore, since it is the final peace at the End of time....

Then the "Gates of the North" will be opened and the strength of those nations which Alexander shut up there will go forth. The whole earth will be terrified at the sight of them; men will be afraid and flee in terror to hide themselves in mountains and caves and graves. They will die of fright and very many will be wasted with fear. There will be no one to bury the bodies. The tribes which will go forth from the North will eat the flesh of men and will drink the blood of beasts like water. They will eat unclean serpents, scorpions, and every kind of filthy and abominable beast and reptile which crawls the earth. They will consume the dead bodies of beasts of burden and even women's abortions. They will slay the young and take them away from their mothers and eat them. They will corrupt the earth and contaminate it. No one will be able to stand against them.

After a week of years, when they have already captured the city of Joppa, the Lord will send one of the princes of his host and strike them down in a moment. After this the king of the Romans will go down and live in Jerusalem for seven and half-seven times, i.e. years. When the ten and a half years are completed the Son of Perdition will appear.

He will be born in Chorazaim, nourished in Bethsaida, and reign in Capharnaum. Chorazaim will rejoice because he was born in her, and Capharnaum because he will have reigned in her. For this reason in the third Gospel the Lord gave the following statement: "Woe to you Chorazaim, woe to you Bethsaida, and to you Capharnaum—if you have risen up to heaven, you will descend even to hell" (Luke 10:13–15). When the Son of Perdition has arisen, the king of the Romans will ascend Golgotha upon which the wood of the Holy Cross is fixed, in the place where the Lord underwent death for us. The king will take the crown from his head and place it on the cross and stretching out his hands to heaven will hand over the kingdom of the Christians to the Father. The cross and the crown of the king will be taken up together to heaven. This is because the Cross on which our Lord Jesus Christ hung for the common salvation of all will begin to appear before him at his coming to convict the lack of faith of unbelievers. The prophecy of David which says, "In the last days Ethiopia will stretch out her hand to God" (Ps. 67:32) will be fulfilled in that these last men who stretch out their hands to God are from the seed of the sons of Chuseth, the daughter of Phol, king of Ethiopia. When the Cross has been lifted up on high to heaven, the king of the Romans will directly give up his spirit. Then every principality and power will be destroyed that the Son of Perdition may be manifest.[569]

The character of the Last Roman Emperor is still taught as standard eschatology in Catholicism. The host of the Catholic television show, *The Last Things*, on the EWTN network, Desmond Birch, billed as an expert on the end times, describes the "Great Monarch" or King:

They (the prophecies by the Church Fathers and other, later, great saints regarding the Great Monarch) all contain prophecy of: (1) Toward the end of time but well prior to anti-Christ, the world will be very troubled (2) which troubles are ended for a time by a great temporal ruler, a great Monarch or King (3) who works closely with a very great and saintly Pope (4) together they reestablish peace in the world which lasts for a significant period of time (5) at the end of which time the people go bad because they cannot withstand the temptations that come with continued peace and prosperity (6) as a result of their becoming worse than "ever before" Anti-Christ comes.[570]

Students of biblical eschatology recognize that those Catholic beliefs are not derived from the Old or New Testaments, but rather later traditions, known as private revelations or "those which have been recorded since the days of Christ."[571] Birch cites numerous scholars and saints throughout Christian history who pointed to a Holy Pope and Great Monarch who institute an era of peace just prior to the Great Tribulation of biblical prophecy.[572]

A seventeenth-century German priest known as "the Venerable Bartholomew Holzhauser" in Catholic literature wrote a famous commentary on the book of Revelation, which is still held in high regard today by Roman Catholics. He argued the seven stars and the seven candlesticks seen by John signify seven periods of Church history, from its formation to the return of Christ for the final judgment. He also advocated that the seven periods correspond to the seven churches of Asia Minor addressed by John in Revelation, a view shared by many protestant premillennialists. According to Holzhauser, "the fifth period of the Roman Catholic Church began in 1520, would extend until the time of the 'Holy Pope,' and that fifth period would be marked by major wars, the loss of Roman Catholic Church influence, moral laxity, and that Moslems would again rise up to cause the Latin Church problems."[573]

Various descriptions of the fifth period well describe recent history within and without the Catholic Church. For example, the once-Christian West has sunk to new lows in terms of promiscuity, birth control, abortion, and the widespread acceptance of homosexuality. Even so, Catholic moral influence waned largely due to the hypocrisy entailed by the institutional cover up of the worldwide pedophile-priest scandal (detailed in our book, *Petrus Romanus*).

Pope Francis seems to match the description of the "Holy Pope" presiding during a modern Muslim uprising. Even more, the "Holy Pope" is prophesied to bring the Eastern Orthodox back into communion with Rome. Right on cue, in an address to the Orthodox Church of St. George in Istanbul (formerly Constantinople), Pope Francis said, "the one thing that the Catholic Church desires and that I seek as Bishop of Rome…is communion with the Orthodox Churches."[574] Francis then followed this in February 2016 by meeting with Patriarch Kirill in a "first-ever papal meeting with the head of the Russian Orthodox Church, an historic development in the 1,000-year schism that divided Christianity."[575]

After the fifth period of darkness, chastisement and restoration, Catholic prophecies predict a Great Monarch will arise to vanquish Islam and turn the world to Rome. Holzhauser prophesied:

> There rise a valiant King anointed by God. He will be a Catholic and a descendant of Louis IX, yet a descendant also of an old German imperial family, born in exile. He will rule supreme in temporal matters.[576]

While many Catholic seers imply a restored French monarchy (almost impossible politically), the hero is predicted to be crowned king of the restored Holy Roman Empire. Dupont commented, "But the restoration of Monarchy will not be a local affair; it will be a world-wide phenomenon. This will mark a near historical epoch and, because of this, many people are finding it hard to believe."[577] Indeed, it's even harder to believe that he will convert the world's Muslims. Other prophecies cited predicting a French Monarch include:

> Take notice that the Kingdom of the Franks is predestined by God for the defense of the Roman Church which is the only true Church of Christ. This kingdom shall someday be great among the kingdoms of the earth, and shall embrace all the limits of the Roman Empire, and shall submit all other kingdoms to its own scepter. (St. Rémi, fifth century)

Certain Doctors truly say that one of the Kings of the Frankish Empire shall possess it in its entirety which King shall live in the last time and shall be the greatest and last of Kings. (St. Anselm, eleventh century)

Peace will return to the world when the White Flower again takes possession of the throne of France. (St. Hidlegard, notably German, twelfth century)

The French people will ask for the good King, he who was chosen by God. He will come, this savior whom God has spared for France, this king who is not wanted now because he is dear to God's Heart. He will ascend to the throne; he will free the Church and reassert the Pope's rights. (The Ecstatic of Tours, nineteenth century)

Is not France "the tribe of Juda of the New Covenant" (St. Pius X)? (L'Abbé de Nantes, twenty-first century)[578]

Leading a divinely inspired crusade, the Great Monarch is predicted to conquer many Middle Eastern nations, leading to the widespread conversion of Muslims to Roman Catholicism. A Catholic expert on private revelations,[579] Dupont has collected many private revelations about the Great Monarch:

The Great Monarch...will conquer the (Middle) East. (Pareus, seventeenth century)

Cyprus, the Turks and Barbarians he will subdue. (Cataldus, fifth century)

The Eagle will also invade the Mohammedan countries. (St. Bridget, fourteenth century)

He shall destroy the Jewish and Mohammedan sects. (St. Bridget)

He shall destroy the Mohammedan sect and the rest of the infidels. (St. Francis of Paola, fifteenth century)

The Empire of the Mohammedans will be broken up (by him). (Ven. Holzhauser, seventeenth century)

He shall subdue to his dominion the Mohammedan Empire. (Gekner, seventeenth century)

He shall reign over the House of Agar (Hagar), and shall possess Jerusalem. (Isidore of Seville, seventh century)

He shall wrestle the Kingdom of the Christians from Ishmael, and conquer it from the Saracens. None of the Saracens shall be able to prevail. (Liber Mirabilis, sixteenth century)[580]

Dupont, naively, credits the following prophecy to the fourth-century theologian St. Methodius of Olympus:

A day will come when the enemies of Christ will boast of having conquered the whole world. They will say, "Christians cannot escape now!" But a Great King will arise to defeat the enemies of God. He will defeat them, and peace will be given to the world, and the Church will be freed from her anxieties.[581]

The Apocalypse of Pseudo-Methodius

Dupont does not cite a specific work for Methodius' prediction, but it must be *The Apocalypse of Pseudo-Methodius* now agreed to by a Syrian pseudepigrapher. Falsely attributed to Methodius of Olympus, a fourth-century Church Father, the work attempts to rationalize the Islamic Conquest of the Levant—troublesome in the seventh century, but not of much concern to the fourth-century Olympian Christian. Written in Syriac in the late seventh century, scholars typically date *The Apocalypse of Pseudo-Methodius'* composition to precisely AD 692.[582] *The Apocalypse* is the earliest surviving witness to the legend of the Last World Emperor. Hence, we believe it is no accident the "legends of the black flag and the Muslim savior, the Mahdi, first circulated during the reign of the Umayyad dynasty, which ruled the Islamic empire from the ancient city of Damascus in the seventh and eighth centuries AD."[583]

While recognizing its obvious dependence on Christian sources, an encyclopedia entry credits the composition with the addition of a new character:

> The Apocalypse of St. Methodius, however, adds a new element to Christian eschatology: the rise of a messianic Roman emperor. He became a hero in Christian apocalyptic literature until the end of the medieval period, "the basis for the most important branch of Byzantine apocalyptic tradition."[584] The original Syriac text was translated into Greek, Latin, Slavonic, Arabic, and other languages from the late seventh century onwards and facilitated the Apocalypse's widespread prophetic influence.[585] According to Paul Julius Alexander, it was "the basis for the most important branch of Byzantine apocalyptic tradition."[586]

It's hard for us as modern folks, used to dramatic storytelling via HDTV and iPods, to understand how important this sort of literature was in the ancient world. In fact, it is no exaggeration to say that in the development of the Byzantine apocalyptic tradition, the translation of the Syriac text of Pseudo-Methodius into Greek marked the end of the era of Antiquity, and the beginning of that of the Middle Ages.[587] *The Apocalypse of Pseudo-Methodius* remained influential until at least the fourteenth century.[588] The region surrounding Damascus that produced this literature is the same area that produced many of the Hadiths. Scholars have only started source criticism of the Hadith and have published concerning the Mahdi's dependence on the Last World Emperor tradition.

Citing this work, O. Livine-Kafri writes: "Is there a reflection of the Apocalypse of pseudo-Methodius in Muslim Tradition?"[589] Scholars today recognize that Pseudo-Methodius not only exercised great influence on later apocalyptic texts, but his Apocalypse was used by "theologians and historiographers too, and was probably known to Muslim traditionalists."[590] Not only is it the earliest surviving witness to the legend of the Last World Emperor, it is likely the source material for the Hadith on the arrival of the Mahdi. It is not terribly surprising that the Muslims created the Mahdi in response to the Last Roman Emperor— the consummate Ottoman antihero:

> As far as the history of the literary transmissions allows us to know, Psueudo-Methodius bears witness to a significant innovation with respect to the patterns of previous eschatological literature: it is the peculiar role of the Last Roman Emperor. After a period of domination by the tribes of Ishmael over the Christian *oikoumene*, a Roman Emperor will arise to fight the Ishmaelites. He will liberate the Christian lands, push the Ishmaelites back to the desert and annihilate their power. Then he will establish a long period of peace and prosperity, which will last until the invasion of the peoples of Gog and Magog, followed by the last Emperors move to Jerusalem.[591]

The early Hadith writers were responding to what was being popularly discussed in seventh-century Syria, and the Syriac Apocalypse of Pseudo-Methodius was hot off the press. In a revisionist style similar to the Qur'an's treatment of Ishmael and Isaac, the Last Roman Emperor becomes the Mahdi of the Hadith.

Syrian Influence

It's no secret amongst scholars that early Syrian Christianity had a profound influence on the fledging pre-Qur'an Islam. McCants writes, "In early Islam, Syrians were particularly partial to the Sufyani because his kin, the Umayyads, had ruled the caliphate from Damascus."[592] The term *Sufyani*, a term referring to his descent from the progeny of Abu Sufyan, is yet another legendary character who will allegedly emerge before the Mahdi from Damascus. He is not the ally of the Mahdi nor the Dajjal. The Hadiths regarding the Sufyani specify that he is a tyrant who will spread corruption and mischief on the earth before the Mahdi.

A man will emerge from the depths of Damascus. He will be called Sufyani. Most of those who follow him will be from the tribe of Kalb. He will kill by ripping the stomachs of women and even kill the children. A man from my family will appear in the Haram, the news of his advent will reach the Sufyani and he will send to him one of his armies. He (referring to the Mahdi) will defeat them. They will then travel with whoever remains until they come to a desert and they will be swallowed. None will be saved except the one who had informed the others about them. (Mustadrak Al-Hakim)

This is from a five-volume Hadith collection written by Hakim al-Nishaburi. He wrote it in approximately AD 1003. It contains 9045 Hadiths and al-Nishaburi claimed all Hadiths in it were authentic, according to the conditions of either Sahih al-Bukhari or Sahih Muslim or both. What makes it especially germane to the present argument concerning Syrian influence on the Qur'an and Hadith is that it connects the Sufyani to Damascus, Syria. Of course, many dispensational theologians assert that God still has plans to annihilate Damascus in an unprecedented destruction that, for many premillennial dispensationalists, excludes all alleged past fulfillments:

The burden of Damascus. Behold, Damascus is taken away from being a city, And it shall be a ruinous heap. The cities of Aroer are forsaken: They shall be for flocks, Which shall lie down, and none shall make them afraid. The fortress also shall cease from Ephraim, And the kingdom from Damascus, and the remnant of Syria: They shall be as the glory of the children of Israel, saith the LORD of hosts. (Isaiah 17:1–3)

Scholars we respect like Michael Brown and Craig Keener have concluded that this was fulfilled by the Syro-Ephraimitic War that raged during the middle 730s BC.[593] However, Brown qualifies, "In principle, I have no problem with the concept that ancient biblical prophecies can refer to contemporary events, since it's clear that there are many prophecies still to be fulfilled, including the future world war against Jerusalem. (See Zechariah 12 and 14.)"[594] While they might be correct about dual fulfillment, the past simply does not match God's Word spoken through Isaiah that "Damascus is taken away from being a city, And it shall be a ruinous heap." Up until recently, the capital of Syria reveled in its status as one of the oldest existing cities in the world, and evidence exists of a settlement in the wider Barada basin dating back to 9000 BC.[595] While we recognize apocalyptic symbolism when we see it, "taken away from being a city" does not seem like figurative language. We expect Damascus to be destroyed, and as of October 21, 2015, pro-Moscow Internet news service, Russia Insider, has published what it says is footage of the battle raging between the Syrian army and US-and-Australian-backed rebels in the Damascus suburb of Jobar.

Furthermore, the Qur'an was likely not originally written in pure classical Arabic, as long believed, but more likely it was originally composed in a mixed Arabic-Syriac language, the traders' language of Mecca known to Muhammad. This argument was presented by a scholar writing under a pseudonym, Christopher Luxemberg, because source-critiquing the Qur'an, even in a scholarly manner, can be a capital offense in some countries—for instance, the death warrant put on Salman Rushdie over his fourth novel, *The Satanic Verses* by the infamous Ayatollah Khomeini of Iran. One sure weakness in all Muslim apologetics is that they have no textual evidence for the development of the Qur'an.

Recall that Muhammad, an illiterate, had a supernatural encounter, allegedly with the immortal Gabriel, a similar claim to that of Mormon founder Joseph Smith, who similarly received a doctrinal correction from the angel Moroni. Both were told the Jews and Christians were given a true revelation that had, over time, been corrupted. According to Oxford scholar and Muslim, Martin Lings, Muhammad was unconvinced and thought an evil *jinn* might be deceiving him. (The *jinn* are the Islamic equivalent of the biblical evil spirits or the trickster of paranormal parlance.)

> But he feared this might mean that he become a jinn-inspired poet or a man possessed. So he fled from the cave, and when he was halfway down the slope of the mountain, he heard a voice above him saying: "Oh Muhammad, thou art the messenger of God, and I am Gabriel."[596]

Because Muhammad could not write those revelations, he turned to his friends who wrote for him "on various available items—parchment, shoulder bones of camels, smooth rocks—the only truly authoritative versions exist in the minds of particular men, the *Qurra*, who have memorized all of, or at least parts of, the Qur'an."[597] For years, parts of today's text existed only in the minds of a few men. It was assembled, around AD 650, by order of Uthman ibn Affan, who had scholars assembling various fragments and transcribing the memories of Muhammad's still living contemporaries. Once they decided upon the final text, they destroyed the evidence. "Uthman sent to every Muslim province one copy of what they had copied, and ordered that all the other Qur'anic materials, whether written in fragmentary manuscripts or whole copies, be burnt."[598] Muslim apologists routinely ascribe this to Allah purifying his word despite the lack of archaeological evidence, historical inaccuracies, and discrepancies with non-Muslim literary sources.[599] By destroying the source material, the Qur'an immunizes itself from the source criticism that biblical scholars use to get back to the original text, the original autograph. In contrast, Muslims neglect or avoid the historical reality that the Qur'an was redacted from a number of sources, over a period of time. Because of this forced agreement, a mythology originated concerning a pure and perfectly consistent Qur'an.

> The Qur'an is the literal word of God, which He revealed to His Prophet Muhammad through the Angel Gabriel. It was memorized by Muhammad, who then dictated it to his Companions. They, in turn, memorized it, wrote it down, and reviewed it with the Prophet Muhammad. Moreover, the Prophet Muhammad reviewed the Qur'an with the Angel Gabriel once each year and twice in the last year of his life. From the time the Qur'an was revealed, until this day, there has always been a huge number of Muslims who have memorized all of the Qur'an, letter by letter. Some of them have even been able to memorize all of the Qur'an by the age of ten. Not one letter of the Qur'an has been changed over the centuries.

Unlike the thousands of New Testament documents that have a rich textual tradition, the documents associated with the compilation of the Qur'an were all burned. Thus, it is impossible for a snarky critic to attack the Qur'an with the sort of arguments leveled against the Bible. James White explains, "The Qur'an is 'corrupt,' in the sense of its having been a handwritten and hand-copied document, and that variations exist among its existing manuscripts from the first centuries of its transmission."[600]

Even more intriguingly, this amalgamation of Syriac and Arabian was based on Christian liturgical texts. Luxemberg's analysis suggests that the prevalent Syro-Aramaic language up to the seventh century formed a stronger etymological basis for the Qur'an's and, consequently, many of the Hadith's true meaning. If so, a significant shift in semantic meaning is implied. Changing the meaning of key terms in the Qur'an and various Hadiths has far-reaching implications for Islamic eschatology, especially the personal eschatology associated with martyrdom.

If Luxemberg is correct then, it seems perversely amusing, that the seventy-two (or seventy, depending on which Hadith) paradise virgins promised to the Muslim suicide victims are more likely only white grapes—originally meant to glorify Jesus as God in heaven in Syrian Christian Church frescos and stained glass. The Muslim misunderstanding results in a despicable but useful lie promising unlimited, Hugh-Hefner-style orgies in order to incite adolescent males into committing suicide bombings. It seems so transparently evil, one marvels why anyone accepts it as from God. Such obvious appeals to the lust of the flesh strongly suggest the promised virgin harem is not from Yahweh. The Bible seems clear enough:

> Not in the lust of concupiscence, even as the Gentiles which know not God: That no man go beyond and defraud his brother in any matter: because that the Lord is the avenger of all such, as we also have forewarned you and testified. For God hath not called us unto uncleanness, but unto holiness. (1 Thessalonians 4:5–7)

But for Mahdists and jihadi, the ends *do* justify the means. For example, a Hamas jihadi, Abu Wardeh, entices would-be suicide bombers promising a licentious afterlife harem: "I described to him how God would compensate the martyr for sacrificing his life for his land. If you become a martyr, God will give you 70 virgins, 70 wives and everlasting happiness."[601] While it's too tawdry to be an actual offer from a Holy

God, the carnal promise appeals to testosterone-fueled but otherwise sexually repressed adolescents amongst a group of brutal menfolk like the members of ISIS with nothing much to lose. In fact, ISIS' main recruitment tactic is to promise young soldiers obedient wives (and/or sex slaves).[602] Accordingly, every time a United States or Russian airstrike kills a few thousand Islamic State terrorists, a few more thousand join from places in Africa, Afghanistan, and Indonesia—often, teenage boys responding to propaganda promising them a wife (and sex slaves) for joining the IS. Muslim apologists must face facts. Such a transparently diabolic enticement to sexual promiscuity and the abuse of women betrays the spirit behind Islam. Even worse, it's probably a misunderstanding due to Qur'anic plagiarism.

It turns out that the seventy (or seventy-two) virgins promised to suicide bombers are probably only white grapes. The word *huri*, universally interpreted by Arab scholars as white-eyed virgins (who will serve the faithful in paradise; Surah 44:54, 52:20, 55:72, 56:22) means, according to Luxenberg, "white grapes." He says that many Syriac Christian depictions of paradise describe it as abounding in pure white grapes. When Luxemberg's book was first promoted, the Western press had a field day asserting that suicide bombers expecting a harem of beautiful young virgins would be shocked and disappointed by a bowl of rasins.[603] The book makes a case that because *hur'in* in Syro-Aramaic is a substantive adjective (functions as a noun) consisting of the Aramaic adjective *hur* (white) substantivized with *'in* to form a noun meaning "white (ones)." After some linguistic discussion, the author identifies "ones" more specifically based on context and philology.

> This is to be found among what the Koran calls the fruits of Paradise. These include, among others, *date palms* and *pomegranates* (Sura 55:68) as well as *grapes* (Sura 78:32). These last-mentioned are conspicuously named only in this passage in connection with Paradise, whereas they occur in no fewer than ten pas-

sages among the other fruits of the earth and of earthly gardens. (Suras 2:266; 6:99; 13:4; 16:11,67; 17:91;18:32; 23:19; 36:34; 80:28)[604]

He also argues based on hur'in as a Qur'anic double expression. In simple terms, double expressions compare two terms that share a certain quality. The most common devices used to achieve this are metaphors and similes in poetic language. Based on parallel usage in Christian hymns by Ephraem the Syrian, Luxemberg makes a reasonable case that, in context, hur'in originally denoted heavenly "white grapes" as opposed to other fruits.

> But not least the internal criteria of the Koran will convince us that with the double expression (*hur 'in*) the Koran is doing nothing more with this metaphor than describing this fruit of Paradise *par excellence in a totally special way* and *emphasizing* it over the other fruits of Paradise, and that by this it finally means nothing more than what Ephraem the Syrian also meant, namely, *grapes.*[605]

If Luxemberg is correct then the original compilers and redactors of the Qur'an borrowed a popular Syriac Christian literary device denoting heavenly white grapes assuming it to be the Arabic word *houri* ("virgin"). The pathetic irony facing suicide bombers it that, ultimately, they will not even get the grapes but rather face the judgment of Jesus Christ at the Great White Throne judgment (John 5:22; Revelation 20:11–15). Even so, there are several reasons not to accept the Qur'an, and while this is not a book of Christian apologetics contra-Islam, it is relevant and we think it important to establish that the Qur'an routinely plagiarizes the Hebrew Bible and, less often, the New Testament while imposing an unsophisticated Islamic spin onto the historical narrative. First keep in mind that we have the revelations of Yahweh, most of the Hebrew Scriptures, preserved in Hebrew, Aramaic, and Greek on papyrus, parchment, and bronze scrolls, famously known as the Dead Sea Scrolls. They devastate Muslim claims that the text was altered to make Ishmael seem to be the "real" son of promise and other such revisionist nonsense.

Errors in the Qur'an

If the Qur'an is truly divine revelation then we would expect Allah's critique of Christian doctrine to be accurate and compelling. Christian apologist, James White, writes, "If the Qur'an is the very words of Allah without admixture of man's insights or thoughts, then it would follow inevitably that its representations will be perfectly accurate and its arguments compelling."[606] In other words, if Allah really is God as President Bush[607] and Obama claim, one would not expect to find fallacious strawman arguments leveled at well-known Christian doctrines. Instead, we find a poorly cobbled together misconstruction of Yahweh's self-revealed triune nature. Muslims routinely assert the idea that the Father, Son, and Virgin Mary are the three Persons of the Christian Trinity—an absurdity to Christians, but, apparently, not to the authors of the Qur'an.

"Say Not Three!"

O People of the Scripture! Do not exaggerate in your religion nor utter aught concerning **Allah** save the truth. The Messiah, **Jesus son of Mary**, was only a messenger of Allah, and His word which He conveyed unto **Mary**, and a spirit from Him. So believe in Allah and His messengers, and say not "Three"—Cease! (it is) better for you!—Allah is only One Allah. Far is it removed from His Transcendent Majesty that He should have a son. His is all that is in the heavens and all that is in the earth. And Allah is sufficient as Defender. (Surah 4:171, emphasis added)[608]

It seems the author, Muhammad, was as confused about the Trinity as are many who claim to be Christians.[609] We boldfaced the obvious: "say not three" refers to: Allah, Jesus, and Mary. Christians believe in one God in three persons based on Jesus' Great Commission baptismal formula "in the name of the Father, and of the Son, and of the Holy Ghost" (Matthew 28:19). Mary is conspicuously not in the formula, suggesting that the Qur'an's author is confused when offering, "He conveyed unto Mary, and a spirit from Him." An early Muslim commentary, the *Tanwīr al-Miqbās min Tafsīr Ibn 'Abbās*, identifies the "three" of Surah 4 as: "a son, father and wife."[610] Where might Muhammad have come to such an errant but understandable mistake? James White offers a plausible historical scenario of what a young Muhammad might see when looking inside a Syrian church:

> Inside a small church in a Syrian village, he would have seen statuary. Possibly God represented as creating all things. The crucifix to be sure. The common artistic representation of the Holy Spirit was a dove, which would not, in and of itself, suggest to a young man from Mecca a divine figure.
>
> But what else? A woman. A woman in various exalted poses, a woman holding the baby Jesus. He would have seen and heard much about Mary, for the slow (and unbiblical) process of Mary's exaltation had begun centuries before Muhammad's birth. So in light of the religious experience that was his in Mecca's polytheistic context, would it not be easy for him to interpret what he saw in the light of Allah, Mary, and their child, Jesus? This is not a possible answer for the believing Muslim, but it surely would explain why the Qur'an seems to impute to Christians a view of God that we have never held.[611]

That misrepresentation of basic Christian theology calls the Qur'an's claim to divine inspiration into serious question. White surmises, "We simply must insist that if its author believed Christians hold to three gods, Allah, Mary, and evidently their offspring, Jesus, then the Qur'an is the result of human effort, is marked by ignorance and error, and so is not what Muslims claim it to be."[612] It not only explains the Qur'an's mistake, it suggests Muhammad was the very fallible human source. If one analyzes the Mahdi tradition in light of current medieval scholarship, it proves similarly fallible.

11

Armageddon
The Battle for the Cosmic Mountain

And I saw three unclean spirits like frogs come out of the mouth of the dragon, and out of the mouth of the beast, and out of the mouth of the false prophet. For they are the spirits of devils, working miracles, which go forth unto the kings of the earth and of the whole world, to gather them to *the battle of that great day of God Almighty*. (Revelation 16:13–14, emphasis added)

GRAND RABBI Moshe Shternbuch of the Eda Charedit, a great-grandson of the Gaon of Vilna—"the saintly genius from Vilnius"[613]—recently said that the times of the Moshiach are here. According to Rabbi Shternbuch, his grandfather, Vilna Gaon, taught accordingly about the coming of Messiah.

> When you hear that the Russians have captured the city of Crimea, you should know that the times of the Messiah have started, that his steps are being heard. And when you hear that the Russians have reached the city of Constantinople (today's Istanbul), you should put on your Shabbat clothes and don't take them off, because it means that the Messiah is about to come any minute.[614]

The Russians took Crimea in 2014[615] and, as we have demonstrated, Constantinople is central to Islamic eschatology. In the IS' trademark Hadith prophecy about Dabiq (which they claimed to be fulfilling), the Muslim army is divided into three groups.

> The Last Hour would not come until the Romans would land at al-A'maq or in Dabiq. An army consisting of the best (soldiers) of the people of the earth at that time will come from Medina (to counteract them). When they will arrange themselves in ranks, the Romans would say: Do not stand between us and those (Muslims) who took prisoners from amongst us. Let us fight with them; and the Muslims would say: Nay, by Allah, we would never get aside from you and from our brethren that you may fight them. They will then fight and a third (part) of the army would run away, whom Allah will never forgive. A third (part of the army) which would be constituted of excellent martyrs in Allah's eye, would be killed and the third who would never be put to trial would win and they would be conquerors of Constantinople.[616]

The first third retreats and suffers damnation as cowards, the second third is killed in battle, and the final third goes on to become the conquerors of Constantinople (Istanbul)—today the fifth-largest city in the world. But more interestingly, the IS' interpretation is not coherent with geopolitical reality; the prophecy seemingly assumes that Constantinople is still the capital of the eastern leg of the Roman Empire, which is no longer the case. Istanbul is a modern Muslim metropolis today. Its destruction by the IS would not advance Islam, but further galvanize the world against the IS. It's also not internally coherent.

This section will address the term "Armageddon"—from a Hebrew Bible perspective down to how it applies in Christian eschatology. We offer an overview and then four key points of analysis. First will be a summary and overview of the Old Testament use of the "Day of the Lord" terminology. This naturally leads to the term "Armageddon" because of the book of Revelation's detailed exposition of the Day of the Lord and mention of in "the Hebrew tongue, Armageddon" (Revelation 16:16b). Solutions to the meaning of the cryptic term will be offered on the basis of plausible Hebrew transliterations as well as contextual and geographic coherence. Then the relationship to the cosmic mountain and Antichrist figure will be explored. Finally, the battle itself will be examined and a novel solution offered in light of the Ezekiel 38 and 39 descriptions of an end-time war. The Hebrew background to the term "Armageddon" entails a confrontation over the divine mountain and a more defined picture of the prophetic scenario.

Day of the Lord

The Day of the Lord is a key theme found in the Old Testament prophetic books. It carries a context of future judgment and foreboding darkness. However, one should not read all of the passages into our future, as some have come and gone. The first appears in Amos and is speaking of the coming Assyrian invasion of the Northern Kingdom (Amos 5:18–20). Zephaniah uses the term to refer to the imminent Babylonian invasion of Judah (Zephaniah 1:7, 14). Nevertheless, other passages do refer to a time of ultimate judgment upon the nations and indicate a much wider scope (Ezekiel 30:3; Joel 3:14; Obadiah 15). Most germane to the task, here are instances when the prophet seems to speak of an eschatological Day of the Lord (Malachi 4:5; Joel 3:2). Even more, the New Testament authors Peter and Paul appropriated the term for the future return of Christ (2 Peter 3:10; 1 Corinthians 1:8). Heiser wrote, "The Day of the Lord does not refer to a specific twenty-four hour day. Rather, it refers to a period of time, much in the way we would today say, 'the day of reckoning' or 'day of vengeance.'"[617] In context, "the battle of that great day of God Almighty" (Revelation 16:14) shows this usage. Heiser also acknowledged its eschatological sense.

> The term refers to a time in the far future with respect to when the prophet lived—from our perspective, to the time of Jesus' first coming and beyond to his second coming. The reason that it can refer to a variety of time periods is that the "Day of Yahweh" indiscriminately meant "judgment was coming."[618]

Depending on context, the Day of the Lord denoted the "wide-sense day" covering the Great Tribulation mentioned by Jesus (Matthew 24:21) and the "narrow-sense day," the literal day upon which Jesus returns for the Battle of Armageddon (Revelation 16:16; 19:11–21).

The broad sense encompasses a span of time known in the Hebrew Bible as "the time of Jacob's distress" (Jeremiah 30:7) and also in Daniel as "a time of trouble, such as never has been since there was a nation till that time" (Daniel 12:1). Jesus referred to it as the "great tribulation" (Matthew 24:21; Revelation 7:14) just prior to His return. This time is described by Him in Matthew's Gospel (24:15–28) and in detail through John with the trumpet and bowl judgments found in the book of Revelation. Prior to Armageddon, a substantial part of the broad Day of the Lord's judgments have occurred concurrent with the trumpets and bowls. Then the armies of the nations will only begin to be gathered by the demonic hordes to Armageddon after the sixth bowl is poured out (Revelation 16:12–16). The Hebrew Bible supplies more detail.

Joel 3:9–16 and Zechariah 14:1–5 both indicate that after the armies of the nations have gathered in Israel, then a specific day will come, e.g., the "Day of the Lord is near" (Joel 3:14) and "a day is coming for the Lord" (Zechariah 14:1). It is apparent that this narrow Day of the Lord will not take place until the armies have gathered in Israel by the miraculous sign-working, unclean frog spirits emerging from the satanic trinity: the Dragon, the Beast, and the False Prophet.

And I saw three unclean spirits like frogs come out of the mouth of the dragon, and out of the mouth of the beast, and out of the mouth of the false prophet. For they are the spirits of devils, working miracles, which go forth unto the kings of the earth and of the whole world, to gather them to the battle of that great day of God Almighty. (Revelation 16:13–14)

The "great day of God Almighty" is a special day that will be within the broad Day of the Lord but utterly distinct. Both Joel 3 and Zechariah 12–14 indicate that their Day of the Lord will be the specific day when the Lord comes to fight against and destroy the armies gathered in Israel. Also, Jesus revealed to John that this will be when Jesus returns to the earth (Revelation 19:11–21). Thus, the narrow Day of Joel 3 and Zechariah 14 will be the *day* on which Christ comes to the earth to fight the Battle of Armageddon.

The prophecy of Zechariah 14 gives us specific details about that future day. At the end of the Tribulation, during the Battle of Armageddon, and after it, the following will occur: First, the nations of the earth will surround Jerusalem (v.2). Second, Jerusalem will be captured, plundered, and women raped (v.2b). Third, a remnant will flee via a valley created by an earthquake (v.5a). Fourth, Jesus will return to the Mount of Olives as was promised by the angel after the ascension (Acts 1:11; Zechariah 14:4). Fifth, He comes with an angelic army to fight the nations (Zechariah 14:5b). Revelation 19 parallels this section and indicates that "from his mouth comes a sharp sword with which to strike down the nations" (v. 19:15a). Furthermore, the text describes a horrible plague cursed upon the combatants (Zechariah 14:12; cf. Revelation 19:15). Finally, the Lord will be King and the whole world will worship Him (Zechariah 14:16).

Daniel 11:40–45 is a parallel passage that suggests the Muslims turn and attack the first beast. It also focuses on Jerusalem, even specifying that "He [The Antichrist] shall enter also into the glorious land [Israel], and many countries shall be overthrown: but these shall escape out of his hand, even Edom, and Moab, and the chief of the children of Ammon" (Daniel 11:41). No known historical sequence corresponds to that which is laid out in those verses, leading us to conclude that it describes the final battle for the mount of assembly in Jerusalem (Zechariah 12:9). Finally, the "glorious holy mountain," indisputably Mt. Zion, is where the Antichrist dies (Daniel 11:45).

According to biblical scholar Charles Torrey, "In Hebrew eschatology Jerusalem was the center of all the predicted gatherings, whether of the people of God or of the heathen nations."[619] The Hebrew Bible is unequivocal in its testimony. Joel 2:32 proclaims that "in Mount Zion and in Jerusalem there shall be those who escape." Obadiah 21 describes the culmination: "Saviors shall go up to Mount Zion to rule Mount Esau, and the kingdom shall be the Lord's." Isaiah 24:23 declares: "Then the moon will be confounded and the sun ashamed, for the Lord of hosts reigns on Mount Zion and in Jerusalem, and his glory will be before his elders." With this prophetic unanimity, one wonders why Armageddon is typically located on the plain of Megiddo.

Armageddon in Revelation 16:16

A principle tenet of this treatment is that Armageddon has nothing to do with the Valley of Megiddo. The cryptic passage in question reads, "And he gathered them together into a place called in the Hebrew tongue Armageddon" (Revelation 16:16). The term in Greek, Ἁρ Μαγεδών, is problematic in that it is a transliteration of a Hebrew term, yet we find no immediate Old Testament analog. It is better represented in English as "Har Magedon," because in Koine Greek of the preceding rough breathing mark, Ἁρ. Biblical scholar Charles Torrey argued that the division into two words is required by the Semitic trilateral root structure. The former word Ἁρ or "Har" means "mountain" (הַר) in Hebrew.[620]

Accordingly, the remainder is Μαγεδών, but the last two letters "ών" are merely a suffix for a place name.[621] Hence, all that remains is a Greek transliteration of a Hebrew word for a mountain, which was written as Μαγεδ.

Many respected dispensational scholars (Missler, Pentecost, Walvoord, Fruchtenbaum) identify Armageddon with the area of the Galilean city of Megiddo and believe that a literal military battle will be fought or staged in that area (known as the Megiddo Plains). Arnold Fruchtenbaum argues:

> Megiddo was a strategic city located at the western end of the Valley of Jezreel, guarding the famous Megiddo Pass into Israel's largest valley. One can see the entire Valley of Jezreel from the mount upon which the city of Megiddo stood. So what is known as the Valley of Armageddon in Christian circles is actually the biblical Valley of Jezreel. The term *Armageddon* is never applied to the valley itself, but only to the mount at the western end.[622]

This sounds convincing at first. Yet the western end of the Jezreel Valley consists of Mount Tabor and Mount Gilboa. It is flanked on the south by Mount Carmel. There is no such "Mount Megiddo." Apparently, this idea became widely accepted in dispensational scholarship since it appeared in the New Scofield Reference Bible notes for Judges 5:19 and Revelation 16:16.[623] Modern scholars no longer assume it to be Megiddo.

> The word "Armageddon" in Hebrew is *har-mĕgiddôn*, meaning "the mount of Megiddo." The city of Megiddo was strategically located in northern Palestine on a plain in the Valley of Jezreel or Esdraelon. Although Megiddo was not a "mountain," it was the site of many significant battles in Israel's history (e.g., Judg. 5:19; 2 Kings 23:29; 2 Chron. 35:22; Zech. 12:11).[624]

The difficulty is that there are no scholarly sources that corroborate a "Mount Meggido" convention prior to modern-era dispensationalism.

The main assets of the Megiddo rendering is that the Greek appears as if it could be a possible transliteration for מְגִדּוֹ (mᵉgid·dô), and that it was the site of some important battles in Israelite history (Joshua 12:21; Judges 5:19; 2 Kings 9:27, 23:29–30).[625] However, the problems demonstrably outweigh the advantages.

The ten-thousand-pound elephant in the room is that there simply is no such place as Mount Megiddo. In the Bible, Megiddo is twice represented as "the plain of Megiddo" (Zechariah 12:11; 2 Chronicles 35:22). The only mountains near it have their own well established names like Mount Hermon. In truth, during the apostle John's day, the only actual hill at Megiddo was a measly seventy-foot high artificial mound known as a "tell" in archaeology.[626] Furthermore, by using Google Earth for geographic investigation, one can see that the town of Megiddo is a full fifty-four miles in a straight line from the Mount of Olives where the Lord defeats the armies in Zechariah 14. Thus a rendering of Megiddo makes the Day of the Lord passages centering on Jerusalem unrealistically distant. In contrast, the Mount of Olives where the Lord lands with His army is a mere one-third of a mile from Mount Zion. Because of the geography and the fact that the text specifies a mountain, the Megiddo Plain or Jezreel Valley is not a viable option. We now explore the more plausible alternative that has been suggested for a Hebrew source term that renders as the Greek term Μαγεδ.

The reference is cryptic and has long evaded unambiguous definition. In effect, scholars must now attempt to reverse transliterate from Greek back to Hebrew. The early commentators Origen, Eusebius, and Jerome did not even think Armageddon was the name of an actual place.[627] R. H. Charles ventured, "it is possible that Ἅρ Μαγεδών may be a corruption either for רֽ מִגְדֹּה = 'his fruitful mountain.'"[628] This connects it to Jerusalem and coheres nicely to Old Testament "Day of the Lord" texts. Another suggestion is that the Hebrew gādad ("a marauding band, troop")[629] appended to har ("mountain") would mean "marauding mountain" and would perhaps allude to Jeremiah's "destroying mountain" (Jeremiah 51:25).[630] Another similar idea suggested by Johnson stems from the secondary sense of the Hebrew *gādad*, which means "to gather in troops or bands," because one can make a noun form a verb in Hebrew by adding the prefix "ma," rendering *magēd*, "a place of gathering in troops."[631] This coheres nicely with the context of Revelation 16. While these all seem plausible, in seeming frustration, Robert Mounce surmises:

> When it takes place, Armageddon is symbolic of the final overthrow of all the forces of evil by the might and power of God. The great conflict between God and Satan, Christ and Antichrist, good and evil, that lies behind the perplexing course of history will in the end issue in a final struggle in which God will emerge victorious and take with him all who have placed their faith in him. This is Har-Magedon. (Mounce 1997, 302)

While this is surely correct, God has given us this strange name for some purpose, albeit enigmatic. Still yet, there is a solution that offers more explanatory scope than the above.

Biblical scholar Charles C. Torrey proposed a solution based on Hebrew mythology back in 1938 that is gaining wider acceptance. Torrey refers to an article in the *Hastings Dictionary of the Bible* that posited an alternate rendering by Hommel. As far back as the nineteenth century, German scholars had made a connection to Isaiah 14:13 and the "Mount of Assembly," but ancient Near Eastern scholarship and archaeology were still in their infancy. Torrey aptly pointed out that interpreters lacking an intimate knowledge of both Hebrew and Greek miss that the Greek letter gamma, which is the "γ" in Μαγεδών; the Hebrew letter gimelin מְגִדּוֹן; or the "g" in the English "Megiddo," can also represent the Hebrew consonant ayin, "ע."[632] In other words, English Bible readers only consider "Megiddo" being unaware of the possibility that John was Hellenizing as well as transliterating. Heiser explained:

Neither Greek nor English has a letter (other than hard "g") that approximates the sound of *'ayin*. That is why it is represented in academic transliteration as a backwards apostrophe. The sound of that letter *ayin* is made in the back of the throat and sounds similar to hard "g." Perhaps the best example of a Hebrew word that begins with the letter *ayin* is "Gemorrah" (*'amorah*). That familiar word is not spelled with the Hebrew "g" (*gimel*) like the "g" in "Megiddo." It is spelled with *'ayin*.[633]

Accordingly, Torrey postulated מוֹעֵד (*mô·'ēḏ*) which harkens the "Mount of Assembly" language used in Isaiah 14:13, an actual mountain corresponding to John's transliteration. American theologian and Old Testament scholar, Meredith Kline, concurred by stating that "representation of the consonant *'ayin* by Greek *gamma* is well attested. Also, in Hebrew, *on* is an affirmative to nouns, including place names."[634] The "Mount of Assembly" rendering was also suggested by Mathias Rissi in his Revelation study *Time and History,* published in 1966.[635] Because of its scholarly support and convincing explanatory scope, the "Mount of Assembly" interpretation is the focus of this presentation.

The Cosmic Mountain

The "mount of assembly in the far reaches of the north" (Isaiah 14:13) was originally a mythological meeting place for the pagan gods and corresponds to Mount Zaphon in Ugaritic texts. These texts describe Mount Zaphon as Baal's "holy mountain," "beautiful hill," and "mighty mountain."[636] According to John Walton:

Saphon/Zaphon is identified with a mountain, Jebel al-*'Aqra,* or Casius in classical sources (deriving from the Hittite Chazzi), which lies north of Ugarit. It is considered holy because it is capped by Baal's palace in the Baal Epic and is also the site of his burial.[637]

Isaiah was drawing on imagery from Baal-Athtar mythology to make a point about the king of Babylon as well as a divine usurper. It may seem odd that Isaiah would reference a Canaanite holy mountain, yet the Hebrew prophets were famous for juxtaposing Yahweh against the Canaanite deities. For instance, the biblical account of Elijah pronouncing a drought on the land was an assault on Baal as fertility god (1 Kings 17:1). His subsequent showdown with the prophets of Baal was a further demonstration of their god's impotence (1 Kings 18:38). In the same way, the prophets appropriate the property of a foreign god to assert Yahweh's superiority.

Jerusalem was located at a higher elevation than much of the surrounding region. The Temple was on a conspicuous summit in Jerusalem, his holy hill Mount Zion (Psalms 2:6; 99:2, 9). Psalm 48 is an explicit example of the connection to Zaphon: "His holy mountain, beautiful in elevation, is the joy of all the earth, Mount Zion, *in the far north*, the city of the great King" (Psalm 48:1b–2). This "far north" reference connects to the Isaiah taunt song. Heiser notes:

> Yahweh's sanctuary is on a mountain, Mount Zion (Ps. 48:1–2) which is located in the "heights of the north (*saphon*)," or on a "very high mountain" (Ezek. 40:2). Zion is the "mount of assembly" again located in the "heights of the north (*saphon*)," (Isa.14:13). (Heiser, 2004, 42)

It is important to note that it is described as "in the far north," yet Jerusalem is hardly the extreme geographic north. There is something much bigger going on. The ancient Near Eastern cosmology was a tripartite conception in which the abode of the gods was "the heights of the north." Thus, the cosmic north is being alluded to designating the divine Mount Zion.[638]

Yahweh was associated with a holy mountain from the very beginning in Eden.[639] Ezekiel 28:13–16 equates the Garden of God with the Mountain of God. Then during in the interim, He relocated to Mount Horeb or Sinai (Exodus 3:1). The assembly or *mô·'ēḏ* terminology alludes to the "tent of meeting," which served temporarily, and then later the Temple proper in Jerusalem on Mount Zion is associated with the *mô·'ēḏ* terminology (Psalm 74:4; Lamentations 2:6).[640] According to Ezekiel, Yahweh vacated the mountain prior to the Temple's destruction by the Babylonians (Ezekiel 10:18). Lamentations 5:16 describes Mount Zion as utterly desolate. Jesus was the fulfillment of Yahweh's return for the Second Temple period. However, the Second Temple was also destroyed. Still yet, Yahweh's glory is promised to return to a new Temple in the end time after the nation has repented and been cleansed (Ezekiel 43:1–9). We argue that this corresponds to what we know about the resolution of Armageddon and the Day of the Lord.

It seems likely that Armageddon refers to the end-time battle for Yahweh's holy mountain. Mounce comments, "Still others interpret the term in reference to some ancient myth in which an army of demons assault the holy mountain of the gods."[641] And indeed, various texts support the idea that this will be a war with divine, demonic, and earthly soldiers. Zechariah describes the Lord returning with his "holy ones" (Zechariah 14:5). Other Old Testament passages also support the idea (Isaiah 13:16; 24:1–21; Joel 3:9–12). The book of Revelation describes the involvement of demonic hordes (Revelation 16:14) and armies from heaven dressed in white linen who accompany the Lord (Revelation 19:14). Finally, the Dead Sea Scrolls also support this future event. Heiser argues, "The conflict described in the *War Scroll* involves both men and heavenly beings fighting side-by-side and against one another."[642] Accordingly, it seems appropriate to believe that just as Jesus leads an army, the Antichrist or Beast is Satan's incarnate general.

The Divine Usurper

There is an interesting parallel involved with the term "Armageddon" in that the phrase "in Hebrew" only appears in one other instance within the book of Revelation. According to Alan Johnson, "It is better to understand the term ["Armageddon"] symbolically in the same manner as 'in Hebrew' in 9:11 alerts us to the symbolic significance of the name of the angel of the Abyss."[643] This is the angel of the bottomless pit, namely Abbadon in Hebrew or Apollyon in Greek. According to Kline, the technique of using a Hebrew term is called *Hebraisti* and was favored by John. It is also used four times in his Gospel, three of which are also place names (John 5:2; 19:13, 17). Because the book of Revelation is full of symbols, word plays, juxtapositions, and parallels, it is not too fanciful to postulate that the Holy Spirit was making a prophetic statement between these two *Hebraisti*.

The "Antipodal to the Abyss" argument offered by Kline further supports the "Mount of Assembly" hypothesis.[644] This line of reasoning derives from the fact that both accounts juxtapose polar opposites in the cosmic scheme of things: the Mountain of God on one end and the pit of hell on the other. For example, the Isaiah passage contrasts the ambition, "I will ascend to heaven; above the stars of God" (v.13) against "But you are brought down to Sheol, to the far reaches of the pit" (v.15). Similarly, we find in the book of Revelation's two *Hebraisti*: the divine mountain and the bottomless pit—a perfect pairing of polar opposites, on the cosmic scale. This is a compelling correlation between the two accounts. Kline argues:

> In short, then, we find that in Isaiah 14 and the book of Revelation there are matching antonymic pairings of *har môcëd* and *har magedön* with the pit of Hades. Within the framework of this parallelism the *har môcëd* of Isaiah 14:13 is the equivalent of the *har magedön* of Revelation 16:16 and as such is to be

understood as its proper derivation and explanation. Accordingly, *har magedön* signifies "Mount of Assembly/Gathering" and is a designation for the supernal realm.[645]

The evidence is compelling that the term "Armageddon" speaks well past the gathering of earthly armies for war and to a deeper supernatural battle for the cosmic Mountain of God.

The context of the *assembling* of the armies by demonic spirits (Revelation 16:14) is practically a word play to the "Mount of Assembly." Furthermore, the allusion to the taunt song in Isaiah 14:12–15 creates astonishing parallels. The Hebrew phrase *helel ben-shachar* in verse 12, meaning "morning star, son of dawn," has been interpreted to be varying entities, including the proper name Lucifer. Modern scholars agree that this most likely is related to Ugaritic mythology concerning Baal and Athtar.[646] While Isaiah could be simply borrowing from local mythology for an illustration, it seems as if the prophet sees through the king of Babylon to the wicked spiritual power behind him. The book of Daniel suggests that earthly kingdoms have cosmic overlords (Daniel 10:13, 20) a paradigm that fits nicely with the Beast of Revelation who is similarly empowered by the great red dragon identified as Satan (Revelation 12:9; 13:2).

In Ugaritic lore, this usurper is argued to be Athtar, who was referred to as Venus ("morning star"), who seeks to displace Baal.[647] Other scholars relate this passage to an ancient Babylonian or Hebrew star-myth similar to the Greek legend of Phaethon.[648] Even so, one can imagine that, in a cosmic sense, all of these myths stem from a common historical event, a shared memory. There was an angelic rebellion.

The New Testament is clear that angels rebelled (Matthew 25:41; Revelation 12:9), and the earth is currently under the power of a usurper (2 Corinthians 4:4; 1 John 5:19). While the king of Babylon could hardly hope to "ascend to heaven above the stars of God," it certainly speaks to Satan's extreme hubris. C. S. Lewis famously said, "It was through pride that the devil became the devil: Pride leads to every other vice: it is the complete anti-God state of mind."[649] *Helel Ben-Shachar's* frustrated divine ambition harkens the account of a war in heaven in Revelation 12:7–17 in which Satan is thrown to earth, suggesting "the man who made the earth tremble" (Isaiah 14:16).

In fact, this taunt song is where the popular name for the devil, Lucifer, is derived from "morning star" as it is rendered in the Latin Vulgate.[650] During the intertestamental period, this account of the angel's fall associated with the morning star was subsequently associated explicitly with the name Satan, as seen in the second Book of Enoch (29:4; 31:4). This association of Lucifer to Satan continued with the Church Fathers because he is represented as being "cast down from heaven" (Revelation 12:7–10; cf. Luke 10:18).[651] Because Peter ascribes "morning star" to Christ (2 Peter 1:19) and the fact that it is also a title John uses for Jesus (Revelation 22:16), it has been suggested that this could be pointing to the Antichrist's parody of Jesus.[652] Accordingly, the prefix "anti" means "instead of" as well as "against"[653]—a fact that led Luther and Calvin to the conclusion that the papacy's claim to *Vicar of Christ* amounted to self-identifying with the Greek equivalent *Anti-Christos*. Paul expounds on him in 2 Thessalonians 2:3–5, writing, "Let no man deceive you by any means: for that day shall not come, except there come a falling away first, and that man of sin be revealed, the son of perdition; Who opposeth and exalteth himself above all that is called God, or that is worshipped; so that he as God sitteth in the temple of God, shewing himself that he is God" (2 Thessalonians 2:3–5). Of course, that "temple of God" would be on Mount Zion as well.

The Battle

This Antichrist figure finds his counterpart in the Hebrew Bible as Gog in Ezekiel 38–39. Much has been written associating the Magog war of

Ezekiel 38–39 with the Battle of Armageddon. There are demonstrable parallels, yet seemingly, the book of Revelation explicitly places it one thousand years after Armageddon (Revelation 20:8). Amillennialists like Kline attempt to conflate the battles described in Revelation 19 and 20.[654] Yet this lacks coherence, as Heiser points out several insurmountable difficulties to this view.[655] Still, both Kline and Heiser agree that Gog can be but isn't necessarily associated with the Antichrist. However, in Revelation 20, the Antichrist has been defeated, and what is described is the release of Satan. Heiser solves this by viewing Gog as both. He writes, "I have argued that Ezekiel 38–39 will be fulfilled in two events: (1) Armageddon, which also is the fulfillment of Daniel 11:40–45; and (2) the subsequent, separate battle of Revelation 20:7–9."[656] Thus, the satanically possessed Beast of Revelation is Gog in the Battle of Armageddon, and Satan himself is Gog in the later war. Heiser also connected this to the Watchers:

> Not only will the second generation Watchers be permitted to attack the holy city of Jerusalem at Armageddon, but according to Revelation 13 another Beast—the Antichrist—emerges from the Abyss prior to Armageddon. This connection with the abode of the Watchers is significant for identifying him for what he is: the incarnation of the fallen sons of God, the Watchers, the false god-man, the consummate seed of the serpent—the ultimate nephilim descendant.[657]

Many other scholars have speculated that the Antichrist is a Nephilim. In our previous work, *Exo-Vaticana*, we cited an Italian Franciscan theologian and advisor to the Supreme Sacred Congregation of the Roman and Universal Inquisition in Rome, Ludovico Maria Sinistrari (1622–1701), who shared the same notion:

> Now, it is undoubted by Theologians and philosophers that carnal intercourse between mankind and the Demon sometimes

gives birth to human beings; that is how is to be born the Antichrist, according to some Doctors, such as Bellarmin, Suarez, Maluenda, etc. They further observe that, from a natural cause, the children thus begotten by Incubi are tall, very hardy and bold, very proud and wicked.[658]

While Heiser argues that the Magog war is fulfilled in stages of the "already but not yet" fulfillment scenario, this present treatment suggests a similar but novel solution.

One of the better arguments against placing the Magog war prior to the Tribulation as some dispensationalists do as well as the recapitulation view of amillennialists is that Ezekiel 38 describes Israel as already completely regathered in the land (vv.8, 12) and dwelling securely without defenses (v.11).[659] Because he assumes the Magog war is necessarily prior to Armageddon, Tim LaHaye wrote:

> The threat of an attack will terrify Israel into turning to God for help. And their cries will not be in vain, for the Almighty will put on a demonstration of power unequaled since the plagues of Egypt and the parting of the Red Sea. The result? Israel will continue in peace and the world will know there is a God in heaven.[660]

That description certainly does not apply to Israel's current situation or to the preconditions for the Battle of Armageddon. Today, Israel is under constant threat and has very real barrier walls. It is also inconsistent with Armageddon, because it is in the latter part of the Great Tribulation. Surely after enduring the trumpet and bowl judgments, they will not be together in a secure peaceful state. Furthermore, the dry-bones prophecy of Ezekiel 37 describes Israel's rebirth contingent with the Messiah (vv.15–28). Only then will the diaspora be completely undone and the nation at peace. This only makes sense in light of it being post-Millennium as per Revelation 20. Thus, I completely agree with Heiser that Ezekiel 38 is the satanic battle after the Millennium. However, from this point forward, an alternative is offered.

It is the proposal here that Ezekiel 38 describes the battle of Armageddon which temporally precedes the Magog war of chapter 39. This makes the players Ezekiel 38 all the more interesting. Gog, Magog, Meshech and Tubal along with "Persia, Ethiopia, and Libya with them; all of them with shield and helmet: Gomer, and all his bands; the house of Togarmah of the north quarters, and all his bands: and many people with thee." (Ezekiel 38:5–6)

Chuck Missler has done a great deal of study on the Ezekiel 38 prophecy. He identifies the players as such:

- Magog is the Southern Steppes of Russia (former Soviet-Bloc countries);
- Meshech and Tubal are Turkey;
- Persia is Iran;
- Ethiopia is Southern Egypt, Sudan, Somalia;
- Libya is Libya (but it may also include Algeria, Morocco, and Tunisia);
- Gomer is North-Central Turkey;
- Togarmah is Eastern Turkey.[661]

John Weldon identifies them accordingly:

—**Gog** (an unidentified leader of the invasion, of the land of Magog, "the prince of Rosh, Meshech and Tubal.")

—**Magog** (Russia and/or Central Asian Muslim nations: Kazakhstan, Tajikistan, Uzbekistan, Kyrgyzstan, Turkmenistan;

Russians of Scythian origin just north of the Black Sea and Caucus Mountains)

—**Meshech** and **Tubal** (cities on the southern coast of the Black Sea, referring to modern Turkey, just south of Russia, a nation which recently supported Israel but is now increasingly Islamist, cooperating with Russia)

—**Persia** (Iran and, perhaps ironically, its ancient territory included both Shiite Iraq and also Afghanistan)

—**Put** (Libya—a few authorities include with her, Algeria, Morocco and Tunis; Somaliland or Somalia, which borders Ethiopia.) As Dr. Mark Hitchcock observes, "Libya would certainly jump at the chance to join forces with the Sudan, Iran, Turkey, and the former Muslim republics of the Soviet Union to crush the Jewish state."

—**Gomer** (Eastern Europe or portions thereof, North Central Asia minor [Turkey], possibly the Ukraine; the identification as Germany is probably incorrect.) Again, Turkey is turning increasingly Islamist and definitely part of the Ezekiel 38 coalition.

—**Togarmah** (Southeastern Europe, or Turkey or the South East portion of Turkey near the Syrian border; also possibly Ukraine: separated by the Black Sea, both Turkey and Ukraine have a long chronology of geographic, cultural and historic contact.)

—**Cush** (The Islamic Republic of Sudan, one of the most militant Islamic nations on earth; and possibly Ethiopia.)

—**The many nations with you**—additional nations not cited who are allied with the Russian confederation.[662]

Heiser said:

This brief survey of the nations of the ancient world surrounding Israel and their modern political equivalents was designed to highlight two truths. First, that the modern Islamic states do correspond to Israel's ancient enemies—nations that are the subject of yet unfulfilled prophetic oracles. Second, that we need not twist such prophecies to target modern political villains, like the former Soviet Union. The Israeli-Muslim feud is both more rational, and more biblical.[663]

While the traditional view is that chapter 39 is a restatement of 38, this is a tacit acknowledgement that chapter 38 can stand alone as a complete battle.[664] Furthermore, chapter 39 is inaugurated with a new "thus says the Lord God." This paper suggests that chapters 38–39 are two distinct wars for the following seven reasons: One, Gog and his armies are described as brought out to battle at the beginning of each chapter in unique circumstances (38:4–9; cf. 39:2). Two, chapter 38 clearly states that the land was restored from war (v.8). It is suggested that this refers to the Ezekiel 39/Armageddon war. Three, the chapter 38 war ties together with the post-Millennium release of Satan (Revelation 20:7–10; cf. Ezekiel 38:16, 22) and the White Throne judgment (Revelation 20:11–15) with "I will enter into judgment with him" (Ezekiel 38:22). Four, the nations will know that their defeat was by the Lord and that Israel will know the Lord from that day forward (39:21–22). This arguably convenes the inauguration of the Millennium. Five, the nations will understand why Israel was exiled and abandoned by God (39:23). This explains the Tribulation. Six, the Lord will restore and gather Israel (39:25–27). This seems to be concurrent with the return of Christ in Ezekiel 37:15–28 and Zechariah 12:9, and is necessarily a precursor to the chapter 38 war. Seven, Israel knows their God from that day forward and God never hides His face from them again (39:28–29 cf. Revelation

20:6). Consequently, the prerequisite "regathered and secure" status of Ezekiel 38 (Revelation 20) is arguably the result of the previous Ezekiel 39 (Revelation 19) war. All that is required for one to accept is that these are two oracles, which are in a non-chronological order, a contention that is hardly unprecedented.

Enemy from the Cosmic North

In the Ezekiel 39 war, it is also compelling that Gog is described as coming "from the uppermost parts of the north" and "against the mountains of Israel" (v. 2). This language strongly concurs with the "mount of assembly in the far reaches of the north" interpretation of Armageddon. Brevard Childs' scholarship on "the enemy from the north and the chaos tradition" suggests a possible connection:

> Isa14:12 ff. is a taunt against the king of Babylon and not directly related to the enemy tradition. Nevertheless, it is quite remarkable that the king who dared to "sit on the mount of assembly in the *far north*" is described as the one "who made the earth tremble, who shook kingdoms."[665]

It may be helpful to view it as cosmic north referring generally to the supernatural realm rather than geography. In light of the case for supernatural warriors, it is interesting to note the distinction made between his hordes and people (39:4). In the aftermath, Gog falls on the mountains of Israel. There is a massive feast of carrion for the birds (39:4; cf. 17–20), which is correlated directly with Revelation 19:17–19. There is only one time on the prophetic timeline about which one could say that God will destroy the nations who attack Jerusalem, revealing Himself to all the nations and no longer tolerate His name being profaned (Ezekiel 39:7; Zechariah 12:9; cf. Revelation 19:15). There is really only one day that he will regather all of Israel to their land while pouring out his spirit (Ezekiel 39:29; cf. Zechariah 12:10). Because these things are established "from that day forward' (Ezekiel 39: 22), this war will necessarily conclude just prior to the Millennium (Revelation 20:4). That necessitates that the war described in Ezekiel 39 concurs with the "narrow sense" Day of the Lord, Armageddon, or the battle of *HarMô·'ēd*.

This chapter offered an analysis of the term "Armageddon" as it relates to eschatology and the Old Testament. After offering a brief summary of the Day of the Lord concept, we sought to illustrate the superiority of the "Mount of Assembly" interpretation over the more popular plains of Megiddo assumption. The case for the "Mount of Assembly" view was made by demonstrating its linguistic plausibility, greater geographical likelihood, and superior explanatory scope. That scope was demonstrated through prophetic connections to the Mountain of God, the Antichrist figure, and the Magog wars. Finally, a novel reading of the Ezekiel 39 war's conflation with Revelation 19 and Zechariah 14 was offered as a separate event from the previous chapter's account, which arguably occurs when Satan is unchained at the end of the Millennium (Revelation 20:8 cf. Ezekiel 38). In the end, it seems that these points strongly support the notion that the Battle of Armageddon is indeed the battle for Mount Zion concurrent with the Second Coming of Jesus Christ.

12

Why Many Christians, Muslims, and Jews Will Accept Antichrist (Last Roman Emperor) as Messiah

By Derek Gilbert, SkyWatch TV host

[Editors' note: This guest chapter is extracted from the upcoming new book by Derek Gilbert, *The Great Inception: False Prophecies and the Antichrist's End-Times End Game* to be released Fall, 2016.]

IT IS HUMAN nature to study a thing primarily as though it's a discrete entity, separate from other factors and influences. For example, an analysis of American colonial history often ignores the impact of events taking place elsewhere in the world such as the English Civil War that broke out barely twenty years after the first boatload of Puritans landed at Plymouth Rock.

So it often is with Christians and a study of Bible prophecy. While Christianity is the largest religion on earth, with an estimated 2.2 billion believers, it represents less than a third of the world's population. Muslims number about 1.6 billion, or 22 percent of the global population. (Jews, surprisingly, don't even make the top ten, placing eleventh with about fourteen million adherents, only 0.22 percent of the world's population.)[666]

It must also be noted that Protestant Christians, especially those holding a premillennial, pre-Tribulation view of end-times prophecy, are a minority within world Christianity. Roman Catholic and Orthodox Christians, who are generally amillennial (rejecting the belief that Jesus will have a literal thousand-year reign on earth), comprise 62 percent of global Christianity.[667] Among Protestants, it is safe to say that most of the mainline denominations (Lutheran, Methodist, Anglican, Presbyterian, etc.) place little emphasis on teaching prophecy.

Biblical illiteracy in America, even among Christians who describe themselves as "born again," is rampant. The Barna Group's 2009 study on the state of American Christianity revealed that only 9 percent of American adults possess a biblical worldview,[668] and among "born-again" believers, only 19 percent were found to hold a biblical worldview.[669] It is no surprise, then, that Christians, especially in the West, know little about Bible prophecy, and what we do know may have been absorbed from movies or popular fiction rather than from the Bible itself.

And therein lies the seed of a great deception, possibly the greatest in all of history—one that may lead millions to destruction and lures an untold number of Jews and Christians into welcoming the Antichrist when he appears on the world stage.

A 2013 survey that was widely reported by conservative media trumpeted the surprising conclusion that 2 in 5 American adults claim to believe that they're living in the end times prophesied by the Bible.[670] Among evangelicals, the proportion rose to 3 out of 4.

But the survey did not ask the key question: What do the end times look like to people who, judging by the Barna Group's research, have a shaky grasp on Christian doctrine at best? Many, if not most, who say they believe they're living in the last days don't actually know what the Bible says about them.

Here is another point to consider: Even those of us who have devoted time to the study of Bible prophecy (and please note that this author is by no means a scholar) usually don't bother to consider what people of other faiths believe about eschatology. Christians aren't the only global religion with prophecies about the end of the world as we know it. Actions are driven by beliefs, and history is filled with irrational actions motivated by faith in things that proved false.[671]

It is in this light that we briefly consider what the world's other monotheistic religions believe about the end of history. Their responses to events that fulfill their faiths' eschatological expectations appear to be revealed to us in the end-times prophecies of the Bible.

A disclaimer first: This author is admittedly not a scholar of the Bible and even less so of the teachings of Jews and Muslims. Further, Islam and Judaism are not equal monolithic religions. Both faiths are subdivided into sects that hold differing and often contradictory beliefs. Thus the summary below should not be taken as authoritative or exhaustive. Not everyone who identifies as a Jew or Muslim will necessarily hold all (or any) of these beliefs.

This analysis is intended only to demonstrate that the enemy—the principalities, powers, thrones, and dominions referred to by the apostle Paul—has set in motion a brilliant end-times deception that may convince many that the Antichrist is actually the Messiah.

Muslim eschatology is dominated by two prophesied figures. The Mahdi, or "rightly-guided one," is similar to the Jewish understanding of the *mashiach*,[672] a mortal man who plays a central role in defeating the enemies of Allah. The Dajjal is the Islamic Antichrist figure. Interestingly, neither the Mahdi or the Dajjal are mentioned in the Quran. All that is known about them comes from the *Hadith*, collections of reports that purportedly preserve the sayings of Muhammad verbatim.

Unlike the Quran, which was compiled under the authority of the early Islamic authorities in Medina, the Hadith were not collected until the eighth and ninth centuries, and the sayings were not evaluated by a central authority. Islamic scholars in the centuries since have divided the

Hadith into *sahih* (authentic), *hasan* (strong), and *daʾif* (weak), although there is no universal agreement on which are which. Sunni and Shia Muslims refer to different collections of Hadith, and there is a small group of Quranists who reject its authority altogether.

This makes it as difficult to compile an authoritative list of what Muslims believe about the end times as it is to identify a universal set of Christian eschatological beliefs—in other words, impossible. There are fundamental differences that have divided Sunnis and Shias for more than thirteen hundred years and they naturally carry over into eschatology. For example: Sunnis believe the Mahdi has yet to appear on earth, while Shias believe they will see his return. Those views are as mutually exclusive as those that distinguish the Christian Messiah from the Jewish *mashiach*.

Two other figures play key roles in Islamic eschatology: Isa, the Muslim conception of Jesus, who will appear in the last hour to kill the Dajjal (or help the Mahdi do so), and the Sufyani, a Muslim tyrant (or national hero, depending on the sect) who will emerge in Damascus before the Mahdi's arrival.

Isa's return, oddly enough, *is* prophesied in the Quran,[673] although Muslims believe Isa/Jesus did not die on the cross but was taken up into heaven by Allah. Isa, in spite of his miraculous birth (Muslims do believe Mary was a virgin) and rescue from the cross, will die like any other mortal man some years after his return.

The Sufyani, like the Mahdi and the Dajjal, is an apocryphal figure mentioned only in the Hadith. This character illustrates the depth of the hostility between Sunnis and Shias. His name stems from his ancestor, one Abu Sufyan, the leader of Muhammad's tribe who initially persecuted the self-proclaimed prophet and his followers. Although he and his family eventually converted to the faith, Abu Sufyan's son fought Muhammad's son-in-law, Ali, for control of the new Islamic empire, and eventually became the caliph.[674]

Ali's supporters, the "Shi'at Ali" ("partisans of Ali" and later just "the

Shi'a"), formed their own sect that persists to this day. The Shia soon began teaching that the Mahdi would return someday to defeat the champion of the Sunnis, the Sufyani, in the Levant. Many Shias today believe the Sufyani's emergence is imminent, which they believe is a bad thing because of his opposition to the Mahdi.

Conversely, some Sunnis see the Sufyani as a sort of national hero, especially in Syria, the historic homeland of the Sufyani's ancestors.[675] And unlike Shia prophecies that portray Syria in a negative light because it will be the birthplace of the Sufyani, it holds a place of honor for Sunnis as the site of the decisive future victory over the forces of Rome.

This adds more fuel to an already incendiary situation. Some 670 million Muslims, including an overwhelming majority in the Middle East and western Asia, expect to see the Mahdi in their lifetimes, which roughly means sometime during the first half of the twenty-first.[676] But Sunnis and Shias, like Jews and (most) Christians, are looking for different men to fulfill their prophecies.

It seems a safe guess that the typical Muslim is not much better informed about his or her faith than the typical Christian. So while large majorities in nations like Syria, Iraq, and Afghanistan expect the Mahdi's return in the near future,[677] their expectations—which are already built on teachings drawn from sometimes contradictory Hadith of dubious authenticity—may be shaped to fit current events by charismatic and persuasive imams or political leaders.

In very broad strokes, then, we can establish some common expectations:

1. The "last hour" will be preceded by corruption, widespread unbelief, oppression of Muslims, declining standards of living, wars and anarchy, sexual immorality, the emergence of false prophets, and an increase in technology.
2. The armies of Rome will land at al-A'maq, a valley near Antakya (Antioch) in southern Turkey, or in Dabiq, a rural village in Syria between Aleppo and the border with Turkey. The Muslims triumph

over the "Romans" and go on to conquer Constantinople (Istanbul). This belief is central to the apocalyptic theology of the Islamic State (ISIS), which as mentioned earlier in this book, named its official magazine *Dabiq* to emphasize its significance.

3. The Dajjal emerges from the East, possibly from Khorasan (the traditional name of a region in eastern Iran and western Afghanistan), and remains on earth, deceiving and oppressing people for forty days, forty months, or forty years.

4. Isa (Jesus) descends from heaven at Damascus and either helps the Mahdi kill the Dajjal or kills the Dajjal himself.

5. The Sufyani fields an army to fight the Mahdi, but the earth swallows the Sufyani and his followers before they reach the Mahdi.

6. When the fighting is over, Isa and the Mahdi will lead prayers at Jerusalem. Al-Mahdi will try to defer to Isa, but Isa will insist on remaining subordinate to the Mahdi. The two will rule over the earth for forty years before dying of old age.

Obviously, there is far more to Islamic eschatology than just the above. However, since much of it is not universally believed or deals with supernatural events that take place after the defeat of al-Dajjal, they do not concern us here.

And then there are multiple variations on the main theme that are unique to either Sunnis or Shias. Some Sunnis believe the Dajjal will come from Iran; some Shias believe the civil war in Syria is a sign that the end times are upon us. Both sects declare that the other will mistake the Dajjal for the Mahdi, and news accounts of the apocalyptic beliefs of young Muslim men fighting each other in the Syrian civil war convey the sense that Sunnis and Shias are slaughtering each other for the privilege of going toe-to-toe with the Dajjal.

It must be noted that while Mecca and Medina are the holiest sites in Islam, future events in Islamic prophecy are focused on the Levant. Damascus and Jerusalem are far more important in Islamic eschatology than the cities that gave birth to Islam. Perhaps not coincidentally, Jerusalem, site of the resurrection of Jesus, and Damascus, where Paul converted, played key roles in the establishment of Christianity.[678]

Because of the Islamic State's surprising resilience, we must consider their interpretation of Islamic eschatology when trying to project into the future. There are important questions about some of the events on the group's prophetic timeline. In particular, when ISIS refers to Rome, we must ask: which one?

When Muhammad reportedly prophesied the future battle at al-A'maq or Dabiq, Rome wasn't Rome anymore. The Western Roman Empire ended in AD 476, 150 years before Muhammad's rise to power. In Muhammad's day, the remnant of the Roman Empire was centered on the Byzantine capital, Constantinople (modern Istanbul). Nor did Rome wield the religious influence most modern readers assume the Vatican possessed until at least a couple hundred years after the time of Muhammad.

So who or what is meant by "Rome"? Even the rank-and-file Islamic State faithful don't agree, variously identifying Rome as the Roman Catholic Church, "Christendom" (Western Europe), the United States, or Turkey (which is ironic, since an uncomfortable amount of evidence suggests that the governments of Turkey, the United States, and other Western allies actively assisted the Islamic State up to and even beyond the point that it declared the caliphate).[679, 680, 681]

More important, as noted above, is the fundamental disagreement between Sunnis and Shias over the identity of the Mahdi. Sunnis, who comprise an estimated 87–90 percent of Muslims worldwide,[682] have traditionally derived religious authority from the caliphate. The first caliph was appointed by the companions of Muhammad at his death as the prophet left no male heir.

Shias, however, follow the bloodline of Muhammad, believing that his true heir descends from the prophet's cousin and son by marriage, Ali. To Shias, and more specifically Twelver Shias, the Mahdi is the

Twelfth Imam, Muhammad al-Mahdi, who went into hiding in AD 873 at the age of four.

Or so it is claimed. His father, Hasan al-Askari, lived his life under house arrest and was poisoned at the age of twenty-eight, probably by the Abbasid caliph, dying without a male heir. That might have been the end of Shia Islam, except that one Abu Sahl al-Nawbakhti of Baghdad saved the day by claiming that al-Askari did, in fact, have a son who had gone into *ghaybah*—"occultation" or "hiding." Like King Arthur, who will return at the hour of England's greatest need, the Twelfth Imam will emerge from occultation at the end of the age to usher in an age of peace and justice, and to establish Islam as the global religion.

In short, the Mahdi's appearance will either be the arrival of a "rightly guided" Sunni Muslim leader, a mortal man who will rule for a time and then die, or the return of a Shiite Imam who has been supernaturally preserved for over eleven hundred years.

This is a key distinction: For Shias, the Mahdi must reappear as one specific person. In Sunni theology, "The mantle of the Mahdi can be appropriated, in the right context, by a charismatic leader megalomaniacal enough to believe Allah is directing him to wage divinely-guided jihad."[683] Unlike Sunnis, Shias do not believe that human action can affect the timing of the last hour's arrival.

Furthermore, there are reasons to believe that Shias, especially in Iran, are not necessarily eager for the Mahdi's return. The ayatollahs, who rule about 40 percent of the world's Shia Muslims, would find the return of al-Mahdi an obstacle to maintaining their positions of authority—and with them, their comfortable lives of nice cars, attractive wives, and big houses.

One Israeli scholar puts it bluntly:

Shi`ism in general, and post-revolutionary Iranian Shi`ism in particular, is *not* only *not* messianic or apocalyptic in character, but is in fact the fiercest enemy of messianism to be found anywhere in the Muslim world or Islamic history.[684]

That may be a surprise to American readers who have listened to conservative media commentators claim for years that Twelver Shias wanted nothing more than to trigger the Apocalypse and expedite al-Mahdi's return by destroying Israel. But beyond the threat that messianism poses to lives and lifestyles of Iran's theocratic elites, since the *truly* faithful believe it wouldn't change the timetable at all and that the Mahdi and Isa/Jesus are prophesied to lead the faithful in prayer at Jerusalem, it would seem the ayatollahs have a compelling reason *not* to turn the Temple Mount into a radioactive crater for the Twelfth Imam.

That said, it is still a safe bet that at least one and perhaps several military battles for Zion are in the future. The Temple Mount is the prize, and its significance is recognized by Muslims, Jews, and Christians. And Sunni Muslims, whose long history of radical Mahdist movements continues in the Islamic State, generally believe the last hour can be jump-started. In that light, some of the more extreme actions of the Islamic State are understandable (but nevertheless unconscionable) as attempts to draw "Rome" into that fateful showdown at Dabiq.

In broad terms, the eschatological beliefs of Jews and Christians are more similar to those of Shia Muslims than those of Sunnis, at least insofar as the influence humans can have on the timeline of the last days. And since Christians and Jews share the prophecies of the Hebrew prophets, it isn't surprising that there are some similarities in their eschatological teachings. However, it is in the differences, and the failure of many professing Christians to understand the basics of Bible prophecy, that danger lies.

As with Christian interpretations of end-times prophecy, Israel will face an existential threat from a coalition of enemies invading from the north—the prophecy of the war of Gog and Magog recorded in Ezekiel chapters 38 and 39. Typically, Christians understand that this war will end when God intervenes and supernaturally destroys the invading army with "torrential rains and hailstones, fire and sulfur" (Ezekiel 38:22, ESV). The Messiah plays no overt role in this battle, and Christians debate whether they will still be on earth during this war, as some believe the conflict takes place after a Rapture of the Church.

However, Jews believe the *mashiach* does participate. In fact, *two* are expected in Jewish prophecy—Mashiach ben Yosef and Mashiach ben David. Both are men of this world, observant Jews, rather than supernatural saviors.

> The origin and character of the Messiah of the tribe of Joseph, or Ephraim, are rather obscure. It seems that the assumed superhuman character of the Messiah appeared to be in conflict with the tradition that spoke of his death, and therefore the figure of a Messiah who would come from the tribe of Joseph, or Ephraim, instead of from Judah, and who would willingly undergo suffering for his nation and fall as victim in the Gog and Magog war, was created by the haggadists.[685]

In short, Mashiach ben Yosef is killed during the Magog invasion and then replaced and later resurrected by Mashiach ben David (or Elijah), who then goes on to purify Jerusalem, gather the Jews to Israel, build the Third Temple, reinstitute the Sanhedrin, and restore the system of sacrifices.

To be sure, not all Jews believe in the literal coming of the *mashiach*. Generally speaking, Orthodox and Hasidic Jews are most likely to await his arrival, while Conservative, Reform, and Deconstructionist Jews tend to view the *mashiach's* appearance as symbolizing the redemption of mankind from the evils of the world.

These divergent views within the body of modern Judaism, as with Islam, allow for a wide range of interpretations when it comes to analyzing the prophetic significance of current events. This is also true for Christianity. The quickest way to start an argument among a group of Christians is to ask, "Pre-, mid-, or post?" The question refers, of course, to the timing of the Rapture and where it falls relative to the Great Tribulation, the prophesied seven-year countdown to the Messiah's return, a time when God pours out His divine judgment on an unbelieving world. And lately, "pre-wrath" has earned a place on that list, an interpretation that places the Rapture during the Great Tribulation but before the Day of the Lord.

There are also differences of opinion between Christian premillennialists, postmillennialists, and amillennialists. Those terms broadly describe people who hold differing beliefs in the timing of the millennial reign of Jesus—whether he returns at the beginning or end of the thousand-year period described in Revelation 20:1–6, or whether the Millennium is symbolic or spiritual (and clearly not a literal period of one thousand years), inaugurated at Christ's resurrection.

In the second half of the twentieth century, charismatic Christians in North America spawned a new teaching about the end times that, frankly, is so far removed from Scripture that it is not even properly called an interpretation. Emerging from the apostolic-prophetic movement, which is itself an outgrowth of the Latter-Rain movement of the 1950s and '60s, the so-called New Apostolic Reformation takes a postmillennial view of prophecy (although that is not universally true in this movement) and teaches a "victorious eschatology" featuring a triumphant Church that completely Christianizes the world before the return of Jesus.

This view is called Dominion Theology, or Kingdom Now. Some under this umbrella teach that a select group of believers will literally defeat the enemies of God, including the Antichrist (if he is mentioned at all), sin, and death. In some iterations of this doctrine, this elite group of super-Christians literally becomes the incarnate Christ. This twist of Revelation 12:5 places the birth of Jesus, the "man child," in the future as a prophecy of His return. It also transforms Christ *into* the Church, a "corporate Christ," the Many-Membered Man-Child. This heretical doctrine, called Manifest Sons of God, is also an outgrowth of the Latter-Rain movement that has survived into the twenty-first century.

Furthermore, some teach that Christ, however He appears, will not or cannot return until Christians physically take back the dominion over the earth that was lost when Satan deceived Adam and Eve in Eden. This doctrine is based on a misapplication of Psalm 110:1:

> The LORD says to my Lord: "Sit at my right hand, until I make your enemies your footstool."

Dominionism thus substitutes the Church for God, making Christians responsible for defeating His enemies, or for Jesus, based on the notion that since Christ is the head of the Church, we Christians are the "feet" with His enemies subservient to us. Either way, this is heresy.

This teaching contradicts Hebrews 2:8, Ephesians 1:20–23, and 1 Corinthians 15:24–28. While it is clear that much of the world is still in bondage to the enemies of God, "He put all things under [Christ's] feet and gave him as head over all things to the church" (Ephesians 1:22, ESV). This is an "already but not yet" prophecy; creation is already subject to Christ, and a day is yet coming when He will return to claim the earth and all that is in it.

Dominionism is a variant of replacement theology, or supersessionism, which teaches that the Church has replaced Israel in all prophecies yet unfulfilled. This includes the land promised to Abraham's descendants in Genesis 15:18–21 and Joshua 1:3–4, the area from the River of Egypt[686] to the Euphrates. This would be problematic in today's world, to say the least—that area includes the Palestinian territories, Jordan, Lebanon, and parts of Syria, Iraq, Kuwait, and Saudi Arabia.

Quite frankly, Dominionist eschatology skips over the uncomfortable bits that foretell a time when the Antichrist will be "allowed to make war on the saints and to conquer them" (Revelation 13:7; also Daniel 7:21, ESV). But just as with the Mahdi of Sunni Islam, modern-day prophets and apostles of the New Apostolic Reformation believe they are anointed to receive new revelations that allow them to interpret Holy Scripture in any way they see fit.

While Dominion theology may sound like an outlier in modern

Christianity, this relatively small group wields a surprising amount of influence with the conservative right in America. Elements of Dominionist doctrine have found their way into such mainstream evangelical events as the National Day of Prayer.[687] And while the trend of moral decay in the West makes it unlikely that Americans will ever elect an openly Dominionist president, the influence of Dominion theology may very well lead some conservative Christians to welcome a world leader who promises to usher in a new Judeo-Christian era.

Admittedly, these are incomplete descriptions the eschatological positions described above, and there is a range of often conflicting opinions within all of them. However, it should be enough to see that end-times expectations of the three major monotheistic religions are widely divided with one another and within themselves. As events unfold, they will be interpreted differently by those religions and their imams, rabbis, ayatollahs, pastors, priests, and teachers.

To outside observers, it must be confusing that adherents of a religion who rely on the same set of holy texts can arrive at conclusions that are so radically different. As this is true of the basic doctrines of the faiths, which are spelled out in the Quran, Torah, Tanakh, and Bible, it is even more true of their interpretations of prophecy, much of which must be drawn from symbolic language that may not even be part of the holy books themselves.

In the Bible, this vagueness is by design. The apostle Paul tells us that prophecy is the "secret and hidden wisdom of God, which God decreed before the ages for our glory. None of the rulers of this age understood this, for if they had, they would not have crucified the Lord of glory" (1 Corinthians 2:7–8, ESV).

Paul was telling the Church at Corinth that Old Testament prophecies of the coming Messiah were vague enough that the fallen angels and their demonic minions did not understand Christ's purpose on earth. If they had, Paul wrote, they would have done everything in their power to prevent the crucifixion.[688] The messianic prophecies that seem obvious today—for example, Psalm 22 and Isaiah 53—were not at all clear to those around Jesus as they were being fulfilled. Only in retrospect did the apostles understand, and apparently the enemy was caught off guard, too.

Think about that. God, in His wisdom, obscured the prophecies of the Messiah just enough to prevent the enemy from devising a convincing false fulfillment. And there have been plenty of false messiahs persuasive enough to lead people astray over the last two thousand years. Most notable was Simon bar Kokhba, who led a revolt that created a short-lived independent Jewish state before it was crushed by Rome in AD 136. More than half a million Jews were killed by the Roman army,[689] leaving Judaea depopulated, Jerusalem destroyed, and the land renamed Syria Palaestina—Palestine. The net result of bar Kokhba's rebellion was the end of hope for an independent Jewish state in the Holy Land for nearly two thousand years.

We should not expect prophecies of Christ's return to be any more specific than those of His birth. And that is the point: The principalities and powers who seek the destruction of humanity have been hard at work spreading extra-biblical teachings over the last two thousand years, both inside and outside the Church. The goal is to use wild misinterpretations of end-times prophecy to lure Christians, Jews, Muslims, and perhaps many of other faiths into welcoming the Antichrist when he appears on the world stage. That is why a firm grasp of the basics of Bible prophecy is critically important.

In spite of the clear warning in Scripture that Satan can appear as an angel of light, Christians should be especially wary of messianic claims as we approach the last days. Getting it wrong means literally siding with the devil.

Consider the following scenario: War erupts between Israel and its nearby Muslim neighbors. This would not be a surprise in 2016, given recent history in the Middle East, but the prophet Daniel was told about this twenty-five hundred years ago:

At the time of the end, the king of the south shall attack him, but the king of the north shall rush upon him like a whirlwind, with chariots and horsemen, and with many ships. And he shall come into countries and shall overflow and pass through.

He shall come into the glorious land. And tens of thousands shall fall, but these shall be delivered out of his hand: Edom and Moab and the main part of the Ammonites.

He shall stretch out his hand against the countries, and the land of Egypt shall not escape.

He shall become ruler of the treasures of gold and of silver, and all the precious things of Egypt, and the Libyans and the Cushites shall follow in his train.

But news from the east and the north shall alarm him, and he shall go out with great fury to destroy and devote many to destruction. (Daniel 11:40–45, ESV)

It is generally accepted by scholars that this is a prophecy of the future wars of the Antichrist. The account is plausible enough that it reads like a summary of one of Israel's wars from the last half-century.

The king of the south is probably Egypt. Although the nation now appears to want Israel as an ally against the Shia power in the region, Iran, Egypt was long an enemy of Israel and holds a special place in the psyche of Jews as the nation that enslaved their ancestors. In recent history, Egypt was a principal belligerent in both 1967's Six-Day War and 1973's Yom Kippur War. And we saw in 2011, when the Muslim Brotherhood ousted former president Hosni Mubarak (with the tacit approval of the United States government), that Egypt is just one change of government away from becoming an enemy again.

The king of the north may represent an Arab coalition against Israel. Other than Egypt, invaders throughout history have tradition-ally attacked Israel from the north—Syria, Assyria, Babylon, Persia, Greece, and Rome all came into the Holy Land from the north. It is not a coincidence that the "uttermost north," the phrase used to describe the location of Magog in Ezekiel 38 and 39, is used elsewhere in the Old Testament to describe the dwelling place of Baal, Mount Zaphon (Jebel al-Aqra in northern Syria).

In today's world, it is not difficult to imagine Sunni nations forming an alliance as they did in 1948, 1967, and 1973, some combination of Syria, Lebanon, Iraq (or parts thereof), Saudi Arabia, and Jordan. Given the apocalyptic expectations of the Sunnis in the Middle East, it is not inconceivable that these nations would unite behind a charismatic leader who might be proclaimed by his followers as the Mahdi.[690]

Naturally, Christians and Jews in today's geopolitical climate would be just as likely to identify this Muslim leader as the Antichrist[691]—albeit incorrectly.

Such a coalition would seem to fulfill the prophecy of Psalm 83:

O God, do not keep silence;
do not hold your peace or be still, O God!
For behold, your enemies make an uproar;
those who hate you have raised their heads.
They lay crafty plans against your people;
they consult together against your treasured ones.
They say, "Come, let us wipe them out as a nation;
let the name of Israel be remembered no more!"
For they conspire with one accord;
against you they make a covenant—
the tents of Edom [Jordan and Palestinians] and the Ishmaelites [Saudi Arabia],
Moab [Jordan and Palestinians] and the Hagrites [Egypt; from Hagar, Sarah's Egyptian servant],
Gebal [Hezbollah and Lebanon] and Ammon [Jordan and Palestinians] and Amalek [Arabs in the Sinai, where ISIS now has a presence],

Philistia [Hamas and Palestinians of Gaza] with the inhabitants
of Tyre [Hezbollah—although Shia, definitely hostile to Israel—
and Lebanon];
Asshur [Syria and northern Iraq] also has joined them;
they are the strong arm of the children of Lot.
(Psalm 83:1–8, ESV)[692]

These verses name all of the Muslim Arab nations in the immediate
vicinity of Israel. If Psalm 83 does foretell a future event, Daniel 11 may
describe how it unfolds.

It is widely agreed that the "him" in Daniel 11:40–44 is the character
called the Antichrist, and that he is distinct from the kings of the north
and south. To many, it logically follows that this leader, who emerges
from this war as the victor over Israel's traditional enemies, will be an
Israeli and will likely present himself to the world as a Jew.

Not all scholars agree with this interpretation, but it makes sense.
First, it points to the most logical national origin of a political figure
who can motivate the Jews to build the Third Temple and reinstitute the
sacrifices and offerings. It is difficult to see that an Antichrist from any
other faith tradition would allow this to happen. Second, it is difficult
to imagine that a European or Muslim Antichrist would conduct the
prophesied war of Daniel 11.

This is not a new idea. In fact, it's a very old interpretation. Some
early Church Fathers, including Irenaeus and Hippolytus, believed the
Antichrist would be a Jew. Interestingly, Hippolytus was a disciple of
Irenaeus, who was a disciple of Polycarp, who was a disciple of the apostle John. So it is possible that the concept of a Jewish Antichrist came
directly from the man who was given the Revelation by Jesus Christ
Himself.

Certainly, this notion will not sit well with American evangelicals, who support the nation of Israel more enthusiastically than most
American Jews. Please note that I only suggest this figure will *present*

himself as a Jew. Given that he will seat himself in the rebuilt Temple and declare himself a god, we can safely conclude that he will not actually *be* a Jew.

The recent popularity of the Muslim Antichrist theory is understandable given the acts of raw, unspeakable evil committed by the Islamic State in the service of their god. The reader may wonder, understandably, why the Antichrist would lead a war to destroy his most enthusiastic followers.

The answer is quite simple: Muslims, in the eyes of the enemy, are already lost. Those who embrace the false teachings of Muhammad are destined for destruction. The real prizes are the followers of Jesus Christ and the people God chose for Himself when he called Abram from the city of Ur. Thus the best use the enemy has for Muslims at this point is as cannon fodder—a bloody sacrifice to lure as many Jews and Christians as possible into worshipping the Beast, whom they will mistakenly see as a literal godsend.

In the interest of brevity, let us bullet-point a potential sequence of events triggered by this Psalm 83/Daniel 11 war:

- Arab nations launch a surprise attack against Israel.
- A dynamic military and/or political figure leads Israel to an overwhelming victory.
- He "comes into the glorious land," possibly by taking the West Bank and Gaza (fulfilling the prophecy of Zephaniah 2).
- "News from the east and the north" provokes the next phase of the Antichrist's war, possibly strikes against Muslim nations joining the conflict from farther away, such as Turkey, Iran, Pakistan, and some of the Muslim republics in central Asia.
- Although it appears the country of Jordan is spared, it is not a stretch to read into Daniel's account an expansion of Israel's territory, which would likely be interpreted as God fulfilling the land promise made to Abraham.

Now, reflect for a moment: Certainly Muslims in the region, where the majority of Sunnis expect the Mahdi's arrival in the very near future, would be tempted (and perhaps encouraged by religious and political leaders) to view a charismatic Israeli leader as the Dajjal. This would accelerate the recent trend of young Muslim men flocking to Syria to take part in what they believe are the final battles leading to victorious global jihad.

After the decisive victory by the Antichrist, Muslim eschatology ceases to be relevant. As mentioned above, their beliefs serve the Enemy's purpose, which is to draw them into a bloody war that they will lose to establish the claim of the Antichrist as the prophesied savior of Israel.

Jews, who are still looking for a geopolitical *mashiach*, could interpret this conflict as the war of Gog and Magog, which is the ultimate battle in Jewish eschatology. Some Orthodox rabbis are openly predicting the imminent arrival of the *mashiach*; in fact, some have already declared that the ongoing Syrian civil war is, in fact, the war of Gog and Magog.[693] The hero of this apocalyptic war would be welcomed by many as Israel's long-awaited *mashiach*.

And how would American Christians receive such a man? Evangelicals typically view strong Israeli leaders, such as the prime minister at the time of this writing, Benjamin Netanyahu, in a very positive light. Conservative American Christians, especially those with a poor understanding of Bible prophecy (or those not expecting a literal fulfillment of Daniel, Ezekiel, and Revelation), might actually work to elevate such a man to the status of a world leader—which, of course, is his ultimate destiny, if only for a short while.

But the Dominionist segment of Christianity, which already ignores the Antichrist in its bizarre mutation of end-times prophecy, is looking instead for a Christianized version of victorious global jihad. In their world, Christ cannot return until Christians take over the earth, perhaps with Jews as a blended body of believers, the One New Man. The apostolic-prophetic movement might just see this victorious Israeli figure as

Christ incarnate, a fulfillment of their expected Manifest Sons of God. Remember, since the apostles and prophets leading this movement claim the authority of their biblical forebears, which includes the men who wrote the New Testament, they have the freedom to twist and supplement Scripture as needed to make their doctrine fit current events.

Now, consider the world's reaction to the next item in the chronicle of the wars of Antichrist:

> And he shall pitch his palatial tents between the sea and the glorious holy mountain. Yet he shall come to his end, with none to help him.(Daniel 11:45, ESV)

The Antichrist sets up his government somewhere between the Mediterranean coast and Jerusalem. But he meets an unexpected end, perhaps by assassination. How could this figure be the Antichrist, then, if he is killed before he commits "the abomination that causes desolation" by desecrating the Temple and declaring his divinity? We look to the Revelation of John:

> And I saw a beast rising out of the sea, with ten horns and seven heads, with ten diadems on its horns and blasphemous names on its heads. And the beast that I saw was like a leopard; its feet were like a bear's, and its mouth was like a lion's mouth. And to it the dragon gave his power and his throne and great authority. **One of its heads seemed to have a mortal wound, but its mortal wound was healed, and the whole earth marveled as they followed the beast.** (Revelation 13:1–3, ESV, emphasis added.)

The seemingly miraculous healing of the Antichrist will amaze the world, convincing many of his divinity. You will have realized by now that this is a chilling parallel with Jewish eschatology. Jews expect Mashiach ben Yosef to die in the war with Magog, after which Mashiach ben David arrives to kill the enemy leader with the breath of his mouth, and then brings Mashiach ben Yosef back to life.

In some traditions, Mashiach ben David goes on to purify Jerusalem and Israel. If the Israeli Antichrist theory is correct, that has disturbing implications. The purification includes removing non-Jews from Jerusalem. It is not our intention to cast aspersions on our Jewish brothers and sisters, but the Antichrist's "war on the saints," prophesied in Daniel 7 and Revelation 13, will happen at some point, and this seems the likely spot in the prophetic timeline.

It should be noted that the final break between early Christians and their Jewish neighbors in Judaea did not occur in the first century. During the revolt led by Simon bar Kokhba, which began in AD 132, he was hailed as the *mashiach* by the prominent Rabbi Akiva. Bar Kokhba's name was actually Simon ben Kosiba; bar Kokhba ("son of the star") was a messianic claim based on his supposed fulfillment of the prophecy of Balaam, son of Beor:

> I see him, but not now;
> I behold him, but not near:
> a star shall come out of Jacob,
> and a scepter shall rise out of Israel
> (Numbers 22:17, ESV)

Christians, who until that point had attended synagogue and were still considered a Jewish sect, could not agree to recognize a mortal man as Messiah and refused to fight for bar Kokhba. Their punishment was confinement and death.[694]

In recent years, a rise in Zionist sentiment among Israelis appears to have rehabilitated the reputation of Simon bar Kokhba. In the aftermath of his disastrous rebellion, he was derisively called bar Koziba ("son of the lie").[695] Today, however, bar Kokhba is something of a national hero.[696] Bonfires are lit on Lag Ba'Omer to celebrate his short-lived Jewish state, and Rabbi Akiva's definition of the *mashiach*, a temporal savior more closely realized in Simon bar Kokhba than in any other Jewish man over the last two thousand years, is still the standard by which Jews will evaluate future claimants to the title.[697]

Sadly, it appears all too likely that this misguided nationalist sentiment will be manipulated by the supernatural Man of Lawlessness to deceive Jews into following him, possibly citing the example of bar Kokhba as he singles out Christians for destruction. And those supporting his reverse pogrom will genuinely believe they are doing God's work—at least until "Mashiach ben David" puts a stop to the sacrifices and declares himself to be God.

Delving into a more detailed, scholarly analysis of end-times prophecy is not the purpose of this chapter. Rather, it is hoped that by highlighting several points of congruence between Islamic, Jewish, and Christian eschatology (especially one particularly dangerous strain of Christian prophetic interpretation), the dangers of a poor grasp of prophecy might become clear.

We will not understand the prophecies of the years to come perfectly in every detail. But our hope is that through study and prayer, those of us still on earth when the prophesied Beast finally emerges will not fall victim to a cosmic deception that has eternal consequences for the unprepared.

13

The Cumaean Sibyl and Visions
of the Final Roman Emperor

THE CUMAEAN SIBYL was the priestess presiding over the Apollonian oracle at a Greek colony named Cumae in today's Naples, Italy. The word *sibyl* is Latin from the ancient Greek word *sibylla*, meaning "prophetess." A famous pagan icon, she predicted the end-time judgment of Rome. Pseudo-Methodius' prediction, whether the Great Monarch for Catholics or the Mahdi for Muslims, has its origin in the legendary sibylline books and possibly the original pagan oracles.[698] The *Sibylline Oracles* are a pseudepigraphal collection of utterances attributed to female visionaries called Sibyls.[699] Although often altered by Christians and Jews, they are a collection of fourteen books and eight fragments, spanning from the second century BC to the early eighth century AD.[700] The surviving texts include remnants of the old Roman *Sibylline Books*, attributed to the pagan prophetess known as the Sibyl. *Eerdman's Bible Dictionary*, a trusted academic source, identifies the extant oracles.

SIBYLLINE ORACLES.† A collection of oracles of Jewish and Christian origin that are part of the Pseudepigrapha. "Sibyl" (Gk. *Sibylla*) may have been the name of a specific legendary

319

Greek prophetess, but it became an international term for a type of oracular literature usually focused on predictions of wide-scale disasters, political upheavals, and, sometimes, *a golden age under a great world leader*. A number of collections of Sibylline oracles from different parts of the Mediterranean world and the Near East existed. (emphasis added)[701]

The oldest collection of Sibylline books was attributed to the Hellespontine Sibyl and was well-kept in the temple of Apollo at Gergis. From Gergis the collection passed to Erythrae, where it became famous as the oracles of the Erythraean Sibyl. It would appear to have been this very collection that found its way to the well-known Cumaean Sibyl and from Cumae to Rome to Syria and finally to the Great Seal of the United States of America, which is, according to occult scholar Manly P. Hall, the Cumaean Sibyl's prophecy of the coming of Apollo/Osiris/Nimrod—whom we call Antichrist.[702] It is especially notable that the eastern division of the original Catholic Church, Islam, and most all of Freemasonic occultism share a similar belief in an end-time king who seems to set the world straight, ushering in a period of peace and prosperity. This is in accord with the first three and a half years of the final seven in Daniel's seventy-week prophecy.

Many ancient references to the Sibyl's prophecies survive in various quotations. For example, Plato and Aristotle mentioned the original oracular poems, which in their original pagan forms seem buried under Jewish and Christian revisionism. Although many of the older books burned in a fire, the original pagan oracles were collected in 76 BC and an official edition was issued by the Roman Empire, an edition mentioned as late as AD 405. This fact makes it seem unlikely that the apologists writing to Romans would try such an obvious alteration. Recall that Justin was a disciple of Irenaeus of Lyons (AD 175),[703] who was mentored by Polycarp who learned from John, the "apostle Jesus loved" (John 21:20).[704] John was the only one who did not run after Jesus' arrest and subsequently composed his Gospel, the strongest statement of Jesus' divinity, the Johannine epistles, exhorting virtue and confession of sin, and, Methodius' alleged Revelation aside, the final inspired *Apocalypse* in the canon of Scripture. One cannot be taught in a better line of tradition as to the inspired author of Revelation's original intention than Irenaeus and Justin, and, preterism aside, these early Christians all still awaited a future Antichrist and Jerusalem Temple. Irenaeus wrote:

> But when this Antichrist shall have devastated all things in this world, he will reign for three years and six months, and sit in the temple at Jerusalem; and then the Lord will come from heaven in the clouds, in the glory of the Father, sending this man and those who follow him into the lake of fire; but bringing in for the righteous the times of the kingdom, that is, the rest, the hallowed seventh day; and restoring to Abraham the promised inheritance, in which kingdom the Lord declared, that "many coming from the east and from the west should sit down with Abraham, Isaac, and Jacob" (Matthew 8:11).[705]

The early Christian Church actually took these oracles quite seriously and codified and even composed many of the extant manuscripts. During the formational period of the Church, the early apologists frequently cited the Sibyl in apologetic arguments. Justin Martyr (AD150),[706] Theophilus, Bishop of Antioch (AD 180), Clement of Alexandria (AD 200), Lactantius (AD 305), and Augustine (AD 400), all cited various versions of the prophecies often reinterpreting or "Christianizing" them. Constantine, the first Christian emperor, quoted a long passage of the Sibylline Oracles (Book 8) containing an acrostic in which the initials from a series of verses read: Jesus Christ Son of God Saviour Cross. Some oracles are decidedly Christian oriented. It doesn't bode well for Rome.

Is the end of the world and the last day And judgment of the immortal God for them That are approved and chosen. And there shall Against the Romans first of all be wrath Implacable, and there, come a time. (Sibylline Book III: 120)

Some fragmentary verses that do not appear in the collections that survive are only known because they were quoted by a Church Father Justin Martyr (ca. 150) in his "Hortatory Address to the Greeks," specifically mentioning the Cumaean Sibyl "having no remembrance of what she had said, after the possession and inspiration ceased."[707] Even so, part of Justin's apologetic was that the pagans, despite their embrace of idols, *did* know of the One True God. He wrote:

We must also mention what the ancient and exceedingly remote Sibyl, whom Plato and Aristophanes, and others besides, mention as a prophetess, taught you in her oracular verses concerning one only God. And she speaks thus:—
"There is one only unbegotten God,
Omnipotent, invisible, most high,
All-seeing, but Himself seen by no flesh."
Then elsewhere thus:—
"But we have strayed from the Immortal's ways,
And worship with a dull and senseless mind
Idols, the workmanship of our own hands,
And images and figures of dead men."
And again somewhere else:—
"Blessed shall be those men upon the earth
Who shall love the great God before all else,
Blessing Him when they eat and when they drink;
Trusting it, this their piety alone.
Who shall abjure all shrines which they may see,
All altars and vain figures of dumb stones,

Worthless and stained with blood of animals,
And sacrifice of the four-footed tribes,
Beholding the great glory of One God."
These are the Sibyl's words.[708]

Since Justin was arguing with Romans, it is hard to believe he simply altered the text to make his points. The original pagan collection was known to exist and was attested until the fifth century, so his opponents would have surely called him out. Justin leaves no doubt by ending his three citations with one remark, "These are the Sibyl's words."[709] His basic argument is that, "Even your own prophetess told you there was one creator God and that your temples are full of useless idols," an idea that nicely parallels the Hebrew prophets (Isaiah 2:8; Jeremiah 50:2; Ezekiel 22:3). However, if they are, in fact, from the ancient Roman Sibylline, they truly are rather shocking coming from the heart of ancient polytheistic paganism. Alternate explanations suggest Justin was "cheating" by putting words in her mouth, including the possibility that he might have accessed versions altered by Jewish scribes or perhaps they reflect monotheism coming from the Judean sibyl (or Babylonian Saba) mentioned later in this chapter. It explains why so many scholars believe books 2 and 3 were heavily altered or even entirely composed by early Christians who simply ascribed their own apologetics to the Sibyl. Even so, if the prophetess truly was not in control of her words as described by Justin, there is no reason to believe the spirit realm truly cared about Rome's imperial opinion, and stated the unvarnished truth of ultimate monotheism, in a Trinitarian sense, of an invisible Creator.

Justin was likely citing an ancient Roman text. Considering the post-Augustinian citations of the Roman Empire's official edition of the Sibylline Oracles, it seems highly unlikely so many well-read Christian apologists would try to convince Roman citizens using obviously altered citations. Roman scholars had access to the Empire's official edition until the fifth century and could easily call Justin—or even, much later, Augustine—out for altering it. We are not aware that any such rejoinders exist, but very little from antiquity is extant so, at best, it's an argument from silence and carries little weight.

We find the character argument more compelling. Jesus taught that honesty was a virtue to be sought. Because the early Church esteemed honesty, it seems unlikely Justin or other serious followers of Jesus intentionally altered the citations to suit a particular point that could have been made with better documentation. These were learned men, schooled in the art of scholarly debate and discourse beyond that which most moderns attain. The sheer output of research and writing still existing from these men demands a strong work ethic at minimum. While such alterations certainly exist, it does not mean every apologist followed such an intellectually dishonest ethic.

While ancient historians do not always agree, there appear to be many Sibylline prophetesses and temples. Between four and twelve such temples appear to be active, simultaneously dispersed across the Roman Empire in major cities after Alexander conquered the known world and Hellenized it. Each temple paid a financial homage to Rome and likely served as an intelligence-gathering arm of the Sibyl. Of course, such information swapping amongst cults is expected.

Perhaps the Sibyl-cult developed and continued to grow in elite circles, especially amongst the wealthiest members of society, some for which money is no object and of whom such occult activity is well attested in the lurid histories of the sorcery-practicing emperors and, later, popes. Throughout the medieval period, belief in such occult traditions reigned. The Roman poet Virgil (70–19 BC) was lauded as a sorcerer of rare expertise.[710]

Such paganism hits home with moderns, given that the New Testament Greek term translated "sorcery" is from the Greek *pharmakeia* or *pharmakon*, depending on the case and tense is where the English "pharmacy" was derived. A basic lexicon notes it is derived from the older word *pharmakeuō*, which meant explicitly "to administer drugs."[711]

However, there is widespread agreement that sorcery involved divination, spirit contact, deception, or curses (including poisoning), rather than the healing arts practiced by doctors like Luke, the esteemed historian of the Christian Church (Luke, Acts).

Lesser known than the Cumaean is the Judean Sibyl, a Jewess who in various incarnations prophesied from the Babylonian captivity into the post-Christian era from Babylon and later, Jerusalem. According to the second-century Greek geographer, Pausanias:

> Later than Demo there grew up among the Hebrews above Palestine a woman who gave oracles and was named Sabbe. They say that the father of Sabbe was Berosus, and her mother Erymanthe. But some call her a Babylonian Sibyl, others an Egyptian.[712]

The Hebrew Sibyl was later known as the Sabbe of Palestine.[713] Reflecting its Roman antiquity, "Sabbe" could be derived from the Aramaic *saba* ("old").[714] Interestingly, the Hebrew term pronounced the same transliterated as *tsaba* means "host," also denoting immortal armies ("host of heaven"). We believe these beings, some of which are fallen, have preserved this tradition to place their "man" in control. The Judean Sibyl was still highly regarded during the New Testament era, even by Jews and Christians.[715] For example, the *Jewish Encyclopedia* stated the Hebrew Sibyl "was regarded as a very ancient personage who perpetuated the wisdom of the past, and the traditions concerning her may consequently be compared with the Jewish legends of Enoch and of Asher's daughter Serah."[716] Finally, the Sybil and/or Pseudo-Methodius might have based the "great monarch" on the Hebrew Bible type of Gideon. The last Roman emperor or Mahdi character is most likely a useful-fiction borrowed from several sources. Even so, the Judean Sibyl may reflect Jewish influence and could explain some of the quotations that seem monotheistic.

In *A Plea for the Christians to Marcus Aurelius* (AD 176), the Christian apologist Athenagoras of Athens quoted the oracles verbatim, amongst many pagan references including Homer and Hesiod, and, stated several times that all these works should already be familiar to the Roman Emperor. Our point is not that he believed in pagan prophecy or deities; his purpose was to cross the cultural divide by reading the pagans' valued books and to speak their language. Much like the apostle Paul's citation of the Greek poet Epimenides (Acts 17:28), the early apologists operated in their own cultural milieu and wrote from a supernatural worldview, which often is alien to our modern, scientific, reductionistic thinking. The *Jewish Encyclopedia* explains the scholarly conundrum of restoring the pagan originals: "Christianity has not only preserved these poems, but has added to them, so that the sibylline utterances in their present form are a mixture of Jewish and Christian elements, imposing upon criticism the task of separating them."[717] To do such work, one must be able to handle Syriac, Greek, and Latin texts, making for a slow process, as not many contributors with ancient language proficiency are available. Even so, there appear to be several literary and character parallels to the popular Sibylline literature, which likely would have been known to a late-sixth-century pseudepigrapher in Damascus or nearby.

As explained in our chapter, *The Last Roman Emperor Becomes the Muslim's Mahdi*, the Mahdi was crafted by Hadith compilers in the seventh and eighth century as a response to the widespread Christian belief in the Apocalypse falsely ascribed to third-century Church Father, Methodius. Many of its prophecies trace back to traditions from the Sibylline literature, which is a hodgepodge of Christian, Jewish, and pagan oracular poems but parallel Bible prophecy in many intriguing ways. Books 2 and 3 of the extant oracles are thought to be the most heavily Christianized but likely have dependence on the previous Jewish Babylonian revisions that would have been most available to the second-century Church. Many parallel the New Testament's final book Revelation in its depiction of Rome as the Great Harlot who rides the

Beast and meets destruction. We continue to watch the world gather together in response to Mahdism.

Freemasonic scholar Manly P. Hall described a Sibylline prophecy in the Great Seal of the United States (as explained in *Zenith 2016*) and now current academic research of medieval literature presents the case that the same Sibylline source inspired the last Roman emperor literary topos resulting in the Catholic monarch and Mahdi traditions via Sibylline paganism and could turn out to be from a very ancient pagan source. Hillary Clinton, whom we identified from her birthdate after the Parsons/Hubbard ritual as the most likely candidate for the Babalon working's "whore of Babalon," is the frontrunner as Democratic presidential candidate.[718] Are we perched at the Zenith? President Obama's ambition to become UN secretary general has become public knowledge. While we label not, we are *very intrigued* by his bravado. More so, Vladamir Putin and Prelate Archbishop Kirill have openly declared a twenty-first century crusade while remaining belligerently pro-Assad/anti-USA, and we cannot help but sense that it is leading to a time when the reptilian spirits will be gathering the world's leaders (Revelation 16:14), and that the world is already perched upon the ultimate battle of biblical prophecy, Armageddon.

What Do Popes and Occultists Believe the Sibyl's Conjure Heralds? Who, Really, Is the Last Emperor of Rome?

[The following information is largely excerpted from the Defender Publishing books *On the Path of the Immortals* and *Zenith 2016*.]

Some years ago I (Tom Horn) was on my way to Roswell, New Mexico, to meet with David Flynn and some other friends. As I recall, we were joining up to support David, who was scheduled to give a presentation during the famous International UFO Festival. While driving, my cell phone rang and on the other end of the line was another friend, filmmaker Chris Pinto. He wanted to know if I would be interested in meeting with him in Washington, DC, in just two days from then to be part of the History Channel's *Brad Meltzer's Decoded* series. Normally I decline all such invitations, as I have witnessed too many times how these programs twist the Christian's worldview, and I'm typically uninterested in sacrificing myself to help somebody's secular ratings. Yet because it was Pinto and the project sounded like it was right down his alley (the *Brad Meltzer's* team was going to "investigate the historical mystery as to what happened to the White House Cornerstone"), I agreed to participate. The History Channel wanted me to speak to the issue of the Washington Monument, why and how it was built, and whether the missing White House cornerstone may lay hidden beneath it. It sounded harmless enough, and so I agreed to turn around and head that way.

Two days later—while Pinto was somewhere across town having already been filmed for the program—I met up with Meltzer's two main field investigators (who can be seen running around the world in the History Channel series checking into whatever the producers pretend to investigate) in DC—Christine McKinley and Scott Rolle. Christine has a mechanical engineering degree from the California Polytechnic University, and Scott Rolle is a circuit court judge in Frederick County, Maryland (and an actor), so I was interested especially in what Christine might think of the engineering feat that the Freemasons had employed in building the largest obelisk of its kind in the world (the Washington Monument). A special permit had been ascertained for the film project, and besides McKinley and Rolle there were at least five camera operators, two producers, technicians, and a huge crowd of people that had gathered to see what was going on. The producer wanted to film McKinley and Rolle (the "investigators") walking up (with the Capitol Dome in their background) while I approached the obelisk from the other direction, and then we would meet up at the base of the monument, greet each other, and begin talking about the mysterious construction project, why it was built, and finally whether I believed the stone was buried beneath it.

But something else happened.

As I started describing the obelisk facing the dome and the rich Egyptian symbolism involving Osiris, Isis, the Freemasons, and how the mechanics of these magical devices were specifically designed to open a doorway or "stargate" that allows Osiris to arise from the underworld to take his rightful place inside every US president (more on that in a bit), the producer became enthralled with the storyline and wanted to continue filming me (for almost two hours) basically describing the plotline from my book *Zenith 2016*. Then Christine McKinley went off-script too, explaining that her father had been a 32nd-Degree Freemason and she wanted to know if I thought he had been part of an occult organization, which led to another half-hour of discussion and, well, we never did get back to the original reason for my being there. The producer then approached me to ask if they could use the film they had shot to pitch a different project to the History Channel, which I agreed to but never heard any more about.

When the *Decoded* episode on the missing White House cornerstone played on television, I was—once again—happy that my face was not included in a History Channel production (and I have since turned them down several times, most recently for their "Search for the Lost Giants" program in which they practically begged me to appear to discuss how transhumanism and the genetics revolution may be repeating what the ancient Watchers did in creating Nephilim). They did, however, include Chris Pinto's interview in the *Decoded* episode filmed that day, followed by the "investigators" at a bar or pool hall somewhere afterward, defending the Freemasons as American heroes and depicting Pinto as a nut-job conspiracy theorist. I only had to watch a couple other episodes of *Decoded* to get that it's a ruse meant for entertainment, ratings, and sales, but not a whit about serious investigative work or "decoding" anything.

That said, I do have to thank the History Channel and Brad Meltzer for that Washington, DC, experience and their disgraceful treatment (frame-up) of award-winning and *real* exploratory filmmaker, Chris Pinto. They unintentionally provided me one of the "thousand points of light" that eventually convinced us to launch SkyWatchTV and to make bona fide investigative reports an integral part of our future media endeavors. In fact, the book you now hold in your hands is only a part of what will be followed by a documentary film and four-part television special into this subject including (to return to my point) fresh insights into the most powerful stargates in the world—America, the Vatican, and the portals of Apollo-Osiris.

How many people know that located right inside Washington, DC, is: 1) a stargate; 2) Seventy-two (72) pentagrams at the base of the stargate to control the "Immortals"; 3) powerful generators (Dome and Obelisk) designed from antiquity to make the stargate work; and 4) ancient prophecies connected to this device that make it clear exactly who will be coming through the mystical doorway in the future? How many also know that similar devices and prophecies are built into the Vatican's headquarters in Rome? We decided this information was so important that we have included it as bonus material in this chapter, which is excerpted from *Zenith 2016*.

The Dome and Obelisk

Undoubtedly, the vast majority of people, when looking at Washington, DC, and at the Vatican, never comprehend how these cities constitute one of the greatest open conspiracies of all time. There, reproduced in all their glory and right before the world's eyes, is an ancient talismanic diagram based on the history and cult of Isis, Osiris, and Horus, including the magical utilities meant to generate the deities' return.

The primeval concept—especially that of sacred Domes facing

Obelisks—was designed in antiquity for the express purpose of regeneration, resurrection, and apotheosis, for deity incarnation from the underworld to earth's surface through union of the respective figures—the Dome (ancient structural representation of the womb of Isis) and the Obelisk (ancient representation of the erect male phallus of Osiris).

This layout, as modeled in antiquity, exists today on the grandest scale at the heart of the capital of the most powerful government on earth—the United States—as well as in the heart of the most politically influential Church on earth—the Vatican. Given this fact and the pattern provided by the apostle Paul and the Apocalypse of John (the book of Revelation) that the end times would culminate in a marriage between political (Antichrist) and religious (False Prophet) authorities at the return of Osiris/Apollo, it behooves open-minded researchers to carefully consider this prophecy in stone, as it defines the spiritual energy that is knowingly or unknowingly being invoked at both locations with potential ramifications for Petrus Romanus…and beyond.

The US capital has been called the "Mirror Vatican" due to the strikingly similar layout and design of its primary buildings and streets. This is no accident. In fact, America's forefathers first named the capital city "Rome." But the parallelism between Washington and the Vatican is most clearly illustrated by the Capitol building and Dome facing the Obelisk known as the Washington Monument, and at St. Peter's Basilica in the Vatican by a similar Dome facing a familiar Obelisk—both of which were, according to their own official records, fashioned after the Roman Pantheon, the circular Domed Rotunda "dedicated to all pagan gods." This layout—a Domed temple facing an Obelisk—is an ancient, alchemical blueprint that holds significant esoteric meaning.

For those who may not know, the US Capitol building in Washington, DC, is historically based on a pagan Masonic temple theme. Thomas Jefferson, who shepherded the antichristian "Roman Pantheon" design, wrote to the Capitol's architect, Benjamin LaTrobe, defining it as "the first temple dedicated to…embellishing with Athenian taste the course of a nation looking far beyond the range of Athenian destinies"[719] (the "Athenian" empire was first known as "Osiria," the kingdom of Osiris). In 1833, Massachusetts Representative Rufus Choate agreed, writing, "We have built no national temples but the Capitol."[720] William Henry and Mark Gray in their book, *Freedom's Gate: Lost Symbols in the US Capitol,* add that, "The US Capitol has numerous architectural and other features that unquestionably identify it with ancient temples."[721] After listing various features to make their case that the US Capitol building is a "religious temple"—including housing the image of a deified being, heavenly beings, gods, symbols, inscriptions, sacred geometry, columns, prayers, and orientation to the sun—they conclude:

> The designers of the city of Washington DC oriented it to the Sun—especially the rising Sun on June 21 and December 21 [the same day and month as the end of the Mayan calendar in 2012]. The measurements for this orientation were made from the location of the center of the Dome of the US Capitol, rendering it a "solar temple." Its alignment and encoded numerology point to the Sun as well as the stars. A golden circle on the Rotunda story and a white star in the Crypt marks this spot.... It is clear that the builders viewed the Capitol as America's sole temple: a solemn...Solar Temple to be exact.[722]

To understand what these statements may soon mean for the future of the world, one needs to comprehend how these [stargate] aparati— the Dome and the Obelisk facing it—facilitate important archaic and modern protocols for invigorating *prophetic* supernatural alchemy. In ancient times, the Obelisk represented the god Osiris' "missing" male organ, which Isis was not able to find after her husband/brother was slain and chopped into fourteen pieces by his evil brother Seth (or Set). The story involves a detailed account of the envious brother and seventy-two conspirators [important numerology we will get to later in this chapter] tricking Osiris into climbing inside a box, which Seth quickly locked and threw into the Nile. Osiris drowned, and his body floated down the Nile River, where it snagged on the limbs of a tamarisk tree. In Byblos, Isis recovered his body from the river bank and took it into her care. In her absence, Seth stole the body again and chopped it into fourteen pieces, which he threw into the Nile. Isis searched the river bank until she recovered every piece, except for the genitals, which had been swallowed by a fish (Plutarch says a crocodile). Isis recombined the thirteen pieces of Osiris' corpse and replaced the missing organ with a magic facsimile (Obelisk), which she used to impregnate herself, thus giving rise to Osiris again in the person of his son, Horus. This legendary ritual for reincarnating Osiris formed the core of Egyptian cosmology (as well as the Rosicrucian/Masonic dying-and-rising myths) and was fantastically venerated on the most imposing scale throughout all of Egypt by towering Obelisks (representing the phallus of Osiris) and Domes (representing the pregnant belly of Isis) including at Karnak where the upright Obelisks were "vitalized" or "stimulated" from the energy of the masturbatory sun god Ra shining down upon them.

There is historical evidence that this elaborate myth and its rituals may have been based originally on real characters and events. Regarding this, it is noteworthy that in 1998, former secretary general of Egypt's Supreme Council of Antiquities, Zahi Hawass, claimed to have found the burial tomb of the god Osiris (Apollo/Nimrod) at the Giza Plateau. In the article, "Sandpit of Royalty," from the newspaper *Extra Bladet* (Copenhagen), January 31, 1999, Hawass was quoted saying:

> I have found a shaft, going twenty-nine meters vertically down into the ground, exactly halfway between the Chefren Pyramid and the Sphinx. At the bottom, which was filled with water, we have found a burial chamber with four pillars. In the middle is a large granite sarcophagus, which I expect to be the grave of Osiris, the god.... I have been digging in Egypt's sand for more

than thirty years, and up to date this is the most exciting discovery I have made.... We found the shaft in November and began pumping up the water recently. So several years will pass before we have finished investigating the find.[723]

As far as we know, this discovery did not ultimately provide the physical remains of the deified person. But what it did illustrate is that at least some very powerful Egyptologists believe Osiris was a historical figure, and that his body was stored somewhere at or near the Great Pyramid. Manly P. Hall, who knew that the Masonic legend of Hiram Abiff was a thinly veiled prophecy of the resurrection of Osiris, may have understood what Zahi Hawass (not to mention Roerich, Roosevelt, and Wallace with their sacred Osiris Casket) was looking for, and why. Consider that he wrote in *The Secret Teachings of All Ages*: "The Dying God [Osiris] shall rise again! The secret room in the House of the Hidden Places shall be rediscovered. The Pyramid again shall stand as the ideal emblem of...resurrection, and regeneration."[724]

In Egypt, where rituals were performed to actually "raise" the spirit of Osiris into the reigning Pharaoh, political authority in the form of divine kingship or theocratic statesmanship was established (later reflected in the political and religious doctrine of royal and political legitimacy or "the divine right of kings," who supposedly derived their right to rule from the will of God, with the exception in some countries that the king is subject to the Church and the pope). This meant, among other things, that the Egyptian pharaoh enjoyed extraordinary authority as the "son of the sun god" (Ra) and the incarnation of the falcon god Horus during his lifetime. At death, Pharaoh became the Osiris, the divine judge of the netherworld, and on earth, his son and predecessor took his place as the newly anointed manifestation of Horus. Thus each generation of pharaohs provided the gods with a spokesman for the present world and for the afterlife while also offering the nation divinely appointed leadership.

Yet the observant reader may wonder, "Was there something more to the pharaoh's deification than faith in ritual magic?" The cult center of Amun-Ra at Thebes may hold the answer, as it was the site of the largest religious structure ever built—the temple of Amun-Ra at Karnak—and the location of many extraordinary mysterious rites. The great temple with its one hundred miles of walls and gardens (the primary object of fascination and worship by the nemesis of Moses—Pharaoh of the Exodus, Ramses II) was the place where each pharaoh reconciled his divinity in the company of Amun-Ra during the festival of Opet. The festival was held at the temple of Luxor and included a procession of gods carried on barges up the Nile River from Karnak to the temple. The royal family accompanied the gods on boats while the Egyptian laity walked along the shore, calling aloud and making requests of the gods. Once at Luxor, the pharaoh and his entourage entered the holy of holies, where the ceremony to raise the spirit of Osiris into the king was performed and the pharaoh was transmogrified into a living deity. Outside, large groups of dancers and musicians waited anxiously. When the king emerged as the "born again" Osiris, the crowd erupted in gaiety. From that day forward, the pharaoh was considered to be—just as the god ciphered in the Great Seal of the United States will be—the son and spiritual incarnation of the Supreme Deity. The all-seeing eye of Horus/Apollo/Osiris above the unfinished pyramid on the Great Seal represents this event.

Modern people, especially in America, may view the symbols used in this magic—the Dome representing the habitually pregnant belly of Isis, and the Obelisk, representing the erect phallus of Osiris—as profane or pornographic. But they were in fact ritualized fertility objects, which the ancients believed could produce tangible reactions, properties, or "manifestations" within the material world. The Obelisk and Dome as imitations of the deities' male and female reproductive organs could, through government representation, invoke into existence the being or beings symbolized by them. This is why inside the temple or Dome, temple prostitutes representing the human manifestation of the goddess were also available for ritual sex as a form of imitative magic. These prostitutes usually began their services to the goddess as children, and were deflowered at a very young age by a priest or, as Isis was, by a modeled Obelisk of Osiris' phallus. Sometimes these prostitutes were chosen, on the basis of their beauty, as the sexual mates of sacred temple bulls who were considered the incarnation of Osiris. In other places, such as at Mendes, temple prostitutes were offered in coitus to divine goats. Through such imitative sex, the Dome and Obelisk became "energy receivers," capable of assimilating Ra's essence from the rays of the sun, which in turn drew forth the "seed" of the underworld Osiris. The seed of the dead deity would, according to the supernaturalism, transmit upward (through the portal) from out of the underworld through the base (testes) of the Obelisk and magically emit from the tower's head into the womb (Dome) of Isis where incarnation into the sitting pharaoh/king/president would occur (during what Freemasons also call *the raising [of Osiris] ceremony*). In this way, Osiris could be habitually "born again" or reincarnated as Horus and constantly direct the spiritual destiny of the nation.

This metaphysical phenomenon, which originated with Nimrod/ Semiramis and was central to numerous other ancient cultures, was especially developed in Egypt, where Nimrod/Semiramis were known as Osiris/Isis (and in Ezekiel chapter 8 the children of Israel set up the Obelisk ["image of jealousy," verse 5] facing the entry of their temple—just as the Dome faces the Obelisk in Washington, DC and in the Vatican City—and were condemned by God for worshipping the sun [Ra] while weeping for Osiris [Tammuz]). The familiar Masonic figure of the point within a circle is the symbol of this union between Ra, Osiris, and Isis. The "point" represents Osiris' phallus in the center of the circle or womb of Isis, which in turn is enlivened by the sun rays from Ra, just as is represented today at the Vatican, where the Egyptian Obelisk of Osiris sits within a circle, and in Washington, DC, where the Obelisk does similarly, situated so as to be the first thing the sun (Ra) strikes as it rises over the capital city and which, when viewed from overhead, forms the magical point within a circle known as a *circumpunct*. The sorcery is further amplified, according to ancient occultic beliefs, by the presence of the Reflecting Pool in DC, which serves as a mirror to heaven and "transferring point" for [the immortals] spirits and energies.

And just what is it the spirits see when they look downward on the Reflecting Pool in Washington? They find a city dedicated to and built in honor of the legendary deities Isis and Osiris complete with the thirteen gathered pieces of Osiris (America's original thirteen colonies); the required Obelisk known as the Washington Monument; the Capitol Dome (of Isis) for impregnation and incarnation of deity into each pharaoh (president); and last but not least, the official government buildings erected to face their respective counterparts and whose cornerstones— including the US Capitol Dome—were dedicated during astrological alignments related to the zodiacal constellation Virgo (Isis) as required for the magic to occur.

Where the Vitality of Osiris/Apollo (the Beast that Was, and Is Not, and Yet Is) Pulsates in Anticipation of His Final "Raising"

The three-hundred-thirty ton Obelisk in St. Peter's Square in the Vatican City is not just any Obelisk. It was cut from a single block of red granite during the Fifth dynasty of Egypt to stand as Osiris' erect phallus at the Temple of the Sun in ancient Heliopolis (Ἡλιούπολις, meaning "city of the sun" or "principal seat of Atum-Ra sun-worship"), the city of "On" in the Bible, dedicated to Ra, Osiris, and Isis. The Obelisk was moved from Heliopolis to the Julian Forum of Alexandria by Emperor Augustus and later from thence (approximately AD 37) by Caligula to Rome to stand at the spine of the Circus. There, under Nero, its excited presence maintained a counter-vigil over countless brutal Christian executions, including the martyrdom of the apostle Peter (according to some historians). Over fifteen hundred years following that, Pope Sixtus V ordered hundreds of workmen under celebrated engineer-architects Giovanni and Domenico Fontana (who also erected three other ancient Obelisks in the old Roman city, including one dedicated to Osiris by Rameses III—at the Piazza del Popolo, Piazza di S. Maria Maggiore, and Piazza di S. Giovanni in Laterano) to move the phallic pillar to the center of St. Peter's Square in Rome. This proved a daunting task, which took over four months, nine hundred laborers, one hundred forty horses, and seventy winches. Though worshipped at its present location ever since by countless admirers, the proximity of the Obelisk to the old Basilica was formerly "resented as something of a provocation, almost as a slight to the Christian religion. It had stood there like a false idol, as it were vaingloriously, on what was believed to be the center of the accursed circus where the early Christians and St. Peter had been put to death. Its sides, then as now, were graven with dedications to [the worst of ruthless pagans] Augustus and Tiberius."[725]

The fact that many traditional Catholics as well as Protestants perceived such idols of stone to be not only objects of heathen adoration but the worship of demons (see Acts 7:41–42; Psalm 96:5; and 1 Corinthians 10:20) makes what motivated Pope Sixtus to erect the phallus of Osiris in the heart of St. Peter's Square, located in Vatican City and bordering St. Peter's Basilica, very curious. To ancient Christians, the image of a cross and symbol of Jesus sitting atop (or emitting from) the head of a demonic god's erect manhood would have been at a minimum a very serious blasphemy. Yet Sixtus was not content with simply restoring and using such ancient pagan relics (which were believed in those days to actually house the pagan spirit they represented) but even destroyed Christian artifacts in the process. Michael W. Cole, associate professor in the Department of the History of Art at the University of Pennsylvania, and Professor Rebecca E. Zorach, associate professor of Art History at the University of Chicago, raise critical questions about this in their scholarly book *The Idol in the Age of Art* when they state:

Whereas Gregory, to follow the chroniclers, had ritually dismembered the city's *imagines daemonem* [demonic images], Sixtus fixed what was in disrepair, added missing parts, and made the "idols" into prominent urban features. Two of the four obelisks had to be reconstructed from found or excavated pieces... The pope was even content to destroy *Christian* antiquities in the process: as Jennifer Montagu has pointed out, the bronze for the statues of Peter and Paul came from the medieval doors of S. Agnese, from the Scala Santa at the Lateran, and from a ciborium at St. Peter's.

[Sixtus] must have realized that, especially in their work on the two [broken obelisks], they were not merely repairing injured objects, but also restoring a *type*... In his classic book *The Gothic Idol*, Michael Camille showed literally dozens of medieval images in which the freestanding figure atop a column betokened the pagan idol. The sheer quantity of Camille's examples makes it clear that the device, and what it stood for, would have been immediately recognizable to medieval viewers, and there is no reason to assume that, by Sixtus's time, this had ceased to be true.[726]

The important point made by Professors Cole and Zorach is that at the time Sixtus was busy reintroducing to the Roman public square restored images and statues on columns, the belief remained strong that these idols housed their patron deity, and further that, if these were not treated properly and even placed into service during proper constellations related to their myth, it could beckon evil omens. Leonardo da Vinci had even written in his Codex Urbinas how those who would adore and pray to the image were likely to believe the god represented by it was alive in the stone and watching their behavior. There is strong indication that Sixtus believed this too, and that he "worried about the powers that might inhabit his new urban markers."[727] This was clearly evident when the cross was placed on top of the Obelisk in the midst of St. Peter's Square and the pope marked the occasion by conducting the ancient rite of exorcism against the phallic symbol. First scheduled to occur on September 14 to coincide with the liturgical Feast of the Exaltation of the Cross and not coincidently under the zodiacal sign of Virgo (Isis), the event was delayed until later in the month and fell under the sign of Libra, representing a zenith event for the year. On that morning, a pontifical High Mass was held just before the cross was raised from a portable altar to the apex of Baal's Shaft (as such phallic towers were also known). While clergy prayed and a choir sang Psalms, Pope Sixtus stood facing the Obelisk and, extending his hand toward it, announced: *"Exorcizote, creatura lapidis, in nomine Dei"* ("I exorcize you, creature of stone, in the name of God"). Sixtus then cast sanctified water upon the pillar's middle, then its right side, then left, then above, and finally below to form a cross, followed by, *"In nomine Patris, et Filij, et Spiritussancti. Amen"* ("In the Name of the Father and of the Son and of the Holy Ghost. Amen"). He then crossed himself three times and watched as the symbol of Christ was placed atop Osiris' erect phallus.

Washington Dome facing Obelisk

Vatican Dome facing Obelisk

Yet if what Sixtus established in the heart of Vatican City gives some readers pause (numerous other signature events by Sixtus aligned the Sistine city with constellations sacred to Osiris and Isis, which we are not taking time to discuss here but that caused Profs. Zorach and Cole to conclude that, in the end, Sixtus wanted to remain *in the good graces of the pagan gods*), in Washington, DC, near the west end of the National Mall, the Obelisk built by Freemasons and dedicated to America's first president brings the fullest meaning to the Nephilim-originated and modern porn-industry impression that "size matters." This is no crude declaration, as adepts of ritual sex-magic know, and dates back to ancient women who wanted to give birth to the offspring of the gods and who judged the size of the male generative organ as indicative of the "giant" genetics or divine seed needed for such offspring. While such phallic symbols have been and still are found in cultures around the world, in ancient Egypt, devotion to this type "obscene divinity" began with Amun-Min and reached its crescendo in the Obelisks of Osiris.

Throughout Greece and Rome the god Priapus (son of Aphrodite) was invoked as a symbol of such divine fertility and later became directly linked to the cult of pornography reflected in the more modern sentiments about "size." This is important because, in addition to the Washington Monument being intentionally constructed to be the tallest Obelisk of its kind in the world at 6,666 (some say 6,660) inches high and 666 inches wide along each side at the base, one of the original concepts for the Washington Monument included Apollo (the Greek version of Osiris) triumphantly returning in his heavenly chariot, and another illustrating a tower "like that of Babel" for its head. Any of these designs would have been equally appropriate to the thirty-three-hundred-pound pyramidal capstone it now displays, as all three concepts carried the meaning necessary to accomplish what late researcher David Flynn described as "the same secret knowledge preserved by the mystery schools since the time of the Pelasgians [that] display modern Isis Osiris worship."[728] This is to say, the "seed" discharged from a Tower-of-Babel-shaped head would magically issue forth the same as would proceed from the existing Egyptian capstone—the offspring of Apollo/Osiris/Nimrod.

The greatest minds in Freemasonry, whose beliefs set the tone for the design of the capital city, its Great Seal, its Dome, and its Obelisk, understood and wrote about this intent. Albert Pike described it as Isis and Osiris' "Active and Passive Principles of the Universe...commonly symbolized by the generative parts of man and woman,"[729] and Freemason writer Albert Mackey described not only the Obelisk, but added the importance of the circle around its base, saying, "The Phallus was an imitation of the male generative organ. It was represented...by a column [Obelisk] that was surrounded by a circle at the base."[730]

In Egypt, where the parodies and rituals for raising Osiris to life through these magical constructs was perfected, Pharaoh served as the "fit extension" for the reborn god to take residence in as the "sex act" was ritualized at the temple of Amun-Ra. The all-seeing eye of Horus/Osiris/Apollo above the unfinished pyramid on the Great Seal of the United States forecasts the culmination of this event—that is, the actual return of Osiris—for the United States closely following the year 2012, and the Dome and Obelisk stand ready for the metaphysical ritual to be performed in secret by the elite. We use the phrase "performed in secret" because what the vast majority of people throughout America do not know is that the "raising" ceremony is still conducted inside the head-quarters of the Scottish Rite Freemasonry in the House of the Temple by the Supreme Council 33rd-Degree over Washington, DC, for at least two reasons. First, whenever a Mason reaches the Master level, the ritual includes a parody representing the death, burial, and future resurrection of Hiram Abiff (Osiris). The world at large finally caught a glimpse of this custom when Dan Brown, in his book *The Lost Symbol*, opened with a scene depicting the start of the tradition:

The secret is how to die.

Since the beginning of time, the secret had always been how to die.

The thirty-four-year-old initiate gazed down at the human skull cradled in his palms. The skull was hollow, like a bowl, filled with bloodred wine.

Drink it, he told himself. You have nothing to fear.

As was tradition, he had begun his journey adorned in the ritualistic garb of a medieval heretic being led to the gallows, his loose-fitting shirt gaping open to reveal his pale chest, his left pant leg rolled up to the knee, and his right sleeve rolled up to the elbow. Around his neck hung a heavy rope noose—a "cable-tow" as the brethren called it. Tonight, however, like the brethren bearing witness, he was dressed as a master.

The assembly of brothers encircling him all were adorned in their full regalia of lambskin aprons, sashes, and white gloves. Around their necks hung ceremonial jewels that glistened like ghostly eyes in the muted light. Many of these men held power-ful stations in life, and yet the initiate knew their worldly ranks meant nothing within these walls. Here all men were equals, sworn brothers sharing a mystical bond.

As he surveyed the daunting assembly, the initiate wondered who on the outside would ever believe that this collection of men would assemble in one place…much less this place. The room looked like a holy sanctuary from the ancient world.

The truth, however, was stranger still.

I am just blocks away from the White House.

This colossal edifice, located at 1733 Sixteenth Street NW in Washington, DC, was a replica of a pre-Christian temple— the temple of King Mausolus, the original mausoleum…a place to be taken after death. Outside the main entrance, two seventeen-ton sphinxes guarded the bronze doors. The interior was an ornate labyrinth of ritualistic chambers, halls, sealed vaults, libraries, and even a hallow wall that held the remains of two human bodies. The initiate had been told every room in the building held a secret, and yet he knew no room held deeper secrets than the gigantic chamber in which he was currently kneeling with a skull cradled in his palms.

The Temple Room.[731]

While such drama makes for excellent fiction, *The Lost Symbol* turns out to be at best a love fest and at worst a cover-up between Dan Brown and the Freemasons. However, one thing Brown said is true— the Temple Room in the Heredom does hold an important *secret*. We've been there, stood inside and prayed for protection under our breath, because according to our sources (who provided facts that have not been denied when we were interviewed by a US Congressman, US Senator, and even a 33rd-Degree Freemason on his radio show), in addition to when a Mason reaches the Master level, the ancient raising ceremony is conducted following the election of an American president—just as their Egyptian forefathers did at the temple of Amun-Ra in Karnak—in keeping with the tradition of installing within him the representative spirit of Osiris until such time as the god himself shall fulfill the Great Seal prophecy and return in flesh.

In the prologue of 33rd-Degree Freemason Manly P. Hall's book, *The Lost Keys of Freemasonry*, detailed recounting of the underlying and familiar story of Hiram Abiff (Osiris) is told, who sets out to construct the temple of the Great Architect of the Universe, but is killed by three spectres. This story, impersonated every time an initiate reaches the level of Master Mason, is by admission of Freemasons a retelling of the death-epic of the god Osiris. In *Lost Keys*, Hall narrates how the Great Architect gives Hiram (Osiris) the trestleboard for the construction of the great temple, and when he is killed by three ruffians, the Great Architect bathes him in "a glory celestial," as in the glory surrounding the all-seeing eye of Osiris above the pyramid on the Great Seal. The Great Architect follows this by charging those who would finish the building with the task of finding the body of Hiram (Osiris) and raising him from the dead. When *this* has been accomplished, the great work will conclude and the god will inhabit the (Third) Temple:

> Seek ye where the broken twig lies and the dead stick molds away, where the clouds float together and the stones rest by the hillside, for all these mark the grave of Hiram [Osiris] who has carried my Will with him to the tomb. This eternal quest is yours until ye have found your Builder, until the cup giveth up its secret, until the grave giveth up its ghosts. No more shall I speak until ye have found and raised my beloved Son [Osiris], and have listened to the words of my Messenger and with Him as your guide have finished the temple which I shall then inhabit. Amen.[732]

Thus the appearance of the uncapped pyramid of Giza on the Great Seal of the United States echoes the ancient pagan as well as Masonic beliefs concerning the old mysteries and the prophecy of the return of Osiris/Apollo/Nimrod. In *Rosicrucian and Masonic Origins*, Hall, who had said in *The Secret Teachings of All Ages* that the Great Pyramid was "the tomb of Osiris,"[733] explains that Preston, Gould, Mackey, Oliver, Pike, and nearly every other great historian of Freemasonry were aware of this connection between Freemasonry and the ancient mysteries and primitive ceremonials based on Osiris. "These eminent Masonic scholars have all recognized in the legend of Hiram Abiff an adaptation of the Osiris myth; nor do they deny that the major part of the symbolism of the craft is derived from the pagan institutions of antiquity when the gods were venerated in secret places with strange figures and appropriate rituals."[734] In *Morals and Dogma*, Albert Pike even enumerated the esoteric significance of the Osiris epic at length, adding that lower-level Masons (Blue Masonry) are ignorant of its true meaning, which is only known to those who are "initiated into the Mysteries."[735] Pike also spoke of the star Sirius—connected to Isis and at length to Lucifer/Satan—as "still glittering" in the Masonic lodges as "the Blazing Star." Elsewhere in *Morals and Dogma*, Pike reiterated that the "All-Seeing Eye...was the emblem of Osiris"[736] and that the "Sun was termed by the Greeks the Eye of Jupiter, and the Eye of the World; and his is the All-Seeing Eye in our Lodges."[737]

Magic Squares, 666, and Human Sacrifice?

While finding the body of Osiris and resurrecting it—either figuratively or literally—is central to the prophetic beliefs of Freemasonry, until Apollo and/or Osiris return, formal procedures will continue in secret for installing within America's national leader the divine right of kingship through the raising of the Osiris ceremony. It is very important to note how, when this ritual is carried out in the Temple Room of the Heredom, it unfolds below a vast thirty-six-paneled skylight that forms a stylized Magic 666 Square. Around the four sides of the skylight can be seen the Winged Sun-Disc. This positioning above the altar is in keeping with historical occultism. Egyptian magicians employed the same symbolism above the altar for invoking the sun deity. In the St. Martin's Press book *Practical Egyptian Magic* it is noted: "Emblematic of the element of air, this consists of a circle or solar-type disk enclosed by a pair of wings. In ritual magic it is suspended over the altar in an easterly direction and used when invoking the protection and co-operation of the sylphs."[738] The Renaissance occultist Paracelsus describes these sylphs as invisible beings of the air, entities that the New Testament book of Ephesians (2:2) describes as working beneath "the prince [Lucifer/Satan] of the power of the air, the spirit that now worketh in the children of disobedience." In applied magic, the "magic square of the sun" itself was associated in antiquity with binding or loosing the sun god Apollo/Osiris and was the most famous of all magical utilities because the sum of any row, column, or diagonal is equal to the number 111, while the total of all the numbers in the square from 1 to 36 equals 666. In the magical Hebrew Kabbalah, each planet is associated with a number, intelligence, and spirit. The intelligence of the Sun is Nakiel, which equals 111, while the spirit of the Sun is Sorath and equals 666. It makes sense therefore that Freemasons built the Washington Monument Obelisk to form a magic square at its base and to stand 555 feet above earth, so that when a line is drawn 111 feet directly below it toward the underworld of Osiris, it equals the total of 666 (555+111=666)—the exact values of the binding square of the Sun God Apollo/Osiris installed in the ceiling above where the Osiris raising ceremony is conducted in the House of the Temple.

6	32	3	34	35	1
7	11	27	28	8	30
19	14	16	15	23	24
18	20	22	21	17	13
25	29	10	9	26	12
36	5	33	4	2	31

Magic 666 Square

36-paneled magic-square skylight above
the altar in the House of the Temple

Freemason and occultist Aleister Crowley practiced such Kabbalah and likewise connected the number 111 with the number 6, which he described as the greatest number of the Sun or sun god. He employed the magic square in rituals to make contact with a spirit described in *The Book of the Sacred Magic of Abramelin the Mage*, a work from the 1600s or 1700s that involves evocation of demons. In Book Four of the magic text, a set of magical word-square talismans provides for the magician's Holy Guardian Angel who appears and reveals occult secrets for calling forth and gaining control over the twelve underworld authorities including Lucifer, Satan, Leviathan, and Belial. In addition to Crowley, the most influential founding father and Freemason, Benjamin Franklin, not only used such magic squares, but according to his own biography and numerous other authoritative sources even created magic squares and circles for use by himself and his brethren. Yet the gentle appearance and keen astuteness of America's most famous bespectacled Freemason might have hidden an even darker history than the story told by those magic squares, which his strong, deft hands once held. Award-winning filmmaker Christian J. Pinto explains:

One of the most influential founding fathers, and the only one of them to have signed all of the original founding documents (the Declaration of Independence, the Treaty of Paris, and the US Constitution) was Benjamin Franklin. Franklin was…without question, deeply involved in Freemasonry and in other secret societies. He belonged to secret groups in the three countries involved in the War of Independence: America, France, and England. He was master of the Masonic Lodge of Philadelphia; while over in France, he was master of the Nine Sisters Lodge, from which sprang the French Revolution. In England, he joined a rakish political group founded by Sir Francis Dashwood (member of Parliament, advisor to King George III) called the "Monks of Medmenham Abbey," otherwise known as the "Hellfire Club." This eighteenth-century group is described as follows:

> The Hellfire Club was an exclusive, English club that met sporadically during the mid-eighteenth century. Its purpose, at best, was to mock traditional religion and conduct orgies. At worst, it involved the indulgence of satanic rites and sacrifices. The club to which Franklin belonged was established by Francis Dashwood, a member of Parliament and friend of Franklin. The club, which consisted of "The Superior Order" of twelve members, allegedly took part in basic forms of satanic worship. In addition to taking part in the occult, orgies and parties with prostitutes were also said to be the norm.

Pinto continues this connection between Benjamin Franklin and dark occultism:

> On February 11, 1998, the *Sunday Times* reported that ten bodies were dug up from beneath Benjamin Franklin's home at 36

Craven Street in London. The bodies were of four adults and six children. They were discovered during a costly renovation of Franklin's former home. The *Times* reported: "Initial estimates are that the bones are about two hundred years old and were buried at the time Franklin was living in the house, which was his home from 1757 to 1762 and from 1764 to 1775. Most of the bones show signs of having been dissected, sawn or cut. One skull has been drilled with several holes."

The original *Times* article reported that the bones were "deeply buried, probably to hide them because grave robbing was illegal." They said, "There could be more buried, and there probably are." But the story doesn't end there. Later reports from the Benjamin Franklin House reveal that not only were human remains found, but animal remains were discovered as well. This is where things get very interesting. From the published photographs, some of the bones appear to be blackened or charred, as if by fire... It is well documented that Satanists perform ritual killings of both humans and animals alike.[739]

While many students of history are aware of the Magic 666 Square and its use by occultists down through time to control the spirit of Apollo/Osiris, what some will not know is how this magical binding and loosing of supernatural entities also extends to the testes of Washington's 6,666-inch-high phallic Obelisk, dedicated by Freemasons seventy-two years following 1776 (note again the magic number 72), where a Bible (that Dan Brown identified as the "Lost Symbol" in his latest book) is encased within the cornerstone of its 666-inch-square base. One wonders what type of Bible this is. If a Masonic version, it is covered with occult symbols of the Brotherhood and Rosicrucianism and the purpose for having it so encased might be to energize the Mason's interpretation of Scripture in bringing forth the seed of Osiris/Apollo from the testes/cornerstone. If it is a non-Masonic Bible, the purpose may be to "bind" its influence inside the 666 square and thus allow the seed of Osiris/Apollo to prevail. The dedication of the cornerstone during the astrological alignment with Virgo/Isis as the sun was passing over Sirius indicates a high degree of magic was indeed intended by those in charge.[740]

Prophecy about the Coming of Apollo/Osiris

[After documenting how Freemason US President Franklin D. Roosevelt and his Vice-President Henry Wallace, also a Freemason, pushed to get the Great Seal of the United States placed on the one-dollar bill, and how both men believed the symbolism and mottoes of the seal were a Masonic-approved prophecy about a New World Order that would start at the second coming of Apollo/Osiris/Nimrod, Tom Horn continued in *Zenith 2016*:]

Whatever the case for Wallace, like Manly Hall, had, he and Roosevelt viewed the all-seeing eye above the unfinished pyramid as pointing to the return (or reincarnation) of this coming savior, whose arrival would cap the pyramid and launch the New World Order. The all-seeing eye on the Great Seal is fashioned after the Eye of Horus, the offspring of Osiris (or Osiris resurrected), as both men surely understood. Aliester Crowley, 33rd-Degree Freemason (the "wickedest man on earth") and a Roerich occult contemporary, often spoke of this as the "New Age of Horus" and the breaking dawn of the rebirth of Osiris. That the United States president, vice president, and such mystics and Freemasons simultaneously used such identical language is telling, given that the Great Seal's mottoes and symbolism relate to both Osiris and Apollo specifically, yet as one. Osiris is the dominant theme of the Egyptian symbols, his resurrection and return, while the *mottoes* of the seal point directly to Apollo, and the eagle, a pagan emblem of Jupiter, to Apollo's father. For instance, the motto *annuiti coeptis* is from Virgil's *Aeneid*, in which Ascanius, the son of Aeneas from conquered Troy, prays to Apollo's father, Jupiter [Zeus]. Charles Thompson, designer of the Great Seal's final version, condensed line 625 of book IX of Virgil's *Aeneid*, which reads, *Juppiter omnipotes, audacibus annue coeptis* ("All-powerful Jupiter favors [the] daring undertakings"), to *Annuit coeptis* ("He approves [our] undertakings"), while the phrase *novus ordo seclorum* ("a new order of the ages") was adapted in 1782 from inspiration Thompson found in a prophetic line in Virgil's Eclogue IV: *Magnus ab integro seclorum nascitur ordo* (Virgil's *Eclogue IV*, line 5), the interpretation of the original Latin being, "And the majestic roll of circling centuries begins anew." This phrase is from the Cumaean Sibyl and involves the future birth of a divine son, spawned of "a new breed of men sent down from heaven" (what Roosevelt, Wallace, and Roerich were looking for) when he receives "the life of gods, and sees Heroes with gods commingling." According to the prophecy, this is Apollo, son of Jupiter (Zeus), who returns to Earth through mystical "life" given to him from the gods when the deity Saturn returns to reign over the Earth in a new Pagan Golden Age.

From the beginning of the prophecy we read:

Now the last age by Cumae's Sibyl sung Has come and gone, and the majestic roll Of circling centuries begins anew: Justice returns, returns old Saturn's reign, With a new breed of men sent down from heaven. Only do thou, at the boy's birth in whom The iron shall cease, the golden race arise, Befriend him, chaste Lucina; 'tis thine own Apollo reigns.

He shall receive the life of gods, and see Heroes with gods commingling, and himself Be seen of them, and with his father's worth Reign o'er a world....

Assume thy greatness, for the time draws nigh, Dear child of gods, great progeny of Jove [Jupiter/Zeus]! See how it totters—

the world's orbed might, Earth, and wide ocean, and the vault profound, All, see, enraptured of the coming time![741]

According to Virgil and the Cumaean Sibyl, whose prophecy formed the *novus ordo seclorum* of the Great Seal of the United States, the New World Order begins during a time of chaos when the earth and oceans are tottering—a time like today. This is when the "son" of promise arrives on earth—Apollo incarnate—a pagan savior born of "a new breed of men sent down from heaven" when "heroes" and "gods" are blended together. This sounds eerily similar to what the Watchers did during the creation of the Nephilim and to what scientists are doing this century through genetic engineering of human-animal chimeras. But to understand why such a fanciful prophecy about Apollo, son of Jupiter, returning to earth should be important to you: In ancient literature, Jupiter was the Roman replacement of Yahweh as the greatest of the gods—a "counter-Yahweh." His son Apollo is a replacement of Jesus, a "counter-Jesus." This Apollo comes to rule the final New World Order, when "Justice returns, returns old Saturn's [Satan's] reign." The ancient goddess Justice, who returns Satan's reign (*Saturnia regna*, the pagan golden age), was known to the Egyptians as Ma'at and to the Greeks as Themis, while to the Romans she was Lustitia. Statues and reliefs of her adorn thousands of government buildings and courts around the world, especially in Washington, DC, as familiar Lady Justice, blindfolded and holding scales and a sword. She represents the enforcement of secular law and is, according to the Sibyl's conjure, the authority that will require global compliance to the zenith of Satan's dominion concurrent with the coming of Apollo. What's more, the Bible's accuracy concerning this subject is alarming, including the idea that "pagan justice" will require surrender to a satanic system in a final world order under the rule of Jupiter's son.

In the New Testament, the identity of the god Apollo, repeat-coded in the Great Seal of the United States as the Masonic "messiah" who returns to rule the earth, is the same spirit—verified by the *same name*—that will inhabit the political leader of the end-times New World Order. According to key Bible prophecies, the Antichrist will be the progeny or incarnation of the ancient spirit, *Apollo*. Second Thessalonians 2:3 warns: "Let no man deceive you by any means: for that day shall not come, except there come a falling away first, and that man of sin be revealed, the son of *perdition* [*Apoleia*; Apollyon, Apollo]" (emphasis added). Numerous scholarly and classical works identify "Apollyon" as the god "Apollo"—the Greek deity "of death and pestilence," and Webster's Dictionary points out that "Apollyon" was a common variant of "Apollo" throughout history. An example of this is found in the classical play by the ancient Greek playwright Aeschylus, *The Agamemnon of Aeschylus*, in which Cassandra repeats more than once, "Apollo, thou destroyer, O Apollo, Lord of fair streets, Apollyon to me."[742] Accordingly, the name Apollo turns up in ancient literature with the verb *apollymi* or *apollyo* ("destroy"), and scholars including W. R. F. Browning believe apostle Paul may have identified the god Apollo as the "spirit of Antichrist" operating behind the persecuting Roman emperor, Domitian, who wanted to be recognized as "Apollo incarnate" in his day. Such identifying of Apollo with despots and "the spirit of Antichrist" is consistent even in modern history. For instance, note how Napoleon's name literally translates to "the true Apollo."

Revelation 17:8 likewise ties the coming of Antichrist with Apollo, revealing that the Beast shall ascend from the bottomless pit and enter him:

> The Beast that thou sawest was, and is not; and shall ascend out of the Bottomless Pit, and go into *perdition* [*Apolia*, Apollo]: and they that dwell on the Earth shall wonder, whose names were not written in the Book of Life from the foundation of the world, when they behold the Beast that was, and is not, and yet is. (emphasis added)

Among other things, this means the Great Seal of the United States is a prophecy, hidden in plain sight by the Founding Fathers and devotees of Bacon's New Atlantis for more than two hundred years, foretelling the return of a terrifying demonic god who seizes control of Earth in the new order of the ages. This supernatural entity was known and feared in ancient times by different names: Apollo, Osiris, and even farther back as Nimrod, whom Masons consider to be the father of their institution.[743]

The Washington Stargate

Through Masonic alchemy, presidential *apotheosis*—that is, the leader of the United States (America's pharaoh) being transformed into a god within the Capitol Dome/womb of Isis in sight of the Obelisk of Osiris (the Washington Monument to those whom Masons call "profane," the uninitiated)—actually began with America's first and most revered president, Master Freemason George Washington. In fact, Masons in attendance at Washington's funeral in 1799 cast sprigs of acacia "to symbolize both Osiris' resurrection and Washington's imminent resurrection in the realm where Osiris presides."[744] According to this Masonic enchantment, Osiris (Horus) was rising within a new president in DC as Washington took his role as Osiris of the underworld. This is further simulated and symbolized by the three-story design of the Capitol building. Freemasons point out how the Great Pyramid of Giza was made up of three main chambers to facilitate pharaoh's transference to Osiris, just as the Temple of Solomon was a three-sectioned tabernacle made up of the ground floor, middle chamber, and Holy of Holies. The US Capitol building was thus designed with three stories—Washington's Tomb, the Crypt, and the Rotunda—capped by a Dome. Each floor has significant esoteric meaning regarding apotheosis, and the tomb of Washington is empty. The official narrative is that a legal issue kept the government from placing Washington's body there. However, just as the tomb of

Jesus Christ was emptied before His ascension, Washington is not in his tomb because he has traveled to the home of Osiris, as depicted high overhead in the womb/Dome of Isis.

When visitors go to Washington, DC and tour the Capitol, one of the unquestionable highlights is to visit the womb of Isis—the Capitol Dome—where, when peering upward from inside Isis' continuously pregnant belly, tourists can see hidden in plain sight Brumidi's 4,664-square-foot fresco, *The Apotheosis of George Washington.* The word "apotheosis" means to "deify" or to "become a god," and explains part of the reason US presidents, military commanders, and members of Congress lay in state in the Capitol Dome. The womb of Isis is where they go at death to magically reach apotheosis and transform into gods.

Those who believe the United States was founded on Christianity and visit the Capitol for the first time will be surprised by the stark contrast to historic Christian artwork of the ascension of Jesus Christ compared to the "heaven" George Washington rises into from within the energized Capitol Dome/womb of Isis. It is not occupied by angels, but with devils and pagan deities important to Masonic belief. These include Hermes, Neptune, Venus (Isis), Ceres, Minerva, and Vulcan (Satan), of course, the son of Jupiter and Juno to which human sacrifices are made and about whom Manly Hall said brings "the seething energies of Lucifer" into the Mason's hands.[745]

For high-degree Masons and other illuminati, the symbolism of Washington surrounded by pagan entities and transformed into a heathen god is entirely appropriate. Deeply rooted in the mysteries of ancient societies and at the core of Rosicrucianism and those rituals of the Brotherhood that founded the United States is the idea that chosen humans are selected by these supernatural forces and their earthly kingdoms are formed and guided by these gods. As a Deist, George Washington believed that by following the enlightened path guided by principles of Freemasonry, he would achieve apotheosis and become deified. Affirming this widespread belief among America's Founding

Fathers are numerous works of art throughout Washington, DC. On an 1865 card titled "Washington and Lincoln Apotheosis," Abraham Lincoln is depicted transcending death to meet Washington among the gods. What god did Lincoln become? Humanist and American poet Walt Whitman eulogized him as the "American Osiris." Horatio Greenough's 1840, government-commissioned statue of George Washington shows the first president enthroned as the god Jupiter/Zeus. On one side of Washington/Zeus is his son Hercules clutching two serpents, and on the other side is his son Apollo. Greenough admitted this vision was based on presenting Washington as a deified figure, the father of Apollo similar to what the Hebrew God is to Jesus. Another representation of Washington as Jupiter/Zeus is a painting by Rembrandt Peale that hangs in the Old Senate Chamber. Peale painted it in a "poetic frenzy" in a stone oval window atop a stone sill engraved "PATRIAE PATER" ("Father of His Country"). The window is decorated with a garland of oak leaves, which was sacred to Jupiter, and is surmounted by the "Phydian head of Jupiter" (Peale's description) on the keystone. The symbol of Jupitor/Zeus, the father of Apollo above Washington's head, reflects the same conviction scripted on America's Great Seal—that the divine being watching over Washington and the founding of the country was Jupiter/Zeus (Lucifer in the Bible), whose son is coming again to rule the *novus ordo seclorum*. Even the name "Capitol Hill" for Government Center in Washington originated with this concept. Thomas Jefferson selected it to reflect Capitoline Hill from ancient Rome, where Jupiter (Jove) was the king of the gods. In more recent times, the Congressional Prayer Room was set up next to the Rotunda, where representatives and senators can go to meditate. The centerpiece in this room is a large, stained-glass window with George Washington between the two sides of the Great Seal of the United States. What is striking about this feature is that the order of the seal is inverted against protocol, with the reverse side of the seal, which should be at the bottom, above Washington's head, and the front of the seal, which should be at the top, under his

The Apotheosis of George Washington above 72 pentagrams

feet. In this position, Washington is seen on his knees praying beneath the uncapped pyramid and the all-seeing eye of Horus/Osiris/Apollo. I leave the reader to interpret what this clearly is meant to signify.

Beside those pagan gods which accompany Washington inside the Capitol Dome, the scene is rich with symbols analogous with ancient and modern magic, including the powerful trident—considered of the utmost importance for sorcery and indispensable to the efficacy of infernal rites—and the caduceus, tied to Apollo and Freemasonic Gnosticism in which Jesus was a myth based on Apollo's son, Asclepius, the god of medicine and healing whose snake-entwined staff remains a symbol of medicine today. Occult numerology associated with the legend of Isis and Osiris is also encoded throughout the painting, such as the thirteen maidens, the six scenes of pagan gods around the perimeter forming a hexagram, and the entire scene bounded by the powerful Pythagorian/Freemasonic "binding" utility—seventy-two five-pointed stars within circles.

Seventy-two (72) Pentagrams to Control the Immortals

Much has been written by historians within and without Masonry as to the relevance of the number seventy-two (72) and the alchemy related to it. In the Kabbalah, Freemasonry, and Jewish apocalyptic writings, the number equals the total of wings Enoch received when transformed into Metatron (3 Enoch 9:2). This plays an important role for the Brotherhood, as Metatron or "the angel in the whirlwind" was enabled as the guiding spirit over America during George W. Bush's administration for the purpose of directing the *future* and *fate* of the United States (as also prayed by Congressman Maj. R. Owens of New York before the House of Representatives on Wednesday, February 28, 2001).

But in the context of the Capitol Dome and the seventy-two stars that circle Washington's apotheosis in the womb of Isis, the significance of this symbolism is far more important. In sacred literature, including the Bible, stars are symbolic of angels, and within Masonic Gnosticism, seventy-two is the number of fallen angels or "kosmokrators" (reflected in the seventy-two conspirators that controlled Osiris' life in Egyptian myth) that currently administer the affairs of earth. Experts in the study of the Divine Council believe that, beginning at the Tower of Babel, the world and its inhabitants were disinherited by the sovereign God of Israel and placed under the authority of seventy-two angels (the earliest records had the number of angels at seventy, but this was later changed to seventy-two) which became corrupt and disloyal to God in their administration of those nations (Psalm 82). These beings quickly became worshipped on earth as gods following Babel, led by Nimrod/ Gilgamesh/Osiris/Apollo. Consistent with this tradition, the design- ers of the Capitol Dome, the Great Seal of the United States, and the Obelisk Washington Monument circled the *Apotheosis of Washington* with seventy-two pentagram stars, dedicated the Obelisk seventy-two years after the signing of the Declaration of Independence, and placed seventy-two stones on the Great Seal's uncapped pyramid, above which the eye of Horus/Osiris/Apollo stares. These three sets of seventy-two (72), combined with the imagery and occult numerology of the Osiris/ Obelisk, the Isis/Dome, and the oracular Great Seal, are richly symbolic of the influence of Satan and his angels over the world (see Luke 4:5–6, 2 Corinthians 4:4, and Ephesians 6:12) with a prophecy toward Satan's final earthly empire—the coming *novus ordo seclorum*, or new golden pagan age.

In order for the "inevitable" worship of Osiris to be "reestablished" on earth, the seventy-two demons that govern the nations must be con- trolled, thus they are set in magical constraints on the Great Seal, the Washington Obelisk, and the pentagram circles around the *Apotheosis of Washington* to bind and force the desired effect.

In *The Secret Destiny of America*, Hall noted as well that the sev- enty-two stones of the pyramid on the Great Seal correspond to the seventy-two arrangements of the Tetragrammaton, or the four-lettered name of God in Hebrew. "These four letters can be combined in seventy-two combinations, resulting in what is called the Shemhamforesh, which represents, in turn, the laws, powers, and energies of Nature."[746] The idea that the mystical name of God could be invoked to bind or loose those supernatural agents (powers and energies of nature, as Hall called them) is meaningful creed within many occult tenets, including Kabbalah and Freemasonry. This is why the seventy-two stars are pentagram-shaped around the deified Freemason, George Washington. Medieval books of magic, or grimoires such as the Key of Solomon and the Lesser Key of Solomon not only identify the star systems Orion (Osiris) and Pleiades (Apollo) as the "home" of these powers, but applies great importance to the pentagram shape of the stars for binding and loosing their influence. Adept Rosicrucians and Freemasons have long used these magical texts—the Key of Solomon and the Lesser Key of Solomon—to do just that. Peter Goodgame makes an important observation about this in "The Giza Discovery":

> One of the co-founders of the occult society known as the Golden Dawn[747] was a Rosicrucian Freemason named S. L. MacGregor Mathers, who was the first to print and publish the Key of Solomon (in 1889) making it readily available to the public. Mathers describes it as a primary occult text: "The fountainhead and storehouse of Qabalistic Magic, and the origin of much of the Ceremonial Magic of mediaeval times, the 'Key' has been ever valued by occult writers as a work of the highest authority." Of the 519 esoteric titles included in the catalogue of the Golden Dawn library, the Key was listed as number one. As far as contents are concerned, the Key included instructions on how to prepare for the summoning of spirits including…demons…. One of the most well-known members of the Golden Dawn was the magician [and 33rd-degree freemason] Aleister Crowley. In 1904 Crowley published the first part of the five-part Lesser Key

of Solomon known as the Ars Goetia,[748] which is Latin for "art of sorcery." The Goetia is a grimoire for summoning seventy-two different demons that were allegedly summoned, restrained, and put to work by King Solomon [according to Masonic mysticism] during the construction of the Temple of YHWH.[749]

Unlike other grimoires including the sixteenth-century *Pseudo-monarchia Daemonum* and the seventeenth-century *Lemegeton*, the Key of Solomon does not contain the "Diabolical Signature" of the devil or demons, which the Ars Goetia describes as numbering seventy-two and who were, according to legend, constrained to assist King Solomon after he bound them in a bronze vessel sealed by magic symbols. Such books routinely contain invocations and curses for summoning, binding, and loosing these demons in order to force them to do the conjurers will. Even members of the Church of Satan sign letters using the Shemhamforash, from the Hebrew name of God or Tetragrammaton, producing a blasphemous reinterpretation of the seventy-two entities. And then there is Michelangelo, who painted what we have called the "Sign of the Sixth Knuckle" inside the Sistine Chapel (mentioned elsewhere in *Zenith 2016*) that tied the prophecy on the Great Seal of the United States from the Cumaean Sibyl to the return of the Nephilim Apollo. But incredibly, Michelangelo also produced the Shemhamforash on the Vatican's famous ceiling, as his fresco has "an architectural design of 24 columns. On each of these columns are two cherubs, which are mirror imaged on the adjoining column totaling 48 cherubs figures. Then on the 12 triangular spandrels flanking the ceiling borders are an additional 24 nude figures (two bronze nude figures per triangular spandrel) also mirror imaging each other. This totals to 72 cherub figures or the 72 angels of God or names of God [or conversely, the 72 angels that fell and are now the demons or kosmokrators over the nations of the earth]."[750]

Once one understands the importance that these mystical keys hold in Kabbalah, Rosicrucianism, Freemasonic mysticism, and other mystery traditions, there can be (and is) but one reasonable interpretation for the connection in the Vatican and the seventy-two pentagrams at the base of the *Apotheosis of Washington*. These are there to bind and control the demons over the nations to honor the dedication made by early American Freemasons and certain Roman devotees for a New Atlantis and New World Order under the coming antichrist deity Osiris/Apollo.[751]

*In other words, what may be the most powerful stargates in the world are in Washington, DC and at the Vatican. They are ready now to open, **that the spirit that is prophesied to inhabit THE FINAL ROMAN EMPEROR may come through them to establish his new and final Golden Pagan Age.***

Notes

1. Katie Zavadski, "ISIS Now Has a Network of Military Affiliates in 11 Countries around the World," New York, November 23, 2014, http://nymag.com/daily/intelligencer/2014/11/isis-now-has-military-allies-in-11-countries.html, accessed May 22, 2015.
2. http://www.christianheadlines.com/columnists/denison-forum/isis-rapidly-becoming-global-movement.html.
3. Reuters, "Jordan's King Abdullah: We Are Facing a Third World War," The Jerusalem Post, November 17, 2015, http://www.jpost.com/Middle-East/ISIS-Threat/Jordans-King-Abdullah-We-are-facing-a-Third-World-War-434408, accessed November 18, 2015.
4. William McCants, *The ISIS Apocalypse: The History, Strategy, and Doomsday Vision of the Islamic State* (St. Martin's Press. 2015)Kindle Location 79.
5. Elisabetta Povoledo, "Benedict Will Live in Vatican City, but Many Details Remain Undecided," February 12, 2013, *The New York Times*, last accessed March 15, 2016, http://www.nytimes.com/2013/02/13/world/europe/pope-benedict-xvi-resignation.html?_r=0.
6. Eric Schmitt, "In Battle to Defang ISIS, U.S. Targets Its Psychology," *New York Times*, December 28, 2014, last accessed February 18, 2016, http://www.nytimes.com/2014/12/29/us/politics/in-battle-to-defang-ISIS-us-targets-its-psychology-.html?_r=0.
7. Ibid.
8. David Commins, *The Wahhabi Mission and Saudi Arabia* (IB Tauris, London, New York: 2006), vi.
9. Front page of the As-Sunnah Foundation of America website, *ASFA*, last accessed February 17, 2016, http://sunnah.org/wp/.

10. Zubair Qamar, "Wahhabism: Understanding the Roots and Role Models of Islamic Extremism," under the "Introduction" header, last accessed February 17, 2016, http://www.sunnah.org/articles/Wahhabiarticleedit.htm.

11. Ibid.

12. "ISIS Spokesman Declares Caliphate, Rebrands Group as 'Islamic State,'" Jihadist News, last updated June 29, 2014, last accessed February 17, 2016, https://news.siteintelgroup.com/Jihadist-News/ISIS-spokesman-declares-caliphate-rebrands-group-as-islamic-state.html.

13. Eric Schmitt, "In Battle to Defang ISIS," http://www.nytimes.com/2014/12/29/us/politics/in-battle-to-defang-ISIS-us-targets-its-psychology-.html?_r=0.

14. George Weigel, "ISIS, Genocide," https://www.firstthings.com/web-exclusives/2016/02/ISIS-genocide-and-us; emphasis added.

15. Anugrah Kumar, "Over 100 NGOs, Leaders to Obama: ISIS Atrocities against Christians, Other Minorities, Are Genocide," *Christian Post*, February 18, 2016, http://www.christianpost.com/news/obama-ISIS-atrocities-christians-minorities-genocide-international-religious-freedom-roundtable-158043/.

16. Ibid.

17. "Leading Sunni Sheikh Yousef Al-Qaradhawi and Other Sheikhs Herald the Coming Conquest in Rome," *MEMRI: The Middle East Media Research Institute*, posted December 6, 2002, last accessed February 18, 2016, http://www.memri.org/report/en/0/0/0/0/0/0/774.htm.

18. "Leading Sunni Sheikh," http://www.memri.org/report/en/0/0/0/0/0/0/774.htm.

19. "In New Message Following Being Declared a 'Caliph,'…" *MEMRI: The Middle East Media Research Institute*, posted July 1, 2014, last accessed February 18, 2016, http://www.memrijttm.org/content/view_print/blog/7607; emphasis added.

20. "Pertaining to the Conquest of Constantinople and the Appearance of Dajjal and Descent of Jesus Son of Mary (Jesus Christ)," *The Only Quran*, last accessed February 18, 2016, http://www.theonlyquran.com/hadith/Sahih-Muslim/?volume=41&chapter=9.

21. Sophie Jane Evans, "ISIS's Chilling Death March to the End of the World: Jihadists Release Video Depicting Their Apocalyptic Vision of a Future Battle Culminating in Rome," *DailyMail*, December 11, 2015, last accessed February 18, 2016, http://www.dailymail.co.uk/news/article-3356503/ISIS-s-chilling-death-march-end-world-Jihadists-release-video-depicting-vision-future-battle-culminating-Colosseum.html.

22. Sam Prince, "WATCH: New ISIS Video Shows Armageddon Battle with the

West," *Heavy News*, December 11, 2015, last accessed February 18, 2016, http://heavy.com/news/2015/12/new-ISIS-islamic-state-news-video-see-you-in-dabiq-rome-muslim-extremists-rome-crusaders-colosseum-malahim-meeting-at-dabiq-italy-west-war-uncensored-full-youtube/.

23. Video can be seen at the following article: Anthony Bond, Kara O'Neill, Kelly-Ann Mills, "ISIS Release Chilling New 'End of the World' Video Showing Final Battle with Crusaders," *Mirror News*, December 11, 2015, last accessed February 18, 2016, http://www.mirror.co.uk/news/world-news/ISIS-release-sickening-new-video-6995563.

24. Tyler Durden, "ISIS Releases New Apocalyptic Video Depicting 'Final' Battle with 'Crusaders' in Syria," December 12, 2015, *Zero Hedge*, last accessed February 18, 2016, http://www.zerohedge.com/news/2015-12-12/ISIS-releases-new-apocalyptic-video-depicting-final-battle-crusaders-syria.

25. David Stout, "Vatican Backs Military Campaign against ISIS," *Time*, March 15, 2015, last accessed March 15, 2016, http://time.com/3745462/vatican-ISIS-syria-iraq-middle-east/.

26. "Pope Francis: US Action against ISIS a 'Just War,'" *CBN News*, September, 8, 2014, last accessed March 15, 2016, http://www1.cbn.com/cbnnews/world/2014/August/Pope-Francis-US-Action-against-ISIS-a-Just-War.

27. "Just War theory," *Wikipedia: The Free Encyclopedia*, last modified March 10, 2016, last accessed March 15, 2016, https://en.wikipedia.org/wiki/Just_war_theory.

28. John L. Allen Jr., "Vatican Backs Military Force to Stop ISIS 'Genocide,'" *Crux News: Covering All Things Catholic*, March 13, 2015, last accessed March 15, 2016, http://www.cruxnow.com/church/2015/03/13/vatican-backs-military-force-to-stop-ISIS-genocide/.

29. Thomas D. Williams, PhD, "After Paris, Pope Francis Tells Christians to Be Ready for the End of the World," *Breitbart*, November 15, 2015, last accessed March 15, 2016, http://www.breitbart.com/big-government/2015/11/15/paris-pope-francis-tells-christians-ready-end-world/.

30. Sophie Jane Evans, "ISIS's Chilling Death March," http://www.dailymail.co.uk/news/article-3356503/ISIS-s-chilling-death-march-end-world-Jihadists-release-video-depicting-vision-future-battle-culminating-Colosseum.html.

31. Robert Windrem, "ISIS Magazine *Debiq* Singled Out Pope Francis Ahead of US Trip," *NBC News*, September 22, 2015, last accessed March 15, 2016, http://www.nbcnews.com/storyline/pope-francis-visits-america/ISIS-magazine-dabiq-singles-out-pope-francis-ahead-u-s-n431681.

32. Chris Perez, "Pope Francis: If I'm Assassinated, at Least Make it Painless,"

New York Post, March 10, 2015, last accessed March 15, 2016, http://nypost. com/2015/03/10/pope-francis-if-im-assassinated-at-least-make-it-painless/.

33. Edward Pentin, "Pope Francis' Consecrating the World to Mary Culminates Fatima Celebration," *National Catholic Register*, October 15, 2013, last accessed March 15, 2016, http://www.ncregister.com/daily-news/ pope-francis-consecrating-the-world-to-mary-culminates-fatima-celebration/.

34. Thomas Horn and Cris Putnam, *Petrus Romanus: The Final Pope Is Here* (Crane, MO: Defender Publishing, 2012), 454.

35. Thomas Horn, *Zenith 2016: Did Something Begin in the Year 2012 that Will Reach its Apex in 2016?* (Crane, MO: Defender Publishing, 2013), 371.

36. For more information on this, see the appendix at the back of this book on the Cumaean Sibyl's prophecy, the Great Seal, and the design and layout of the Vatican and Washington, DC.

37. "Was Pope Francis Canonically Elected?" *Catholic Truth*, last accessed March 15, 2016, http://catholictruthblog.com/2013/12/30/ was-pope-francis-canonically-elected/.

38. Rev. Herman Bernard Kramer, *The Book of Destiny* (Belleville, IL: Buechler Publishing Company, 1955), 277.

39. Leah Barkoukis, "Report: Obama Wants to Become UN Secretary General, Netanyahu Doing Everything He Can to Stop Him," *Fox News*, January 10, 2016, last accessed March 15, 2016, http://nation.foxnews. com/2016/01/10/report-obama-wants-become-un-secretary-general- netanyahu-doing-everything-he-can-stop-him.

40. "End of Time Prophecies, Apocalypse & Eschatology," *Discovering Islam*, last accessed March 15, 2016, http://www.discoveringislam.org/end_of_time. htm.

41. Benny Morris, *1948: A History of the First Arab-Israeli War* (Yale University Press, New Haven and London: 2008), 179.

42. Rabbi Yechiel Eckstein, "Ancient Jewish History: The Bible on Jewish Links to the Holy Land," *Jewish Virtual Library*, last accessed February 8, 2016, https://www.jewishvirtuallibrary.org/jsource/Judaism/biblejew.html.

43. Herb Scribner, "15 Christian Women Who Are Changing the World," *Deseret National News*, August 7, 2014, last accessed March 15, 2016, http://national.deseretnews.com/article/2079/15-christian-women-who-are- changing-the-world.html.

44. "The Holy Club," *Christianity Today*, last accessed January 28, 2016, http:// www.ctlibrary.com/ch/1983/issue2/216.html.

45. John Charles Ryle, *A Sketch of the Life and Labors of George Whitefield* (New York: Anson D. F. Randolf, 1854; Kindle Edition), 25–27.

46. Richard McNemar, *The Kentucky Revival* (Lawton, OK: Trumpet Press,

1808; Kindle Edition, Great Plains Press: 2011), Kindle Locations 467–477; emphasis added.

47. Kevin Belmonte, *D. L. Moody—A Life: Innovator, Evangelist, World Changer* (Chicago, IL: Moody Publishers: 2014; Kindle Edition), 62.

48. Sid Roth, *The Incomplete Church: Unifying God's Children* (Shippensburg, PA: Destiny Image, 2007), 14.

49. Cris Putnam, *The Supernatural Worldview: Examining Paranormal, Psi, and the Apocalyptic* (Crane, MO: Defender Publishing, 2014), 205–210.

50. Fred R. Shapiro and Joseph Epstein, eds., *The Yale Book of Quotations* (New Haven, CT: Yale University Press, 2006), 708.

51. John Marszalek, "Scorched Earth: Sherman's March to the Sea," http://www.civilwar.org/hallowed-ground-magazine/fall-2014/scorched-earth.html, accessed November 25, 2015.

52. "Heimbach, Daniel; Senior Professor of Christian Ethics," Southeastern Baptist Theological Seminary, http://apps.sebts.edu/FacultyInfo/FacultyPage.cfm?id=)%23*W%22R%3FW%23K*11%0A.

53. Daniel R. Heimbach, "The Bush Just War Doctrine: Genesis and Application of the President's Moral Leadership in the Persian Gulf War," in *From Cold War to New World Order: The Foreign Policy of George H. W. Bush.* Edited by Meena Bose and Rosanna Perotti (Westport, CoT: Greenwood, 2002), 441–464.

54. Daniel R. Heimbach, "Introduction to Christian Ethics Lecture 36," Southeastern Baptist Theological Seminary (Wake Forest, NC: 2013).

55. Ibid.

56. David Rosch, "ISIS Terror Threat Gives Impetus To 'Just War,' Strategists Say," Baptist Press, September 3, 2014, http://www.bpnews.net/43278/isis-terror-threat-gives-impetus-to-just-war-strategists-say.

57. Nick Goutteridge, "Putin Has Achieved More against ISIS in a Fortnight than US Did in a Whole YEAR, Syrian MP," *The Guardian UK,* October 27, 2015, http://www.express.co.uk/news/world/612978/Islamic-State-ISIS-Vladimir-Putin-airstrikes-ISIS-Syria-US-coalition-Assad, accessed November 25, 2015.

58. Charles Guthrie and Michael Quinlan, *Just War: The Just War Tradition* (London: Bloomsbury, 2007), 11.

59. J. Scarisbrick, *Henry Viii,* (New Haven, CT: Yale University Press, 1997), 341.

60. James White, "Debate with Bother John, Resolved: The Church of the Council of Nicaea Is Not the Roman Catholic Church," Alpha & Omega Ministries, http://vintage.aomin.org/JRWReb1.html, accessed November 24, 2015.

61. Thomas F. X. Noble, "Lecture One: What Is Papal History and How Did it Begin?" notes for course, *Popes and the Papacy: A History* (The Teaching Company, 2006), 3.

62. Russ Houck, *Epidemic Examining the Infected Roots of Judaism and Christianity: How Do We Find God with All This Mess?* Volume 1 (Negev Publishing, 2012).

63. Alexander Hislop, *The Two Babylons: or, The Papal Worship Proved to Be the Worship of Nimrod and His Wife* (Edinburgh: James Wood, 1882), 120, https://play.google.com/store/books/details?id=GooEAAAAQAAJ&rdid=book-GooEAAAAQAAJ&rdot=1.

64. Eusebius, *Vita Constantini*, 4.62.4.

65. Christopher Tyerman, *God's War: A New History of the Crusades,* (Cambridge, MA: Belknap Press of Harvard University Press, 2006), 33.

66. Augustine of Hippo, "The City of God," in *St. Augustin's City of God and Christian Doctrine*, ed. Philip Schaff, trans. Marcus Dods, vol. 2, A Select Library of the Nicene and Post-Nicene Fathers of the Christian Church, First Series (Buffalo, NY: Christian Literature Company, 1887), 15,http://www.sacred-texts.com/chr/ecf/102/1020027.htm.

67. "Catholic Education Resource Center," retrieved25 April 2015.

68. Thomas Aquinas, S., & Fathers of the English Dominican Province(2009), *Summa theological,* Translation of: Summa theologica.; Includes index. (Complete English ed.) (STh., II–II q.40 a.1 resp.). (Bellingham, WA: Logos Research Systems, Inc.)

69. Gerard O'Connell, "Full Text of Pope Francis' Press Conference on Plane Returning From Korea," *America the National Catholic Review*, August 18, 2014, http://americamagazine.org/content/all-things/full-text-pope-francis-press-conference-plane-returning-korea, accessed July 23, 2015.

70. Aquinas, S., *Summa theological.*

71. O'Connell, "Full Text."

72. Laurence H. Silberman, "The Dangerous Lie That 'Bush Lied,'" *The Wall Street Journal,* February 8, 2015, http://www.wsj.com/articles/laurence-h-silberman-the-dangerous-lie-that-bush-lied-1423437950, accessed November 4, 2015.

73. Aquinas, S., *Summa theologica.*

74. O'Connell, "Full Text." http://americamagazine.org/content/all-things/full-text-pope-francis-press-conference-plane-returning-korea.

75. Karen Yourish, K. K. Rebecca Lai, and Derek Watkins, "Death In Syria," *The New York Times,* September. 14, 2015, http://www.nytimes.com/interactive/2015/09/14/world/middleeast/syria-war-deaths.html, accessed November 4, 2015.

76. "Iraq 2014: Civilian Deaths Almost Doubling Year on Year," https://www.iraqbodycount.org/analysis/numbers/2014/, accessed November 4, 2015.

77. Anthony Colangelo, "Islamic State's Shocking Death Toll," *The New Daily*, June 29, 2015, http://thenewdaily.com.au/news/2015/06/29/islamic-states-shocking-death-toll/ accessed November 24, 2015.

78. Yourish, et al., "Death In Syria."

79. In Iraq, "The Christian population is down from as many as 1.5 million in 2003 to around 400,000 [in 2014]." Robin Emmott, "Iraq's Christians Flee Violence, Fear End of Long History," Reuters, July 9, 2014,http://uk.reuters.com/article/2014/07/09/uk-iraq-security-chrisitianity-idUKKBN0FE1L920140709.

80. Heng Chu, David A. Plaisted (1994), "Model Finding in Semantically Guided Instance-Based Theorem Proving," *Fundam. Inform,* .**21** (3): 221–235.

81. Daniel A. Plainsted, "Estimates of the Number Killed by the Papacy in the Middle Ages and Later."

82. John Wesley, "Doctrine of Original Sin," Part I, section II.8, 1757, Wesley's Works, vol. 9, edited by Thomas Jackson, pp. 217–19.

83. Brownlee, *Lectures on Romanism* (Philadelphia, PA: D. Weidner, 1840), p. 6.

84. Plainsted, "Estimates," 19.

85. *Halley's Bible Handbook* (1965), p. 726.

86. Plainsted, "Estimates," 19.

87. Ibid., 21.

88. Ibid.

89. Ibid., 5.

90. R. F. Foster, *Modern Ireland, 1600–1972* (New York: Penguin Books, 1989), pp.72, 130.

91. "The Saint Bartholomew's Day Massacre," http://www.reformation.org/bart.html accessed November 28, 2015.

92. Cushing B. Hassell, *History of the Church of God,* 470. linkhttps://books.google.com/books?id=L_QPAAAAYAAJ&vq=1492&pg=PA470#v=onepage&q=persecution%20was%20begun%20against%20the%20Jews&f=false.

93. Plainsted, citing an independent source Joseph McCabe, *The Story of Religious Controversy* in "Estimates," 8.

94. Johannes P. Louw and Eugene Albert Nida, *Greek-English Lexicon of the New Testament: Based on Semantic Domains* (New York: United Bible Societies, 1996), p. 542.

95. "Table 1 Death by Government," https://www.hawaii.edu/powerkills/DBG.TAB1.2.GIF, accessed November 28, 2016.

96. "Selected Pre-20th Century Democide Totals," https://www.hawaii.edu/powerkills/PRE-20TH.GIF.

97. P. Schaff, (1997), *The Nicene and Post-Nicene Fathers Vol. IV.* St. Augustin: The Writings against the Manichaeans and against the Donatists (Oak Harbor: Logos Research Systems) 249.

98. "Unam Sanctum," in *Catholic Encyclopedia*, New Advent, http://www.newadvent.org/cathen/15126a.htm, accessed November 4, 2015.

99. Francis X. Rocca, "Vatican to Sign First Treaty with 'State of Palestine,'" *The Wall Street Journal*, May 13, 2015, http://www.wsj.com/articles/vatican-to-sign-first-treaty-with-state-of-palestine-1431531609, accessed November 25, 2015.

100. Pope Francis, *SULLA CURA DELLA CASA COMUNE*, Libreria Editrice Vaticana, http://w2.vatican.va/content/francesco/en/encyclicals/documents/papa-francesco_20150524_enciclica-laudato-si.html, 129.

101. Benedict XVI, *Caritas In Veritate* ("Charity in Truth"), *Vatican*, June 29, 2009, http://w2.vatican.va/content/benedict-xvi/en/encyclicals/documents/hf_ben-xvi_enc_20090629_caritas-in-veritate.html accessed October 9, 2015.

102. Paul VI, Speech at the UN October 4, 1965, as quoted in: *The Power Puzzle: A Compilation of Documents and Resources on Global Governance*, edited by Carl Teichrib, Copyright 2004, second edition, 43.

103. Marilyn Ferguson, *Aquarius Now: Radical Common Sense and Reclaiming Our Personal Sovereignty* (York Beach, ME: Red Wheel/Weiser, 2005), 41.

104. Barbra Marx Hubbard, "Marx Hubbard Responds to Cardinal Müller's LCWR Comments," *National Catholic Reporter*, May.13, 2014, http://ncronline.org/news/vatican/marx-hubbard-response-cardinal-m-ller, accessed October 10, 2015.

105. Cris D. Putnam and Thomas Horn, *On the Path of the Immortals* (Crane MO: Defender, 2015), p. 92.

106. Hubbard.

107. Robert Muller, "World Care Curriculum," Robert Muller.org, http://robertmuller.org/rm/R1/World_Core_Curriculum.html, accessed October 10, 2015.

108. Robert Muller, *The Desire to be Human: A Global Reconnaissance of Human Perspectives in an Age of Transformation* (Miranana, 1983), p. 304.

109. "Iraq: Abp Tomasi on Pope's Appeal to UN's Ban Ki-moon," Vatican Radio, August 13, 2014, http://en.radiovaticana.va/news/2014/08/13/iraq__abp_tomasi_on_pope%E2%80%99s_appeal_to_un%E2%80%99s_ban_ki-moon_/1104468, accessed November 4, 2015.

110. John F. Walvoord, "Revelation," in *The Bible Knowledge Commentary: An Exposition of the Scriptures*, ed. J. F. Walvoord and R. B. Zuck, vol. 2 (Wheaton, IL: Victor Books, 1985), 963.

111. David Rockefeller, *Memoirs* (New York: Random House Trade Paperbacks, 2011), p. 405.

112. Martin Kramer, "Bernard Lewis". *Encyclopedia of Historians and Historical Writing*1. London: Fitzroy Dearborn., 1999), 719–720. http://www.webcitation.org/query?url=http%3A%2F%2Fwww.martinkramer.org%2Fsandbox%2Freader%2Farchives%2Fbernard-lewis%2F&date=2010-11-13.

113. Bernard Lewis, *The Crisis of Islam: Holy War and Unholy Terror*, Kindle Edition, (New York: Random House Publishing Group, 2003), Kindle Locations 1208–1211.

114. According to Iraqi government statistics, the rate of cancer in the country has skyrocketed from 40 per 100,000 people prior to the First Gulf War in 1991, to 800 per 100,000 in 1995, to at least 1,600 per 100,000 in 2005. http://www.aljazeera.com/indepth/features/2013/03/2013315171951838638.html.
Chris Busby, MalakHamdan and EntesarAriabi, "Cancer, Infant Mortality and Birth Sex-Ratio in Fallujah, Iraq 2005–2009," *International Journal of the Environmental Research and Public Health*,2010, 7(7), 2828–2837.

115. "Obama Bows to the Saudi King, Why? It's Obvious!" YouTube, April 10, 2009, https://youtu.be/ltjdtbTMzCQ accessed October 18, 2015.

116. William McCants, *The ISIS Apocalypse: The History, Strategy, and Doomsday Vision of the Islamic State*, Kindle Edition (St. Martin's Press, 2015), Kindle Locations 2629–2632.

117. Associated Press, "Bush Bank Tied to Nazi Funding," *The Washington Times*, October 17, 2003, http://www.washingtontimes.com/news/2003/oct/17/20031017-110534-8149r/, accessed November 23, 2015.
Cindy Rodríguez, "Bush Ties to bin Laden Haunt Grim Anniversary," *The Denver Post*, August 12, 2006, http://www.denverpost.com/rodriguez/ci_4319898, accessed November 23, 2015.

118. Craig Unger, *House of Bush, House of Saud: The Secret Relationship between the World's Two Most Powerful Dynasties* (New York: Scribner, 2004), p. 4.

119. "Islamic Black Magic (Voodoo)," Islam Watch, http://www.islam-watch.org/abulkasem/IslamicVoodoos/Part5b.htm.

120. Diane Morgan, *Essential Islam: A Comprehensive Guide to Belief and Practice*, (ABC-CLIO 2010), p. 87.

121. Bernard Lewis, *The Political Language of Islam* (Chicago: University of Chicago Press, 1988), p. 72.

122. Ibid.

123. Laruent Murawiec, *The Mind of Jihad* (Cambridge, Cambridge University Press, 2008), 2–3.

124. Wood, "What ISIS Really Wants."

125. Murawiec, *Mind of Jihad, 12.*

126. Aakov Katz, "Witness Hamas Fired from School," *Jerusalem Post*, January 6, 2009, http://www.jpost.com/Israel/Witnesses-Hamas-fired-from-school, accessed November 27, 2015.

127. Amira Hass, Amos Harel, AviIssacharoff, AkivaEldar, The Associated Press and AnshelPfeffer, "UN Rejects IDF Claim Gaza Militants Operated from Bombed-out School," *Haaretz*, July 1, 2009, http://www.haaretz.com/news/un-rejects-idf-claim-gaza-militants-operated-from-bombed-out-school-1.267630.

128. Lloyd Steffen, *Holy War, Just War: Exploring the Moral Meaning of Religious Violence*, (Rowman& Littlefield, 2007), p. 221.

129. MOSCOW (AFP), "Church Says Russia Fighting 'Holy Battle' in Syria," *France 24*, September 30, 2015, http://www.france24.com/en/20150930-church-says-russia-fighting-holy-battle-syria, accessed October 7, 2015.

130. Daniel R. Heimbach, Lecture 35 Crusade, ETH 5100, Introduction to Christian Ethics, Southeastern Baptist Theological Seminary.

131. Clinton E. Arnold, "Can We Still Believe in Demons Today?," in *The Apologetics Study Bible: Real Questions, Straight Answers, Stronger Faith*, ed. Ted Cabal et al. (Nashville, TN: Holman Bible Publishers, 2007), p. 1475.

132. Aki Peritz, Tara Maller, "The Islamic State of Sexual Violence," *Foreign Policy*, September 16, 2014, http://foreignpolicy.com/2014/09/16/the-islamic-state-of-sexual-violence/,accessed November 4, 2015.

133. Douglas Stuart, "What Were the Characteristics of Holy War in the Old Testament?" *Biblical Training.org*, June 19, 2012, https://www.biblicaltraining.org/blog/curious-christian/6-19-2012/what-were-characteristics-holy-war-old-testament, accessed October 10, 2015.

134. 276 *charam* in *New American Standard Hebrew-Aramaic and Greek Dictionaries: Updated Edition,* edited by Robert L. Thomas (Anaheim, CA: Foundation Publications, Inc., 1998).

135. Leon J. Wood, "744 חָרַם, *charam*" *Theological Wordbook of the Old Testament,* ed. R. Laird Harris, Gleason L. Archer Jr., and Bruce K. Waltke(Chicago: Moody Press, 1999), p. 324.

136. Johannes P. Louw and Eugene Albert Nida, *Greek-English Lexicon of the New Testament: Based on Semantic Domains* (New York: United Bible Societies, 1996), p. 146–147.

137. Ahmed ibn Naqib al-Misri, *Reliance of the Traveller: A Classic Manual of Islamic Sacred Law*, trans. Nuh Ha Mim Keller (Amana Publications, 1999), p. 99.

138. La Sor, W. S., Hubbard, D. A., & Bush, F. W. (1996),*Old Testament Survey: The Message, Form, and Background of the Old Testament* (2nd ed.) (147) (Grand Rapids, MI: William B. Eerdmans Publishing Company).

139. Michael S. Heiser, "What's Ugaritic Got to Do with Anything?," Logos, https://www.logos.com/ugaritic.

140. "OT Scholar Bruce Waltke Resigns Following Evolution Comments," http://www.christianitytoday.com/gleanings/2010/april/ot-scholar-bruce-waltke-resigns-following-evolution.html.

141. Douglas Stuart, Gordon-Conwell Seminary, http://www.gordonconwell.edu/academics/view-faculty-member.cfm?faculty_id=15891&grp_id=8946.

142. Douglas Stuart, "What Were the Characteristics of Holy War in the Old Testament?" *Biblical Training.org*, June 19,2012, https://www.biblicaltraining.org/blog/curious-christian/6-19-2012/what-were-characteristics-holy-war-old-testament, accessed October 10, 2015.

143. Richard Dawkins, *The God Delusion*(Great Britain: Bantam Press, 2006), p. 31.

144. Michael Heiser, "Genesis 6 Hybridization: Sons of God, Daughters of Men and the Nephilim," Ancient of Days Conference (2005), http://ancientofdaysbibleufo.podomatic.com/entry/2009-01-03T14_25_07-08_00, accessed November 23, 2015.

145. James Swanson, *Dictionary of Biblical Languages with Semantic* Domains : Hebrew (Old Testament) (Oak Harbor: Logos Research Systems, Inc., 1997).

146. Michael Heiser, "The Nephilim," Sitchin Is Wrong,http://sitchiniswrong.com/nephilim/nephilim.htm, accessed November 24, 2015.

147. In *On the path of the Immortals* we explained the immorality of the messenger-angels (Hebrew: *malak*) and hosts or soldiers (Hebrew: *tsaba*) (Psalm 148: 2, 5–6) and explained the Hebrew word *tsaba*, "hosts," is a most often used of military personnel and is often translated "armies" in English, as discussed in *Brown, Driver, and Briggs,Enhanced Hebrew and English Lexicon*, 838.

148. Francis Brown, Samuel Rolles Driver, and Charles Augustus Briggs, *Enhanced Brown-Driver-Briggs Hebrew and English Lexicon* (Oxford: Clarendon Press, 1977), p. 839.

149. Chuck Missler, *The Book of Joshua: An Expositional Commentary* (Coeur d'Alene, ID: Koinonia House, 1996), p. 30.

150. Missler, *Book of Joshua*, 30.

151. W. S. La Sor, D. A. Hubbard, , &F. W. Bush, F. W. (1996),*Old Testament Survey: The Message, Form, and Background of the Old Testament* (2nd ed.) (Grand Rapids, MI: William B. Eerdmans Publishing Company), p. 144.

152. John Noble Wilford, "Believers Score in Battle Over the Battle of Jericho," *The New York Times*, February 22, 1990, http://www.nytimes. com/1990/02/22/world/believers-score-in-battle-over-the-battle-of-jericho. html, Accessed October 9, 2015.

153. "Silos and Bunkers for Sale," http://www.hardenedstructures.com/bunkers-for-Sale.php.

154. Missler, *Book of Joshua*, 31.

155. Heiser.

156. J. F. Walvoord (1990),*The Prophecy Knowledge Handbook,* Includes indexes. (Wheaton, Ill.: Victor Books), p. 318.

157. Robert Alter, "Discourse, Direct and Indirect," *The Anchor Bible Dictionary* edited by D. N. Freedman (New York: Doubleday. 1996), 6:505

158. Alter, "Discourse, Direct and Indirect," *ABD*, 2:213.

159. Millard J. Erickson, *Christian Theology.*, 2nd ed. (Grand Rapids, MI: Baker Book House, 1998), p. 468.

160. Jesse Childs, "How to Plan a Crusade by Christopher Tyerman Review— The Role of Reason in Medieval Religious Wars," *The Guardian*, September 25, 2015, http://www.theguardian.com/books/2015/sep/25/ how-to-plan-a-crusade-reason-and-religious-war-in-the-middle-ages-christopher-tyerman-review, accessed October 5, 2015.

161. Martin Luther, Thesis 32 from "Luther's 95 Thesis" http://www. biblestudytools.com/history/creeds-confessions/luther-95-theses.html, accessed October 15, 2015.

162. Ibid., Thesis 16.

163. Bamber Gascoigne, "History of the Reformation," HistoryWorld.com, http://www.historyworld.net/wrldhis/PlainTextHistories.asp?ParagraphID= hnl#ixzz3sNxZwTky, accessed November 23, 2015.

164. Philip Daileader, "How the Crusades Changed Everything," The Teaching Company.

165. Tom Kington, "Vatican Offers 'Time Off Purgatory' to Followers of Pope Francis Tweets," *The Guardian*, July 16. 2013, http://www.theguardian. com/world/2013/jul/16/vatican-indulgences-pope-francis-tweets, accessed October 5, 2015.

166. Max Fisher, "News from 1096 AD: Pope Discusses Military Force against Middle Eastern Caliphate," *Vox*, August 18, 2014, http://www.vox.

com/2014/8/18/6031559/news-from-1096-ad-pope-endorses-military-force-to-destroy-middle, accessed September 15, 2015.

167. George W. Bush, *Public Papers of the Presidents of the United States, George W. Bush, 2001, Book 2, July 1 to December 31, 2001* (Washington DC: Office of the Federal Register, 2004), 1116,https://books.google.com/books?id=YnuegHp61zgC&lpg=PA1116&ots=QNoC8QmeDH&dq=This%20crusade%2C%20this%20war%20on%20terrorism%20is%20going%20to%20take%20a%20while.%20And%20the%20American%20people%20must%20be%20patient.%20I'm%20going%20to%20be%20patient.&pg=PA1116#v=onepage&q&f=false.

168. Alexander Cockburn, "The Tenth Crusade," Counterpunch, September 7, 2002, http://www.counterpunch.org/2002/09/07/the-tenth-crusade/, accessed November 5, 2015.

169. Malachi Martin, *The Keys of This Blood: The Struggle for World Dominion between Pope John Paul Ii, Mikhail Gorbachev, and the Capitalist West* (New York: Simon and Schuster, ©990), 1.

170. "Pope Francis Warns on 'Piecemeal World War III'" BBC News, September 13, 2014, http://www.bbc.com/news/world-europe-29190890, accessed May 22, 2015.

171. O'Connell, "Full Text of Pope Francis' Press Conference on Plane Returning from Korea," *National Catholic Review* August 18, 2014, http://americamagazine.org/content/all-things/full-text-pope-francis-press-conference-plane-returning-korea accessed May 22, 2015.

172. Hal Lindsey, *The Final Battle* (Palos Verdes, CA: Western Front,1995), xiv.

173. Lyndon H. LaRouche, Larouche for President, ABC-TV Nationwide Broadcast, http://web.archive.org/web/20010414022653/http://www.etext.org/Politics/LaRouche/102592.tv, accessed October 4, 2015.

174. Edwin Charles Knuth; William GuyCarr, *The Money Power: Empire of the City* and *Pawns in the Game—Two Books in One*, Kindle Edition (Progressive Press, 2014) Kindle Locations 3276–3283.

175. Cardinal Caro y Rodriguez, Archbishop of Santiago, Chile,*Mystery of Freemasonry Unveiled*, 118.

176. "Originally published in 1925, this book remains the best summary and reference book on the deceits and evils of Masonry. Exposes the Worldwide Plans for the Destruction of the Christian Order, as Well as its Anti-Catholic Fury throughout the World,"http://angeluspress.org/Mystery-Of-Freemasonry-Unveiled.

177. Keelan Balderson, "Albert Pike's 3 World Wars Letter Hoax," Wide Shut, http://wideshut.co.uk/albert-pikes-3-world-wars-letter-hoax-wideshut-webcast/, accessed October 4, 2015.

178. William Guy Carr, *Satan Prince of this World*, 71. https://www.scribd.com/doc/3221212/carr-william-guy-satan-prince-of-this-world-1959#scribd.

179. Rod Dreher, "The Anti-Benedict Conspiracy," The American Conservative, September 25, 2015, http://www.theamericanconservative.com/dreher/the-anti-benedict-conspiracy/ accessed October 6, 2015.

180. Ibid.

181. St. Francis of Assisi, *Works of the Seraphic Father St. Francis Of Assisi*, (Washbourne, 1882), 248–250. https://archive.org/details/worksseraphicfa00frangoog.

182. Cris Putnam and Thomas Horn, *Petrus Romanus* (Crane MO: Defender, 2012), 94–95.

183. Malachi Martin, *Windswept House*, 600.

184. Albert Pike, *Morals and Dogma of the Ancient and Accepted Scottish Rite of Freemasonry* (L.H. Jenkins, 1871), 325,https://books.google.com/books/reader?id=cMtJAAAAMAAJ&printsec=frontcover&output=reader&pg=GBS.PA321.

185. Malachi Martin, *The Jesuits: The Society of Jesus and the Betrayal of the Roman Catholic Church* (New York: Linden Press, Simon & Schuster, 1987), 13.

186. Cheryl K. Chumley, "Vatican Makes History: Pope Allows Islamic Prayers, Koran Readings," *The Washington Times*, June 9, 2014, http://www.washingtontimes.com/news/2014/jun/9/vatican-makes-history-pope-allows-islamic-prayers-/, accessed October 4, 2015.

187. Jack Khoury and the Associated Press, "Pope Francis: Abbas Is An 'Angel of Peace,' read more: http://www.haaretz.com/news/world/1.656737,*Haaretz*, May 16, 2015, http://www.haaretz.com/news/world/1.656737, accessed September 23, 2015.

188. "Palestinian Leader: Number of Jewish Victims in the Holocaust Might be 'Even Less Than a Million...' Zionist Movement Collaborated with Nazis to 'Expand the Mass Extermination' of the Jews," http://www.memri.org/report/en/print672.htm.

189. http://www.jpost.com/landedpages/printarticle.aspx?id=300397.

190. http://www.jpost.com/landedpages/printarticle.aspx?id=403133#.

191. http://www.algemeiner.com/2015/05/17/pope-francis-whitewashes-a-terrorist/.

192. "Chronic Kleptocracy: Corruption within the Palestinian Political Establishment," http://archives.republicans.foreignaffairs.house.gov/112/74960.pdf, accessed May 22, 2015.

193. Ibid., 2.

194. Katie Zavadski, "ISIS Now Has a Network of Military Affiliates in 11

Countries around the World," New York, November 23, 2014, http://nymag.com/daily/intelligencer/2014/11/isis-now-has-military-allies-in-11-countries.html, accessed May 22, 2015.

195. http://www.christianheadlines.com/columnists/denison-forum/isis-rapidly-becoming-global-movement.html.

196. Adam Withnall, "Iraq Crisis: ISISChanges Name and Declares Its Territories a New Islamic State with 'Restoration of Caliphate' in Middle East," *The Independent*, June 29 2014, accessed May 22, 2015, http://www.independent.co.uk/news/world/middle-east/isis-declares-new-islamic-state-in-middle-east-with-abu-bakr-albaghdadi-as-emir-removing-iraq-and-syria-from-its-name-9571374.html.

197. "This Is the Promise of Allah," http://myreader.toile-libre.org/uploads/My_53b039f00cb03.pdf, accessed July 25, 2015.

198. Pew Forum, "Mapping the Global Muslim Population," http://www.pewforum.org/2009/10/07/mapping-the-global-muslim-population/, accessed July 25, 2015.

199. Ibid.

200. "'They're Delusional': Rivals Ridicule ISIS Declaration of Islamic State," CBS News, June 30, 2014, http://www.cbsnews.com/news/theyre-delusional-rivals-ridicule-isis-declaration-of-islamic-state/, accessed July 25, 2015.

201. Timothy R. Furnish, *Holiest Wars: Islamic Mahdis, Their Jihads, and Osama bin Laden*, Kindle Edition, Kindle Locations 60–61.

202. A. R. Kelani, *The Last Apocalypse: An Islamic Perspective*, 2nd ed. (Arlington, TX.: Fustat, 2003), 22–23.

203. Shane Harris and Nancy Youseff, "Exclusive: 50 Spies Say ISIS Intelligence Was Cooked," *The Daily Beast*, September 9, 2015, http://www.thedailybeast.com/articles/2015/09/09/exclusive-50-spies-say-isis-intelligence-was-cooked.html, accessed September 16, 2015.

204. Reuters, "ISIS Gains Syrian Area Near Border."

205. Graeme Wood, "What ISIS Really Wants," *The Atlantic*.

206. http://www.theonlyquran.com/hadith/Sahih-Muslim/?volume=41&chapter=9.

207. Farzana Hassan Shahid, *Prophecy and the Fundamentalist Quest: An Integrative Study of Christian and Muslim Apocalyptic Religion* (Jefferson, N.C.: McFarland, 2008), 41.

208. Jessica Stern and J. M. Berger *ISIS: The State of Terror* (HarperCollins, 2013), 224–225.

209. Timothy R. Furnish, MahdiWatch.org, http://www.mahdiwatch.org/ accessed July 23, 2015.

210. Timothy R. Furnish, *Holiest Wars: Islamic Mahdis, Their Jihads, and Osama Bin Laden* (Westport, Conn.: Praeger Publishers, 2005), 1.

211. Sara A. Carter, "Islamic State Recruitment Document Seeks to Provoke 'End of the World,'" *USA Today*, July 28, 2015, http://www.usatoday.com/story/news/world/2015/07/28/ami-isil-document-pakistan-threatens-india/30674099/, accessed July 30, 2015.

212. https://americanmediainstitute.com/investigations/islamic-state-recruitment-document-seeks-to-provoke-end-of-the-world/.

213. http://www.motherjones.com/politics/2014/07/sigar-afghanistan-us-weapons-wind-up-insurgents.

214. Jeremy Bender, "ISIS Is Turning US Humvees into Iraq's Worst Nightmare,"http://www.businessinsider.com/isis-turning-us-humvees-into-iraqs-nightmare-2015-6, accessed July 27, 2015.

215. Furnish, "Through a Glass Darkly: A Comparison of Self-Proclaimed 'Mahdist' States throughout History to the Theory of the (True) Mahdist State Yet to Come," Scientific Committee of the International Conference of Mahdism Doctrine, 2008, http://mahdaviat-conference.com/vdchtqnkd23nz.102.html, accessed July 30, 2015.

216. Wood, "What ISIS Really Wants."

217. http://www.judicialwatch.org/document-archive/pgs-287-293-291-jw-v-dod-and-state-14-812-2/, accessed July 23, 2015.

218. "Pgs. 287–293 (291) JW v DOD and State 14-812," http://www.judicialwatch.org/wp-content/uploads/2015/05/Pg.-291-Pgs.-287-293-JW-v-DOD-and-State-14-812-DOD-Release-2015-04-10-final-version11.pdf?D=1 Page 5.

219. Ibid.

220. "The US War in Syria Begins Now...," http://forum.prisonplanet.com/index.php?topic=247150.1040, accessed October 4, 2015.

221. Providence Research, The ISIS Threat: The Rise of the Islamic State and Their Dangerous Potential, https://books.google.com/books?id=0e6rBAAAQBAJ&lpg=PP12&ots=_KfoGvrr8d&dq=Zionists%2C%20Crusaders%20and%20Safavids%20%2B%20ISIS&pg=PP13#v=onepage&q=Zionists,%20Crusaders%20and%20Safavids%20&f=false.

222. http://www.huffingtonpost.co.uk/2014/08/14/cia-israel-isis-conspiracy-theories-hilary-clinton_n_5677687.html.

223. "French Report ISIL Leader Mossad Agent," http://www.veteranstoday.com/2014/08/04/french-report-isil-leader-mossad/.

224. http://www.veteranstoday.com/2014/08/04/french-report-isil-leader-mossad/.

225. "Pentagon Confirms ISIS 'Dirty Bomb' claims."

226. John Blosser, "ISIS Vows to Smuggle Nuke Over Mexican Border," NewsMax, http://www.newsmax.com/Newsfront/ISIS-smuggle-nuclear-weapon/2015/06/03/id/648560/, accessed July 27, 2015.

227. http://americamagazine.org/content/all-things/full-text-pope-francis-press-conference-plane-returning-korea.

228. http://americamagazine.org/content/all-things/full-text-pope-francis-press-conference-plane-returning-korea.

229. Charles Guthrie and Michael Quinlan, *Just War: The Just War Tradition: Ethics in Modern Warfare*, (New York, Walker and Company), 17.

230. Ibid, 35.

231. http://www.cruxnow.com/church/2015/03/21/why-a-peace-pope-may-reluctantly-back-force-against-isis/.

232. World Watch List, Open Doors International, https://www.opendoorsusa.org/christian-persecution/world-watch-list/.

233. Ibid.

234. Caroline Wheeler, "The World Must Act NOW: Plea to Save Christians in Syria from ISIS Barbarians," http://www.express.co.uk/news/world/609728/Christian-genocide-Syria-Islamic-State-ISIS-persecution-religious-leaders.

235. "Islamic State: Vatican Backs Using Military Force," BBC, http://www.bbc.com/news/world-europe-31893351, accessed May 22, 2015.

236. John Bingham, "'I Beg You—Send Troops,' Iraqi Archbishop Tells Parliament," *The Telegraph*, February 10, 2015, http://www.telegraph.co.uk/news/religion/11402354/I-beg-you-send-troops-Iraqi-Archbishop-tells-Parliament.html.

237. Thomas D. Williams, "Vatican Relaunches 'Just War Doctrine' to Stop Isis Genocide," Breitbart, March 16, 2015, http://www.breitbart.com/national-security/2015/03/16/vatican-relaunches-just-war-doctrine-to-stop-isis-genocide/, accessed September 8, 2015.

238. http://americamagazine.org/content/all-things/full-text-pope-francis-press-conference-plane-returning-korea.

239. Francesco Antonio Grana, "Pope Francis: 'That Was the First Armenian Genocide. But We See Even Today,'" April 12, 2015, http://www.ilfattoquotidiano.it/2015/04/12/papa-francesco-armeno-fu-genocidio-ne-vediamo-oggi/1582036/, accessed May 22, 2015. (Translated with Google Translate).

240. Jeannie Law, "Christian Teenagers Crucified, Unborn Babies Hung From Trees in Syria," BreatheCast, April 29, 2014, http://www.breathecast.com/articles/christian-teenagers-crucified-unborn-babies-hung-on-trees-and-more-deaths-in-syria-by-jihadists-for-refusal-to-convert-to-islam-15371/, accessed June 2, 2015.

241. "U.S. Investigating 'Credible'Reports That ISIS Used Chemical Weapons," CNN, August 14, 2015,http://www.cnn.com/2015/08/13/politics/isis-mustard-gas-chemical-weapons/, accessed September 17, 2015.

242. Mark Mazzetti, Gordon, Michael R.; Landler, Mark, "Syria Has Used Chemical Arms on Rebels, U.S. and Allies Find," *New York Times*, June 13, 2013, http://www.nytimes.com/2013/06/14/world/middleeast/syria-chemical-weapons.html& Middle Eastern media coverage, "Bodies Still Being Found after Alleged Syria Chemical Attack: Oopposition,"*The Daily Star* (Lebanon), August 22, 2013, http://www.dailystar.com.lb/News/Middle-East/2013/Aug-22/228268-bodies-still-being-found-after-alleged-syria-chemical-attack-opposition.ashx#axzz2chzutFua, accessed September 17, 2015.

243. Theodore Shoebat, "Pope Francis Releases This Statement: I Only Have A Few Years Left to Live (THE CRUSADES ARE RETURNING VERY SOON)," March 13, 2015, http://shoebat.com/2015/03/13/pope-francis-releases-this-statement-i-only-have-a-few-years-left-to-live-the-crusades-are-returning-very-soon/ accessed September 17, 2015.

244. Ibid.

245. http://americamagazine.org/content/all-things/full-text-pope-francis-press-conference-plane-returning-koreahttp://americamagazine.org/content/all-things/full-text-pope-francis-press-conference-plane-returning-korea.

246. PaulVI, Speech at the UN October 4, 1965, as quoted in: *The Power Puzzle: A Compilation of Documents and Resources on Global Governance,* edited by Carl Teichrib, 2004, 2nd ed., 43.

247. Yasir Ghazi, Tim Arango, "Iraq Fighters, Qaeda Allies, Claim Falluja as New State," *New York Times,* January 3, 2014, http://www.nytimes.com/2014/01/04/world/middleeast/fighting-in-falluja-and-ramadi.html?_r=0 accessed March 10, 2016.

248. *Jamaat al-Tahwidwa-i-Jihad:* JTWJ.

249. "A Brief History of Isis," *Chosen People Ministries*, http://chosenpeople.com/main/index.php/ministry-news/926-a-brief-history-of-isis.

250. William Maclean, "Militants Plan al Qaeda Cartoon for Kids, Monitors Say," Reuters, July 20, 2011, http://af.reuters.com/article/worldNews/idAFTRE76J58820110720 accessed March 10, 2016.

251. *ISIS: A Comprehensive Guide on ISIS*. Kindle Edition (Fanton Publishing Inc., 2015), Kindle Locations 51–56.

252. Adl, "Tajrubati," 20, as cited by William McCants, *The ISIS Apocalypse: The History, Strategy, and Doomsday Vision of the Islamic State,* Kindle Edition (St. Martin's Press, 2015) Kindle Locations 141–145.

253. Zarqawi, "al-Bay'a li-tanzim al-Qa'ida bi-qiyadat al-Shaykh Usama bin

Ladin," Kalimatmudi'a, October 17, 2004, 171. In McCants,. *The ISIS Apocalypse*, Graeme Wood, 2016, accessed March 9, 2016.

254. Adam Hanieh, "A Brief History of ISIS," Jacobin, December 2015, https://www.jacobinmag.com/2015/12/isis-syria-iraq-war-al-qaeda-arab-spring/, accessed March 1, 2015.

255. http://www.jewishpress.com/news/breaking-news/analysis-iran-isis-likely-to-unite-for-wwiii/2016/02/28/.

256. Graeme Wood, "Donald Trump and the Apocalypse," *The Atlantic*, February 22, 2016, accessed March 9, 2016, http://www.theatlantic.com/international/archive/2016/02/donald-trump-pope-isis/470307/.

257. Sahih Muslim, "Pertaining to the Conquest of Constantinople and the Appearance of the Dajjal and Descent of Jesus Son of Mary (Jesus Christ), "http://www.theonlyquran.com/hadith/Sahih-Muslim/?volume=41&chapter=9.

258. "ISIS Attack on Funeral Risks Reigniting Sunni-Shi'ite Bloodbath," ArutzSheva, February 29, 2016, http://www.israelnationalnews.com/News/News.aspx/208705#.VuHJc_krIee, accessed March 12, 2016.

259. Tom Wyke, "Gaza Rocked by Suspected ISIS Car Bomb Attacks on Hamas," *Daily Mail*, July 19, 2015,http://www.dailymail.co.uk/news/article-3167516/Gaza-rocked-suspected-ISIS-car-bomb-attacks-Hamas-Islamic-Jihad-officials-jihadis-continue-struggle-power.html, accessed March 1, 2016.

260. Dietrich Jung, ed., *The Middle East and Palestine: Global Politics and Regional Conflict* (New York: Palgrave Macmillan, 2004), 135.

261. "Foreword" *Dabiq*4,http://media.clarionproject.org/files/islamic-state/islamic-state-isis-magazine-Issue-4-the-failed-crusade.pdf page 4.

262. Natasha Culzac, "Islamic State: Pope Is 'Being Targeted by Isis,' Iraqi Ambassador to the Holy See Warns," *The Independent*, September 16, 2014, http://www.independent.co.uk/news/world/middle-east/islamic-state-pope-being-targeted-by-isis-iraqi-ambassador-to-the-holy-see-warns-9736110.html, accessed May 22, 2015.

263. "New Measures Seek to Prevent ISIS Drone Attack on Vatican in Year of Mercy," *The Catholic Herald*, http://www.catholicherald.co.uk/news/2015/11/18/new-measures-seek-to-prevent-isis-drone-attack-on-vatican-in-year-of-mercy/.

264. O'Connell, "Full Text," accessed July 23, 2015.

265. Sara Malm, Sam Tonkin, Will Stewart, "Helpless Russian Pilots 'Were Shot Dead as They Parachuted to the Ground': Furious Putin Accuses Turkey of 'Treachery' after It Downs Jet over Syrian Rebel Territory,'" *Daily Mail*, November 30, 2015, http://www.dailymail.co.uk/news/article-3331558/

Turkey-shoots-fighter-jet-Syrian-border-Local-media-footage-flaming-plane-crashing-trees.html accesses February 14, 2016.

266. Nancy A. Youssef, Michael Weiss, Tim Mak, "U.S. Admits: We Can't Protect Syrian Allies From Russia's Bombs," *The Daily Beast,* http://www.thedailybeast.com/articles/2015/10/01/u-s-admits-we-can-t-protect-syrian-allies-from-russia-s-bombs.html?via=newsletter&source=DDAfternoon, accessed October 5,2015.

267. Kristina Wong, "US Officials: Russia Is Not Striking ISIS Targets in Syria," *The Hill,* October 1, 2015, http://thehill.com/policy/defense/255637-officials-russia-not-striking-isis-in-syria-despite-claims, accessed October 5, 2015.

268. Youssef, et al, "U.S. Admits: We Can't…".

269. Ibid.

270. "Putin, Erdogan Discuss Syrian Crisis," VOA, November 4, 2015, http://m.voanews.com/a/putin-erdogan-discuss-syrian-crisis/3036177.html, accessed November 4, 2015/.

271. Nick Gutteridge, "ISIS Jihadis OBLITERATED: Putin Jets Blast Terrorist HQ in Syria with Bunker-buster Bombs," *The Express,* October 4, 2015, http://www.express.co.uk/news/world/609665/Islamic-State-ISIS-command-post-destroyed-Russian-airstrike-Putin accessed October 6, 2015.

272. Douglas Woodward, "Is Gog Just a Turk?" *Prophecy Watchers Magazine,* October 2015, http://faith-happens.com/exposing-the-dark-forces-behind-gog-and-magog/, accessed October 6, 2015.

273. Michael Heiser, *Islam and Armageddon,* 73.

274. Ibid., 82–83.

275. Woodward, "Is Gog Just a Turk?"

276. Ibid.

277. Ibid.

278. Jack Smith, *Islam the Cloak of Antichrist* (Last Mile Books, 2011), 246, https://books.google.com/books/about/Islam_the_Cloak_of_Antichrist.html?id=ihvaoAEACAAJ.

279. Benni Kleynhans, *Die laastewaarskuwing,* (V.G. Uitgewers, Springs, S.A, 1993). 54.

280. "Church Says Russia Fighting 'Holy Battle' in Syria," France 24, September 30, 2015, http://www.france24.com/en/20150930-church-says-russia-fighting-holy-battle-syria, accessed October 7, 2015.

281. Raymond Ibrahim, "RUSSIA DECLARES 'HOLY WAR' ON ISLAMIC STATE / While Obama Sides with Christian-murdering 'Freedom Fighters,'" *Front Page Magazine,* October 7, 2015, http://www.

frontpagemag.com/fpm/260372/russia-declares-holy-war-islamic-state-raymond-ibrahim, as reprinted by *The United Jerusalem Foundation*, Paragraph 5, http://www.unitedjerusalem.org/index2.asp?id=1952135, accessed October 7, 2015.

282. KesavanUnnikrishnan "Russia's Orthodox Church Backs 'Holy War' against ISIS," *Digital Journal*, October 4, 2015,http://www.digitaljournal.com/news/world/russian-orthodox-church-backs-holy-war-against-isis/article/445605, accessed October 7, 2015.

283. Rod Dreher, "The Anti-Benedict Conspiracy," *The American Conservative*, September 25, 2015, http://www.theamericanconservative.com/dreher/the-anti-benedict-conspiracy/ accessed October 8, 2015.

284. Howard Fineman, "Pope Francis Wants to Be President of the World," *The Huffington Post*, September 24, 2015, http://www.huffingtonpost.com/entry/pope-francis-world-leader_56041e79e4b00310edfa4d0f.

285. "Barack Obama Is 'President of the World'," CNN, November 5, 2008, http://edition.cnn.com/2008/POLITICS/11/05/international.press.reaction/.

286. Michael Day, "Pope Francis Assures Atheists: You Don't Have to Believe in God to Go to Heaven," *Independent*, September 11, 2013, http://www.independent.co.uk/news/world/europe/pope-francis-assures-atheists-you-don-t-have-to-believe-in-god-to-go-to-heaven-8810062.html, accessed October 9, 2015.

287. "Pope Francis: New York Pizza Rat Symbolizes Jesus' Burden," *National Report*, September 28, 2015, http://nationalreport.net/pope-francis-new-york-pizza-rat-symbolizes-jesus-burden/#sthash.CWfJflXl.dpuf, accessed October 11, 2015.

288. "Rat" synonyms, Thesaurus.com,http://www.thesaurus.com/browse/rat, accessed October 7, 2015.

289. William H. Kennedy, *Lucifer's Lodge: Satanic Ritual Abuse in the Catholic Church* (Sophia Perennis, 2004)180, 178–179.

290. "Malachi Martin," Coast to Coast AM, http://www.coasttocoastam.com/guest/martin-malachi/5751, accessed October 7, 2015.

291. "Two Eminent Churchmen Agree: Satanism Is Practiced in Vatican," The Fatima Network Crusader, http://www.fatimacrusader.com/cr54/cr54pg96.asp, accessed October 13, 2015.

292. *Petrus Romanus*, 93.

293. Former Vaticaninsider.

294. Malachi Martin, *The Jesuits: The Society of Jesus and the Betrayal of the Roman Catholic Church* (New York: Linden Press, Simon & Schuster, 1987), 14.

295. Malachi Martin, *Keys of This Blood: Pope John Paul II Versus Russia and the West for Control of the New World Order*, (New York: Simon & Schuster, 1990), 15.

296. Raphael Poch, "ISIS Looking to Build Nuclear Weapons, Turning to Moldovan Gangs for Materials," *Breaking Israel News*, October 11, 2015, http://www.breakingisraelnews.com/50839/ isis-looking-build-nuclear-weapons-turning-moldovan-gangs-materials- terror-watch/#Is2RA70ukhRLX5SD.99, accessed October 12, 2015.

297. Martin, *Keys of This Blood*, 20.

298. St. Francis of Assisi, *Works of the Seraphic Father St. Francis of Assisi* (London, R. Washbourne. 1882), 250.

299. Ibid.

300. "Pope Urban VI," in *Catholic Encyclopedia*, New Advent, http://www. newadvent.org/cathen/15216a.htm, accessed December 18, 2015.

301. St. Francis Of Assisi, *Works of the Seraphic Father*, 248.

302. Horn and Putnam, *Petrus Romanus*, 478–479.

303. Rod Dreher, "The Anti-Benedict Conspiracy," *The American Conservative*, September 25, 2015, http://www.theamericanconservative.com/dreher/the- anti-benedict-conspiracy/ accessed October 8, 2015.

304. *Petrus Romanus*, 15, citing Arnold de Wion, *Lignum Vitae*, (1595), 307– 311.

305. Arnold de Wion, *Lignum Vitae*, (1595), 307–311, available here: https:// books.google.com/books?id=UJommEJQ5o0C&dq=Lignum%20 Vitae%20book%202&pg=PA307#v=onepage&q&f=false.

306. See Carl Popper material in *Petrus Romanus*, page 43.

307. Craig S. Keener, *The IVP Bible Background Commentary: New Testament* (Downers Grove, IL: Intervarsity Press, 1993), Re 13:11–12.

308. Ibid.

309. Paul D. Wegner and Iain Duguid note on "Daniel 8:3" in *The ESV Study Bible* (Wheaton, IL: Crossway Bibles, 2008), 1602.

310. Thomas Horn and Cris Putnam, *On the Path of the Immortals: Exo- Vaticana, Project L.u.c.i.f.e.r., and the Strategic Locations Where Entities Await the Appointed Time* (Crane, MO: Defender, 2015), 283–284; CortLindahl, "The Geomancy of St. Peter's Square and the Vatican," http://survivalcell. blogspot.com/p/geomancy-of-st-peters-square-and.html, (accessed October 13, 2015).

311. Horn and Putnam, *On the Path*, 319–352.

312. Jeremy Hobbs, "Annual Income of Richest 100 People Is Enough to End Global Poverty Four Times Over," *Oxfam International*, January 19, 2013, https://www.oxfam.org/en/pressroom/pressreleases/2013-01-19/annual-

income-richest-100-people-enough-end-global-poverty-four accessed October 7, 2015.

313. Pope Francis, "Address of Pope Francis to the UN System Chief Executives Board for Coordination," LibreriaEditriceVaticana, May 9, 2014, http://w2.vatican.va/content/francesco/en/speeches/2014/may/documents/papa-francesco_20140509_consiglio-nazioni-unite.html, accessed October 7, 2015.

314. Karl Marx, "Des VerzweiflendenGebet" ("Invocation of One in Despair"), *Archiv fur die Geschichte des Sozialismus und der Arbeiterbewegung* (Archives for the History of Socialism and the Workers' Movement), MEGA, I, i (2),30.

315. Karl Marx, *Ueber die Differenz der Demokritischen und EpikureischenNaturphilosophieVorrede (The Difference between Democritus' and Epicurus' Philosophy of Nature,* Foreword), 10.

316. Richard Wurmbrand, *Marx and Satan* (Westchester, IL: Crossway Books, 1985), 12–13.

317. Prominent examples include Cardinal Henry Edward Manning the Lord Archbishop of Westminster as discussed in *Petrus Romanus*, 438, and the revelation commentary by Father Francisco Ribera S.J. discussed in *Petrus Romanus*, 274.

318. "Its colour for cardinals is ordinarily red, and for bishops violet," from "Cope" in *Catholic Encyclopedia*, http://www.newadvent.org/cathen/04351a.htm, accessed October 12, 2015.

319. Dave Hunt, *A Woman Rides the Beast*, (Eugene, OR: Harvest House Publishers, 1994), 56.

320. BBC Latin America, "Brazil Says Amazon Deforestation Rose 28% in a Year," BBC News, November 15, 2013, http://www.bbc.com/news/world-latin-america-24950487 accessed October 7, 2015. Also see: Alonso Martinez, Ivan de Souza, and Francis Liu, "Multinationals vs. Multilatinas: Latin America's Great Race," *Strategy + Business*, Issue 32 Fall 2003, http://www.strategy-business.com/article/03307?gko=85c85, accessed October 7, 2015.

321. Martin, *The Jesuits*, 132.

322. Tony Halpin, "Russian Orthodox Church Chooses between 'ex-KGB Candidates' as Patriarch," *The Times* (of London), January 26 2009, http://www.thetimes.co.uk/tto/faith/article2100100.ece, accessed October 12, 2015.

323. Ion Mihai Pacepa, "The Secret Roots of Liberation Theology" *National Review*, April 23, 2015, http://www.nationalreview.com/article/417383/

secret-roots-liberation-theology-ion-mihai-pacepa?target=author&
tid=901039, accessed October 8, 2015.

324. Stephenson Billings, "Should the CIA Stop Patriarch Kirill, The Murderous
Billionaire Cult Leader Leading the Soviets to Satanism?" http://christwire.
org/2012/04/should-the-cia-stop-patriarch-kirill-the-murderous-billionaire-
cult-leader-leading-the-soviets-to-satanism/ accessed January 4, 2016.

325. Pacepa, "The Secret Roots of Liberation Theology."

326. D. D. Webster, "Liberation Theology" in *Evangelical Dictionary of Theology:
Second Edition,* A. W. Elwell (Grand Rapids, MI: Baker Academic: 2001),
686.

327. "Francis: Refugees Are the Tip of the Iceberg, Europe Must Welcome
Them," *Vatican Insider,* September 14, 2015, http://vaticaninsider.
lastampa.it/en/the-vatican/detail/articolo/francesco-francis-francisco-
profughi-43342/, accessed October 7, 2015.

328. Karl Marx and Friedrich Engels, *The Manifesto of the Communists*
(International Publishing Co., 1886), http://www.bl.uk/learning/
histcitizen/21cc/utopia/methods1/bourgeoisie1/bourgeoisie.html; also see
Kory Schaff, ed., *Philosophy and the Problems of Work: A Reader,* (Lanham,
MD.: Rowman & Littlefield, 2001), 224.

329. Ibid.

330. Greg Tomlin, "Defector: 'Liberation Theology' a Soviet Plot of the Cold
War," *Christian Examiner,* May 6, 2015, http://www.christianexaminer.
com/article/defector.liberation.theology.a.soviet.plot.of.the.cold.war/48895.
htm, accessed October 7, 2015.

331. "Francis: Refugees."

332. B. W. Segel, *A Lie and a Libel: The History of the Protocols of the Elders of
Zion* (Lincoln: University of Nebraska Press, 1995), 99.

333. Bishop B. C. Butler, "Pope John's Announcement of an Ecumenical
Council," Vatican II—Voice of the Church, http://www.vatican2voice.
org/91docs/announcement.htm accessed October 12, 2015.

334. *Petrus Romanus,* 50.

335. John XXIII, *Address* of October 11, 1962, states, "In truth, at the present
time, it is necessary that Christian doctrine in its entirety, and with nothing
taken away from it, is accepted with renewed enthusiasm, and serene and
tranquil adherence delivered to the exact words of conceiving and reducing
to the form, which especially shines forth from the acts of the *Council
of Trent* and the First Vatican Council." "ALLOCUTIO IOANNIS PP.
XXIII IN SOLLEMNI SS. CONCILII INAUGURATIONE," Section
6 final paragraph translated from Latin by C. D. Putnam,http://www.

vatican.va/holy_father/john_xxiii/speeches/1962/documents/hf_j-xxiii_
spe_19621011_opening-council_lt.html (emphasis added).

336. Pope John XXII encyclical *Pacem in Terris*, LibreriaEditriceVaticana,April
11, 1963, http://w2.vatican.va/content/john-xxiii/en/encyclicals/
documents/hf_j-xxiii_enc_11041963_pacem.pdf, p. 15.

337. Malachi Martin, *Keys of This Blood: Pope John Paul II Versus Russia and the
West for Control of the New World Order* (New York: Simon & Schuster,
1990), 632.

338. Point 17, Pope Paul VI, *OctogesimaAdveniens,* LibreriaEditriceVaticana,
May 14, 1971, http://w2.vatican.va/content/paul-vi/en/apost_letters/
documents/hf_p-vi_apl_19710514_octogesima-adveniens.html,accessed
October 7, 2015.

339. Pope Paul VI, *OctogesimanAdveniens,* LibrerianEditricenVaticana, May 14,
1971, http://w2.vatican.va/content/paul-vi/en/apost_letters/documents/
hf_p-vi_apl_19710514_octogesima-adveniens.html, accessed October 7,
2015.

340. Vicomte de Poncins, *Freemasonry and the Vatican: A Struggle for Recognition*,
translated from French by Timothy Tindal-Robertson (London: Britons
Publishing Co. 1968), 2.

341. John Daniel, *Scarlet and the Beast*, Vol. 1, 3rd ed. (Longview, TX: Day
Publishing, 2007), 938. Also see David A. Yallop, *In God's Name* (New
York: Constable & Robinson, 2012).

342. Kennedy, *Lucifer's Lodge*, 178–179.

343. Martin, *Keys of This Blood*, 632.

344. David A. Yallop, *In God's Name* (New York: Constable & Robinson, 2012).
clviii.

345. Pope John Paul II, Sollicitudo Rei Socialis Point 42,
LibreriaEditriceVaticana, http://w2.vatican.va/content/john-paul-ii/en/
encyclicals/documents/hf_jp-ii_enc_30121987_sollicitudo-rei-socialis.htm
accessed October 9, 2015.

346. Ibid., Point 43 http://w2.vatican.va/content/john-paul-ii/en/encyclicals/
documents/hf_jp-ii_enc_30121987_sollicitudo-rei-socialis.html.

347. Petrus Romanus, 243, citing from *Caritas in Veritate*,
LibreriaEditriceVaticana, June 29, 2009,http://w2.vatican.va/content/
benedict-xvi/en/encyclicals/documents/hf_ben-xvi_enc_20090629_caritas-
in-veritate.html, accessed October 12, 2015.

348. *Exo-Vaticana*, 452.

349. Ibid.

350. Malachi Martin, *The Jesuits: The Society of Jesus and the Betrayal of the*

Roman Catholic Church (New York: Linden Press, Simon & Schuster, 1987), 19.

351. Ibid.

352. Ibid., 20.

353. Cliff Kincaid, "Who Will Probe the U.N.-Vatican Connection?" *Accuracy in Media*, August 4, 2009, http://www.aim.org/aim-report/who-will-probe-the-u-n-vatican-connection accessed October 9, 2015.

354. Mauri, *Vatican Ratline: the Vatican, the Nazis and the New World Order* (BookSurge Publishing, 2006), 108–109. https://www.createspace.com/Special/L/TransitionGuide.jsp.

355. Pope Francis, *SULLA CURA DELLA CASA COMUNE*, LibreriaEditriceVaticana, http://w2.vatican.va/content/francesco/en/encyclicals/documents/papa-francesco_20150524_enciclica-laudato-si.html, 129.

356. http://espresso.repubblica.it/attualita/2015/06/15/news/papa-bergoglio-e-la-lezione-di-francesco-d-assisi-in-anteprima-l-enciclica-sull-ambiente-laudato-si-mi-signore-1.216897?ref=HRBZ-1.

357. KhwajaKhusro Tariq, "In Praise of Pope Francis: A Muslim Perspective," *The Huffington Post*, October 1, 2015, http://www.huffingtonpost.com/khwaja-khusro-tariq/in-praise-of-pope-francis_b_8200944.html, accessed October 14, 2015.

358. Joshua Barajas , "Death Toll During Recent Hajj Pilgrimage Worst on Record," PBS, October 9, 2015, http://www.pbs.org/newshour/rundown/death-toll-during-recent-hajj-pilgrimage-worst-on-record/, accessed October 14, 2015.

359. Faith Karimi and SchamsElwazer, "Stampede Kills More than 700 at Hajj Pilgrimage in Mecca," CNN, September 25, 2015, http://www.cnn.com/2015/09/24/middleeast/stampede-hajj-pilgrimage/, accessed October 14, 2015.

360. Emily Shapiro, "Read What Pope Francis Said at New York's St. Patrick's Cathedral," ABC News, September 23, 2015, http://abcnews.go.com/US/read-pope-francis-yorks-st-patricks-cathedral/story?id=34023376, accessed October 14, 2015.

361. KhwajaKhusro Tariq, "In Praise of Pope Francis."

362. The Catechism of the Catholic Church,http://www.scborromeo.org/ccc/p123a9p3.htm#841, paragraph 841.

363. M. H. Shakir, ed., *The Quran* (Medford, MA: Perseus Digital Library, n.d.).

364. James R. White, *What Every Christian Needs to Know About the Qur'an* (Minneapolis, MN: Bethany House Publishers, 2013), 72.

365. Shelby lin Erdman, Laura Smith-Spark and HadaMessia, "Pope Francis

Begins Mending the Schism with Orthodox Christians," CNN, December 14, 2014, http://www.cnn.com/2014/11/30/world/europe/turkey-pope-visit/index.html, accessed October 12, 2015.

366. Pope Francis, "Pope Francis: Discourse to Representatives of the Churches, Ecclesial Communities and Other Religions," *Vatican Radio*, March 20 2013, http://en.radiovaticana.va/storico/2013/03/20/pope_francis_discourse_to_representatives_of_the_churches%2C_ecclesia/en1-675184, accessed October 6, 2015.

367. Muhammad M. Pickthall, ed., *The Quran* (Medford, MA: Perseus Digital Library).

368. John Hospers, *An Introduction to Philosophical Analysis*, 4th ed. (London: Routledge, 1997), 58. Also see Bertrand Russell, *An Inquiry into Meaning and Truth*, 2nd ed. (Hoboken, NY: Taylor and Francis, 2013), 274.

369. Joshua J. McElwee, "Vatican Signs Treaty with 'State of Palestine,' Calls for Two-State Solution," *National Catholic Reporter*, June 26, 2015, http://ncronline.org/news/vatican/vatican-signs-treaty-state-palestine-calls-two-state-solution, accessed October 7, 2015.

370. Ibid.

371. Victor Harold Matthews, Mark W. Chavalas, and John H. Walton, *The IVP Bible Background Commentary: Old Testament*, electronic ed. (Downers Grove, IL: Intervarsity Press, 2000), Joel 3:2.

372. Note Joel 3:2, *The ESV Study Bible* (Wheaton, IL: Crossway Bibles, 2008), 1652.

373. Victor Harold Matthews, Mark W. Chavalas, and John H. Walton, *The IVP Bible Background Commentary: Old Testament*, electronic ed. (Downers Grove, IL: Intervarsity Press, 2000), Joe 3:2.

374. Robert B. Chisholm, Jr., "Joel," in *The Bible Knowledge Commentary: An Exposition of the Scriptures*, ed. J. F. Walvoord and R. B. Zuck, vol. 1 (Wheaton, IL: Victor Books, 1985), 1421.

375. H. W. Wolff, and S. D. McBride (1977), *Joel and Amos : A Commentary on the Books of the Prophets Joel and Amos*. In *Hermeneia—A Critical and Historical Commentary on the Bible* (Philadelphia: Fortress Press 1977), 76.

376. Heiser, *Islam and Armageddon*, 41.

377. James Lewis, "To Become UN Sec. General Obama Must 'Solve' the Existence of Israel," *American Thinker*, February 10, 2015, http://www.americanthinker.com/articles/2015/02/to_become_un_sec_general_obama_must_solve_the_existence_of_israel_.html#ixzz3oJBkDUhr, accessed October 11, 2015.

378. See "Obama Claims He's Visited 57 States," YouTube, https://www.youtube.com/watch?v=EpGH02DtIws.

379. Douglas Belkin, "For Obama, Advice Straight Up: Valerie Jarrett Is Essential Member of Inner Set," *Wall Street Journal*, May 12, 2008, http://www.wsj.com/articles/SB121055336572783989, accessed October 10, 2015.

380. Ibid.

381. "Inside Iran's Missile Tunnels: Tehran Shows Off "Secret' Ballistic Missiles," *The Telegraph*, October 15, 2015, http://www.telegraph.co.uk/news/worldnews/middleeast/iran/11933008/Inside-Irans-missile-tunnels-Tehran-shows-off-secret-ballistic-missiles.html, accessed October 15, 2015.

382. Michael Heiser, *Islam and Armageddon* (Self-published book, 2002), 41.

383. A. F. Johnson (1981), "Revelation," in F. E. Gaebelein (Ed.), *The Expositor's Bible Commentary, Volume 12: Hebrews Through Revelation* (F. E. Gaebelein, Ed.) (Grand Rapids, MI: Zondervan Publishing House), 530.

384. Max Weber, "Politics as Vocation," http://anthropos-lab.net/wp/wp-content/uploads/2011/12/Weber-Politics-as-a-Vocation.pdf, accessed October 11, 2015.

385. Elizabeth Tenety, "Pope Francis, the 'Humble Pope'?" *The Washington Post*, July 26, 2013, https://www.washingtonpost.com/national/on-faith/pope-francis-the-humble-pope/2013/07/25/959d62d2-f572-11e2-a2f1-a7acf9bd5d3a_story.html, accessed October 8, 2015.

386. Commission for Religious Relations with the Jews, "The Gifts and the Calling Of God are Irrevocable," http://www.vatican.va/roman_curia/pontifical_councils/chrstuni/relations-jews-docs/rc_pc_chrstuni_doc_20151210_ebraismo-nostra-aetate_en.html,, accessed December 18, 2015.

387. "About Craig Keener," Bible Background Research and Commentary by Dr. Craig Keener, http://www.craigkeener.com/about-craig/, accessed December 18, 2015.

388. Craig S. Keener, *The IVP Bible Background Commentary: New Testament* (Downers Grove, IL: InterVarsity Press, 1993), Ro 11:28–29.

389. Gerald F. Hawthorne, Ralph P. Martin, and Daniel G. Reid, eds., *Dictionary of Paul and His Letters* (Downers Grove, IL: InterVarsity Press, 1993), 508.

390. "The Relationship between the Old and New Testament and the Old and New Covenant 27," http://www.vatican.va/roman_curia/pontifical_councils/chrstuni/relations-jews-docs/rc_pc_chrstuni_doc_20151210_ebraismo-nostra-aetate_en.html#4._The_relationship_between_the_Old_and_New_Testament_and_the_Old_and_New_Covenant.

391. D. ArnoldoVvion, *Lignvm Vitae,* book two, 307.

392. *Petrus Romanus*, 308.

393. "Relics," *Gale Encyclopedia of Religion*, vol. 11 (Farmington MI: MacMillian Reference USA, 2005), 7686.

394. Benge Nsenduluka , "Pope Francis Performs 'Miracle' In Naples; Turns Dry Blood to Liquid (Video)," *Christian Post* March 23, 2015, http://www.christianpost.com/news/pope-francis-performs-miracle-in-naples-turns-dry-blood-to-liquid-video-136174/.

395. Hazel Torres, "Another Pope Francis Miracle: Paralyzed Girl Set to Junk Wheelchair and Walk Again," *Christian Post*, October 7, 2015, http://www.christiantoday.com/article/another.pope.francis.miracle.paralyzed.girl.set.to.junk.wheelchair.and.walk.again/66795.htm, accessed October 8, 2015.

396. Ibid.

397. Bryan West, KPNX, Phoenix, "Pope Held Sick Baby, What Happened Next Is Amazing," *USA Today*, September 23, 2015, http://www.usatoday.com/story/news/inspiration-nation/2015/09/23/inspiration-nation-pope-holds-baby/72671356/, accessed October 8, 2015.

398. *Petrus Romanus*, 210, citing: E. M. Butler, *The Myth of the Magus* (Cambridge University Press, 1948), 96.

399. For documentation see *News that Matters* "Vatican Skulls and Bones" http://ivarfjeld.com/category/vatican-skulls-and-bones/, accessed October 9, 2015.

400. Brendan M. Case, "Pope Beatifies 2 Martyrs before Returning Home," *The Dallas Morning News,* August 2, 2002, http://articles.sun-sentinel.com/2002-08-02/news/0208011016_1_juan-bautista-pope-john-paul-ii, accessed October 9, 2015.

401. Martin, *The Jesuits,* 21.

402. Michael W. Cuneo, *American Exorcism: Expelling Demons in the Land of Plenty.* Kindle Edition, (Crown/Archetype, 2002), 14–15.

403. Jones, *One or Two*, Kindle Locations 1221–1224.

404. Cris Putnam, *Supernatural Worldview,* 89.

405. Alan Machado, *Sarasvati's Children: A History of the Mangalorean Christians* (Bangalore: I.J.A. Publications, 1999), 115.

406. St. Francis of Assisi, *Works of the Seraphic Father St. Francis of Assisi* (London, R. Washbourne, 1882), 248, 250.

407. St. Francis of Assisi, *Works of the Seraphic Father St. Francis of Assisi* (London, R. Washbourne. 1882), 250.

408. Adolf Hitler, *Mein Kampf,* translated by Ralph Manheim (Boston: Houghton Mifflin, 1971), 65.

409. Sahih Muslim, 41:6985: http://www.usc.edu/org/cmje/religious-texts/hadith/muslim/041-smt.php#041.6985.

410. "'Moderate' Palestinian Leaders Encourage Attacks, More Israelis Stabbed," *IPT News,* October 8, 2015,http://www.investigativeproject.org/4997/moderate-palestinian-leaders-encourage-attacks accessed October 14, 2015.

411. "Israeli Leader Vows 'Aggressive Steps' to Halt Wave of Violence," *Chicago Tribune*, October 13, 2015, http://www.chicagotribune.com/news/nationworld/ct-jerusalem-palestinian-attacks-20151013-story.html, accessed October 14, 2015.

412. "Temple Mount Violence Escalates," http://www.al-monitor.com/pulse/originals/2015/09/temple-mount-jewish-new-year-stone-throwing-east-jerusalem.html#.

413. MuḥammadḤusaynHaykal, *The Life of Muhammad*, (Petaling Jaya, Malaysia: Islamic Book Trust, 1976), 27.

414. Heiser, *Islam and Armageddon*, 47.

415. "ADL Poll: Anti-Semitic Attitudes on Rise in USA,"*Jerusalem Post*, http://www.jpost.com/Jewish-World/Jewish-News/ADL-poll-Anti-Semitic-attitudes-on-rise-in-USA.

416. Ibid.

417. "Warrant for Genocide: The Myth of the Jewish World-conspiracy and the Protocols of the Elders of Zion," http://www.history.ucsb.edu/faculty/marcuse/classes/33d/projects/protzion/DelaCruzLinksBib.htm.

418. José Delacruz, "The Protocols of the Learned Elders of Zion—Plagiarism at its Best," University of California, Santa Barbara Department of History, http://www.history.ucsb.edu/faculty/marcuse/classes/33d/projects/protzion/DelaCruzProtocolsMain.htm, accessed October 11, 2015.

419. Barry W. Segel, *A Lie and a Libel: The History of the Protocols of the Elders of Zion.* (University of Nebraska Press 1995), 30.

420. Stephen Eric Bronner, *A Rumor about the Jews: Reflections on Antisemitism and the Protocols of the Learned Elders of Zion*, (New York: St, Martin's Press, 2014), 67.

421. Ibid.

422. Bronner, *A Rumor About The Jews,* 67–68.

423. Horn, Putnam, *Petrus Romanus.* 343–362. Also see Michael L. Brown, *Our Hands Are Stained with Blood* (Shippensburg, PA: Destiny Image Publishers, 1992).

424. David Cook, *Contemporary Muslim Apocalyptic Literature*, Kindle Edition. (Syracuse, NY: Syracuse University Press, 2005), Kindle Locations 258–261.

425. Bassam Abu Sharif, a top Arafat aide and PLO spokesman, quoted by theKuwait News Agency, May 31, 1986, http://www.wnd.com/2000/0

1/5383/#BhkYMBiLLRcsmik8.99; also cited in Randall Price, *Unholy War* (Eugene, OR: Harvest House Publishers, 2001), 51.

426. John Rossomando, "ISIS Threatens Holocaust Against Jews," July 4, 2014, http://www.investigativeproject.org/4446/isis-threatens-holocaust-against-jews#, accessed June 5, 2015.

427. Muhammad M. Pickthall, ed., *The Quran* (Medford, MA: Perseus Digital Library).

428. F. F. Bruce (1977),*Paul: Apostle of the Free Spirit*, American ed. published under title: *Paul, Apostle of the Heart Set Free*.; Includes index. (69). Milton Keynes, UK: Paternoster.

429. George J. Marlin, "Chopping up Christians in the Middle East," *The Washington Times*, September 22, 2015, http://www.washingtontimes.com/news/2015/sep/22/george-marlin-christians-persecution-in-the-middle/, accessed October 8, 2015.

430. "Pope Francis' Speech to the United Nations General Assembly," http://www.popefrancisvisit.com/schedule/address-to-united-nations-general-assembly/, accessed October 9, 2015.

431. Ibid.

432. Pope Francis, *SULLA CURA DELLA CASA COMUNE*, *LibreriaEditriceVaticana*, http://w2.vatican.va/content/francesco/en/encyclicals/documents/papa-francesco_20150524_enciclica-laudato-si.html, 129.

433. Ibid.

434. Ibid.

435. Joshua J. McElwee, "Vatican Signs Treaty with 'State of Palestine,'Calls for Two-State Solution" *National Catholic Reporter*, June 26, 2015, http://ncronline.org/news/vatican/vatican-signs-treaty-state-palestine-calls-two-state-solution, accessed October 8, 2015.

436. "Pope Francis Calls Palestinians' Abbas 'Angel of Peace,'" BBC News, May 16,2015, http://www.bbc.com/news/world-middle-east-32769752, accessed October 8, 2015.

437. "Historic First: Islamic Prayers Held at the Vatican," *CBN News*, June 10, 2014, http://www.cbn.com/cbnnews/world/2014/June/Historic-First-Islamic-Prayers-Held-at-the-Vatican/ accessed October 8, 2015.

438. Ibid.

439. Jimmy Akin, "Pope Francis on 'Proselytism,'" *Catholic Answers*, October 21,2013, http://www.catholic.com/blog/jimmy-akin/pope-francis-on-%E2%80%9Cproselytism%E2%80%9D, accessed October 8, 2015.

440. Shaykh Professor Abdul Hadi Palazzi, "What the Qur'an Really Says," online publication, http://www.templemount.org/quranland.html.

441. Ion Mihai Pacepa, *Red Horizons: The True Story of Nicolae and Elena Ceausescus' Crimes, Lifestyle, and Corruption* (Washington, D.C.: Regnery Gateway, 1990), 118.

442. *Arabic Language, Analysis, Literature and Criticism,* grade 12, p. 104, cited at "Palestinian Textbooks: New Palestinian Textbooks Present A World Without Israel," Jewish Virtual Library, February 2007, http://www.jewishvirtuallibrary. org/jsource/arabs/patext2006.html, accessed October 8, 2015.

443. Deborah Snow, "Palestinian Authority Foreign Minister Riad al-Malki Says Australia Lacks Balance on Israel and Palestine," *The Sydney Morning Herald,* May 1, 2015, http://www.smh.com.au/federal-politics/ political-news/palestinian-authority-foreign-minister-riad-almalki-says- australia-lacks-balance-on-israel-and-palestine-20150430-1mwx57.htm accessed October 8, 2015.

444. Obituary, "Laurent Murawiec (1951–2009)" Right Web, April 4 2013, http://www.rightweb.irc-online.org/profile/Murawiec_Laurent, accessed October 8, 2015.

445. Mark Thompson, "Inside the Secret War Council," *Time* 160, 9, August 26, 2002, 36.

446. Laurent Murawiec, *The Mind of Jihad* (Cambridge: Cambridge University Press, 2008), 324.

447. Ibid., 325.

448. William McCants, *The ISIS Apocalypse: The History, Strategy, and Doomsday Vision of the Islamic State*, Kindle Edition. (St. Martin's Press, 2015) Kindle Locations 1879–1880.

449. Muhammad M. Pickthall, ed., *The Quran* (Medford, MA: Perseus Digital Library, n.d.).

450. Ibid.

451. Ibid.

452. http://dictionary.reference.com/browse/semite.

453. Gordon D. Fee and Douglas K. Stuart, *How to Read the Bible for All Its Worth*, 3rd ed. (Grand Rapids, MI: Zondervan Publishing House, 1993), 182.

454. J. F. Walvoord (1990). *The Prophecy Knowledge Handbook,* Includes indexes. (Wheaton, IL: Victor Books) 14.

455. Fee & Stuart, *How to Read the Bible,* 194–197.

456. Michael Heiser, "What Has Ugaritic Have to Do With Anything?" Logos Bible Software, https://www.logos.com/ugaritic accessed October 8, 2015.

457. John H Walton, *Zondervan Illustrated Bible Backgrounds Commentary* (Old Testament) Volume 4: Isaiah, Jeremiah, Lamentations, Ezekiel, Daniel (Grand Rapids, MI: Zondervan, 2009), 7.

458. John Oswalt, *The NIV Application Commentary: Isaiah* (Grand Rapids, MI: Zondervan Publishing House, 2003), 72.

459. "U.S. Religious Landscape Survey," Pew Forum on Religion and Public Life, 2008, http://religions.pewforum.org/reports# , accessed January 19, 2011.

460. Explained by Putnam in the chapter, "Historicism Back to the Future," in *Petrus Romanus*, 277.

461. Alan Kurschner, "Maybe the Bible Is Wrong and the Koran Is Right After All?" http://www.alankurschner.com/2014/11/23/maybe-the-bible-is-wrong-and-the-koran-is-right-after-all/.

462. Joel Richardson, *When A Jew Rules the World: What the Bible Really Says About Israel in the Plan of God,* Kindle Edition.(WND Books, 2015), Kindle Locations 122–140 .

463. Arnold G. Fruchtenbaum, *Israelology: The Missing Link in Systematic Theology,* Revised Edition (Tustin, CA: Ariel Ministries: 1994), 797.

464. Ibid., 797.

465. Barry E. Horner, *Nac Studies in Bible and Theology*, vol. 3, *Future Israel: Why Christian Anti-Judaism Must Be Challenged* (Nashville, TN: B & H Academic, 2007), 65.

466. Uri Goldberg, *What's Next for the Startup Nation?: A Blueprint for Sustainable Innovation,* Kindle Edition (AuthorHouse, 2012). Kindle Locations 356–360.

467. Fruchtenbaum, *Israelology*, 806.

468. רָקַע, *Enhanced Brown-Driver-Briggs Hebrew and English Lexicon*, edited by Francis Brown, Samuel Rolles Driver, and Charles Augustus Briggs(Oxford: Clarendon Press, 1977), 201.

469. ἐκκεντέω in *Greek-English Lexicon of the New Testament: Based on Semantic Domains, Johannes P. Louw and Eugene Albert Nida* (New York: United Bible Societies, 1996), 223.

470. Louis Jacobs, *The Jewish Religion: A Companion* (Oxford: Oxford University Press, 1995), 150.

471. "In the Bible the references to Asshur are always to the land, people, and king of Assyria." In ASSHUR (PLACE), *The Anchor Bible Dictionary,* edited by D.N. Freedman, (New York: Doubleday. 1992) 1:500.

472. Daniel J. Elazar, "The Jewish People as the Classic Diaspora: A Political Analysis," Jerusalem Center for Public Affairs, http://www.jcpa.org/dje/articles2/classicdias.htm, accessed October 6, 2015.

473. Primarily in book 14 of *Antiquities of the Jews* according to the Flavius Josephus biography at the Jewish Virtual Library, https://www.

jewishvirtuallibrary.org/jsource/judaica/ejud_0002_0011_0_10345.html, accessed October 6, 2015.

474. 891 "ἄχριachri or ἄχριςachris"in *New American Standard Hebrew-Aramaic and Greek Dictionaries: Updated Edition,* edited by Robert L. Thomas (Anaheim: Foundation Publications, Inc., 1998).

475. Gerald F. Hawthorne, Ralph P. Martin, and Daniel G. Reid, eds., *Dictionary of Paul and His Letters* (Downers Grove, IL: InterVarsity Press, 1993), 386.

476. M. L. Brown (2003),*Answering Jewish Objections to Jesus, Volume 3: Messianic Prophecy Objections*(Grand Rapids, MI: Baker Books) 148.

477. Sid Roth, *The Incomplete Church: Unifying God's Children* (Shippensburg, PA: Destiny Image, 2007), 14.

478. Ralph Woodrow, "Message from Ralph Woodrow Regarding the Book BABYLON MYSTERY RELIGION," Ralph Woodrow Evangelistic Association,http://www.ralphwoodrow.org/books/pages/babylon-mystery.html, accessed October 8, 2015.

479. "VFTB 164: Did Constantine Steal Christianity?" *View From the Bunker,* November 17, 2013, http://vftb.net/?p=4974, accessed October 7,2015. Also see Natalina, "Russ "Pappy" Houck vs. Cris Putnam Trinity Debate Breakdown" *Extraordinary Intelligence,*http://extraordinaryintelligence.com/trinity-debate-cris-putnam-russ-houck/, accessed October 8, 2015.

480. *The Ante-Nicene Fathers Vol. III: Translations of the Writings of the Fathers Down to A.D. 325,* Latin Christianity: Its Founder, Tertullian (Oak Harbor: Logos Research Systems, 1997), 606.

481. Roth, *The Incomplete Church,* 82.

482. http://www.clearquran.com/002.html.

483. Shaykh Professor Abdul Hadi Palazzi, "What the Qur'an Really Says," http://www.templemount.org/quranland.html, accessed September 11, 2015.

484. Heiser, *Islam and Armageddon,* 44.

485. Ibid., 46.

486. "Remaining and Expanding," *Dabiq* 5: 29.

487. Sahih Muslim Book 041, Hadith Number 6985, http://www.hadithcollection.com/sahihmuslim/169-Sahih%20Muslim%20Book%2041.%20Turmoil%20And%20Portents%20Of%20The%20Last%20Hour/15311-sahih-muslim-book-041-hadith-number-6985.html, accessed October 5, 2015.

488. Muhammad M. Pickthall, ed., *The Quran* (Medford, MA: Perseus Digital Library).

489. "Major Signs of the End of the World," http://www.khorasaan.net/major-signs-of-end-of-the-world.php.

490. Muhammad Nasir al-Din al-Albani, Takhrijahadithfada'il al-Sham wa-Dimashq (Riyadh: Maktabat al-Ma'arif, 2000), 38.

491. Allen P. Ross, "Genesis," in *The Bible Knowledge Commentary: An Exposition of the Scriptures*, ed. J. F. Walvoord and R. B. Zuck, vol. 1 (Wheaton, IL: Victor Books, 1985), 46.

492. Cheryl K. Chumley, "4 in 10 American Adults: We're Living in the End Times," *The Washington Times* September 12, 2013, http://www.washingtontimes.com/news/2013/sep/12/4-in10-american-adults-were-living-end-times/, accessed January 4, 2016.

493. C. H. Spurgeon, *The C.H. Spurgeon Collection, Metropolitan Tabernacle Pulpit*, 1, no. 28, 1855 (Albany, Oregon: Ages Software, 1998), 382.

494. Grant Jeffrey, "Ezekiel's Vision of the Rebirth of Israel in 1948," http://www.grantjeffrey.com/pdf/JeffBIBLE-EzekVision2.pdf, accessed January 3, 2016.

495. Ibid.

496. "Sunnah" in *Encyclopedia Britannica*, http://www.britannica.com/topic/Sunnah, accessed January 13, 2016.

497. Joel Richardson, *Antichrist: Islam's Awaited Messiah* (Enumclaw, WA: Pleasant Word, 2006), 34.

498. "Eschatology: Islamic Eschatology" in Lindsay Jones, *Encyclopedia of Religion*, 2nd ed. (Detroit: Macmillan Reference USA, 2005), 2838.

499. Sahih Muslim, Book 41, 6924, http://searchtruth.com/book_display.php?book=041&translator=2&start=0&number=6924 accessed January 13, 2016.

500. David Cook, *Contemporary Muslim Apocalyptic Literature,* Kindle Edition, (Syracuse, NY: Syracuse University Press, 2006) Kindle Location 109.

501. Chris White (2015-04-06), The *Islamic Antichrist Debunked: A Comprehensive Critique of the Muslim Antichrist Theory* (Kindle Locations 2620–2624). CWM Publishing. Kindle Edition.

502. Muhamad M. Pickthall, ed., *The Quran* (Medford, MA: Perseus Digital Library, n.d.).

503. Various Hadiths are available on the Trials and Fierce Battles (Kitab Al-FitanWa Al-Malahim), Sunnah.com,http://sunnah.com/abudawud/37, accessed January 12, 2016.

504. M. H. Shakir, ed., *The Quran* (Medford, MA: Perseus Digital Library, n.d.).

505. Sunnah,"*Encyclopædia Britannica. Encyclopædia Britannica Online* 2016, http://www.britannica.com/topic/Sunnah accessed January 4, 2016.

506. Ṣamū'īl'Abd al-Shahīd, *The Last Trumpet: A Comparative Study in Christian-Islamic Eschatology* (Longwood, Fla.: Xulon Press, 2005), 29.

507. Shahīd, *The Last Trumpet*, 40.

508. "Theologians have divided these apocalyptic signs into two groups: the Lesser and the Greater Signs of the Hour," David Cook, *Contemporary Muslim Apocalyptic Literature*, Kindle Locations 121–122.

509. Ibid., 122–123.

510. Ibid., 127–129.

511. Shahīd, *The Last Trumpet*, 30–42. My list of minor signs is drawn largely from this section of this book citing numerous Hadiths.

512. Church of God, "Earthquakes Today and Bible Prophecy: Has There Been an Increase in Major Earthquakes?" http://www.cogwriter.com/earthquakes-today.php, accessed January 4, 2016.

513. *Sahih Muslim*, 6924 http://www.theonlyquran.com/hadith/Sahih-Muslim/?volume=41&chapter=9.

514. "Islamic State Threatens to Attack Saudi Arabia," ENCA, December 20, 2015, https://www.enca.com/world/islamic-state-threatens-attack-saudi-arabia, accessed January 12, 2016.

515. Alim, *Sunanan of al-Tirmidhi*, #1236.

516. Ibid., #1446.

517. Shahid, *The Last Trumpet*, 41–42.

518. Alim, *Sunanan of al-Tirmidhi* #1450.

519. *Shahih of Muslim*, v.8, page 174 (English translation).

520. Paige Patterson, *Revelation*, ed. E. Ray Clendenen, vol. 39, *The New American Commentary* (Nashville, TN: B&H, 2012), 310.

521. Joel Richardson, *The Islamic Antichrist*, second ed. (Washington, D.C.: WND Books, 2015), 79.

522. Chris White, *The Islamic Antichrist Debunked: A Comprehensive Critique of the Muslim Antichrist Theory*, Kindle Edition, (Nashville TN, CWM Publishing, 2015), Kindle Locations 2489–2491.

523. Musnad of Ahmad 2: 537–538; and *Shahih of Muslim #2949* (Arabic version) as translated by Shahid, *Last Trumpet*, 41.

524. Al-Fitanwa al-Malhim 183–187, as translated by Shahid, *Last Trumpet*, 41.

525. Ibn Kathir, *The Signs Before the Day of Judgement*(London, Dar Al-Taqwa, 1991), 18.

526. "The World's Muslims: Unity and Diversity," Pew Research Center, April 6 2012, http://www.pewforum.org/2012/08/09/the-worlds-muslims-unity-and-diversity-executive-summary/ accessed December10, 2015.

527. Timothy Furnish, "Mahdism (and Sectarianism and Superstition) Rises in the Islamic World" History.com August 13, 2012, http://

historynewsnetwork.org/article/147714#sthash.F5v4ndOR.AY0ZuBzB.
dpuflt, accessed January 12, 2016.

528. Bernard Lewis, "Islam and the West: A Conversation with Bernard Lewis,"
http://www.catholiceducation.org/en/culture/catholic-contributions/islam-
and-the-west-a-conversation-with-bernard-lewis.html, accessed September
11, 2015.

529. "Islamic 'Messiah' al-Mahdi to Return by 2016, Followed By Jesus? Islamic
'Messiah' al-Mahdi to Return by 2016, Followed By Jesus?" *Israel, Islam
and the End Times* May 19, 2015, http://www.israelislamandendtimes.com/
islamic-messiah-al-mahdi-to-return-by-2016-followed-by-jesus/accessed
January 3, 2016.

530. "About Ṣaḥīḥ Muslim" Sunnah.com, http://sunnah.com/muslim/about,
accessed October 6, 2015.

531. "Major Signs of the End of the World," http://www.khorasaan.net/major-
signs-of-end-of-the-world.php.

532. Sh. G. F. Haddad, "Various Issues about Hadiths," Living Islamic Tradition,
https://www.abc.se/~m9783/n/vih_e.html, accessed October 6, 2015.

533. Furnish, *Holiest Wars*, 150.

534. Timothy R Furnish, "Thursday, August 21, 2014: IS[IS]: Still Beheading
Like It's the End of the World," Mahdi Watch.org,http://www.mahdiwatch.
org/2014.08.01_arch.html, accessed August 10, 2015.

535. Joel C. Rosenberg, *The First Hostage: A J. B. Collins Novel* (Carol
Stream, Illinois: Tyndale House Publishers, 2015), sample: http://www.
joelrosenberg.com/product-details/?isbn=978-1-4964-0615-6#sthash.
fXS9J1hE.dpuf, accessed October 8, 2015.

536. lla Landau-Tasseron, *History of Al-Tabari, Volume 39: Biographies of the
Prophet's Companions and Their Successors*, Suny Series in Near Eastern
Studies (Albany: State University of New York Press, 1996) 39–40,https://
books.google.com/books?id=ztahJV58oLcC&printsec=frontcover#v=onepa
ge&q&f=false.

537. "Mapping the Global Muslim Population," Pew Research Center, October
7, 2009,http://www.pewforum.org/2009/10/07/mapping-the-global-
muslim-population/, accessed December 19, 2015.

538. Mathieu Guidère, *Historical Dictionary of Islamic Fundamentalism*,
Historical Dictionaries of Religions, Philosophies, and Movements
(Lanham, Maryland: The Scarecrow Press, Inc., 2012), 319.

539. William McCants, Brookings Institute, http://www.brookings.edu/experts/
mccantsw accessed October 9, 2015.

540. Jean-Pierre Filiu, *Apocalypse in Islam*, translated by M. B. DeBevoise,
(Berkeley: University of California Press, 2011), 121–140.

541. Filiu, *Apocalypse in Islam*, 131.

542. William McCants, "How ISIL Out-Terrorized Bin Laden," *Politico Magazine*, August 15, 2015, http://www.politico.com/magazine/story/2015/08/isis-jihad-121525#ixzz3o6YPGmIx, accessed October 9, 2015.

543. Bernard Lewis, *The Crisis of Islam: Holy War and Unholy Terror*, Kindle Edition, (New York: Random House Publishing Group, 2003), Kindle Locations 1208–1211.

544. "The World's Muslims: Unity and Diversity," Pew Research Center, August 9, 2012, accessed October 6, 2015.

545. "GRAPHIC IMAGES: East Jerusalem Arab Rams Car into Ultra-Orthodox Jews, Then Stabs Them" *JerusalemPost*, October 13, 2015, http://www.jpost.com/Arab-Israeli-Conflict/GRAPHIC-IMAGES-East-Jerusalem-Arab-rams-car-into-ultra-Orthodox-Jews-then-stabs-them-423831, accessed December 28, 2015.

546. William McCants (2015-09-22), *The ISIS Apocalypse: The History, Strategy, and Doomsday Vision of the Islamic State* (Kindle Locations 529–530). St. Martin's Press. Kindle Edition.

547. am l Abd al-Shah d, *The Last Trumpet: A Comparative Study in Christian-Islamic Eschatology* (Longwood, Fla.: Xulon Press, 2005), 28.

548. Christine Huda Dodge, *The Everything Understanding Islam Book: A Complete Guide to Muslim Beliefs, Practices, and Culture*, 2nd ed., An Everything Series Book (Avon, MA: Adams Media Corp., 2009), 185.

549. Timothy R. Furnish, *Holiest Wars: Islamic Mahdis, Their Jihads, and Osama bin Laden* (Kindle Locations 114-116). Kindle Edition.

550. Timothy R. Furnish, "Through a Glass Darkly: A Comparison of Self-Proclaimed "Mahdist" States throughout History to the Theory of the (True) Mahdist State Yet to Come," International Conference of Mahdism Doctrine, http://www.mahdaviat-conference.com/vdchtqnkd23nz.102.html.

551. Furnish, "Through a Glass Darkly."

552. William McCants, *The ISIS Apocalypse: The History, Strategy, and Doomsday Vision of the Islamic State*, Kindle Edition, (St. Martin's Press, 2015). Kindle Location 79.

553. Ibid., 185–186.

554. Ibid. 237–239.

555. Ibid., 525–530.

556. Louise Sassoon, "Russia Refuses to Rule Out Use of Nuclear Weapons in Fight against ISIS," Mirror Online, UK, http://www.mirror.co.uk/news/

world-news/russia-refuses-rule-out-use-6985903 accessed December 14, 2015.

557. Atoosa Moinzadeh, "Islamic State Claims It Downed Russian Airliner—But Cause Remains Unclear," Vice News,November 1, 2015, https://news.vice.com/article/islamic-state-claims-it-downed-russian-airliner-but-cause-remains-unclear accessed December 19, 2015.

558. Barbara Starr and Catherine E. Shoichet, "Russian Plane Crash: U.S. Intel Suggests ISIS Bomb Brought Down Jet" CNN, Novembern4, 2015, http://www.cnn.com/2015/11/04/africa/russian-plane-crash-egypt-sinai/index.html, accessed December 14, 2015.

559. Sassoon, "Russia 'Refuses to Rule Out.'"

560. Andras Kraft, "The Last Roman Emperor and the Mahdī—On the Genesis of a Contentious Politico-Religious Topos," Proceedings of the international Symposium Byzantium and The Arab World Encounter of Civilizations (Thessaloniki, 16–18 December 2011) https://ceu.academia.edu/AndrasKraft.

561. Paul Julius Alexander, *The Byzantine Apocalyptic Tradition*, ed. Dorothy deFAbrahamse (Berkeley: University of California Press, 1985), 15.

562. CatalinNegru, "About," Reason and Religion,http://reasonandreligion.org/index.php/about/, accessed December 19, 2015.

563. Ernst Sackur, *SibyllinischeTexte und Forschungen: Pseudomethodius, Adso und die TiburtinischeSibylle* (Halle : Max Niemeyer , 1898), 185.

564. Ibid, 186.

565. Ibid.

566. CatalinNegru, *History of Apocalypse*.

567. "Apocalypse of Pseudo-Methodius," Orthodoxwiki, http://orthodoxwiki.org/Apocalypse_of_Pseudo-Methodius#cite_note-0, accessed December 19, 2015.

568. Ernst Sackur, *SibyllinischeTexte und Forschungen: Pseudomethodius, Adso und die TiburtinischeSibylle* (Halle : Max Niemeyer , 1898), 80–83,http://ubsm.bg.ac.rs/engleski/dokument/624/sibyllinische-texte-und-forschungen-pseudomethodius-adso-unit-die-tiburtinische-sibylle.

569. Sackur, *SibyllinischeTexte*, 89–94.

570. Desmond A. Birch, *Trial, Tribulation and Triumph: Before, During, and After Antichrist* (Santa Barbara, CA.: Queenship Publishing, 1996).

571. Dupont, *Catholic Prophecy*, 9.

572. Birch, *Trial, Tribulation and Triumph*.

573. Dupont, *Catholic Prophecy*, 38–44.

574. "Pope Francis: I Seek Communion with Orthodox Churches," Vatican

Radio, http://en.radiovaticana.va/news/2014/11/30/pope_francis_i_seek_communion_with_orthodox_churches/1113017, accessed July 29, 2015.

575. http://www.usatoday.com/story/news/2016/02/12/pope-francis-patriarch-kirill-roman-catholic-church-russian-orthodox-church-meet/80278172/.

576. Yves Dupont, *Catholic Prophecy: The Coming Chastisement* (Rockford IL, Tan Books, 1970), 43.

577. Yves Dupont, "More about the Great Monarch and the Glorious Age of Peace to Come Under the Reign of the Great Monarch," *Today's Catholic World*, October 17.2006, http://www.todayscatholicworld.com/great-catholic-monarch.htm, accessed July 29, 2015.

578. Walter Adams, "What Is the Counterrevolutionary and Royal Army of America?" *Catholic Monarchy*, October 25, 2016, http://catholicmonarchy.com/, accessed July 29, 2015.

579. Dupont has authored many books on the subject for Tan Publishing.

580. Dupont, "More About the Great Monarch."

581. Dupont, *Catholic Prophecy*, 13.

582. Pseudo-Methodius, *Dumbarton Oaks Medieval Library*, trans. Benjamin Garstad, vol. 14, *Apocalypse* (Cambridge, Massachusetts: Harvard University Press, 2012), vii.

583. William McCants, *The ISIS Apocalypse: The History, Strategy, and Doomsday Vision of the Islamic State*, Kindle Edition, (St. Martin's Press, 2015), Kindle Locations 374–376.

584. Paul Julius Alexander, *The Byzantine Apocalyptic Tradition*, ed. Dorothy deFAbrahamse (Berkeley: University of California Press, 1985), 13, https://books.google.com/books?id=nw-rR_Skb-cC&lpg=PA13&vq=most%20important%20branch&dq=Apocalypse%20of%20Pseudo-Methodius&pg=PA13#v=snippet&q=most%20important%20branch&f=false.

585. http://www.cyclopaedia.fr/wiki/Syriac_Apocalypse_of_Pseudo-Methodius.

586. Alexander, *Byzantine Apocalyptic Tradition*.

587. Ibid., 13.

588. E. J. van Donzel and Andrea B. Schmidt, *Brill's Inner Asian Library*, vol. 22, *Gog and Magog in Early Eastern Christian and Islamic Sources: Sallam's Quest for Alexander's Wall* (Leiden: Brill, 2010), 30, accessed June 22, 2015, http://public.eblib.com/choice/publicfullrecord.aspx?p=682249.

589. O. Livbe-Kafri, "Is There a Reflection of the Apocalypse of Pseudo-Methodius in Muslim Tradition?" *Proche-Orient Chrerien*56 (2006), 112–118.

590. Van Donzel and Schmidt, *Brill's Inner Asian Library*, 30.

591. Charles Kannengiesser, Les Pères de L'egliseDans Le Monde D'aujourd'hui:

Actes Du Colloque International Organisé Par Le New Europe College En Collaboration Avec La Ludwig Boltzmann Gesellschaft (Bucarest, 7–8 Octobre 2004) (Paris: Beauchesne, 2006), 224–25.

592. William McCants, *The ISIS Apocalypse: The History, Strategy, and Doomsday Vision of the Islamic State*, Kindle Edition, (St. Martin's Press, 2015), Kindle Locations 1904–1905.

593. Victor Harold Matthews, Mark W. Chavalas, and John H. Walton, *The IVP Bible Background Commentary: Old Testament*, electronic ed. (Downers Grove, IL: InterVarsity Press, 2000), Is. 17:1.

594. Michael Brown, "Does the Bible Predict the Destruction of Syria?," *Charisma*, September 11, 2013, http://www.charismanews.com/opinion/in-the-line-of-fire/40946-does-the-bible-predict-the-destruction-of-syria, accessed October 19, 2015.

595. Ross Burns, *Damascus: A History* (London: Routledge, 2007), 2.

596. Martin Lings, *Muhammad: His Life Based on the Earliest Sources* (Rochester, VT: Inner Traditions, 2006), 44.

597. James R. White, *What Every Christian Needs to Know About the Qur'an* (Minneapolis, MN: Bethany House Publishers, 2013), 254–255.

598. Ibid., 260.

599. Patricia Crone, "What Do We Actually Know about Mohammed?" Open Democracy, June 10, 2008, https://www.opendemocracy.net/faith-europe_islam/mohammed_3866.jsp, accessed October 21, 2015.

600. James R. White, *What Every Christian Needs to Know About the Qur'an* (Minneapolis, MN: Bethany House Publishers, 2013), 172.

601. Ibn Warraq, "Virgins? What Virgins?" *The Guardian*, January 11, 2002, http://www.theguardian.com/books/2002/jan/12/books.guardianreview5, accessed October 19, 2015.

602. "Inside ISIS: Fighters Promised '72 Eternal Virgins in Heaven' While Christian Women Raped as Husbands Beheaded, Says Ex-Member," *Christian Post*, September 14, 2014, http://www.christianpost.com/news/inside-isis-fighters-promised-72-eternal-virgins-in-heaven-while-christian-women-raped-as-husbands-beheaded-says-ex-member-126710/, accessed October 19, 2015.

603. Warraq, "Virgins? What Virgins?"

604. Christoph Luxenberg, *The Syro-Aramaic Reading of the Koran: A Contribution to the Decoding of the Language of the Koran* (Berlin: H. Schiler, 2007), 257.

605. Ibid.

606. White, *What Every Christian*, 75.

607. "Bush: All Religions Pray to 'Same God'" WND, October 7,2007, http://

www.wnd.com/2007/10/43906/#IAtv5sfOG4i4t4h2.99, accessed October 19, 2015.

608. Muhammad M. Pickthall, ed., *The Quran* (Medford, MA: Perseus Digital Library, n.d.).

609. Cris Putnam, "Reply to Rob Skiba on the Denial of the Personhood of the Holy Spirit," LogosApologia.org, September 9, 2013, http://www.logosapologia.org/reply-to-rob-skiba-on-the-denial-of-the-personhood-of-the-holy-spirit/, accessed October 13, 2015.

610. White, 78.

611. Ibid., 87.

612. Ibid., 97.

613. Marius Povilas Šaulauskas and Alfredas Bumblauskas, "The Threefold Step of Academia Europeana: ACase of Universitas Vilnensis," (Universite to id ja, 2009), 24, http://www.zurnalai.vu.lt/problemos/article/viewFile/1946/1179, accessed October 15, 2015.

614. "Rabbi Moshe Shternbuch: We Hear the Footsteps of the Moshiach," Lazer Beams, March 30, 2014, http://lazerbrody.typepad.com/lazer_beams/2014/03/rabbi-moshe-sternbuch.html#sthash.PjoWhtfa.dpuf, accessed November 25, 2015.

615. Matt Smith and Alla Eshchenko, "Ukraine Cries 'Robbery' as Russia Annexes Crimea," CNN, March 18, 2014, http://www.cnn.com/2014/03/18/world/europe/ukraine-crisis/index.html, accessed October 15, 2015.

616. Sahih Muslim by Imam Muslim, translation by Abdul Hamid Siddiqui, *Volume: The Book Pertaining to the Turmoil and Portents of the Last Hour,* http://www.theonlyquran.com/hadith/Sahih-Muslim/?volume=41&chapter=9, accessed November 25, 2015.

617. Heiser, *Islam and Armageddon* (Self-published book, 2002), 83.

618. Ibid., 84.

619. Charles C. Torrey, "Armageddon," *Harvard Theological Review* 31, 3 (1938): 246.

620. James Swanson, *Dictionary of Biblical Languages with Semantic Domains: Hebrew (Old Testament),* electronic ed (Oak Harbor: Logos Research Systems, Inc., 1997).

621. Meredith Kline, "Har Magedon: The End of the Millennium."*Journal of the Evangelical Theological Society,* 39, 2.I (1996): 208.

622. Arnold G. Fruchtenbaum, *The Footsteps of the Messiah: A Study of the Sequence of Prophetic Events,* Rev. ed. (Tustin, CA: Ariel Ministries, 2003), 311.

623. Alan F. Johnson, "Revelation," in *The Expositor's Bible Commentary, Volume*

12: Hebrews Through Revelation, ed. Frank E. Gaebelein (Grand Rapids, MI: Zondervan Publishing House, 1981), 551.

624. "Armageddon" in*Dictionary of Biblical Prophecy and End Times*,ed. J. Daniel Hays, J. Scott Duvall, and C. Marvin Pate (Grand Rapids, MI: Zondervan Publishing House, 2007), 43.

625. Johnson, "Revelation," 551.

626. Robert H. Mounce, "The Book of Revelation,"*The New International Commentary on the New Testament* (Grand Rapids, MI: Eerdmans Publishing Co., 1997), 301.

627. Torrey, "Armageddon," 238.

628. R. H. Charles, *A Critical and Exegetical Commentary on the Revelation of St. John* (Edinburgh: T&T Clark International, 1920), 2:50.

629. R. Laird Harris, Robert Laird Harris, Gleason Leonard Archer and Bruce K. Waltke, *Theological Wordbook of the Old Testament*, electronic ed. (Chicago: Moody Press, 1999, c1980), 150.

630. Johnson, "Revelation," 552.

631. Ibid.

632. Torrey, "Armageddon," 245.

633. Michael S. Heiser, *The Unseen Realm: Recovering the Supernatural Worldview of the Bible* (Bellingham, Wash.: Lexham Press, 2015), 371.

634. Kline, "Har Magedon," 208.

635. Mathias Rissi, *Time and History* (Louisville: John Knox Press, 1966), 84–85.

636. John H. Walton, *Zondervan Illustrated Bible Backgrounds Commentary* (Old Testament) *Volume 5: The Minor Prophets, Job, Psalms, Proverbs, Ecclesiastes, Song of Songs* (Grand Rapids, MI: Zondervan, 2009), 362.

637. Walton, 2009b, 73.

638. H. Niehr, "Zaphon" in *Dictionary of Deities and Demons in the Bible DDD*, 2nd extensively rev. ed. K. van der Toorn, Bob Becking and Pieter Willem van der Horst (Leiden; Boston; Grand Rapids, MI: Brill; Eerdmans, 1999), 927.

639. Michael S. Heiser, "The Divine Council in Late Cannonical and Non-Cannonical Second Temple Jewish Literature," (Ph.D. diss., University of Wisconsin-Madison, 2004), 43.

640. Torrey, "Armageddon," 246.

641. Mounce, The Book of Revelation, 301.

642. Michael S. Heiser, *Islam and Armageddon,* (Self-published book, 2002), 111.

643. Johnson, "Revelation,"551.

644. Kline, "Har Magedon," 208.

645. Ibid.

646. Michael S. Heiser, "The Mythological Provenance of Is. XVIV 12–15: A Reconsideration of the Ugaritic Material," *Vestus Testamentum* LI,3,(2001): 356–357.

647. Heiser, "The Mythological," 356–357.

648. Kaufmann Kohler, "Lucifer," http://www.jewishencyclopedia.com/view. jsp?artid=612&letter=L, accessed March 5, 2011.

649. C. S. Lewis, *Mere Christianity* (NY: Harper Collins. 2001), 122.

650. G. J. Riley, "Devil," in *Dictionary of Deities and Demons in the Bible,* 2nd extensively rev. ed. K. van der Toorn, Bob Becking, and Pieter Willem van der Horst (Leiden; Boston; Grand Rapids, MI: Brill; Eerdmans, 1999), 246.

651. Tertullian, *Contra Marcionem,* 11, 17.

652. M. Eugene Boring, *Revelation, Interpretation, a Bible Commentary for Teaching and Preaching* (Louisville: John Knox Press, 1989), 177.

653. L. J. Lietaert Peerbolte, "Antichrist" in DDD, 62.

654. Kline, "Har Magedon," 219.

655. Heiser, *Islam,* 98–101.

656. Ibid., 102.

657. Ibid., 135.

658. Ludovico Sinistrari, *De Daemonialitate et Incubis et Succubis* (Demoniality; or, Incubi and succubi), from the original 1680 Latin manuscript translated into English (Paris, I. Liseux, 1872), 53. (The 1879 English translation of the book is available in full and for free online in scanned format by the *California Digital Library* here [last accessed December 4, 2012]: http:// archive.org/details/ demonialityorinc00sinirich).

659. Heiser, *Islam,* 100.

660. Tim LaHaye, *The Coming Peace in the Middle East* (Grand Rapids, MI: Zondervan, 1984), 7.

661. Chuck Missler, *Ezekiel an Expositional Commentary* (Coeur d'Alene, ID: Koinonia House, 2008), 248–255.

662. John Weldon, *The Ezekiel 38 Psalm 83 Prophecies: Russia, Iran and Muslim Nations in Biblical Prophecy* (ATRI Publishing: 2012), 30–34.

663. Heiser, *Islam and Armageddon,* 73.

664. Ralph H. Alexander, "Ezekiel" In , in *The Expositor's Bible Commentary, Volume 6: Isaiah, Jeremiah, Lamentations, Ezekiel,* ed. Frank E. Gaebelein (Grand Rapids, MI: Zondervan Publishing House, 1986), 934.

665. Childs 1959, 196.

666. "Major Religions of the World Ranked by Number of Adherents,"

adherents.com, http://www.adherents.com/Religions_By_Adherents.html, retrieved February 28, 2016.

667. "Global Christianity—A Report on the Size and Distribution of the World's Christian Population," Pew Research Center, December 19, 2011,http://www.pewforum.org/2011/12/19/global-christianity-exec/.

668. For the purposes of the survey, a biblical worldview was defined as accepting all of the following points of doctrine: Believing that absolute moral truth exists; the Bible is totally accurate in all of the principles it teaches; Satan is considered to be a real being or force, not merely symbolic; a person cannot earn his or her way into heaven by trying to be good or do good works; Jesus Christ lived a sinless life on earth; and God is the all-knowing, all-powerful Creator of the world who still rules the universe today.

669. "Barna Survey Examines Changes in Worldview among Christians over the Past 13 Years," Barna Group, March 9, 2009,https://barna.org/barna-update/transformation/252-barna-survey-examines-changes-in-worldview-among-christians-over-the-past-13-years#.VtMY3hj5hE4.

670. Jeff Schapiro, "Poll: 4 in 10 Americans Believe They Are Living in the End Times," *The Christian Post*, September 12, 2013,http://www.christianpost.com/news/poll-4-in-10-americans-believe-they-are-living-in-the-end-times-104423/.

671. For example, the mass suicide of the Heaven's Gate cult in 1997, which was motivated by their belief that they'd be joining an alien spacecraft flying behind Comet Hale-Bopp.

672. I will use *mashiach* when referring to the Jewish "anointed one" to distinguish him from the Christian understanding of the Messiah.

673. Qur'an 43:61. "'And indeed, Jesus will be [a sign for] knowledge of the Hour, so be not in doubt of it, and follow Me. This is a straight path.'"

674. William McCants, "The Foreign Policy Essay: The Sectarian Apocalypse," October 26, 2014, http://www.brookings.edu/research/opinions/2014/10/26-foreign-policy-essay-sectarian-apocalypse-mccants.

675. Ibid.

676. Dr. Timothy R. Furnish, "Mahdism (and Sectarianism and Superstition) Rises in the Islamic World," *History News Network*, August 13, 2012, http://historynewsnetwork.org/article/147714#sthash.uCCjkns0.dpuf.

677. Ibid.

678. Interestingly, al-A'maq, the valley where the Islamic State believes it may confront the forces of Rome, lies next to Antioch, the modern Antakya, the city where Christians were first called by that name in the first century. The valley also lies next to Mount Aqraa, formerly Mount Zaphon, which

was known to the ancient world as the site of the palace of Ba'al. I do not believe this is a coincidence, but that theory will be explored more fully elsewhere.

679. "Newly-Declassified U.S. Government Documents: The West Supported the Creation of ISIS," *Washington's Blog*, May 24, 2015,http://www.washingtonsblog.com/2015/05/newly-declassified-u-s-government-documents-the-west-supported-the-creation-of-isis.html.

680. Tyler Durden, "Secret Pentagon Report Reveals US 'Created'ISIS As A 'Tool' To Overthrow Syria's President Assad," *ZeroHedge*, May 24, 2015,http://www.zerohedge.com/news/2015-05-23/secret-pentagon-report-reveals-us-created-isis-tool-overthrow-syrias-president-assad.

681. Nafeez Ahmed, "Pentagon Report Predicted West's Support for Islamist Rebels Would Create ISIS," *Medium*, May 22, 2015,https://medium.com/insurge-intelligence/secret-pentagon-report-reveals-west-saw-isis-as-strategic-asset-b99ad7a29092#.xk748ht7r.

682. "Mapping the Global Muslim Population," Pew Research Center, October 7, 2009,http://www.pewforum.org/2009/10/07/mapping-the-global-muslim-population/.

683. Dr. Timothy R. Furnish, "A Western View on Iran's WMD Goal: Nuclearizing the Eschaton, or Pre-Stocking the Mahdi's Arsenal?," Institute for Near East & Gulf Military Analysis, January 2011, p. 4.

684. Ze'ev Maghen, "Occultation in Perpetuum: Shi`ite Messianism and the Policies of the Islamic Republic," *Middle East Journal*, Vol. 62, No. 2 (Spring 2008), p. 237 (cited by Furnish).

685. Kaufmann Kohler, "Eschatology," *Jewish Encyclopedia*, http://www.jewishencyclopedia.com/articles/5849-eschatology.

686. Not the Nile, but the Wadi al-Arish, the traditional border between Egypt and Israel.

687. This event, held annually on the first Thursday in May, is not in itself a bad thing. It is endorsed by many respected American evangelical leaders. Since at least 2010, the National Day of Prayer Task Force has encouraged Americans to pray for the "seven centers of power": Government, Military, Media, Business, Education, Church, and Family. Those centers of power are virtually identical to the Seven Mountains of Culture that Dominionists believe must be captured by Christians to speed Christ's return.

688. The Greek word translated "rulers" (*archontes*) is used in Scripture to refer to human political leaders and to supernatural entities—which are undoubtedly the forces directing human action opposed to God in either case.

689. Based on the account by Roman historian Cassius Dio.

690. Something like this has happened in recent history. A 1979 rebellion in Saudi Arabia was led by Juhayman al-Otaybi, who declared that his brother-in-law, Mohammed Abdullah al-Qahtani, was the Mahdi.

691. In Jewish eschatology, this would be Armilus, "a king who will arise at the end of time against the Messiah, and will be conquered by him after having brought much distress upon Israel." Kauffman Kohler and Louis Ginsberg, *Jewish Encyclopedia,* http://www.jewishencyclopedia.com/articles/1789-armilus.

692. Psalm 83:1–8 (ESV). Analysis per Joel Richardson, "Which Nations Does Psalm 83 Really Include?" *WND,* August 2, 2012,http://www.wnd.com/2012/08/which-nations-does-psalm-83-really-include/. Richardson was citing the work of Bill Salus, author of *Psalm 83: The Missing Prophecy Revealed.*

693. An interesting interpretation, since Ezekiel's prophecy is very specific about the war taking place in Israel. Adam Eliyahu Berkowitz, "Hassidic Rabbi: War of Gog and Magog Already Began in Syria," October 9, 2015,http://www.breakingisraelnews.com/50649/hassidic-rabbi-reveals-god-sweetened-judgementon-israel-by-moving-war-gog-magog-syria-jewish-world/.

694. Early Church writers Justin (*First Apology*) and Eusebius (*Chronicle*) mention bar Kokhba's treatment of Christians. Cited at "Wars between the Jews and Romans: Simon ben Kosiba (130–136 CE)," Livius.org, http://www.livius.org/ja-jn/jewish_wars/jwar07.html.

695. By Akiva's disciple, Yose ben Halafta, in his historical work, the *Seder Olam Rabbah.*

696. Elon Gilad, "The Bar Kochba Revolt: A Disaster Celebrated by Zionists on Lag Ba'Omer," *Haaretz,* May 6, 2015, http://www.haaretz.com/jewish/features/.premium-1.655052.

697. Dr. Manfred R. Lehmann, "Rabbi Akiva and Bar Kokhba: Two National Heroes," http://www.manfredlehmann.com/news/news_detail.cgi/35/0. In his essay, Dr. Lehmann describes the Judaean Christians of Bar Kokhba's day as disloyal and treasonous.

698. P. Alexander, *The Oracle of Baalbek. The Tiburtine Sibyl in Greek Dress,* (Washington, DC, 1967), 21.

699. Robert C. Kashow, "Sibylline Oracles," ed. John D. Barry et al., *The Lexham Bible Dictionary* (Bellingham, WA: Lexham Press, 2012, 2013, 2014, 2015).

700. Ibid.

701. Allen C. Myers, *The Eerdmans Bible Dictionary* (Grand Rapids, MI: Eerdmans, 1987), 947.

702. Manly P. Hall, *The Secret Destiny of America.* Gaillard Hunt, *The History of*

the *Seal of the United States* (Washington, D.C.,1909), Horn and Putnam, *Petrus Romanus*, 105–106.

703. Ireaneus of Lyons, "Early Christian Writings," http://www. earlychristianwritings.com/irenaeus.html,, accessed February 22, 2016.

704. Irenaeus, *AdversusHaereses*, III.3.

705. Irenaeus, *Against Heresies* Book V, Chapter 30, 4.

706. Justin Martyr, "Horatory Address to the Greeks" in *The Apostolic Fathers with Justin Martyr and Irenaeus* , http://www.ccel.org/ccel/schaff/anf01/Page_273.html.

707. Justin Martyr, "Horatory Address to the Greeks", http://biblehub.com/library/justin/justins_hortatory_address_to_the_greeks/chapter_xxxvii_of_the_sibyl.htm.

708. Justin Martyr, "Justin's Hortatory Address to the Greeks," in *The Apostolic Fathers with Justin Martyr and Irenaeus,* ed. Alexander Roberts, James Donaldson, and A. Cleveland Coxe, trans. M. Dods, vol. 1, The Ante-Nicene Fathers (Buffalo, NY: Christian Literature Company, 1885), 280.

709. Ibid.

710. "The Wonderful History of Virgilius the Sorcerer of Rome" (London, D. Nutt, 1893), https://archive.org/details/wonderfulhistory00lond.

711. Robert L. Thomas, *New American Standard Hebrew-Aramaic and Greek Dictionaries*: Updated Edition (Anaheim: Foundation Publications, Inc., 1998).

712. Pausanias X 12.9.

713. Rieuwerd Buitenwerf, *Studia in Veteris Testamenti Pseudepigrapha, vol. 17, Book Iii of the Sibylline Oracles and Its Social Setting* (Leiden: Brill, 2003), 121.

714. "Sibyl" in Jewish Encyclopedia,http://www.jewishencyclopedia.com/articles/13629-sibyl,accessed February 20, 2016.

715. *A History of the Jewish People in the Time of Jesus Christ*, Part 2, Volume 3 (Scribner, 1896), 273, https://books.google.com/books?id=piRNAQAAM AAJ&pg=PA273&lpg=PA273&dq=Pausanias+X+12.9&source=bl&ots=V KFzkCdxTT&sig=Zbu2rTAc0yeiBZvRG9x9fof7xsU&hl=en&sa=X&ved =0ahUKEwju_9vf9evKAhXINiYKHVjOBrcQ6AEIITAC#v=onepage&q= Pausanias%20&f=false.

716. Richard Gottheil and Samuel Krauss, "Sibyl" in *Jewish Encyclopedia*.com, http://www.jewishencyclopedia.com/articles/13629-sibyl, accessed January 9, 2016.

717. Ibid.

718. Putnam and Horn, *On the Path of the Immortals.*

719. "Growth of a Young Nation," *U.S. House of Representatives: Office of the*

Clerk, last accessed January 30, 2012, http://artandhistory.house.gov/art_artifacts/virtual_tours/splendid_hall/young_nation.aspx.

720. "1964–Present: September 11, 2001, The Capitol Building as a Target," *United States Senate*, last accessed January 30, 2012, http://www.senate.gov/artandhistory/history/minute/Attack.htm.

721. William Henry and Mark Gray, *Freedom's Gate: Lost Symbols in the U.S.* (Hendersonville, TN: Scala Dei, 2009), 3.

722. Ibid., 4.

723. "Sandpit of Royalty,"*Extra Bladet* (Copenhagen, January 31, 1999).

724. Manly P. Hall, *Secret Teachings*, 104.

725. James Lees-Milne, *Saint Peter's: The Story of Saint Peter's Basilica in Rome* (Little, Brown, 1967), 221.

726. Rebecca Zorach and Michael W. Cole, *The Idol in the Age of Art* (Ashgate, 2009), 61.

727. Ibid., 63.

728. David Flynn, *Cydonia: The Secret Chronicles of Mars* (Bozwman, MT: End Time Thunder, 2002), 156.

729. Albert Pike, *Morals and Dogma: Of the Ancient and Accepted Scottish Rite of Freemasonry* (Forgotten Books), 401.

730. Albert Mackey, *A Manual of the Lodge* (1870), 56.

731. Dan Brown, *The Lost Symbol* (Anchor; Reprint edition, 2010), 3–4.

732. Manly P. Hall,*Lost Keys*, Prologue.

733. Manly P. Hall, *Secret Teachings*, 116–120.

734. Manly P. Hall, "Rosicrucianism and Masonic Origins," from *Lectures on Ancient Philosophy—An Introduction to the Study and Application of Rational Procedure* (Los Angeles: Hall, 1929), 397–417.

735. Albert Pike, *Morals and Dogma*,335.

736. Ibid., 16.

737. Ibid., 472.

738. Hope, Murry, Practical Egyptian Magic (New York: St. Martin's Press, 1984), p. 107. Quoted by Fritz Springmeier, The Watchtower & the Masons, 1990, 1992 pp. 113, 114.

739. Horn, *Apollyon Rising 2012*, 7–10.

740. Horn, *Zenith 2016*, 324–348.

741. John Dryden, trans., as published by Georgetown University Online; also appears in: Thomas Horn, *Apollyon Rising 2012*.

742. Peter Goodgame, *The Giza Discovery, Part Nine: The Mighty One*, last accessed January 23, 2012, http://www.redmoonrising.com/Giza/Asshur9.htm.

743. Horn, *Zenith 2016*,136–140.

744. Martin Short, *Inside the Brotherhood: Explosive Secrets of the Freemasons* (UK: HarperCollins, 1995), 122.

745. Manly P. Hall, *The Lost Keys of Freemasonry*, 48.

746. Manly P. Hall, *Secret Destiny of America* (Penguin Group, 2008), chapter 18.

747. See: http://en.wikipedia.org/wiki/Hermetic_Order_of_the_Golden_Dawn.

748. See: http://en.wikipedia.org/wiki/Ars_Goetia#Ars_Goetia.

749. See: http://www.redmoonrising.com/Giza/DomDec6.htm.

750. "Shemhamphorasch," *Wikipedia*, last modified December 6, 2011, http://en.wikipedia.org/wiki/Shemhamphorasch.

751. Horn, *Zenith 2016*, 348–356.